Career and College Readiness Counseling in P–12 Schools

Jennifer R. Curry, PhD, is an associate professor in the counselor education program at Louisiana State University. Her professional experience includes investigating sexual assault of children ages 11 and under, and serving as a professional school counselor in elementary, middle, and high school settings. Her research interests include career and college readiness and school counselor development. She has published three books: *P–12 Career Counseling*, published by Springer; *African Americans Career and College Readiness: the Journey Unraveled*, coedited with M. Ann Shillingford-Butler; and *Integrating Play Therapy in Comprehensive School Counseling Programs*, coedited with Laura Fazio-Griffith. She has presented her work nationally and internationally on a wide range of school counseling topics at over 50 professional conferences. Additionally, she has served as guest editor of the American School Counselor Association's (ASCA) *Professional School Counseling* journal and as an editorial board member for 6 years. Dr. Curry has also served as a delegate of ASCA's national assembly, president of the Louisiana School Counselor Association, and president of the Association for Spiritual, Ethical, and Religious Values in Counseling. She is the recipient of the Vanderbilt's Roger Aubrey Northstar Award, the American Counseling Association's Ross Trust Award for School Counseling, the Biggs-Pine publication award, ASERVIC's Meritorious Service Award and Judi Miranti Lifetime Service Award, LSU's College of Education Early Career Award, Louisiana School Counselor Association's Publication Award, and Louisiana Counseling Association's Advocacy Award.

Amy Milsom, DEd, LPC-S, NCC, is a professor of counselor education at Clemson University and the coordinator of the school counseling program. She received a Bachelor of Arts degree in psychology, a Master of Education degree in counselor education, and a Doctor of Education degree in counselor education from Penn State University. She has over 20 years of experience in the counseling field as a counselor educator, a middle and high school counselor, and provider of counseling services to children, adolescents, and college students. A past editor of *Professional School Counseling*, she has a strong record of peer-reviewed publications and editorial experience. Her research focuses on counselor preparation in general but mainly on school counselor education and students with disabilities, with an emphasis on postsecondary transition planning and college readiness for students with disabilities. Dr. Milsom serves on multiple journal editorial boards and regularly conducts CACREP accreditation site visits. Most recently, she has assisted in the development of training modules for school counselors and others working with P–12 students, which are produced as part of the College and Career Counseling Initiative by the Southern Region Education Board.

Career and College Readiness Counseling in P–12 Schools

Second Edition

Jennifer R. Curry, PhD

Amy Milsom, DEd, LPC-S, NCC

SPRINGER PUBLISHING COMPANY

NEW YORK

Springer Publishing Company, LLC
11 West 42nd Street
New York, NY 10036
www.springerpub.com

Acquisitions Editor: Nancy Hale
Compositor: diacriTech

ISBN: 978-0-8261-3614-5
e-book ISBN: 978-0-8261-3615-2

Instructor's Materials: Qualified instructors may request supplements by e-mailing textbook@springerpub.com:

Instructor's Manual: 978-0-8261-3616-9
Instructor's PowerPoints: 978-0-8261-3617-6

17 18 19 20 21 / 5 4 3 2 1

Library of Congress Cataloging-in-Publication Data
Names: Curry, Jennifer R., author. | Milsom, Amy, author.
Title: Career and college readiness counseling in P-12 schools / Jennifer R. Curry, PhD and
    Amy Milsom, DEd, LPC-S, NCC.
Other titles: Career counseling in P-12 schools
Description: Second edition. | New York, NY : Springer Publishing Company, LLC, [2017] |
Title of first edition: Career counseling in P-12 schools. | Includes bibliographical references and index.
Identifiers: LCCN 2016054625 | ISBN 9780826136145
Subjects: LCSH: Career education. | Vocational education. | College preparation programs.
Classification: LCC LC1037 .C875 2017 | DDC 370.113—dc23 LC record available at https://lccn.loc.gov/2016054625

Printed in the United States of America by Gasch Printing.

For Daniel, I hope you will always explore your options, especially when your path becomes unclear or confusing. In the moments of your life when you seek clarity, the light of adventure will shine before you; and, if you listen with an open mind and heart, the music of possibility will play the song of your future.

—Jennifer R. Curry

Contents

Preface   *xi*

Acknowledgments   *xiii*

1. P–12 Career and College Readiness: Ecosystemic, Developmental Considerations   1
Current Trends in Career and College Readiness   3
Federal Initiatives   10
An Ecosystems Approach to P–12 Career and College Readiness   12
Historical Developments in Career Theory Related to Children and Adolescents   17
Career and College Readiness Skills   22
The Roles of Stakeholders in Career and College Readiness   24
How to Use This Book to Prepare for P–12 Career and College Readiness Programming in Schools   27
Summary   29
References   29

2. P–12 Career and College Readiness: Preparing All Students for a Postsecondary Plan   33
The School Counselor's Role: Creating a Career and College Readiness Culture   33
Does College Pay Off?   34
Understanding the Value of a Degree in Context   38
Advising the College-Bound Student   40
The Career-Bound Student   47
Helping Students Research Career and Technical Programs   51
Resources to Facilitate College Decision Making   52
Final Thoughts   54
Summary   56
References   56

3. P–12 Career and College Readiness: Professional Preparation   59
Career and College Readiness Counseling Competencies   60
Preparation for Providing Career and College Readiness Interventions in Schools   69
Summary   71
References   72

4. **P–12 Career and College Readiness: Cultural Considerations**   **73**
   Special Population Considerations   74
   Advocacy and Equity in P–12 Career and College Readiness   92
   Summary   95
   References   95

5. **P–12 Career and College Readiness:**
   Assessment and Evaluation   **103**
   Purpose of Career and College Readiness Assessment   104
   Choosing Career and College Readiness Assessments   105
   Career and College Readiness Assessments   108
   Using Assessment Results: Evaluation   116
   Summary   118
   References   119

6. **P–12 Career and College Readiness: Curriculum Development**   **121**
   Choosing a Curriculum Foundation   121
   Writing Curriculum Objectives   122
   Choosing Interventions and Writing Lesson Plans   125
   Implementing the Curriculum   128
   Evaluating Outcomes   129
   Summary   136
   References   136

7. **Career and College Readiness for Grades P–1: Exposure and**
   Awareness   **139**
   Career and College Readiness for PreK, Kindergarten,
   and First Grade   139
   Developmental Overview   140
   Relevant Career Theory for PreK, K, and First-Grade Students: Gottfredson (1981)
   and Young (1983)   143
   Play Techniques and Career and College Exposure for P–1 Students   145
   The School Counselor and the Core Counseling Curriculum   149
   Importance of Stakeholders   153
   Summary   159
   References   160

8. **Career and College Readiness for Grades 2 and 3: Career Play and**
   Exploration   **163**
   Developmental Overview   163
   Relevant Career and Systems Theory: Bourdieu (1977) and Gottfredson (1981)   167
   The School Counselor and Core Counseling Curriculum   169
   School Counseling Interventions   170
   Importance of Stakeholders   175
   Summary   182
   References   183

9. **Career and College Readiness for Grades 4 and 5: Preparing for the Middle School Transition**   *185*

Developmental Overview   *185*
Relevant Career Theory: Bandura (1977), Gottfredson (1981), Young (1983), and Super (1980)   *189*
The Middle School Transition   *196*
The School Counselor and the Core Counseling Curriculum   *196*
Importance of Stakeholders   *198*
The Fifth- to Sixth-Grade Transition   *203*
Summary   *207*
References   *208*

10. **Career and College Readiness for Grades 6 and 7: Promoting Self-Awareness**   *211*

Developmental Overview   *211*
Career Theory and Development: Gottfredson (1981), Holland (1973), and Young (1983)   *215*
Middle School Career and College Readiness   *218*
The School Counseling Curriculum   *218*
Promoting STEM Careers in Middle School   *221*
Engaging Stakeholders   *225*
Summary   *231*
References   *232*

11. **Career and College Readiness for Grade 8: High School Transition Planning**   *235*

Developmental Overview   *236*
Relevant Career Theories: Gottfredson (1981), Holland (1973), and Young (1983)   *237*
Eighth-Grade Student Career and College Readiness Outcomes   *239*
Career and College Readiness Interventions   *239*
Partnering With Parents and the Community   *247*
Facilitating the Eighth- to Ninth-Grade Transition   *249*
Summary   *253*
References   *254*

12. **Career and College Readiness for Grade 9: Focus on Academic and Work Habits**   *257*

Developmental Overview   *258*
Relevant Career Theories: Gottfredson (1981), Holland (1973), and Super (1980)   *260*
Facilitating the Eighth- to Ninth-Grade Transition: Follow-Up Activities   *262*
The High School Academic Pathway   *263*
Ninth-Grade Student Career and College Readiness Outcomes   *264*
Career and College Readiness Interventions: Collaborating With Teachers   *267*
Summary   *274*
References   *275*

13. **Career and College Readiness for Grade 10: Career and College Planning** *277*
Developmental Overview *277*
Relevant Career Theory: Super (1980) and Lent, Brown, and Hackett (1994) *280*
Mindsets and Behaviors for 10th Grade *285*
Summary *296*
References *297*

14. **Career and College Readiness for Grade 11: Beginning the Career and College Transition** *299*
Developmental Overview *299*
Relevant Career Theory: Lent, Brown, and Hackett (1994) and Savickas (2005) *301*
11th-Grade Curriculum Development *304*
Interventions: Collaborating With Teachers *305*
Targeted Counseling Interventions *308*
Summary *316*
References *317*

15. **Career and College Readiness for Grade 12: Postsecondary Transitions** *319*
Developmental Overview *319*
Relevant Career Theory: Savickas (2005) and Brown (2002) *320*
12th-Grade Curriculum Development *322*
Counseling and Educational Interventions *322*
Celebrating the High School Transition *332*
Summary *335*
References *335*

16. **Appendices**
A: National Career Development Association Minimum Competencies for Multicultural Career Counseling and Development *339*
B: Career Counselor Assessment and Evaluation Competencies *343*
C: ASCA Mindsets & Behaviors for Student Success: K–12 College and Career-Readiness Standards for Every Student *347*
D: ASCA Ethical Standards for School Counselors *353*

Author Index *375*
Subject Index *381*

Preface

Our decision to write this book stemmed from our desire to provide school counselors with a resource that could help them easily conceptualize the career and college readiness needs of P–12 students and design relevant and meaningful interventions. We wanted to develop a book that not only was practical but also pushed readers to be intentional in their work. Further, we believed it was important to respond to national initiatives that emphasize a focus on career and college readiness. The unique aspect of our book, compared to many other career counseling textbooks, is that we present a comprehensive, integrated, and practical approach to counseling, specifically targeting career and college readiness in P–12 schools.

In this book, our second edition, we continue to provide a review of developmental, ecosystemic, and career theories to inform relevant P–12 career and college readiness interventions. Given the variation that exists in the psychosocial, cognitive, and academic development of P–12 students, we review numerous developmental theories and assist readers in using them as a foundation to design sequential and developmentally appropriate career and college readiness curricula and interventions. We also help readers understand the ecosystemic influences (e.g., family, school, community, society) on career development and college readiness, and we discuss both why it is important to involve various stakeholders in career and college readiness initiatives and how to involve them. Finally, we provide readers with concrete examples of how to apply various career counseling theories when working with P–12 students.

We start this book with six foundational chapters in which we review (a) current data and issues related to college and career readiness, (b) information to assist with postsecondary planning and career and college advising, (c) professional preparation standards for individuals who will provide career and college readiness interventions, (d) cultural considerations in career and college readiness, (e) career and college readiness assessment, and (f) career and college readiness curriculum development. We then address career development and college readiness needs by grade level. Our focus in each grade level chapter is to help readers apply knowledge of ecosystems, developmental theories, and career theories, and identify ways that multiple stakeholders can become involved in career and college readiness interventions. We also provide concrete, practical examples, including case examples as well as Voices From the Field written by practicing school counselors to demonstrate some of the concepts and interventions we highlight in each chapter.

We greatly enjoyed writing this book, but it was challenging at times for us to decide in which chapter to include certain information. In that vein, we encourage readers not to limit themselves to implementing career and college readiness interventions exactly as we outline them. Many of the activities and ideas we share could be applicable across numerous grade levels if modified to accommodate developmental differences. Also, P–12 students can benefit from repetition, so it never hurts to target something more than once. Our hope is that both preservice and practicing school counselors find this book useful in helping identify career and college readiness needs and design developmentally appropriate interventions that are grounded in theory and research.

In addition to the textbook, we have provided an Instructor's Manual and PowerPoints intended to support instructors in developing a graduate level course on P–12 career and college readiness. The manual includes a sample syllabus that reflects the content of the textbook. We designed this sample course with a number of useful tools for each chapter including discussion questions, project-based activities, quizzes and essay questions, and social media that may be useful for teaching this course. These materials may also be additive to an existing course as supplemental materials. **The Instructor's Resources are available to qualified instructors by e-mailing textbook@springerpub.com.**

Acknowledgments

We wish to acknowledge the help and support of Patrick Akos, Logan Chandler, Julie Coughlin, Tanya K. Dupuy, Ainsley Pellerin, Jennie F. Trocquet, Brienna Floyd, and Samantha J. Latham, in addition to the individuals who were generous enough to share their Voices From the Field.

ONE

P–12 Career and College Readiness: Ecosystemic, Developmental Considerations

In the book *Callings: The Purpose and Passion of Work* (2016), Dave Isay, the founder of StoryCorps, shares transcribed interviews conducted with individuals from many walks of everyday life who work in a variety of careers. Individuals in Isay's book range from a surgeon, bridgetender, "street" telescopist, and garbage collector, to a man who filets salmon every day. The common thread throughout the book is the transformative power of the careers to empower people to impact their communities. Throughout the interviews in the book, individuals convey how their work has helped them to have hope, change their own circumstances, and recognize how much their contributions matter to their friends, family, patients, clients, and society at large.

Work should be an exciting blend of challenge and accomplishment that is engaging and that meets an individual's personal and professional growth needs. Beyond providing fiscal support, a person's chosen career ideally should provide mental stimulation, a creative outlet, an opportunity to contribute to society and the well-being of others, and feelings of personal value, pride, mattering, and mastery (Curry & Bickmore, 2012; Myers, Sweeney, & Witmer, 2000). When individuals make informed career decisions based on an assessment of aptitude, values, interests, and person–environment fit, they are more likely to be satisfied with their careers and be committed long term to their career choices.

To ensure students' future career success, contemporary schools need to offer diverse curricula and educational options that afford students opportunities to develop comprehensive skills and competencies to meet the demands of the 21st century workplace. As global economies, industry, and technology change, so must the preparation of students (Akos, Niles, Miller, & Erford, 2011). Johnson (2000) noted that employment in the future will include more contractual work, more temporary assignments, and decentralized work locations (e.g., site or field based, home office) rather than stable, long-term appointments. Thus, young adults entering the workforce must be more flexible, adaptable, and committed to lifelong learning as they approach postsecondary life (Johnson, 2000).

Yet, many students and families are concerned about what preparation is required to be successful in the workforce of the future. They also feel confusion about the college payoff and the value of a college degree. The costs of postsecondary education and training in comparison to the income afforded to college graduates and the employment rates of degree earners has come under heavy scrutiny in recent years. In fact, much of the national discourse on (a) *who* should pay for college and (b) *how* to pay for college is very politically charged (Blumenstyk, 2015). Moreover, college access and equity remains at the forefront of these debates.

In discussing trends in higher education, Brock (2010) indicated that although access to higher education has greatly improved in recent years, success (measured by college retention and degree completion) has not improved. Demographically, postsecondary schools are more diverse than ever, but Brock (2010) discussed how most of that diversity is accounted for by enrollment at 2-year colleges and less selective institutions. Women now outnumber men at 4-year institutions, but women and individuals from minority populations are overrepresented at 2-year colleges. When considering college readiness, practitioners would be remiss if they neglected to identify the unique needs of populations like first-generation college students, English-language learners (ELLs), students with identified disabilities, and students from lower socioeconomic backgrounds, to name a few. Moreover, according to the National Poverty Center (using data from the U.S. Census Bureau) in 2014, more than one in five children in the United States lived in poverty. Students living in poverty may have fewer familial resources to facilitate career and college readiness in the home. Therefore, school counselors need to be prepared to assist those students through equity-based programming. We continue to examine the needs of these and other specific populations throughout this book.

Although many researchers, educators, and policy makers agree that career and college readiness are essential components of a P–12 education, there is no clear definition of what this means. Because the terms *college readiness* and *career readiness* are distinct enough from each other, we define them separately. Most of what has been written about college readiness focuses on readiness to succeed at 4-year institutions. Conley (2007) proposed that the construct of *college readiness* is multifaceted, with academic skills being only one component. He wrote that:

> The college-ready student envisioned by this definition is able to understand what is expected in a college course, can cope with the content knowledge that is presented, and can take away from the course the key intellectual lessons and dispositions the course was designed to convey and develop. In addition, the student is prepared to get the most out of the college experience due to a thorough understanding of the culture and structure of postsecondary education and the ways of knowing and intellectual norms that prevail in this academic and social environment. The student has both the mindset and disposition necessary to enable this to happen. (pp. 5–6)

College preparation expectations differ depending on whether students attend 4-year colleges, 2-year colleges, or vocational and technical schools. Aside from obvious academically related differences among 4-year, 2-year, and vocational/technical schools, Conley's definition of college readiness seems broad enough to apply to various types of postsecondary education. In essence, he suggested that on top of possessing requisite academic and higher order thinking skills that enable students to retain and apply knowledge and skills, students do better when they have an idea of what to expect and are committed to developing the skills and knowledge to successfully navigate postsecondary school. We believe that better preparation for college via P–12 interventions could help to improve these success rates, and we discuss numerous interventions throughout this book.

In addition to college readiness, defining *career readiness* is of vital importance. According to the Association for Career and Technical Education (ACTE, 2010),

Career readiness involves three major skill areas: *core academic skills* and the ability to apply those skills to concrete situations in order to function in the workplace and in routine daily activities; *employability skills* (such as critical thinking and responsibility) that are essential in any career area; and *technical, job-specific skills* related to a specific career pathway. (p. 1)

Regarding academics, the ACTE (2011) emphasized that basic math and English/language arts skills are critical for all students planning to enter the workforce. Additionally, ACTE noted collaboration, professionalism, ability to use technology, responsibility, flexibility, and problem solving as important employability skills.

Students who choose not to pursue college or technical school need to possess academic, employability, and technical skills upon high school graduation in addition to possessing basic job search knowledge and skills (e.g., fill out a job application, write a resume and cover letter, search for job openings, answer interview questions appropriately) to secure employment. As mentioned, for students who do intend to pursue college, academic skills and employability skills will be necessary by graduation in order for them to be successful in college.

CURRENT TRENDS IN CAREER AND COLLEGE READINESS

Before we focus on interventions that may help students develop the skills and knowledge to be successful in careers and college, we want to provide an overview of what students do after high school. As we present the information that follows, you will see fairly consistent trends. Specifically, gaps in achievement and opportunity for minorities and individuals from lower socioeconomic groups are reflected in much of the data. These gaps unfortunately start during P–12 education and are demonstrated in high school matriculation data. According to the U.S. Census Bureau's *Statistical Abstract of the United States* (2011), in 2010, 87.1% of citizens ages 25 or older had completed a high school degree. However, high school graduation rates were reported at 88.9% for Asians, 87.6% for Whites, 84.2% for Blacks, and 62.9% for Hispanics. This is concerning as individuals without a high school diploma are at a disadvantage when it comes to career outcomes; they earn less and are more likely to be unemployed than high school graduates. We explore this issue later in this chapter.

College Attendance and Degree Attainment

[handwritten margin note: More employers are requiring higher levels of education & training]

According to a summary of U.S. Bureau of Labor Statistics (Ryan & Bauman, 2016), by the year 2024 there will be a 13.8% increase in jobs requiring a master's degree, and a 12.2% increase in jobs requiring a doctoral degree, but only a 3.9% increase in jobs requiring only a high school diploma or equivalency (i.e., office and administrative support, production occupations). Carnevale, Smith, and Strohl (2010) reported that by the year 2018, the United States will need 22 million new college degree earners, but we will most likely be short by three million. The shortage will be based on an increase in the number of retirees coupled with the demand by employers to hire workers with higher levels of education and training. Ryan and Bauman found that of people ages 25 and older in 2015, approximately 42.3% had completed an associate's degree or higher but only 12.0% had completed a graduate or professional degree. These data are in sharp contrast to the estimations of occupations aforementioned that will require advanced degrees; thus, one may deduce that of the students currently pursuing postsecondary education, many are not seeking the level of degree necessary for the demands of the workforce. Compounding this issue, of students enrolled in college, an estimated 40% attend community colleges, but for students whose families earn less than $40,000 annually, 50% attend community colleges. The information from Carnevale et al. coupled with these data suggest that an increase in number of people pursuing college degrees, and in particular advanced degrees, will be important for the future. Additionally, efforts to address issues related to college accessibility for diverse populations, including individuals from low-income families, will be equally important.

College attendance rates have increased in recent years. The Chronicle of Higher Education (2011) reported an overall average growth rate of 39% in undergraduate college enrollment (2-year and 4-year colleges) from 1999 to 2009; during that time frame, growth rates for enrollment in graduate school averaged 36%. Average growth rates for undergraduate enrollment were 93% for Hispanic students and 78% for Black students; growth rates for American Indians and Asians averaged 45%, and rates for Whites were the lowest at 24%. Despite increased college enrollment growth for Hispanics and Blacks, smaller percentages of minority students attend college compared to their majority peers. That is, the average college enrollment in 2009 was 41% of the U.S. population. Breaking down the percentages by specific subgroups, we see that 45% of White students, compared to 38% of Black and 28% of Hispanic students, were enrolled in college. Carnevale et al. (2010) also noted that college education attainment continues to elude individuals from lower socioeconomic classes, with the greatest number of college graduates coming from the middle and upper classes.

According to the U.S. Census Bureau (2011), only 29.9% of U.S. citizens had attained a 4-year college degree. Four-year college degree attainment rates were reported as 52.4% for Asians, 30.3% for Whites, 19.8% for Blacks, and 13.9% for Hispanics (with intragroup differences identified among Cubans, Puerto Ricans, and Mexicans). Although we have no specific knowledge regarding the causes for these differences, numerous intrapersonal and environmental factors, to be discussed later, likely play important roles in the career and college success of these individuals.

We want to examine more specifically the concern expressed by Brock (2010) presented earlier in this chapter related to stagnant college success rates (i.e., retention and completion). In their longitudinal study of students attending and matriculating through college in 2008 to 2009, the National Center for Education Statistics (NCES, 2011a) revealed that 44% completed their bachelor's degree in 48 months, 23% in 49 to 60 months, and 9% within 61 to 72 months. A disheartening 24% did not finish within 72 months (6 years). Interestingly, approximately 30% of all students started their degrees at 2-year schools, and those who started at 2-year schools tended to take longer to complete their degrees (e.g., 50.6% of students who started at a 4-year school completed their degree in 4 years, compared to only 25.4% of students who started their degrees at 2-year schools). Myriad possible explanations exist for these differences in time to completion. Research suggests, however, that the types of students who are more likely to attend community college (i.e., those of nontraditional age, first-generation college students, single parents, veterans, and students from low socioeconomic status [SES] families) may have to attend part time and may have to devote more time to work or family to the exclusion of solely focusing on school (Blumenstyk, 2015).

Examining the data (NCES, 2011a) more closely, as parental educational attainment increases, so does degree completion (e.g., 20% of students whose parents attained a high school diploma or less completed their degrees compared to 29.8% of students whose parents had a graduate or professional degree). Furthermore, the data suggested that Black and Hispanic students who completed their degrees tended to have parents with less education than did their White and Asian counterparts (e.g., approximately 38% of Black and Hispanic students reported parents having a bachelor's degree or higher, compared to approximately 60% of the White and Asian students). Black and Hispanic students also were more likely to have dependents than were White and Asian students.

NCES (2011a) did not reveal the reason it takes some students longer than others to matriculate or why some students do not complete college at all. As mentioned previously, and based on the trends noted, it seems likely that a number of intrapersonal and environmental factors affect long-term career and college outcomes for students. We discuss many of these factors throughout this book. One major concern, however, is that many students don't appear to be ready to do college level work.

In fact, college instructors estimate that up to 42% of college students are not adequately prepared by their high schools to meet college course expectations (Hart Research Associates, 2005). Of interest, nearly 90% of graduating seniors in the United States take the ACT®, an assessment that can provide a comparison of students' achievement in relation to Math, Science, Reading, and English college readiness benchmarks. Based on a report released by ACT, Inc. (2015), *The Condition of College and Career Readiness 2015,* 40% of students achieved at or above the minimum college readiness benchmark scores in three or four content areas. More specifically, 64% of students taking the ACT met the English benchmark, 46% met the Reading benchmark, 42% met the Math benchmark, and 38% met the Science benchmark. Unfortunately, 31% of high school graduates who took the ACT did not meet benchmarks in any of the four content areas. While it is difficult to ascertain the exact reasons for these trends, one alarming concern noted by ACT in the executive summary of *The Forgotten Middle* (ACT, Inc., 2008), was that only 2 out of 10 eighth-grade students are actually on track to take the courses in high school that will prepare them for college. In other words, many of our middle and high school students are not taking courses that are rigorous enough to prepare them for postsecondary education options. We revisit this problem throughout this book.

Career and Employment Outcomes

What happened to the students who did not graduate from high school or who did not attend college? According to an executive summary of the Georgetown University Center on Education and the Workforce report *Projections of Jobs and Education Requirements Through 2018* (Carnevale et al., 2010), individuals who do not attend some college and have only a high school diploma or less are mainly relegated to work in three main occupation clusters: food and personal services, sales and office support, and blue-collar employment. Further, inasmuch as the college payoff has been questioned, the cost of not going to college is undebatable. Tabulating data collected in the March 2013 *Current Population Survey,* the Pew Research Center (2014) noted three distinct and concerning issues for individuals ages 25 to 32 who held only a high school diploma: (a) they earned far less annual median income, (b) they were substantially more affected by unemployment rates, and (c) they were significantly more likely to live in poverty (see Figures 1.1–1.3, respectively). The U.S. Bureau of Labor Statistics (2015) revealed that in a 10-year span from 2003 to 2013, a rising wage inequality existed between the lowest and highest paid workers in the United States. In particular, annual wages above the 90th percentile increased 4.6% while those in the lowest 10th percentile decreased by 2.2% when adjusted for inflation.

FIGURE 1.1   Disparity Among Millennials Ages 25 to 34, by Education Level in Terms of Annual Earnings

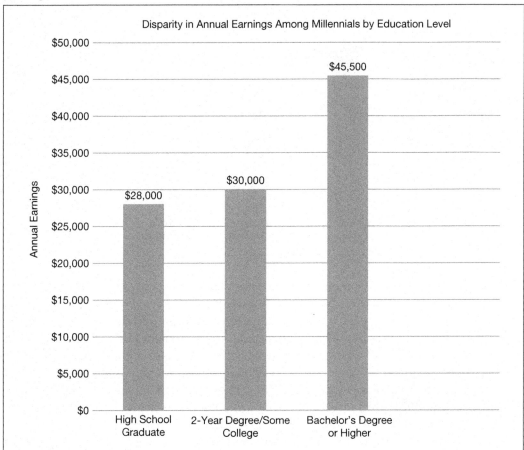

FIGURE 1.2   Unemployment Rates Among Individuals Ages 25 to 34, by Degree Attainment

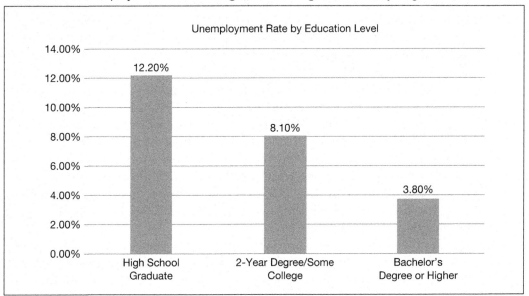

FIGURE 1.3   Percent of Millennials Ages 25 to 34 Living in Poverty, by Education Level

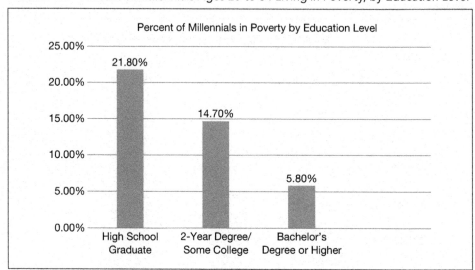

Indeed, employment and income both highly correlate with education attainment. Based on NCES (2014) data, trends in employment by education from 1975 to 2014 have a distinct pattern. In 2014, individuals ages 25 to 34 with a bachelor's degree or higher had an employment rate of 84%, those with some college had an employment rate of 74.5%, those with high school diplomas had an employment rate of 68.2%, and those without high school completion had employment rates of 57.8%. These same data, collected all the way back to 1975, are fairly stable over time; the same degrees and employment rates in 1975 were, respectively, 82%, 71.7%, 65.5%, and 52.9%.

Noteworthy, a significant number of individuals ages 18 to 24 with high school diplomas or less were at historically low employment levels from 2009 to 2014 (NCES, 2014). This is likely due to the impact of the economic recession. While unemployment for individuals with high school diplomas remained stable at rates between 9% and 14% from 1995 to 2009, in 2009, that rate rose sharply to 22.7% and decreased slightly to 21.1% through 2014. These data reflect that during recessions, the most economically vulnerable populations are those groups with the lowest degree attainment.

With regard to career outcomes for college graduates, of those students completing their bachelor's degrees in 2013, 72.1% were employed in full-time jobs. Comparatively, 67.5% of individuals earning associates degrees were in full-time jobs and 61.7% of high school completers were in full-time jobs (NCES, 2015). Nevertheless, what these numbers don't reflect is whether or not individuals were hired in their fields of study, what their advancement opportunities look like, how their occupations are projected to grow, and what skills they will need to advance in order to remain employable.

Another consideration, beyond employability issues, is that the disparity of earnings across ethnic groups, race, and gender persists (see Figure 1.4). Although we know who is getting hired based on their level of education, the divergence of pay across groups is more apparent when we view disaggregated data. For example, women continue to earn significantly less than men, regardless of race or ethnicity (American Association of University Women, 2016; U.S. Bureau of Labor Statistics, 2015). Additionally, according to an executive summary of Georgetown University's Center on Education and the Workforce, *The College Payoff: Education, Occupations, Lifetime Earnings* (Carnevale, Rose, & Cheah, 2011), women, African Americans, and Latinos continue to earn less than White and Asian males even when they have similar degree attainment and work in the same occupations Nevertheless, regardless of gender, race, or ethnicity, the level of education achieved drives earnings, and generally, for most occupations, the higher the degree, the greater the income (see Table 1.1).

FIGURE 1.4 Median Usual Weekly Earnings of Women and Men Who Are Full-Time Wage and Salary Workers, by Race and Hispanic or Latino Ethnicity, 2014 Annual Averages

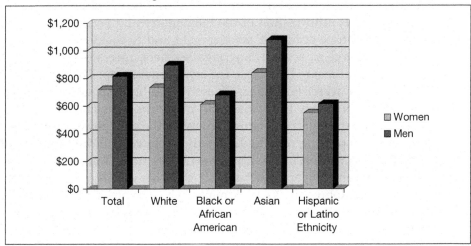

TABLE 1.1 Lifetime Earnings by Educational Attainment Based on Race and Ethnicity

Degree Earned	Asian ($)	Latino ($)	African American ($)	White ($)
Less than high school	950,000	875,000	950,000	1,200,000
High school diploma	1,150,000	1,160,000	1,200,000	1,333,000
Some college/ no degree	1,450,000	1,400,000	1,350,000	1,600,000
Associate's	1,650,000	1,550,000	1,500,000	1,750,000
Bachelor's	2,250,000	1,800,000	1,850,000	2,400,000
Master's	3,100,000	2,500,000	2,400,000	2,700,000
Doctorate	3,500,000	2,900,000	2,850,000	3,500,000
Professional	3,800,000	2,500,000	2,850,000	3,750,000

Source: Adapted from Carnevale et al. (2011).

FEDERAL INITIATIVES

As career and college readiness has gained importance in the U.S. educational discourse, federal policy has changed to give prominence to P–12 student development in these areas. Although innumerable state, regional, and district level policies exist that should be considered when planning career and college interventions, we will focus on current federal initiatives that school counselors need to understand for effective practice. In this section, we highlight the No Child Left Behind (NCLB) Act, the Every Student Succeeds Act (ESSA), the National Math and Science Initiative (NMSI), and the Reach Higher Initiative.

No Child Left Behind Act

The NCLB Act of 2001 (PL 107-110) was signed into federal law in January 2001 (U.S. Department of Education, 2004). The overarching goal of this legislation, a reauthorization of the Elementary and Secondary Education Act, was to improve academic achievement and to focus attention on minority populations (e.g., second language learners, migratory children, children with disabilities) to help close the achievement gap. The most salient points of this law were: (a) increased accountability—specifically in relation to student proficiency in reading and math; (b) more choices for parents and students—students can change schools if the one they attend is deemed failing; and (c) putting reading first—all students should be competent readers by third grade. NCLB instituted a 12-year time frame for schools to close the achievement gap and have all students achieving at proficient levels (Martin & Robinson, 2011). A major criticism of NCLB is that because the main focus was academics, particularly strengthening math and reading as measured through standardized testing, less emphasis was placed on learning in nontested subjects such as arts, physical education and health, music, social studies, science, and foreign language.

Every Student Succeeds Act

The ESSA (PL 114-95) was signed into law by President Barack Obama on December 10, 2015. It is the latest reauthorization of the Elementary and Secondary Education Act and, unlike NCLB, ESSA has a primary focus on academically preparing students for careers and college. Several notable aspects of this law include (a) more support for expanding preschool programming, (b) requirements for all students to be taught at an academic standard that prepares them for success in careers and college, and (c) maintaining annual student learning assessment while reducing unnecessary and excessive testing protocols (Executive Office of the President, 2015). The foci on high academic rigor, teacher effectiveness, increasing technology in low SES classrooms, and making college affordable and equitable are salient features of this law noteworthy for P–12 career and college preparation.

Reach Higher

Reach Higher, an initiative sponsored by former first lady Michelle Obama, and in conjunction with the American School Counselor Association (ASCA), is an effort to get all students to commit to pursue some sort of postsecondary education. As part of President Obama's North Star goal 2020, a goal that the United States would be the leader in college graduates in the world again by 2020, Mrs. Obama challenged students, parents, and school counselors to work together within their communities to focus on completion and submission of Free Application for Federal Student Aid (FAFSA) forms, applications for scholarships, and applications to colleges across the country. Reach Higher is meant to prevent students from making foreclosed decisions about college, such as believing that college is unaffordable and therefore not an attainable option. The goal is to make students aware of the financial support available to them and to assist school counselors by providing them essential resources to help students make college choices. Reach Higher provides school counselors with strategies and materials such as the College Signing Day Toolkit, the College Signing Day pocket card, the College Scorecard, Net Price Calculator, College Navigator, and the Financial Aid Shopping Sheet (www.whitehouse.gov/reach-higher).

National Math and Science Initiative

According to the NMSI (as reported in Fleisher, 2012), the United States is falling behind in science, technology, engineering, and math (STEM), a potential threat to our global standing. Based on data reported by NMSI, in a ranking of 31 countries by the Organization for Economic Cooperation and Development, students in the United States rank 15th in reading, 19th in math, and 14th in science. Furthermore, when it comes to science, only 29% of fourth graders in the United States are proficient; and even more astounding, only 18% of 12th graders are at or above the proficient level in science (NMSI, 2011). Major corporate sponsorship for this initiative comes from Exxon, the Bill and Melinda Gates Foundation, and the Michael and Susan Dell Foundation. With so many potential career opportunities available, what makes STEM careers so critical? Who currently excels in STEM and how can we expand success to multiple populations?

STEM Careers, Women, and Minorities

Projections for STEM careers continue to show a great deal of growth and high demand for workers in these areas. This is no surprise given that the efforts in fields such as aeronautical engineering have made space travel and research possible, and have expanded our understanding of the complexities of our universe. Advancements in the frontier of sustainability engineering and the use of renewable energy sources (e.g., wind and solar power) hold promise for the health and integrity of our planet and the long-term needs of our growing population. Progress in the medical field in the treatment of illness and in understanding how the human body functions at a microscopic level have increased longevity and quality of life for millions of people.

The need for expertise in STEM areas is apparent, and long-term projections continue to show job growth in these areas and the need for a workforce to occupy these positions, in spite of economic recession and a loss of jobs in most sectors. For example, from July 2010 to July 2011, 299,000 jobs were added in the health care industry and 246,000 were added to professional and technical service industries such as computer systems design, bookkeeping, and payroll services (NCES, 2011b). That same period saw drops or no growth in the areas of government employment, leisure, and hospitality. Moreover, recent data show that health and technical careers are the highest paid professions for individuals with bachelor's degrees (NCES, 2011b). Yet, are students entering these professions?

According to the NCES (2011b), 16.1% of 2008–2009 graduates majored in STEM areas. However, a demographic breakdown of this number proves concerning. In particular, 25.5% of college males, but only 9.7% of college females, majored in STEM areas. Differences in race were also present among STEM majors: 31.4% of Asian students enter STEM majors, as do 16% of White students, 14.9% of Black students, and 12.3% of Hispanic students.

Many initiatives have been proposed to promote student interest and development in STEM areas, including the Race to the Top Fund where STEM is a priority in P–12 education, National Lab Day, and a plethora of grants for teachers, counselors, and others to provide STEM opportunities for P–12 students. Moreover, corporate sponsorship of federal initiatives for STEM has grown to include prestigious donors such as the Bill and Melinda Gates Foundation, the Carnegie Corporation, Time Warner Cable, Discovery Communications, and The MacArthur Foundation. In this book, we look at ways to engage P–12 students in STEM education.

AN ECOSYSTEMS APPROACH TO P–12 CAREER AND COLLEGE READINESS

Ecological and systems theories have become more prominent in recent years as both school-based professionals and researchers in many fields have begun to place greater appreciation on the role of family and community in the lives of P–12 students. In fact, school–family–community partnerships are frequently discussed in relation to addressing academic and behavioral concerns. We believe that three particular theories—Bronfenbrenner's *Bioecological Theory*, Young's *Career Concepts*, and Bordieu's *Social Capital Theory*—provide a strong foundation for conceptualizing when and how school counselors might involve a variety of stakeholders in their efforts to address career and college readiness.

Bronfenbrenner's Bioecological Theory

Urie Bronfenbrenner's Bioecological Theory (1977) is helpful in understanding the importance of students' environments on their preparation for careers and college. In his theory, Bronfenbrenner indicates that a child's own biology is the most important "environment" that affects his or her development.

Then, layers of environments (such as family, community, school, and society) interact to shape a child's development. These interactions become more complex as children develop increased cognitive abilities. As such, Bronfenbrenner supports the importance of choosing and implementing interventions that take into consideration a child's developmental level and involve individuals with whom the child interacts.

In describing the various environments that shape development, Bronfenbrenner defined multiple contexts including microsystems, mesosystems, exosystems, macrosystems, and chronosystems. *Microsystems* are the small environmental systems that exist in a child's immediate surroundings. Microsystems typically include a child's family, school, and neighborhood; the relationships that exist within microsystems are bidirectional, which is sometimes called reciprocity. For example, parental beliefs and actions are believed to affect those of the child, and vice versa. Bronfenbrenner indicates that the relationships that exist within microsystems are the most influential to a child. As such, we have chosen to devote a good amount of space in this text discussing the individuals who typically exist in a child's microsystems (e.g., parents, teachers, counselors, community members) and the roles they can and do play in shaping career and college readiness development.

The remaining environmental layers described by Bronfenbrenner are important in relation to their indirect influence on children. *Mesosystems* are the interactions that occur between microsystems (e.g., communication between home and school); for example, the interaction between family members and school staff at a parent–teacher conference. *Exosystems* are the structures that interact with microsystems (e.g., resources available in a school, policies made by the school board). The *macrosystem* comprises the cultural beliefs and values held by a society. According to Bronfenbrenner, the macrosystem directly affects the exosystem, which directly affects the mesosystem. For example, societal values (macrosystem level) that reinforce the idea that only schools are responsible for preparing students for careers and college may result in community microsystems feeling little obligation to offer career- or college-related services or resources (exosystem level). Because the community has no resources or services, they would have no relevant structures in place and therefore no need to interact (mesosystem level) with the school. In a system like this, one might expect parents, teachers, and students to receive inadequate information or insufficient training related to careers and college. School counselors may need to examine macrosystem level factors to understand how and why interactions at lower environmental levels occur as they do.

It could be argued that a mesosystem in which frequent communication and collaboration occurs among microsystems might be more desirable in relation to fostering career and college readiness than would a mesosystem in which there are few interactions (Milsom, 2007). With greater communication comes greater understanding of expectations. Career and college transitions can create challenges as new microsystems come into play. Diamond, Spiegel-McGill, and Hanrahan (1988) discussed Bronfenbrenner's theory specifically in relation to transitions for students receiving special education services. They indicated that "the transition process can be seen as one of expanding the child's immediate environments, which in turn results in a greater number of environments which must relate to each other within the mesosystem" (pp. 245–246). Students transitioning to careers and college in essence eventually lose a familiar microsystem (e.g., public school system) and replace it with an unfamiliar one (e.g., college or employment setting). Milsom (2007) suggested that the more familiar a student becomes with an anticipated future microsystem, the more opportunities there are to develop the requisite knowledge, skills, and attitudes for success in that microsystem. It is likely that some skills and knowledge areas required for a successful transition to careers or college may be unfamiliar to many students. In line with Bronfenbrenner's theory is the idea that students who have high school experiences that are similar to their anticipated careers and college experiences should be fairly successful in their transition. An awareness of skill, knowledge, behavioral, and attitudinal components related to success in careers and college is critical for high school personnel in assessing student strengths and weaknesses in those areas. By planning ahead and allowing adequate time for students to develop new skills, school counselors and other stakeholders can help to "minimize the stress involved for children and their families and . . . maximize the chances of the child being successful in the new environment" (Kemp & Carter, 2000, p. 393). The development and maintenance of a collaborative mesosystem (to include communication with future microsystems) is in alignment with current thinking about school, family, and community partnerships. Figure 1.5 depicts the concentric circle of ecosystems.

FIGURE 1.5   Ecosystems

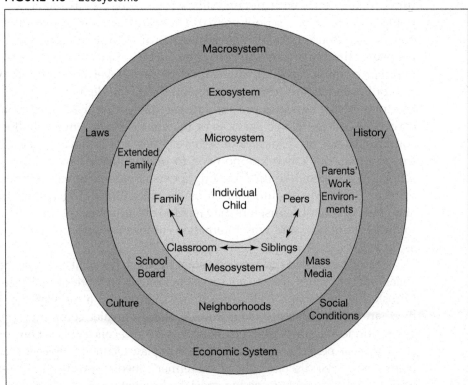

Young's Career Concepts

[handwritten margin note: Young – CC Readiness framework @ each ecosystemic level to help counselors develop a systems approach to intervention.]

Young (1983) contended that while many career theories address developmental aspects of the individual, most fail to address the environmental contexts in which individuals live that influence career development. Using Bronfenbrenner's (1977) model, Young (1983) provided a framework for career and college readiness counseling at each ecosystemic level that could help school counselors conceptualize a systems approach to intervention. For example, Young noted that at the microsystem level both family and school have a large impact on the individual. He highlighted five familial characteristics that interchangeably influence career development: (a) birth order, (b) early parent–child interaction, (c) the child's identification with parents, (d) the amount of contact the child has with parents, and (e) the child's perception of parent(s) influence. We address each of these influences in subsequent chapters.

[handwritten margin note: interventions that involve family; familial influences on career development.]

As previously mentioned, the school is also a microsystem that can hold great influence on career development, and Young (1983) explained that the school can exert two types of influence, *explicit* and *implicit*. The explicit influences at the school microsystems level include things that are directly done with the purpose of promoting career and college readiness, such as individual and small group counseling, career and college curriculum, and grade-level or school-wide activities. The implicit influences at the school microsystems level include things that are indirect influences on student career and college readiness, such as integration of careers and college in the educational curriculum, socialization experiences, access to extracurricular opportunities, and diversified course offerings that allow students to explore interests.

[handwritten margin note: Explicit influences on career development @ school]

[handwritten margin note: Implicit influences @ school]

Other microsystem influences include peers and social support networks and, for many adolescents, workplace microsystems for seasonal and part-time employees. The positive developmental influences of part-time work on adolescents, according to Young (1983), include increased autonomy, realistic understanding of adult workplace expectations, and overall career knowledge. Negative career developmental influences of the workplace included decreased involvement with school, family, and peers (such as reduced participation in extracurricular activities like clubs and sports) and a focus in the workplace on task skills rather than higher order thinking skills. For example, for an adolescent working in a fast-food restaurant, he or she may be trained to make fries and hamburgers but never understand the concepts of marketing (i.e., branding), the economic development of the fast-food industry, and the reasons for safety requirements and industry regulation.

[handwritten margin note: + impact of workplace; ↑ autonomy; ↑ understanding of adult workplace expectations; ↑ overall career knowledge; – impact of workplace; ↓ involvement in other microsystems; ↓ focus on higher order thinking skills, task skills]

Young (1983) believed that multiple mesosystems influence students' career development: school-to-work transition, school-to-school transition, and family and school interactions. These interactions can become very complex and may involve more than one mesosystem. For instance, in the transition from middle to high school, the family may be interacting both with the middle school teachers, counselors, and administrators and the same personnel at the high school level. However, beyond these major mesosystem interactions, many small-scale mesosystem interactions impact career development, including career shadowing, field observations, field trips, and

[handwritten margin note: Mesosystems that impact career development]

cross-age programming (e.g., older students providing mentoring or tutoring for younger students).

Exosystemic influences on career development appear to be prominent for many students. According to Young (1983), the exosystem influences include the social support network and employment of parents (especially maternal employment), family socioeconomic status, public policy, and social media. All of these systems can have positive and negative outcomes for the developing individual. For example, state policy requiring career and college readiness information may be very helpful for students. However, financial constraints and budget cuts may make some career and college readiness programs vulnerable with the potential for being cut. Likewise, social media that promotes minorities and females in nontraditional roles (such as STEM careers) may promote career development (Choate & Curry, 2009). However, media that sexually objectifies women or stereotypes minorities may undermine career development. Another exosystem influence, according to Young (1983), is the impact child labor laws have on the amount and type of work exposure adolescents can have. Similarly, federal initiatives, such as those explored earlier in this chapter, are exosystem interventions based on cultural expectations of the importance of STEM careers and postsecondary success for students.

At the macrosystem level, work is an important aspect of each individual's unique identity in modern U.S. culture. According to Young (1983), the cultural aspects of education include social consensus on the purpose of education, work ethic, and job entitlement (in particular, a decreasing work ethic coupled with an increasing expectation that jobs will be available), technological changes, and cultural changes in the belief that a person has one career for a lifetime. In 1983, Young projected that many of the cultural career expectations of the current generation of students who are growing up in a fairly financially stable environment may be drastically altered with the advent of large-scale economic decline both in the United States and in global economies. Because we are currently living in an era of economic concern (10% unemployment), it is presumable that cultural shifts in career expectations regarding work ethic, job entitlement, and life-span career transitions and change will occur.

Bordieu's Social Capital Theory

Bourdieu's Social Capital Theory (1986) essentially notes the importance of the resources available to individuals within their social structures, both informally (i.e., relationships with family members) and formally (e.g., parent's work or a student's school). Through relationships developed within their social structures, students and their families form networks in which resources can be accrued that are both tangible (such as getting a job) and intangible (such as acquiring enrichment-based knowledge). Social capital may be inherited through connections by birth. Individuals who inherit capital expend less time and energy seeking to gain capital, as they have the opportunity to take advantage of networks of support and resources that already exist in their immediate systems. A few examples of students who might have more social capital would be members of a royal family, children born to wealthy parents, or children born into families with middle class, professional, and educated parents. The other way that social capital may be acquired is through supportive interactions with individuals who will share their resources and capital through investing energy and assets in an individual with lower social capital.

We can illustrate social capital by providing a comparison. John and Lydia are both 5 years old. Lydia is a single child who loves art. Her parents bought her an easel when she was 3 and she has finger paints, paper, crayons, and PlayDoh at home. Lydia enjoys sculpting, painting, and coloring. Her parents have a membership at the local art museum and they take Lydia there about once per month. In contrast, John lives with his grandmother and four siblings. His grandmother has difficulty making ends meet and does not have money for extra toys or supplies in the home. John and Lydia both end up in the same first-grade class. It turns out that they both love to draw and both are quite artistic. Lydia's parents send her to a Saturday morning art class where she learns to paint on canvas. At school, both Lydia and John show promising signs of talent in the area of art and both are sent for screening for a talented program. Both qualify. Moving forward, both will have access to teachers and programs that will enhance their art performance; however, Lydia will still have the advantage of having parents who can afford art supplies, art camps, and enrichment activities that allow Lydia to explore her art interests. John may also build more capital around his art talent through a growing network of support from teachers, but he will also have to compensate for not having informal networks that can promote his art talent and interests through expending energy of his own to find mentors and access opportunities.

HISTORICAL DEVELOPMENTS IN CAREER THEORY RELATED TO CHILDREN AND ADOLESCENTS

Numerous career development theories exist that guide the work of counseling professionals. However, we believe that school counselors can benefit most from a few specific theories for which practical application for children and adolescents is well documented. We have chosen in this text to highlight a number of individuals whose work provides a strong foundation for school-based career and college readiness interventions, and in the chapters that follow we introduce their theories and articulate how their work relates to students in grades P–12. In this introductory chapter, however, we focus on five key career theorists: Frank Parsons, John Holland, Donald Super, Linda Gottfredson, and John Krumboltz.

Frank Parsons

It is commonly accepted that Parsons (1909), author of *Choosing a Vocation*, is one of the most influential individuals in relation to career development. In his model, Parsons emphasized the importance of self-awareness, occupational awareness, and making logical occupational choices. He believed that people could be matched with occupations if they knew enough about themselves and about work requirements to determine if they would be a good fit for a particular occupation. His ideas served as the precursor to the trait and factor career theories that are so prominently used today in career counseling.

John Holland

Trait and factor theories emphasize finding a match between an individual's personality and a work environment. Holland (1973) developed the *Theory of Vocational Choice*, one of the most practical and commonly applied career theories. He, like Parsons, believed that job success and job satisfaction result from a strong person–environment match. Of prominence in Holland's theory is what he describes as an individual's personality. He believes that a career personality emerges as a result of the interaction of inherent characteristics and the activities to which someone is exposed. The resulting personality is reflected in a person's interests, abilities, and values.

Holland developed a classification system, based on personality types, through which he is able to categorize people and occupations. In his theory, Holland postulates that in order to be successful and satisfied, an individual needs to choose an occupation that is congruent with his or her personality. The six personality types are Realistic, Investigative, Artistic, Social, Enterprising, and Conventional. Holland displays these codes on a hexagon (Figure 1.6).

Realistic personalities interact with the environment by focusing on concrete and physical activities through which they can manipulate objects, tools, and machines. In contrast, *investigative* personalities interact with the environment by using their intellect. They prefer working with concepts and words. *Artistic* personalities interact with the environment through creativity, preferring to engage in activities like art, drama, and others that allow them to express themselves creatively. People who fall into the *social* personality type prefer to interact with the environment through use of their interpersonal skills. They like engaging in activities that allow them to interact with others.

FIGURE 1.6 Holland Codes

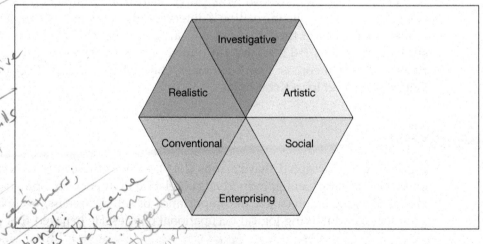

Enterprising personalities interact with the environment typically through activities that allow them to exhibit dominance and power over others and to experience recognition for their efforts. Finally, people who fall into a *conventional* personality type prefer activities for which they will receive approval from others. Their behaviors are expected and routine.

Through the identification of a Holland Code, the classification system captures the nuances that exist within people and occupations. The three-letter Holland Code (e.g., SAI) reflects the most prominent personality types exhibited by an individual or occupation. The first letter represents the most influential characteristics in describing an individual's career decisions; the second letter is the next most influential, and the third letter the third most influential. Holland indicates that the clarity of a person's identity is reflected in how well his or her personality code is differentiated and if the code is consistent. A personality code is well differentiated when the scores for the main personality types (i.e., Holland Code) are much higher than those for the remaining personality types. A consistent personality code is one that includes personality types that are adjacent on the hexagon (see Figure 1.6).

Assessment plays an important role in Holland's theory and the concrete application of his theory is likely what makes it so appealing to counselors. Holland's Self-Directed Search (SDS; see Chapter 5), an instrument that can be used to identify an individual's Holland Code, contains items that examine interests, abilities, and values. The self-report instrument has been validated for use with adolescents and adults. In Holland's Occupations Finder, occupations are categorized by Holland Code. Once individuals identify their Holland Code through the SDS, they can search the Occupations Finder to identify congruent occupations.

Donald Super

While trait and factor theories focus on identifying characteristics related to the fit between people and occupations, developmental theories focus on understanding career development across the life span. Super's (1953) *Life-Span, Life-Space Theory* is the most well-known developmental career theory. He explains that career choice results from a developmental process rather than from a onetime decision. He also believes that people may be happy engaging in more than one occupation. In his theory, Super outlined five developmental stages (growth, exploration, establishment, maintenance, and disengagement) and explains that different career tasks occur throughout those stages. He also emphasized the importance of various life roles (e.g., child, worker, parent) on career development. Of most importance in Super's theory is self-concept, which consists of a person's view of himself or herself and the person's life situation. Super believes that career choices result from a person attempting to find work that fits his or her self-concept. As life roles change over time, naturally a person's self-concept will change, and therefore occupational preferences and choices may change over time.

Linda Gottfredson

In her *Theory of Circumscription and Compromise*, Gottfredson (1981) explains how career aspirations develop over time, beginning in childhood. Similar to its role in Super's theory, self-concept plays a prominent role in Gottfredson's theory; she indicates that people usually choose occupations that are consistent with their self-concept. According to Gottfredson, self-concept consists of a social self (e.g., perceptions of sex, ability, and social status) and psychological self (e.g., values).

Gottfredson described a four-stage model of career development. The first stage, *Orientation to Size and Power*, typically occurs from ages 3 to 5. During this stage, children develop the ability to picture themselves in adult roles. Their self-concept begins to develop but is limited to dichotomous views of self. During the second stage, *Orientation to Sex Roles*, children between the ages of 6 and 8 start to expand their knowledge of careers beyond those they see in their immediate family. They tend to become aware of careers to which they have frequently been exposed. Furthermore, during this stage children start to categorize people based on salient characteristics including sex and race, and these characteristics become prominent in their own self-concept; in particular, sex typing becomes highly influential. In this sense, sex refers to the biological differences between males and females, whereas gender refers to the social or cultural differences between male and female identity. Both gender and sex matter to children in stage two. Stage three, *Orientation to Social Valuation*, typically occurs in the middle school years (ages 9–13). During stage three, children and young adolescents become aware of the existence of different socioeconomic levels and indicators of social status. They also develop an awareness of the connection between high-status jobs and increased educational requirements. Furthermore, they become keenly aware of their own academic abilities and social status, integrating those into their self-concept. The final stage, *Orientation to Internal, Unique Self*, is when adolescents are able to articulate their idealistic and realistic career aspirations.

A few key terms are critical to understanding Gottfredson's (1981) theory. *Circumscription* is the process of narrowing down or ruling out occupations. According to Gottfredson, individuals circumscribe occupations based on perceptions of their social self and perceptions of the accessibility of those occupations. During stages two, three, and four, occupations are ruled out when individuals do not perceive them to be consistent with their own sex, social status, or interests and abilities. Gottfredson describes the resulting list of occupations as the *Zone of Acceptable Alternatives*. She believes that once an occupation is circumscribed, reversing the process can be challenging but not impossible. A second important term, *compromise*, is when individuals give up occupations that are compatible for ones that are most accessible. According to Gottfredson, as people compromise they first consider their perceptions of sex type, then prestige, and finally interests.

John Krumboltz

According to Krumboltz (2009), *Happenstance Learning Theory* is applicable to career and college readiness in a number of noteworthy ways. Basic tenets include that learning is constant and may occur from experiences that are positively or negatively consequential. Similarly, career and college aspirations may be influenced by prior learning that has led to positive or negative feedback for the individual. Similarly, associated learning may occur by vicarious experience or through observing the experiences of others. Associative learning may happen through social media, television, or through the direct environment, and interactions with parents, teachers, and peers. Settings may have negative or positive effects on learning.

For example, P–12 schools, which should offer support for positive learning, often set students up for a series of disappointments by not adequately or effectively addressing social injustices, economic hardships, bullying, and learning disabilities (Krumboltz, 2009). However, unplanned events are a natural and necessary part of career development. Indeed, in direct opposition to Social Capital Theory, in which assets and structures help individuals, Happenstance Learning Theory asserts that unplanned events are also helpful and necessary. Krumboltz offered several fundamental suggestions for career counseling:

1. The goal of career counseling is to help clients learn to take actions to achieve more satisfying career and personal lives—not to make a single career decision. (p. 141)
2. Career assessments are used to stimulate learning, not to match personal characteristics with occupational characteristics. (p. 143)
3. Clients learn to engage in exploratory actions as a way of generating beneficial unplanned events. (p. 144)
4. The success of counseling is assessed by what the client accomplishes in the real world outside the counseling session. (p. 145)

Consider suggestion number 3. Jamilia had never considered being a girl scout, but all her friends begged her to do so. She didn't really know much about the organization other than they sold cookies, and she definitely didn't like the outfits they wore. She wanted to spend time with her friends, however, so she asked her parents and they allowed her to join. Through membership in the organization, Jamilia was exposed to so many things—she learned about sales and first aid and science and writing. Her only career aspiration up until that point was to be a dancer, but after participating in some of the science and nature activities, she started to reconsider. She found that she really liked figuring things out, and it turns out she was good at science—something she had never realized from school. Seeing Jamilia's interest, one of her scout leaders told her about a science camp for girls that she thought Jamilia might enjoy, and with her help, Jamilia's parents were able to secure a scholarship for her to attend. At that camp, she made connections to a staff member who later would play a critical role in her getting a college scholarship. Had Jamilia's friends not begged her to join them, her parents not permitted her to do so, and her scout leader not suggested the camp, it is possible that Jamilia never would have developed a love for science or found a way to college. This is just one example of how unplanned events can positively impact future outcomes.

CAREER AND COLLEGE READINESS SKILLS

The career theories we just reviewed emphasize the importance of self-awareness (knowing one's interests, aptitudes, values, and beliefs) and career awareness (knowing specific occupational training and skill requirements) so that meaningful career goals can be identified and pursued. Knowledge of the skills needed for success in careers and college in general also can be important in helping students identify strengths and weaknesses and in helping counselors and other educators identify areas for intervention. As we discussed previously, 21st-century students need multiple skills to be successful in careers and college. We talked about academic, employability, and technical skills, as well as important intrapersonal factors and dispositions. We want to look now at a few specific skills that all students, no matter what their career path, need to possess. These skills fall into six major categories: career exploration, social interaction and communication, higher order thinking, financial literacy, self-regulation, and employability.

Career Exploration Skills

As students enter the 21st-century workforce, it is most likely that their career paths will change multiple times. Students need to have the skills to explore various occupations, including having an understanding of how their own aptitudes, interests, and values impact overall career satisfaction and career decision making. Moreover, they also need to know how to comprehensively engage in career exploration tasks to access accurate information regarding the training required to enter an occupation, what a typical day on the job is like, what additional skill sets are required, what specialty areas exist within an occupation, average earnings/wages, and the projected outlook for the growth or decline of an occupation. To be able to find this information, students need to be provided opportunities to engage in activities such as completing career assessments, reviewing technical websites, engaging in job shadowing, and understanding interview protocols. Career exploration skills are more salient than ever as students are often exposed, via social media, to unrealistic careers. For example, many students may like the idea of entering the area of forensics as a result of watching crime scene investigation shows; however, careers are often inaccurately portrayed in such Hollywood creations. Being able to accurately explore a career allows students to develop a realistic view of the day-to-day realities of a particular occupation.

Social Interaction and Communication Skills

In addition to knowing how to explore a career, students need to have the skills to be successful in the workplace. There are myriad social and communication skills necessary for career success. Being able to work collaboratively with others as well as function autonomously are vital. Other skills include active listening; communicating effectively in writing, verbally, and electronically; compromising; managing conflict; and interacting effectively with a group (Sharf, 2006). Students also need to have self-awareness of their own values, cultural heritage, beliefs, and biases and how these may affect their interactions with others; most importantly, they need to have a true appreciation for diversity and a propensity for cultural sensitivity and positive affirmation of others (ASCA, 2012; Holcomb-McCoy & Chen-Hayes, 2011).

Higher Order Thinking Skills

As suggested by Brock (2010) in his discussion of college readiness, students in the most basic sense need to possess cognitive skills that will enable them to retain and apply knowledge. We suggest that a continuum of cognitive skills would be important to assess when working on career and college readiness. At the most basic level, students need to possess the cognitive skills that would enable them to do things like focus their attention, concentrate on a task, and comprehend instructions. At a middle level, critical thinking skills would be required—the ability to identify problems and generate solutions. Finally, for students pursuing 4-year college degrees, higher order thinking skills would be necessary to enable them to successfully engage in tasks like solving complex algebraic equations, writing fluent essays, and understanding scientific research methodology.

Financial Literacy Skills

Financial literacy may be defined as "possessing the skills and knowledge on financial matters to confidently take effective action that best fulfills an individual's personal, family and global community goals" (National Financial Educators Council, n.d.). For P–12 students, financial literacy skills related to postsecondary life include things such as learning how to create and manage a budget based on projected income and lifestyle, saving for college, and managing debt (e.g., credit cards, student loans). Related to budgets, all P–12 students can benefit from learning about financial matters that would relate to living on their own and supporting or contributing to a family. Understanding things like basic budgeting, mortgage rates, compound interest, and car loans can help them determine what they can and cannot afford based on their income. Learning how to manage debt also is important for all students, but particularly for students who need to take out loans to pay for their postsecondary education.

[handwritten margin notes: Info needed by middle school; HOPE covers 100% of tuition & $300 for Books]

An estimated 66% of first-time bachelor's degree recipients borrowed to finance their education, with their average debt equaling $24,700 (NCES, 2011a). Skills to navigate the financial aid system (e.g., filling out an FAFSA; exploring loan, scholarship, and other funding sources) can help students and their families develop a more realistic understanding of whether or not postsecondary school is possible. At least 13 states have scholarship programs that cover tuition and other costs for eligible students (Brandon, 2006). For example, Georgia's HOPE (Helping Outstanding Students Educationally) scholarship requires a high school grade point average of 3.0 in a college preparatory curriculum; it covers 100% of tuition and provides $300 for books (Brandon, 2006). Students and their families ideally must understand the requirements for these types of scholarships by middle school so that they can make appropriate high school curricular choices. Furthermore, in order to determine what might be realistic financially, students and families also need to understand what expenses (e.g., residence hall fees, institutional fees, transportation costs, extracurricular activities, materials needed such as notebooks and laptops) the scholarships do and do not cover.

Self-Regulatory Skills

[handwritten margin note: Mastery of task = skills + feelings of efficacy in that area]

Self-regulation (Bandura, 1977) refers to the ability to set goals and manage behavior toward those goals. Self-regulation requires approximating consequences, determining the action required to meet a desired outcome, and evaluating one's abilities to successfully complete a desired behavior and reach a goal (Bandura, 1977). Additionally, it includes directing oneself in day-to-day activities with discipline, and it is a particularly important skill for facing challenges and being able to problem solve, break goals down into manageable tasks, and focus on task completion. According to Bandura (1986), mastery of any given task requires the minimal skills necessary to perform the task *and* feelings of efficacy in one's ability to effectively apply skills. Thus, in order for students to achieve in school and move through postsecondary educational programs and careers with success, they must possess the skills to set and attain goals as well as the belief that they can achieve those goals.

Employability

Employability skills include those skills necessary to secure a position in one's chosen field. Skills such as developing a resume that accurately and effectively highlights one's achievements, writing a cover letter that distinguishes one from other job competitors, and confidently participating in an interview are all critical. Finding open positions in one's field and discerning the necessary qualifications for consideration of employment are also included in this skill set.

THE ROLES OF STAKEHOLDERS IN CAREER AND COLLEGE READINESS

Who is responsible for promoting career and college readiness? The obvious answer is the school counselor (ASCA, 2012); however, in today's educational environment, all educators are expected to play a role in assisting students to become career and college ready. According to a policy brief in the *Alliance for Excellent Education* (Miller, 2009), teachers must be prepared to teach to higher standards than ever before. Rather than just focusing on content, they also need to assist students in connecting academic content to careers and college. Moreover, parents, administrators, and community partners all play a role in developing students' career and college awareness and potential. In this book, we highlight the role of the school counselor in career and college readiness while also looking at the counselor's role in fostering stakeholders' ability to promote career and college readiness. We also focus on adult stakeholders we believe to be most consistently and directly involved in students' lives: counselors, teachers, administrators, parents/guardians, and community partners.

Counselors

Counselors are positioned to promote student development in three specific areas: academic, career, and personal/social domains (ASCA, 2012). Through a comprehensive school counseling program, counselors design, implement, manage, and evaluate services to students and other stakeholders (i.e., parents, teachers, administrators, and community partners). In order to help all stakeholders understand the importance and purpose of a comprehensive career and college readiness approach in schools, it is important that school counselors involve these individuals in the coordination and development of the program (Niles & Harris-Bowlsbey, 2009). Moreover, career and college readiness programming should be consistently delivered, based on measurable goals and objectives, and evaluated. In this way, students receive quality services rather than piecemeal or sporadic interventions, and school counselors are able to monitor the effectiveness of their interventions (ASCA, 2012; Niles & Harris-Bowlsbey, 2009). School counselors provide students with career and college information, assessments, and skills. Further, they assist students in understanding the connections between academics and the world of work. School counselors are trained to deliver the following career and college interventions for students and stakeholders: classroom lessons, small-group interventions, individual counseling and advising sessions, school-wide and grade-level career- and college-related activities, faculty in-service programs, parent workshops, and community partner programs. Examples of all of these services are provided throughout this book.

Teachers

Teachers play a pivotal role in students' career and college readiness. Because students often question the need for academic knowledge (e.g., "Why do we have to learn algebra? I'm never going to use it!"), it can be helpful for teachers to introduce ways that academic content in the classroom relates to future career and college opportunities. Although career education has historically been the school counselor's role, many states are requiring teacher candidates to also demonstrate competency in developing student career and college readiness (Curry, Belser, & Binns, 2013). For instance, the South Carolina Department of Education (2012), in order to align teacher preparation programs with the Education and Economic Development Act, states that, "educator preparation units must provide assessment evidence to indicate that all candidates enrolled in educator preparation, school guidance counseling, and education administration programs possess the knowledge, skills, and dispositions" (p. 4) to integrate career-related content into the P–12 curriculum. However, many teachers may view the integration of careers and college in the classroom curriculum as extra work. Therefore, it is important that teachers are provided with strategies that are manageable and that engage students. In order to effectively do this, teachers need professional development opportunities to learn about technology and curriculum materials that can be used to integrate career and college information into classroom instruction (Curry et al., 2013). In this book, we explore how school counselors can provide teachers with such professional development and collaborate to provide career and college readiness interventions.

In addition, to proactively integrate career and college content into their classrooms, teachers should become aware of how their actions may encourage or discourage students from certain career and college options. They often are the first to identify students who possess aptitudes in certain areas or who have strong interests for certain subjects. With an appreciation for how their encouragement and support can make a difference in students' career and college aspirations, teachers can be intentional about how they work with students.

Administrators

Administrators play a major role in the types of programming that students receive. Effective principals and education leaders understand current policies and best practices, and know that career and college readiness is a critical component of P–12 education. Principals ensure that quality and rigor are maintained in the school's curriculum and work closely with the school counselor to promote the integration of career and college information in the school's education agenda. The principal works to foster collaboration among teachers, parents, students, and the school counselor to improve students' access to rigorous course offerings, college planning, academic advisement, and assessment resources. Further, the principal and school counselor coordinate efforts to ensure that a comprehensive school counseling program is in place and utilized by all stakeholders.

Parents and Guardians

Families play a pivotal role in a child's career and college readiness. Indeed multiple family factors are correlated with career and college decision making, including parents' education level (NCES, 2011a), parents' educational expectations and support for the child, family socioeconomic status, and financial resources (Hossler, Schmit, & Vesper, 1999; Patton & Creed, 2007). Specifically, the higher the educational attainment of the parents, the more likely the child will earn a college degree. In a study of students attending college in the United States, 29.8% of students had a parent with a graduate or professional degree, 26.4% had a parent with a bachelor's degree, 23.7% had a parent with some postsecondary education, and 20.1% had a parent with high school education or less (NCES, 2011a). Because parents convey family values about education, it is important that they understand their role in promoting postsecondary educational options for their children.

Most notably, it is important that school counselors and educators not assume that parents without postsecondary degrees do not value such experiences for their child. However, those parents may need more help assisting their children in navigating admissions, financial aid, registration, and so on; therefore, the resources they receive to do this are vital. School counselors also can educate parents about the ways in which they can promote interest in school, foster the innate talents their children possess, and provide opportunities for their children to explore careers and colleges.

Community Partners

Community partners play an invaluable role in students' career and college readiness. They assist school counselors by providing insight on local workforce needs, providing student career mentorship, serving as career and college guest speakers, providing resources for career and college fairs, and facilitating job-shadowing opportunities. Throughout this book, we offer a variety of examples of how school counselors can engage community partners in career and college readiness initiatives.

HOW TO USE THIS BOOK TO PREPARE FOR P–12 CAREER AND COLLEGE READINESS PROGRAMMING IN SCHOOLS

Developmental Overview

In each chapter of this book, we present a holistic overview of the typical chronological ages present within the grade level under discussion. Children's social, physical, emotional, cognitive, and educational development are interrelated with and greatly influence career and college readiness (Gibson & Mitchell, 2006). Therefore, we begin each chapter with a review of the holistic developmental milestones and developmental tasks for the age group(s) presented in that chapter. However, as an important caution to readers, it is critical to note that development is personal and continues throughout the life span, so the information presented in these chapters is general in nature and may not apply to each individual child. Indeed, development varies among children as rates of growth and personal factors (i.e., temperament, intelligence, support systems) are unique to each individual.

Sequential Career and College Readiness Programming

In this book, we use a sequential format. By this we mean that with each grade level we cover, we show the reader how student competence builds on prior learning in the areas of career knowledge and skills. For example, when learning math, a student is introduced to addition before multiplication. The same is true for careers and college content; each subsequent grade level will build on prior knowledge and skills.

Pedagogy, Learning Objectives, and Curriculum Development

School counselors need to be able to develop a career and college readiness curriculum to meet the needs of the population at the school they serve (ASCA, 2012). However, many school counselors do not have a background in education. Therefore, in this book we use a two-part approach to help novice school counselors write their curriculum: (a) Bloom's Taxonomy, and (b) the *ASCA Mindsets and Behaviors for Student Success: K-12 College- and Career-Readiness Standards for Every Student* (2014; see Appendix C). In counseling and education, pedagogy that paces higher cognitive development is often based on Bloom's Taxonomy. The taxonomy (see Chapter 6) denotes how learning begins with lower-level thinking (memorization, recognition, recall) and moves to more complex, higher order thinking (proposing and using an evaluative criteria). All learning can be paced to higher order thinking.

The ASCA Mindsets and Behaviors (2014) are used to assist school counselors in identifying developmentally appropriate student learning objectives and conceptualizing associated career and college readiness interventions. This book covers practical applications for school counselors to include whole-school programs, grade-level programs, classroom presentations, small-group counseling, individual career and college counseling, individual planning/academic advisement, parent workshops, and faculty in-service on career- and college-related topics.

Sample Activities and Case Studies

Throughout this book, we share examples of career and college readiness interventions that are empirically supported, grounded in theory, and/or already successfully implemented in schools. Our examples reflect counselors' direct work with students (e.g., classroom and individual interventions) as well as their work for the benefit of or in collaboration with parents, teachers, and community partners. Many of the examples are suggested for a specific grade level or type of student, but could easily be adjusted for use with other populations. Further, given the cultural differences and variations possible within any school population, it is important that readers consider culturally sensitive career and college readiness practices (see Chapter 4).

SUMMARY

In this chapter, we defined career and college readiness and the role of the school counselor in helping students develop relevant skills and knowledge. We reviewed federal initiatives that are impacting career and college readiness for students, particularly in the STEM areas, and looked at current trends in postsecondary enrollment and matriculation as well as in employment. We then discussed the type of skills students will need to be successful for college and the world of work and the importance of all stakeholders in promoting students' understanding of careers and college. In the following chapters, we examine career and college readiness by education levels for students in P–12 schools.

⋯❭ Test Your Knowledge

1. Explain how federal initiatives have impacted career and college readiness.
2. Based on the data and statistics shared in the beginning of this chapter, identify one or two specific populations you believe should be targeted in an effort to help close the achievement gap.
3. Compare and contrast the skills needed for career readiness with those needed for college readiness.

REFERENCES

ACT, Inc. (2008). *The forgotten middle: Ensuring that all students are on target for college and career readiness before high school (Policy brief)*. Iowa City, IA: Author.

ACT, Inc. (2015). *The condition of college & career readiness 2015*. Iowa City, IA: Author. Retrieved from http://www.act.org/content/act/en/research/condition-of-college-and-career-readiness-report-2015.html?page=0&chapter=0

Akos, P., Niles, S. G., Miller, E. M., & Erford, B. T. (2011). Promoting educational and career planning in schools. In B. T. Erford (Ed.), *Transforming the school counseling profession* (3rd ed., pp. 202–221). Upper Saddle River, NJ: Pearson.

American Association of University Women. (2016). *The simple truth about the gender pay gap*. Washington, DC: Author.

American School Counselor Association. (2012). *The ASCA national model: A framework for school counseling programs* (3rd ed.). Alexandria, VA: Author.

American School Counselor Association. (2014). *ASCA mindsets & behaviors for student success: K-12 college- and career-readiness standards for every student*. Alexandria, VA: Author.

Association for Career and Technical Education. (2010). *What is career ready?* Alexandria, VA: Author.

Association for Career and Technical Education. (2011). *What is "career ready?"* Retrieved from https://www.acteonline.org/search.aspx?q=what is "career ready"?

Bandura, A. (1977). *Social learning theory*. Englewood Cliffs, NJ: Prentice Hall.

Bandura, A. (1986). *Social foundations of thought and action: A social cognitive theory*. Englewood Cliffs, NJ: Prentice Hall.

Blumenstyk, G. (2015). *American higher education in crisis? What everyone needs to know*. New York, NY: Oxford University Press.

Bourdieu, P. (1986). The forms of capital. In J. G. Richardson (Ed.), *Handbook of theory and research for the sociology of education* (pp. 241–258). Westport, CT: Greenwood Press.

Brandon, E. (2006, September 18). Better yet, no tuition. *U. S. News & World Report, 141*(10), 74–75. Retrieved from http://www.cbsnews.com/news/better-yet-no-tuition

Brock, T. (2010). Young adults and higher education: Barriers and breakthroughs to success. *Future of Children, 20*(1), 109–132.

Bronfenbrenner, U. (1977). Toward an experimental ecology of human development. *American Psychologist, 32,* 513–531. http://dx.doi.org/10.1037/0003-066X.32.7.513

Carnevale, A. P., Rose, S. J., & Cheah, B. (2011). *The college payoff: Education, occupations, lifetime earnings.* Retrieved from http://cew.georgetown.edu/collegepayoff

Carnevale, A. P., Smith, N., & Strohl, J. (2010). *Help wanted: Projections of jobs and education requirements through 2018.* Retrieved from http://cew.georgetown.edu/jobs2018

Choate, L. H., & Curry, J. (2009). Addressing the sexualization of girls through comprehensive programs, advocacy and systemic change: Implications for professional school counselors. *Professional School Counseling, 12*(3), 213–221. http://dx.doi.org/10.5330/PSC.n.2010-12.213

Conley, D. T. (2007). *Redefining college readiness.* Eugene, OR: Educational Policy Improvement Center.

Curry, J., Belser, C. T., & Binns, I. C. (2013). Integrating post-secondary college and career options in the middle school curriculum: Considerations for teachers. *Middle School Journal, 44*(3), 26–32.

Curry, J., & Bickmore, D. (2012). School counselor induction and the importance of mattering. *Professional School Counseling, 15*(3), 110–122. http://dx.doi.org/10.5330/PSC.n.2012-15.110

Diamond, K. E., Spiegel-McGill, P., & Hanrahan, P. (1988). Planning for school transition: An ecological-developmental approach. *Journal of the Division for Early Childhood, 12,* 245–252.

Executive Office of the President. (December, 2015). *Every student succeeds act: A progress report on elementary and secondary education.* Executive Summary. Retrieved from https://www.whitehouse.gov/sites/whitehouse.gov/files/documents/ESSA_Progress_Report.pdf

Fleisher, G. (2012). *Addressing America's STEM crisis: Taking proven programs to national scale.* Dallas, TX: National Math and Science Initiative. Retrieved from https://www.eplc.org/notebook2012/GreggFleisher_May17.pdf

Gibson, R. L., & Mitchell, M. H. (2006). *Introduction to career counseling for the 21st century.* Upper Saddle River, NJ: Pearson.

Gottfredson, L. S. (1981). Circumscription and compromise: A developmental theory of occupational aspirations. *Journal of Counseling Psychology, 28*(6), 545–579. http://dx.doi.org/10.1037/0022-0167.28.6.545

Hart Research Associates. (2005). Rising to the challenge: Are high school graduates prepared for college and work? A study of recent high school graduates, college instructors, and employers. Retrieved from http://www.achieve.org/files/pollreport_0.pdf

Holcomb-McCoy, C., & Chen-Hayes, S. F. (2011). Culturally competent school counselors: Affirming diversity by challenging oppression. In B. T. Erford (Ed.), *Transforming the school counseling profession* (3rd ed., pp. 90–109). Upper Saddle River, NJ: Pearson.

Holland, J. L. (1973). *Making vocational choices: A theory of careers.* Englewood Cliffs, NJ: Prentice Hall.

Hossler, D., Schmit, J., & Vesper, N. (1999). *Going to college: How social, economic and educational factors influence the decisions students make.* Baltimore, MD: The Johns Hopkins University Press.

Isay, D. (2016). *Callings: The purpose and passion of work* (a StoryCorps Book). New York, NY: Penguin Publishing.

Johnson, L. S. (2000). The relevance of school to career: A study in student awareness. *Journal of Career Development, 26*(4), 263–276. http://dx.doi.org/10.1177/089484530002600403

Kemp, C., & Carter, M. (2000). Demonstration of classroom survival skills in kindergarten: A five-year transition study of children with intellectual disabilities. *Educational Psychology, 20*, 393–411. http://dx.doi.org/10.1080/713663756

Krumboltz, J. D. (2009). The happenstance learning theory. *Journal of Career Assessment, 17*(2), 135–154. http://dx.doi.org/10.1177/1069072708328861

Martin, P. J., & Robinson, S. G. (2011). Transforming the school counseling profession. In B. T. Erford (Ed.), *Transforming the school counseling profession* (pp. 1–18). Upper Saddle River, NJ: Pearson.

Miller, M. (2009). *Teaching for a new world: Preparing high school educators to deliver college- and career-ready instruction.* Retrieved from ERIC database (ED507351).

Milsom, A. (2007). Interventions to assist students with disabilities through school transitions. *Professional School Counseling, 10*(3), 273–278.

Myers, J. E., Sweeney, T. J., & Witmer, J. M. (2000). The wheel of wellness counseling for wellness: A holistic model for treatment planning. *Journal of Counseling & Development, 78*(3), 251–266. http://dx.doi.org/10.1002/j.1556-6676.2000.tb01906.x

National Center for Education Statistics. (2011a). *2008–2009 baccalaureate and beyond longitudinal study (B&B:08/09).* Washington, DC: U.S. Department of Education.

National Center for Education Statistics. (2011b). *Digest of education statistics, 2010. (NCES 2011-015).* Washington, DC: U.S. Department of Education. Retrieved from http://nces.ed.gov/fastfacts/display.asp?id=59

National Center for Education Statistics. (2014). *Digest of education statistics. Table 501.50. Employment to population ratios of persons 16 to 64 years old, by age group and highest level of educational attainment: Selected years, 1975 through 2014.* Retrieved from https://nces.ed.gov/programs/digest/d14/tables/dt14_501.50.asp

National Center for Education Statistics. (2015). *Enrollment and percentage distribution of enrollment in public elementary and secondary schools, by race/ethnicity and region: Selected years, fall 1995 through fall 2025.* Washington, DC: U.S. Department of Education. Retrieved from http://nces.ed.gov/programs/digest/d15/tables/dt15_203.50.asp

National Financial Educators Council. (n.d.). Financial literacy definition. Retrieved from http://www.financialeducatorscouncil.org/financial-literacy-definition.html

Niles, S. G., & Harris-Bowlsbey, J. (2009). *Career development interventions in the 21st century* (3rd ed.). Upper Saddle River, NJ: Merrill.

Parsons, F. (1909). *Choosing a vocation.* Boston, MA: Houghton Mifflin.

Patton, W., & Creed, P. (2007). The relationship between career variables and occupational aspirations and expectations for Australian high school adolescents. *Journal of Career Development, 34*(2), 127–148. http://dx.doi.org/10.1177/0894845307307471

Pew Research Center. (2014, February 11). The rising cost of not going to college. Pew Research Center Social and Demographic Trends. Retrieved from http://www.pewsocialtrends.org/2014/02/11/the-rising-cost-of-not-going-to-college

Ryan, C. L., & Bauman, K. (2016, March). *Educational attainment in the United States: 2015. Population characteristics* (Report #P20-578). Washington, DC: U.S. Census Bureau.

Sharf, R. S. (2006). *Applying career development theory to counseling* (4th ed.). Belmont, CA: Thomson.

South Carolina Department of Education. (2012). Standards, policies, and procedures for South Carolina educator preparation units. Retrieved from http://ed.sc.gov/scdoe/assets/File/educators/educator-preparation/educator-units/081012Standards_Policies_Procedures_Board_Approved_2015(1).pdf

Super, D. E. (1953). A theory of vocational development. *American Psychologist, 8,* 185–190.

The Chronicle of Higher Education. (2011). *Almanac of higher education 2011.* Retrieved from http://chronicle.com/section/Almanac-of-Higher-Education/536

U.S. Bureau of Labor Statistics. (2015). *TED: The economics daily. Rising wage inequality 2003–13.* Washington, DC: U.S. Department of Labor. Retrieved from http://www.bls.gov/opub/ted/2015/rising-wage-inequality-2003-13.htm

U.S. Census Bureau. (2011). Educational attainment by race, Hispanic origin, and sex: 1970-2010. In *Statistical Abstract of the United States: 2012* (131st ed., Table 230, p. 151). Washington, DC: Author. Retrieved from https://www2.census.gov/library/publications/2011/compendia/statab/131ed/2012-statab.pdf

U.S. Census Bureau. (2014), *Income and poverty in the United States: 2014* (Table B 2, pp.54–56; Current Population Reports, P60-252)., Retrieved from http://www.npc.umich.edu/poverty/#5

U.S. Department of Education. (2004). *NCLB overview: Executive summary.* Archived information. Washington, DC: Author. Retrieved from http://www2.ed.gov/nclb/overview/intro/execsumm.html

Young, R. A. (1983). Career development of adolescents: An ecological perspective. *Journal of Youth and Adolescence, 12*(5), 401–417. http://dx.doi.org/10.1007/BF02088723

TWO

P–12 Career and College Readiness:
Preparing All Students for a Postsecondary Plan

In this chapter, we discuss the factors involved in students' postsecondary decision making. In addition to 4-year college degrees, we give attention to career-bound students pursuing industry recognized credentials (IRCs) as well as those hoping to transition to technical schools or community colleges for certificate programs or associate's degrees (ADs). In terms of students pursuing 4-year college degrees, we focus on the importance of options including dual enrollment (DE), Advanced Placement (AP) courses, and college entrance exams. This chapter includes interventions designed to help students make the best possible postsecondary educational choices.

THE SCHOOL COUNSELOR'S ROLE: CREATING A CAREER AND COLLEGE READINESS CULTURE

In Chapter 1, we addressed many federal initiatives aimed at career and college readiness (i.e., Every Student Succeeds Act, Reach Higher) and two important documents created by the American School Counselor Association (ASCA): the National Model (2012) and Mindsets and Behaviors (2014). Yet, in order to truly create postsecondary opportunities for students, school counselors need to create a sustained culture of career and college readiness spanning P–12 that includes all stakeholders (e.g., parents, students, community partners, administrators). One group that has done an excellent job defining specific ways to do this is the National Association for College Admission Counseling (NACAC). Originally approved by their executive board in 1990, NACAC continues to develop and maintain a *Statement on Precollege Guidance and Counseling and the Role of the School Counselor*. This document is important because it offers a perspective from outside the P–12 setting of how best to assist students in preparing for and transitioning to higher education.

The NACAC statement (1999) includes several noteworthy considerations. First, the statement highlights elements of an effective precollege program that is highly aligned with the ASCA National Model and addresses issues of equity in the precollege educational environment. Second, the NACAC underscores the need for ethical practice, administrative support, and that individuals working on college preparation with students are adequately trained. This is

[handwritten margin note: Professional development of S. Counselors crucial to CC-Readiness program]

critical given that higher education is evolving and so are students. What is expected today in the college admission process and for college success is qualitatively different than in years past, as we discuss in this chapter. Therefore, having school counselors who are adequately prepared with the most accurate and up-to-date information is necessary for students' success. In essence, the professional development of school counselors is a crucial investment.

The NACAC (1999) statement also takes a developmental approach (similar to this book) in how college preparation should be approached at the middle school and high school levels. At the middle school level, NACAC advocates for interventions designed to promote self-awareness about interests, values, and attitudes; career and educational planning; and an understanding of high school academic options related to careers and college. We agree that these are core developmental issues related to career and college preparation for middle school students and we address these topics in Chapters 10 and 11. For high school students, NACAC recommends a focus on career and college planning, goal setting, decision making, assisting parents and students in understanding the financial aid process, college visits, interviewing skills, and timelines for college applications. We agree that these are helpful skills to develop with high school students and address these in Chapters 12 to 15.

The degree of national interest in the topic of career and college readiness is directly related to the high stakes for America's future. As noted in Chapter 1, careers matter. Here, in Chapter 2, we focus on the pathway to careers through postsecondary education and training. Yet, more than ever before, that pathway may be a bit confusing, and both students and families may be unsure of the best option. We begin by exploring why college decision making has become so complicated.

DOES COLLEGE PAY OFF?

The answer is "yes" and "it depends." When thinking about college, traditionally, most people think of a 4-year degree. Numerous types of certificates, degrees, and postsecondary options exist in many different fields. How do we help students choose the right one(s) for them? An important part of school counselors' work will be to help students (and their families) become aware of the sometimes multiple options and pathways they could take to achieve their long-term career goals.

Recently, I, the first author, was on a high school visit observing a school counselor advising students in a career track class. It was part of a track in which students earn a Certified Nurse Assistant (CNA) certificate for completing specified course work in high school. The school counselor was advising the high school students on nursing degree options after high school through 2-year community college and 4-year university programs. After the lesson, the school counselor stated to me that most of the students completing the certificate were likely to go on to a complete 2-year Associate of Science in Nursing (ASN) degree but not a Bachelor of Science in Nursing (BSN) as the students in this track did not have the prerequisites for 4-year college admission. The school counselor confessed that she often felt she had no other career options to tell the students in the CNA program about in group advisement other than nursing. I asked whether or not she had ever considered talking about other certificate and 2-year options in the medical field, like sonography. The school counselor asked me what a sonographer does, and I explained that some do MRI and others do ultrasounds, while others are even more specialized (e.g., cardiovascular).

I walked with her to a computer and helped her look up sonographer on the *Occupational Outlook Handbook* (U.S. Department of Labor, n.d.). In 2015, a sonographer needed an AS (2 year) and the occupation was growing by 24% (to put this in perspective, the average occupation for 2015 is growing by 7%). Median pay for sonographers in the United States is $63,630 per year (U.S. Bureau of Labor Statistics, 2015). In this case, a 2-year AS would definitely pay off if you consider that the degree is very quick to obtain, an individual would not need to accrue much debt to receive the degree, and once obtained, the likelihood of employability is high. Yet there are bachelor's and master's degrees that may not have this high of a payoff.

You can probably think of countless scenarios like this, one where you or other school personnel did not have comprehensive information to share with students. Indeed, it would be impossible to know of every potential career that exists. Yet, it is critical that school counselors are aware of the types of training programs offered in their schools, educational options available to students, and resources available to help broaden students' career and college exploration to view a large range of careers and postsecondary options. Another important activity school counselors can engage in is to help teachers learn about career and college options related to the courses they teach and point them to resources that will assist them in linking classroom content with the world of work. Teachers who are knowledgeable about their content areas may be the best allies in helping to determine what occupational areas are showing promising growth, sustainable income, and manageable degree or certification attainment costs.

Four Rules to the College Payoff

Carnevale, Rose, and Cheah (2011) noted that there are four basic rules in determining whether or not college pays off. *Rule Number One* is that degree level matters. Typically, this means the higher the degree, the greater the pay. *Rule Number Two* is occupational choice can mean more than degree level. For example, someone with a bachelor's degree in engineering may earn more than a person with a doctoral degree in History. The higher degree does not *always* mean a higher salary in this case because engineers generally receive greater remuneration than historians.

Rule Number Three is that although occupation may determine salary more than a particular degree, the level of education within occupations still matters in terms of salary (Carnevale et al., 2011). In our previous example, we stated that an engineer with a bachelor's degree may make a greater salary than a historian with a doctoral degree. Rule three basically states that within the field of engineering, engineers with higher degrees (i.e., master's or doctoral) make higher salaries than those with lower degree attainment (i.e., bachelor's).

Rule Number Four is that race or ethnicity and gender are complicating factors that actually matter more than education or occupation in determining earnings (Carnevale et al., 2011). Consider Carissa, an African American female who is the director of a human resources department in her company in Texas. She has a master's degree and 10 years of experience. In spite of her experience and education, the likelihood that she receives equal compensation to a White male in her same position with the same degree and same years of experience is not promising. In fact, according to the American Association of University Women's *The Simple Truth About the Gender Pay Gap* (2016), in Texas, median annual earnings for women are 79% of that for men. So for every dollar a man with her same credentials would earn, Carissa would earn $0.79.

The States' Historic Disinvestment in Higher Education

As a result of the 2008 economic recession, unprecedented widespread and deep cuts to funding for higher education were made across the United States. From 2009 to 2012, 48 states decreased funding to higher education through direct support to public institutions, and these cuts ranged from 14.8% to 69.4% (Mortenson, 2012). Concomitantly, due to unemployment or poor employment possibilities during the recession era, many individuals left the workforce and returned to higher education to seek degrees or certifications that would make them more marketable (Baylor, 2014). Also, student enrollments increased by 13.7% in the years 2008 to 2012, and federal student loan borrowing increased in those same years by 54.6% (Baylor, 2014). In sum, as states decreased funding to higher education to make up for budget deficits, student tuition increased substantially. At the same time, student enrollments increased. This leaves institutions of higher education in somewhat of a quagmire in that it is unlikely that states will reinvest fully the funding that was cut during this historic period. Yet, keeping college affordable and providing the necessary revenue to keep higher education afloat is a difficult balance.

Blumenstyk (2015) noted three trends that emerge as colleges and universities now have to compete for tuition revenue that offsets the loss of state investments: (a) greater recruitment of graduate students who often pay a higher differential per credit hour, (b) greater recruitment of out-of-state and international students who pay higher rates, and (c) placing more courses and programs online to offset the cost of instructors, materials, buildings, maintenance, and being able to retrieve a higher per hour credit amount. These trends are concerning, especially because they place an incredible financial strain on the most academically vulnerable populations (e.g., low socioeconomic status [SES], first-generation students). These are the students who most often need greater access to higher education in terms of affordability.

Student Loan Debt

According to *The Economist* (2015), student loan debt tripled from 2004 to 2014, and in the United States currently, student loans now total over $1.2 trillion. Additionally, student loan debt has increased at twice the rate of inflation (The Institute for College Access & Success, 2015). Students whose degrees were from for-profit colleges seem to struggle the most in terms of repaying their loans, with almost 20% defaulting on their loans within 3 years (The Economist, 2015). Based on information from the Institute for College Access & Success's Project on Student Debt (2015), 69% of college graduates from public and nonprofit colleges in 2014 had student loan debt, and the average debt per borrower was $28,950. According to *U.S. News and World Report* (2015), the average loan default amount is $14,000 or less.

Given the increase in cost of college and the high likelihood that students will incur some debt to attend college, school counselors need to be cognizant of ensuring that (a) students have full access and exposure to a career and college readiness curriculum, (b) students are aware of opportunities to earn college credit while in high school, (c) students and parents are provided with financial literacy training pertaining to budgeting for college throughout the P–12 experience, and (d) students explore the many paths to the field of their choice to determine the best college payoff option.

The Value of a Liberal Arts Degree

In an era where the cost of college is increasing dramatically, and student loan debt is skyrocketing, students and their families may wonder if it would be more prudent to pursue shorter degree options. For example, rather than seeking a Bachelor of Science degree in Computer Science, a student might wonder if her career goals in the Computer Science industry are achievable with an AS. As a school counselor, it is important to know each student's hoped for outcomes when giving postsecondary advisement. What, ultimately, is the student's career goal? Is the student able to work and go to school? Does the student have access to financial support (scholarships, grants, family support)? What degree aligns to the student's career interest? It is important to help students and their families weigh all of this information rather than just deciding to go with the cheapest or quickest option.

It is also essential to remember that many students and their families may not know what is additive about the college experience beyond academic content. As McNutt (2014) underscored, the value of a 4-year liberal arts degree is more than just learning about humanities; it is critical thinking, problem solving, and group work. Although there are many shorter options to satisfying career outcomes, we do want to note that the value of college is often beyond the classroom walls. Opportunities for leadership, mentorship by professors, and access to labs and research may be very important to developing career and life experiences for many students. As we review various postsecondary options, we do not want to exalt one option over others.

We are simply highlighting each in the hope that school counselors will expose students to a variety of opportunities and help them explore the potential benefits and limitations of each.

UNDERSTANDING THE VALUE OF A DEGREE IN CONTEXT

All postsecondary educational options have to be understood in context. What can a person do with a particular certificate or degree? Are subsequent degrees necessary to accomplish the goals particular to an individual's career aspirations? Is there high selectivity within programs and, if so, are the selection criteria based on grade point average (GPA), test scores, or other data? Beyond the degree, are there certifications, licenses, board exams, or other credentials that must be obtained to practice in the field? All of these questions are important to examine in considering how much education, training, experience, and cost will be incurred to pursue a particular career path or achieve a career goal. Additionally, understanding both how a career is trending in terms of projected outlook for growth and the anticipated need for a career within different geographical locations are important considerations when working with students to consider careers within context.

For example, imagine a student, Jorge, is interested in psychology and believes he would like to be a clinical psychologist. His school counselor, Mr. Rabin, explores with Jorge the pathway to becoming a clinical psychologist. Together, they discover that Jorge will need to obtain a bachelor's and a doctoral degree. In addition, he will need to complete an internship or residency. Based on the *Occupational Outlook Handbook* (U.S. Department of Labor, n.d.), they note that this career path is growing at a higher-than-average rate (projected at 19% growth). Jorge has no concerns about attending school all the way through a doctoral degree. He is fully committed to this path and to making the financial choices to make this happen.

College Decision-Making Factors

Many factors influence students' decisions about where to attend college. The choice of school is a major life decision, and much has been studied about how students make their decisions. The salience of certain factors has been found to vary to some degree by race, ethnicity, and gender; yet, the overarching main factors identified in literature as influencing students' college choices include cost, cost savings, academic reputation of the institution, peer influence, and parent involvement and expectations (Holland, 2011; Lee, Almonte, & Youn, 2013; Lillis & Tian, 2008). In a study of college tour participants, Curry, Latham, and Sylvest (2015) found that students fell along a spectrum of college decision-making readiness factors including: financial literacy, family influence, social influence, knowledge of academics, personal awareness, career choice and program alignment, understanding of campus culture, and understanding college resources. Curry et al. (2015) found that financially literate students made college decisions from a comprehensive understanding of money. They understood debt, credit (good and bad credit), subsidized versus unsubsidized loans, the difference between a grant and a loan, and how a credit card was different from a debit card; they had been to a bank and had balanced a checkbook, and some had a planned budget for their first year of college. Curry et al. suggest that to be truly financially literate and ready for college, students do not necessarily need to avoid colleges where they will take on debt. They should, however, be able to describe types of debt, the amount of debt, and how long debt will take to pay off along with how much they will realistically earn.

Sometimes, the financial choices students will need to make are more nuanced. For example, imagine a student, Karen, is awarded a scholarship to a state university that will fully cover her tuition. Her parents urge her to go there. She also applies to a very expensive private college and finds out that she has been given a scholarship that will cover her tuition and fees. The cost of living will be higher at the private school, and there is a required meal plan for first-year students. However, she would have to pay fees, and room, and board at the state school as well. After her family calculates the annual difference in cost, it comes to $900. For the difference in class size, program offerings, faculty mentoring, and institutional reputation, Karen decides the $900 per year is well worth it to accept admission at the private college. In this example, Karen's values and her estimation of the difference in cost and the benefits from each school were weighed in making an informed decision.

In terms of knowledge of academics, students should be aware of the types of programs offered at specific schools, whether or not programs are accredited, and whether or not credit is transferrable to other institutions. For example, if a student plans to start at a community college, does the 4-year state university she is interested in have an articulation agreement to accept credit earned? Students and families also are encouraged to gather information about what enrolling in college as "undecided" or in a program for students who are unsure of what to initially major in might look like academically. Many students enter college undecided, but every college has different requirements for how soon a student is required to choose a major and also for the types of courses they would be eligible to enroll in prior to formally selecting a major.

Finally, the college-ready student also should be able to weigh the interests of social, peer, and family influences in making a college decision in a healthy and balanced way. During Curry et al.'s college tour study, one participant, who we'll call Chris, told members of the research team, "I plan to attend X university because my family and I have tailgated there since I was born. My parents would disown me if I went anywhere else." This young man had not chosen a major but had chosen a university based on the football team. Although we agree tailgating is fun, our recommended practice is to challenge students to weigh many factors. Another participant, who we'll call Levi, made a different choice based on personal awareness. He stated, "I really know myself too well to pick a party school. I don't want to go to a large university like X because every weekend is football and tailgating. I don't think I would focus on my classes. I want to have fun, but I need to remember why I am in school, I'm going to get a degree. Yes, I want to have fun, but in the end, I want to have my degree. I can't do that if I don't focus."

ADVISING THE COLLEGE-BOUND STUDENT

Students wishing to go to college must begin preparing very early in their academic careers. Colleges review a wide variety of data when making decisions about who to admit, but understanding what goes into admission decisions is critical for students to determine how best to prepare academically in order to be competitive. School counselors should provide this information to students and their families to help them understand how various factors are weighed by different schools in the admissions process.

In the 2011 *State of College Admission Counseling* report by the NACAC (Clinedinst, Hurley, & Hawkins, 2011), admissions officers identified grades in college preparatory courses, strength of high school curriculum, college admission test scores, and overall high school GPA as the top factors considered in the admissions process. The next most important factors included essays, letters of recommendation, and extracurricular activities. Students' background information such as race, ethnicity, first-generation status, and related factors were considered by 25% to 31% of the colleges included in the study.

College Application Assistance

Some things we know about college enrollment came from the Consortium on Chicago School Research (CCSR; Roderick, Nagaoka, Coca, & Moeller, 2008), a large study of students in the Chicago Public School system. One key finding from this landmark study is that regardless of students' academic achievement level or GPA, they still had general difficulty applying to and enrolling in 4-year colleges. This finding underscores the myth that somehow gifted or very bright students don't need assistance with college applications or college transitions. Kim and Gasman (2011) noted that this same phenomenon happens frequently with Asian American students who often fall under the preconceived notion of the model minority and are presumed to have a college plan. This kind of mistaken assumption about certain students contradicts what is common sense: Applying for college is a new task to most people and therefore is not a skill they have already developed. This new task comes with anxiety and confusion for most students and it should not be assumed that students will be able to just figure things out for themselves.

The second key finding from the CCSR (Roderick et al., 2008) is that attending a K–12 school with a college-going culture strongly influences the college aspirations of all students. Thus, all students, whether they are in AP, honors, regular course work, or special education, should be exposed to a college-bound culture because all students need a postsecondary educational option. Some discouraging findings from the CCSR indicated that even students with high college aspirations don't always submit applications, and even when they do, only about half who applied actually enrolled in college (Roderick et al., 2008).

Further compounding the concern of the CCSR findings, Smith, Pender, and Howell (2013) found that of those students who do apply to and enroll in 4-year colleges, approximately 40% are undermatched—meaning they could attend a more selective postsecondary institution but choose to go to a less selective one instead. Smith et al. found that undermatching was most likely to happen to first-generation college students from low SES, rural areas. According to Smith, Hurwitz, and Howell (2014), undermatch occurs for a variety of reasons including distance from home, financial considerations, isolation, lack of information, application behavior (i.e., only applying to schools where they know a current student, for example). In summary, the college application process is tenuous for most students and their families regardless of academic achievement or college aspiration, and school counselors will need to be prepared to assist all students in the college decision making and application process.

These findings are helpful because they lend to noteworthy implications for school counselors. Specifically, counselors should ensure that all students receive college application information and that all students (and their families) receive support or assistance in filling out applications. For students with language or cultural barriers or who come from low SES families, school counselors should consider ways to ensure families have support and access to information. One state school counselor director relayed the following story. A school counselor in a school with nearly 50% Latino students held a Free Application for Federal Student Aid (FASFA) night at her school to try to encourage students and their families to fill out the FASFA form to determine how much financial aid students qualified for as part of the college application process. She invited a Spanish translator and advertised that families in need of translation services would be provided a separate area to fill out their FASFA forms with a translator to provide assistance. Attendance was low (about 15% of all families including Latino families) and the school counselor wondered why her provision of a translator had not brought in more families. A colleague suggested to her that the next year she provide dinner, child care for younger children, and a completely separate night for Spanish-speaking families. By doing so, Spanish-speaking families would not have to remove themselves and be dismissed from the larger, English-speaking group of families, which might feel alienating. The school counselor took this advice and tripled participation the following year. By accommodating families with younger children who needed childcare and dinner, and providing translation without making anyone feel embarrassed or different, the school counselor improved the FASFA form completions and found more potential funding for students to go to college. As a result, the number of completed college applications also improved.

College Admissions Terminology

School counselors also should ensure that students and their families are familiar with terminology related to college admissions. Clinedinst et al.

(2011) defined a few terms important to understanding college admissions processes:

Early Action is when students apply to a preferred institution and receive an answer well before the institution's regular response time.

Early Decision is when students make commitments to institutions, indicating that, if admitted, they will definitely enroll.

Legacy Applicants are students who are applying to a college that a relative has graduated from. According to The College Board (2016a), these students, known as "legacies," are given preference in admissions decisions by some colleges.

Need-Blind Admission occurs when an applicant's financial needs are not considered in the admission process.

Open Admission involves accepting any applicant regardless of high school rank or GPA as long as the applicant is a high school graduate. However, as noted by The College Board (2016a), colleges with open admission may have major/program-specific entrance criteria.

Regular Decision refers to an application time period and decisions made on a specific timeline.

Rolling Admission is when an institution reviews applications as they are turned in and makes decisions continually rather than on timelines.

Selectivity is defined as, "the proportion of candidates who are offered admission" (p. 13). The most selective higher education institutions are considered to be those with a 50% or less acceptance rate. According to Clinedinst et al. (2011), the average acceptance rate for 4-year institutions in the United States is 65.5% with a range of 10%–90%.

Yield is "the percentage of admitted students who decide to enroll" (p. 14). The average U.S. 4-year institution yield rate is about 45%.

School counselors will need to familiarize themselves with many terms in order to provide adequate advisement in the career and college counseling process, and the list provided here is certainly not exhaustive. For a more comprehensive review, we encourage school counselors to visit the College Admission Glossary: Learn the Lingo page provided by The College Board (2016a).

By understanding important college admissions-related terms, school counselors are better prepared to help students navigate the college application process. For example, if a school counselor is working with a student who is a junior and has a 34 on the ACT and a weighted GPA of 4.3, the school counselor might recognize that the student will likely be competitive in the early admissions process through Early Action. By understanding both the language and the process of college applications, school counselors are better able to demystify and explain those things to students and their families.

Evidence of Academic Rigor and College Preparation

Another critical piece of the advisement process related to college is preparing students for the level of rigor needed for their intended career and major.

For example, a student planning to be a chemical engineer and who wants to enroll immediately in a 4-year college (as opposed to starting at a 2-year college) will need to have high-rigor preparation while in high school in the areas of math and science (i.e., calculus, chemistry, physics) and will need to score well on college entrance exams. Part of academic advisement is ensuring that students understand that colleges and academic programs will look at the type of course work they have completed, not just their GPA. Sometimes, students and their parents are under the misguided assumption that a good GPA is enough to get into a great university. They don't realize that competitive schools look at the kinds of courses students have taken while in high school. Throughout this section, we review criteria related to academic rigor and college preparation that are reviewed in the college admission process.

ACT®

The ACT is a nationally standardized test that is used for college admissions. Students receive scores in four areas (Math, Science, Reading, and English) including a composite score on a scale of 1 to 36 and subscale scores in each area. Historically, students typically took the ACT in their junior year. However, many school counselors now encourage students to take the ACT early and often to become familiar with the exam and to increase their score. Additionally, ACT preparation courses are offered by many high schools either after school or during the summer. Although these test preparation courses vary in how they are designed from after school tutoring to weekend courses, to workshops, they tend to be designed to familiarize students with the content and format of the ACT test. However, Allensworth, Correa, and Ponisciak (2008) found that ACT test prep actually did not result in improved test scores and, in some cases, test scores appeared to decrease. Allensworth et al. speculated that the reason for the decrease is that students, although motivated to do well on the ACT, were not connecting the ACT to their course work or to anything meaningful in their academic or career life. Therefore, a better strategy is to improve career and college readiness skills within content courses via a focus on metacognition (critical thinking, problem solving, analysis) rather than merely focus on test-taking skills. Indeed, students across the United States do not appear to be excelling at the ACT benchmarks in spite of resources expended to improve scores (see Table 2.1).

TABLE 2.1 Percent of 2015 ACT-Tested High School Graduates by Number of Benchmarks Attained

No. of Benchmarks Met	Percent of Graduates
0	31
1	15
2	14
3	12
4	28

Adapted from ACT, Inc. (2015).

SAT®

The SAT, another standardized exam used for college admissions, changed dramatically in 2015, and features of the new SAT touted by The College Board (2016b) include an optional essay, no penalty for guessing answers, free practice exams, and real world vocabulary. The SAT is scored by benchmarking. In other words, a student's score is measured against an ideal score for students in a particular content area at a specific year in school. For example, 8th, 9th, 10th, 11th, and career and college grade benchmarks exist for Math and for evidence-based reading and writing content areas.

In 2015, 1.7 million students took the SAT (The College Board, 2015). Of special interest, 32.5% of those taking the SAT in 2015 were underrepresented minorities and 25.1% of all test takers took the exam using a fee waiver. This indicates that there is increasing access to the SAT from previous years. However, a closer examination shows that the percent of students meeting career and college readiness benchmarks by race is very concerning (see Table 2.2).

AP Courses

To create greater rigor for high school students, many districts and schools offer AP courses that allow students to take college level courses while still in high school. These courses allow students to experience both the content and the rigorous expectations of the college classroom. Through participating in such courses, high school students build greater capacity to manage their time, stress, and workload, which are essential for success in college. Additionally, many AP courses require more project-based learning and term papers, and promote critical thinking, problem solving, and other metacognition skills that are required in college courses. As noted in a report to the College Board by Wyatt, Patterson, and Di Giacomo (2015), students taking AP courses for college credit must "demonstrate proficiency by taking a nationally standardized end of course exam" (p. 5). Additionally, to ensure standards of rigor are maintained, all high school AP courses designated as potential college credit-bearing courses are subject to audits by the College Board (Wyatt et al., 2015). According to The College Board (2015), 2.5 million students took AP exams in 2015, up from 2.3 million in 2014.

Dual Enrollment

DE differs from AP in that students are actually enrolled in a college course that is taught either at a high school, on a college campus, or via distance

TABLE 2.2   Percent of SAT-Tested High School Students That Met the SAT Career and College Readiness Benchmark, by Race

Race	Percent of Graduates
African American	16.1
Asian	61.3
Hispanic	22.7
Native American	32.7
White	52.8

Adapted from The College Board (2016c).

learning courses (Wyatt et al., 2015). To determine how effective AP or DE courses were in terms of first year college GPAs, Ewing and Howell (2015) examined the relationship of GPA and participation in AP Biology, AP Chemistry, AP Physics, studying 5 hours per week, taking any AP course, living in a residential program, living in an honors college, taking a DE course at a community college, and taking a DE course at a 4-year college. They found that AP Biology, Chemistry, and Physics had the strongest relationship with college GPA. Interestingly, while DE at a 4-year college had a small positive relationship (i.e., taking the class resulted in increases in GPA), taking a DE class at a 2-year school had a small negative relationship with GPA, calling into question the expectations for rigor that were likely established during the DE course (Ewing & Howell, 2015; Table 2.3).

Remedial Courses in U.S. Colleges and Universities

Although many students enter college with a lot of academic rigor and preparation from AP and DE credit, more and more students are entering college without the requisite course work. Students entering colleges unprepared for college level course work may choose to, or might be required to, enroll in remedial classes. Although some experts have pointed to this phenomenon as evidence that U.S. students are unprepared for college academics, Sparks and Malkus (2013) cautioned that data about remedial courses is difficult to evaluate conclusively. Specifically, in a report issued in 2013 on First Year Undergraduate Remedial Course taking, the National Center for Education Statistics (NCES) pointed to several issues that problematize outcome data: (a) remedial course enrollment is predominantly self-report data, (b) transcripts do not indicate if courses are remedial or developmental, and (c) students who need remediation are not always the same students who actually enroll in and complete remedial courses (Sparks & Malkus, 2013). Thus, data should be considered within that context.

Within that frame, we do know that the most recent self-report data analyzed by Sparks and Malkus (2013) suggested that nearly 24% of first-year students attending public, 2-year institutions take at least one remedial course compared to 21% of first-year students attending public, 4-year institutions. Private not-for-profit 4-year institutions had first-year students that reported 15% remedial course enrollment, while private for-profit students reported 11% at institutions that were 2+ years and 5.5% at institutions 2 years or less. Variance occurred among 4-year institutions based on selectivity, with the

TABLE 2.3 College Outcomes by Number of AP Courses Taken and Type of DE Courses Taken

Variable	No AP/DE	<3 AP	3 + AP	DE 2 Year	DE 4 Year
4-year enrollment	57.3%	75.2%	87.6%	60.7%	82.1%
4-year persistence	71.2%	80.1%	88.7%	74.4%	77.9%
4-year graduation	30.2%	38.6%	60.6%	39.6%	44.1%
6-year graduation	56.4%	66.5%	82.1%	64.3%	67.3%
4-year GPA	2.69	2.76	3.21	2.78	2.94

Adapted from Ewing and Howell (2015).

more selective schools having first-year students report lower enrollment in remedial courses and less selective schools having first-year students report greater enrollment in remedial courses. The percent of students reporting enrollment in remedial courses by selective 4-year institutions follows: very selective (12.8%), moderately selective (18.8%), minimally selective (20.7%), and open admission (25.6%).

The school counselor's role in preparing students is to ensure that they are as ready as they can be for their postsecondary path. In some instances, students who were able to complete more advanced or rigorous course work in high school and gain acceptance to a 2-year or 4-year college simply might not have developed the skills needed to take college-level course work in certain subject areas. That is, they might have passed their high school classes, but with low grades and limited understanding of the material. Other students might not have been able to enroll in or complete college preparatory course work for a variety of reasons. Students who begin with a deficit in terms of academic preparation or skills might choose to, or might be required to, enroll in remedial course work prior to or during their first year of college. During advising meetings, school counselors can prepare students and their families for this kind of possibility so that it is not a surprise. A number of programs could be put into place proactively, however, to help students prepare for college. One option to consider is Bridge programs.

Bridge Programs: Pathways to 4-Year College

Bridge programs are meant to create academic connections between postsecondary institutions. In most cases, academic credit or a degree at one institution is transferred as credit into a similar degree or major field of study at another institution through agreements between the institutions. These agreements, known as articulation agreements, are meant to create a simplified pathway and smooth transition process for students moving from 2-year institutions to 4-year institutions. Many community colleges have such articulation agreements with 4-year universities such that students earning an AS may transfer to the 4-year institution and receive credit for their AS toward their 4-year bachelor's degree.

Other types of bridge programs include programs meant to create pathways between secondary and postsecondary education for students in underrepresented groups. One example is TRIO, funded by the Higher Education Act (U.S. Department of Education, 2016), which includes multiple programs:

1. *Upward Bound.* Upward Bound programs target low-income high school students who are first-generation college bound. The program provides academic support for college entrance requirements including math, science, composition, literature, and foreign languages. Other types of college preparation include cultural enrichment, financial literacy, and college application assistance (U.S. Department of Education, 2016, CFDA 84.047).

2. *Gaining Early Awareness and Readiness for Undergraduate Programs* (GEAR UP). GEAR UP is an early intervention grant program that is highly competitive. The program is meant to increase college attendance for low-income students. Students begin the program no later than seventh grade and remain in the program all the way through high school (U.S. Department of Education, 2016, CFDA 84.334A).

3. *Talent Search.* Talent Search is a comprehensive program that encourages individuals to complete or reenter secondary and postsecondary education. Services provided through the program include career exploration and assessment; academic, financial, career, and personal counseling; tutoring; college campus tours, college program information, college entrance exam preparation, and mentoring; family workshops; college admissions assistance; and special activities for sixth, seventh, and eighth graders. Funding is generally allocated to programs that serve students with disabilities, homeless children and youth, students in foster care or those aging out of foster care, traditionally underrepresented groups, and students with limited English proficiency (U.S. Department of Education, 2016, CFDA Number 84.044).

Most of the TRIO programs run adjunctively to P–12 schools through entities that work in collaboration, such as community partners, local universities, and government agencies. These groups will likely reach out to school counselors and administrators asking for access to students for the various programs they provide or for help coauthoring grant proposals, developing programs, and soliciting participants. Thus, school counselors may wish to know the efficacy of such programs before agreeing to such partnerships. The good news is that, overall, TRIO programs have been shown to be very effective. For example, in a study conducted by The Pell Institute (2009), three key findings about TRIO participants (compared to their non-TRIO participating and demographically similar cohort counterparts) were found: TRIO participants were (a) more likely to remain in higher education (12% more likely to be retained after year one and 23% after year two), (b) accrued more college credits (6% in year one, 4% in year two), and (c) earned higher GPAs (7% higher after year one, 5% higher after year two).

THE CAREER-BOUND STUDENT

Although some students may want to seek employment upon high school graduation, it is critical to ensure that they are informed of their options and that they are fully prepared with the employability skills as well as credentials they need for their chosen career path. In this section, we examine the growth of IRCs, career and technical education, ASs, and resources to help school counselors working with students seeking career/technical certificates.

Industry Recognized Credentials *(or IBC)*

IRCs, sometimes referred to as Industry-Based Certifications (IBCs), are certificates or credentials earned either in secondary schools or in postsecondary institutions that signify an individual has attained a standard set of skills recognized by a particular industry (National Research Center for Career and Technical Education, n.d.). Many of these certificates are issued by national organizations. For example, a certified welder must be certified by the American Welding Society (AWS), and according to the AWS website (2016).

> The Certified Welder (CW) program tests welders to procedures used in the structural steel, petroleum pipelines, sheet metal, and chemical refinery welding industries. There is a provision to test to a company-supplied or noncode welding specification. Tests for Certified Welder (CW) are performed at AWS Accredited Testing Facilities located throughout the world.

Many high schools around the country provide career and technical education leading to IBC or DE credit in a technical postsecondary school. Many advantages exist to this approach for both students and the workforce.

Advantages of IRCs for Students

One key advantage for students is that IBCs are based on an analysis of workforce needs and should reflect the needs in students' surrounding labor market; students can expect to find jobs in these areas. For example, in areas of high construction growth, IBCs available in the secondary school system might include drafting, carpentry, pipefitting, welding, and electric. Students ideally would choose high school academic courses with content that aligns to the skills needed for the career path chosen so that any additional postsecondary course work needed would be minimized. For example, students choosing welding as an option will need chemistry, as welding requires knowledge of the elements of metals when heated. Thus, a school counselor working with a student choosing a high school welding path would want to ensure that the student has taken the science and math courses necessary to be successful in completing a welding training program. Nationally recognized certificates are generally portable; therefore, once students complete these certificates, they are able to move to most places in the United States and their skills and competencies are recognized and transferrable to other labor markets (Wilcox, 2006).

Advantages of IRCs/IBCs for the Workforce

One advantage of IRCs for the workforce is accountability. That is, by setting standards of agreed-upon competencies and skills for individual occupations, the certificates help to ensure a competent workforce. Additionally, high school training programs are based on relevance, or current trends in the labor force; thus, the IRCs that are awarded are for occupations that are most needed. Specifically, in many states, workforce commission or workforce investment councils regularly meet with state boards of education to identify areas of growth and opportunities to ensure certificate programs are offered to secondary students in areas of high employability. Finally, because IRCs can be awarded through career and technical education in high school or students can apply credit (DE) earned in high school to their postsecondary certificate training, the educational costs of IRCs are controlled, creating a larger pipeline into the labor market (Wilcox, 2006). More specifically, students who might otherwise not be able to afford postsecondary education could potentially graduate high school having met all or nearly all of the requirements for an IBC. With this knowledge, students might be more inclined to pursue these kinds of career paths.

Associate's Degrees

ADs are generally 2-year degrees that may be earned through community colleges or specialized institutions. ADs typically have specialized course work that focuses on the development of skills related to a particular occupation, rather than generalized course work meant to develop critical thinking or problem-solving skills. According to the *Occupational Outlook Handbook* (U.S. Department of Labor, n.d.), an example of a high-paying career that can be obtained with an AD is an electrical engineering technician. The median pay for this career is $61,130 per year with an AD, and no experience is required. However, this occupation's projection is declining by 2%. Thus, researching the growth rate of careers associated with ADs is just as essential as with 4-year college degrees.

Community College Stigma

Holland (2015) described college aspiration in the United States as a "college for all and community college for none" (p. 1) phenomenon, as the concept of college has become synonymous with 4-year institutions and 2-year institutions have garnered a stigma as somewhat less than college. The national discourse on the importance of college has had a desired effect in increasing students' college aspirations across diverse groups. For example, based on a survey of seniors in Chicago Public Schools, the CCSR (Roderick et al., 2008) found that 83% of students aspired to a bachelor's degree, with only 13% aspiring to an AS. However, many students expect to get into college and have success without realizing the degree of preparation or rigor necessary to be successful in a 4-year institution. This is particularly true for low SES, minority first-generation college students who have little direct exposure to college through others in their lives (Holland, 2015).

Consequently, many students have had to create strategies for coping with the stigma of attending community college. In a qualitative study conducted by Holland (2015), some of the stigma-mitigating strategies employed by students who were going to be attending 2-year colleges rather than 4-year colleges follow.

1. *Transfer.* Some students talked about college in terms of their intended transfer school. In other words, they would not mention the 2-year college

where they were starting but would instead talk about the 4-year college where they were planning to transfer to after 2 years.

2. *Disengagement.* This strategy was used when students wanted to separate academic achievement, intelligence, and 2-year college attendance from their identity. Holland noted this most often happened with African American males who would state that they were simply attending a 2-year college to prepare for a vocation or career as an athlete.

3. *Taking a Year Off and Avoidance.* Some students talked about taking off a year or avoided talking about school rather than going to a 2-year college. They either did this because they did not want to acknowledge not getting accepted in a more selective school or were not ready to think about college or simply needed a break.

4. *Refusal.* Students who could not accept the stigma of community college fell into this category. They were not willing to go to a 2-year college and had no other options—many had not made grades that would make other options possible.

Based on Holland's (2015) findings, it is important that school counselors introduce postsecondary school options early for students. Technical schools, community colleges/2-year colleges, and 4-year institutions are all necessary options for a wide range of students. The earlier in life students have exposure to these options, the better. Thus, we advocate for introducing a broad, college-going culture that embraces many options in elementary schools and keeping these options open for students throughout their P–12 experience.

Further, helping students understand the benefits of 2-year colleges may be helpful. Some of these benefits, according to an analysis by Wood and Harrison (2014), included availability of financial aid, job placement record, less rigorous admission policies, and a greater likelihood of accepting college credit earned in high school. Some helpful ways to promote these connections may be to have question-and-answer panels, guest speakers, or to allow students to interview individuals with careers of interest that received ASs from 2-year colleges. See Exhibit 2.1. for an interview conducted with a radiological technician with an AS—this interview provides an example of the type of information students could learn through such an activity.

EXHIBIT 2.1
An Interview With a Radiological Technician

JC: Could you tell me a little bit about how you chose to become a radiological technician?

Patricia: Actually, I thought I wanted to be a nurse, but I applied for a nursing program and didn't get in. I wasn't sure what to do. I had a friend who was an x-ray tech and he asked his supervisor if I could shadow him at work one day. After doing that I thought, this seemed like a good alternative. Growing up

(continued)

EXHIBIT 2.1 (*continued*)

I had only heard of doctors and nurses. I literally had never heard the term *radiological technician*.

JC: So what degree do you hold?

Patricia: My degree is an Associate's degree. An Associate of Science.

JC: How long did it take you to complete your degree?

Patricia: 2 years.

JC: Could you tell me a little about what types of things radiological technicians do?

Patricia: I have had three different jobs in 12 years. I started out in x-ray but was only there for a year. Then I was doing bone density scans and stayed there for 5 years. I really enjoyed that. I have been doing mammograms for the last 6 years and I love it.

JC: What did you like or not like about each of those?

Patricia: Well, in x-ray there is a lot of trauma, like car wrecks, gun shots, severe injuries, and I felt really anxious a lot. I don't think trauma work is the best place for me. I have seen some people who are very good at doing that and seem really calm. I felt very worried and anxious and had a hard time leaving work at work because I would worry about each person. I liked doing bone density because I could do a lot of education with patients and talk about nutrition and preventing bone loss. I felt like I made an impact. But mammogram is my favorite. I think it is life changing. Women's health matters. This is my calling. Many women come in to get their checkup and they are worried because they have a family history or because they don't know what to expect and I get to talk about their fears, their worries, but also to talk about prevention and how to do their monthly self-exams. I know I am making a difference.

JC: Thinking back on your radiological technician degree, would you choose to do anything differently now?

Patricia: No, I am so glad I found this job! I can also do MRIs if I want. There really are so many options. I think it's one of the best kept secrets in the health field. Everyone knows about doctors and nurses but what I do is great, I work amazing hours, and I feel I am paid well. I wouldn't change a thing about this.

HELPING STUDENTS RESEARCH CAREER AND TECHNICAL PROGRAMS

As previously mentioned, many states have begun to align workforce development needs with secondary certificate and technical education offerings. School counselors should refer to the training credentials offered through their district and the paths offered to students when advising students in their particular schools. Another great resource for informing students about potential careers where they may wish to pursue IRCs or ASs is CareerOneStop. The CareerOneStop website (careeronestop.org), sponsored by the U.S. Department of Labor, provides key information on occupations in technical and labor fields. Information on this website is current and quite rich, including fastest growing occupations, occupations with declining employments, employment trends based on growth rates and earnings by region, and occupations by required education level. The website also includes information about certifications available by occupation and certifying agency. More advanced search options include exploring occupations by selected criteria, such as education level, state and national wages, and career videos (useful for career exploration activities with students).

O*Net is another great resource. O*Net (onetonline.org), sponsored by the U.S. Department of Labor, provides a wealth of information about careers including a summary or description of the work, tools and technology, knowledge, skills, ability, work activities, and work context. Other information includes the job zone for each career that provides related careers and the amount of preparation needed (degree, related and on-the-job experience). O*Net also provides the Holland codes associated with the career, work values, and related occupations.

[handwritten margin note: Shouldn't these 2 sites cross-reference each other?]

RESOURCES TO FACILITATE COLLEGE DECISION MAKING

School counselors play a critical role in creating a college-going culture in their schools. Through developing a core counseling curriculum that prepares students for careers and college, providing academic and college counseling, and coordinating and collaborating to provide large scale events such as college fairs and college tours, school counselors facilitate students' career and college exploration and decision making. Following are some key resources school counselors may access to assist students in considering the value, cost, and institutional quality of colleges in the United States. Although there are myriad resources for school counselors to use in assisting students in making postsecondary decisions, we are limited in this chapter in the breadth, depth, and scope of resources we can provide. Therefore, we highlight a few online resources that capture key elements of college decision-making information.

The College Scorecard

The College Scorecard (collegescorecard.ed.gov), a website hosted by the U.S. Department of Education, allows students and their parents to compare 2-year and 4-year institutions based on a variety of data. The intention of the website is to increase institutional accountability by benchmarking information about a specific institution compared to the national average so that families might determine the value of an education at a particular school. This practice also holds higher education programs and institutions to a high degree of accountability in their reporting and in their service and program quality. The data reported includes: programs, regions/geographical location, institution size, and type of institution (public, private, private for profit, religious affiliation) or those with a specialized mission (i.e., historically Black colleges and universities [HBCU], women only). Students can enter their search criteria in an easy-to-navigate site, and they are immediately given options for institutions that came up meeting their criteria. Information on the scorecard includes (a) current number of attendees, (b) annual average cost of attendance compared to national average for similar degrees, (c) graduation rate compared to national average, and (4) salary after attending compared to national average.

The Net Price Calculator Center

The U.S. Department of Education (https://collegecost.ed.gov/netpricecenter .aspx) links students to potential colleges and universities where they answer a series of questions to determine the total net price they would pay annually for their degree. Questions pertain to potentially qualifying for grants and scholarships (based on GPA, ACT and SAT scores), parents' and students' income, parents' assets, and state of residency. The projected tuition, fees, and living expenses are projected for each individual based on the information the student provides.

College Navigator

The College Navigator (nces.ed.gov/collegenavigator) allows students and families to compare similar programs and colleges using a search engine through the NCES. Options include choosing specific schools to search or choosing a state, programs/majors, level of award/degree, and type of institution. From there, the College Navigator provides information on the identified college(s) including general information, tuition, fees, and estimated student expenses; financial aid, net price, enrollment, admissions, retention and graduation rates, programs/majors, service members and veterans, accreditation, campus security, and cohort default rates. The College Navigator allows students and their families to look at colleges and universities by viewing the same benchmark data across all institutions to compare and contrast resources, finances, and other measures of quality.

Financial Aid Shopping Sheet

The Financial Aid Shopping Sheet is hosted by the U.S. Department of Education (2016). The sheet is a tool that provides potential students with a template for viewing financial packages and expenses at higher education institutions so that they can make informed decisions based on comparable data. The tool allows students to compare costs and financial aid packages for programs and services.

College Signing Day

College Signing Day is a milestone event and a time when students across the country, as part of Michelle Obama's Reach Higher initiative, participate in acknowledging that after leaving high school they are committing to taking another step on their educational journey: postsecondary education. This should be an exciting time for school counselors, teachers, parents, students, families, and communities. College Signing Day can be done without a lot of expense by procuring donations ahead of time for snacks, setting up a photo booth, having lots of music, and, of course, asking students to wear their college colors! Ask teachers, community partners, volunteers, family members, and administrators to wear shirts from their alma maters or a local college or university. Reach Higher provides a free downloadable College Signing Day Kit, including the College Signing Pocket Card (ReachHigher.gov). Most importantly, school counselors may share this important activity with the media so that a culture continues to build as students in lower grades see the prominence of College Signing Day and the community sees the positive celebration happening at your school!

FINAL THOUGHTS

Although many resources exist that school counselors may access to promote college exploration and decision making, the most important asset for promoting college readiness is a comprehensive, developmental school counseling program that integrates the ASCA Mindsets and Behaviors (2014; see Appendix C). It is the intentional programming in classrooms, individual advisement, and dissemination of career and college information via parent workshops and faculty in-service that will foster a culture of planning for future success. So how does daily career and college planning, as part of the whole school curriculum, actually look? How do students experience school culture in this regard? Exhibit 2.2 contains one graduate student's reflection on her high school experience where career and college exploration and preparation were key components of the daily curriculum.

EXHIBIT 2.2
Voices From the Field: A Graduate Student's Reflection on Comprehensive Career and College Exploration

Samantha J. Latham

Alumna, Legacy High School

Attending a high school in a middle class neighborhood that continuously scored high on academic rankings naturally gave me access to career and college readiness opportunities. I had access to bountiful AP courses and honors classes, and a team of five school counselors, one of whom had continued her education to earn a certification in college counseling.

Moreover, I was in a program unique to my high school called Legacy 2000 (L2K), which focused on the intangible and tangible skills needed for career success. Dedicated to science, math, and technology careers, this 4-year program extensively developed the skills for presentations, teamwork and collaboration, research, and writing at a college level, as well as career exploration. Beginning on the first day of our freshmen year we had to present a

(continued)

EXHIBIT 2.2 (*continued*)

90-second speech and our development continued all the way through all 4 years, culminating with our final 30-minute senior speech. We completed countless research papers, presentations, and projects that pushed us out of our comfort zones and helped us develop our confidence to succeed in future careers and through the rigorous demands of college.

With an emphasis on career and college exploration, L2K provided numerous opportunities for students to discover what we wanted out of both our future education and work. A college study project was assigned once in freshmen year and again junior year. We had to research and present on at least three different colleges, one of which had to be out of state. Perhaps the most significant part of this project was that we had to contact students at the colleges and interview them about their experience and the different traditions and opportunities their college provided. This would be the first of many opportunities in which we began to develop our networking skills.

The cornerstones of the program are the 20-hour job shadow and 40-hour internship project completed junior and senior year, respectively. The teachers did not set up the different job shadow experiences so it was incumbent upon the students to capitalize on their social networks and interpersonal skills to find a professional to shadow. I was very much interested in medicine and, for my job shadow, I was able to follow an occupational medicine doctor who patiently took the time to explain every aspect of her job to me. For my senior year, I contacted one of the head surgeons at the local city hospital. After explaining my project and why I was interested in surgery, she graciously allowed me to shadow her and her residents for 2 months and I was able to observe numerous surgeries and patient consults.

My job shadow experience with the occupational medicine doctor demonstrated to me the importance of quality patient interaction and how crucial it is to really listen to the patient. Furthermore, my experience at the hospital with the surgical residents provided me with a firsthand account of what life was really like in residency and to witness the competitive, stressful nature of that work environment. I enjoyed being in the operating room and observing the various surgeries, but I did not enjoy what I perceived as the competitive nature of the residency and how that overshadowed the patient interactions. Consequently, both experiences contributed to my decision to not pursue surgery.

Nonetheless, if I had never had that opportunity to shadow different medical professionals, I probably would not have made the decision to switch career paths until much later, perhaps causing me to miss the inspiring opportunities I have now. Moreover, if I had never been pushed to search for out of state schools early on in my high school career, I may not have had the confidence to attend a university in a state where I did not know a single soul. Not only did this program instill a sense of career confidence, it provided opportunities for us to develop the crucial skills of time management, presentation styles, teamwork, and writing that undoubtedly contributed to success in other areas beyond the confines of the program.

SUMMARY

Deil-Amen and Tevis (2010) noted a complication of college-bound research: Although more students than ever aspire to attend college, have exposure and access to college, and enroll in college, we know very little about what happens from enrollment to college graduation. What high school factors might help us better predict college persistence, retention, and matriculation? Based on the work of Engberg and Wolniak (2010) and others, the acquisition of career and college readiness capital in high school contexts pays large dividends in the college setting. School counselors help students gain college readiness capital through promoting access to college, by exposing students to career and college exploration, providing resources, and assisting students in considering their full range of postsecondary options. The options available to students are vast, from IRCs to doctoral degrees, and school counselors need to be knowledgeable about what is available for their students and how to help students and their families navigate the college decision-making process. Indeed, in many cases, the school counselor may be the only person with the knowledge and resources to help students do this critical, life-changing work. We explore this relationship throughout this book and encourage school counselors to conceptualize their role as a creator of career and college readiness capital.

••▶ Test Your Knowledge

1. Name and describe two different types of bridge programs.
2. Give an example of an online resource that allows students and their families to accurately estimate the cost of 1 year of college tuition, including fees, books, and living expenses.
3. Describe three things a school counselor can do to promote a college-going culture.

REFERENCES

ACT, Inc. (2015). *Profile report-national: Graduating class 2015.* Iowa City, IA: Author.

Allensworth, E., Correa, M., & Ponisciak, S. (2008, May). *From high school to the future: ACT preparation—Too much, too late: Why ACT scores are low in Chicago and what it means for schools. Consortium on Chicago school research* (Research Report). Retrieved from https://consortium.uchicago.edu/sites/default/files/publications/ACTReport08.pdf

American Association of University Women. (2016). *The simple truth about the gender pay gap.* Washington, DC: Author.

American School Counselor Association. (2012). *The ASCA national model: A framework for school counseling programs* (3rd ed.). Alexandria, VA: Author.

American School Counselor Association. (2014). *ASCA mindsets & behaviors for student success: K-12 college- and career-readiness standards for every student.* Alexandria, VA Author.

American Welding Society. (2016). Certified welding program. Retrieved from http://www.aws.org/certification/detail/certified-welder-program

Baylor, E. (2014). *State disinvestment in higher education has led to an explosion of student-loan debt*. Washington, DC: Center for American Progress. Retrieved from https://www.luminafoundation.org/files/resources/state-disinvestment-increases-debt.pdf

Blumenstyk, G. (2015). *American higher education in crisis? What everyone needs to know*. New York, NY: Oxford University Press.

Carnevale, A. P., Rose, S. J., & Cheah, B. (2011). The college payoff: Education, occupations, lifetime earnings. Retrieved from http://cew.georgetown.edu/collegepayoff

Clinedinst, M. E., Hurley, S. F., & Hawkins, D. A. (2011). *2011 state of college admission*. Alexandria, VA: National Association for College Admission Counseling.

Curry, J. R., Latham, S. J., & Sylvest, K. (2015). College decision making maturity factors: The development of a spectral scale. Unpublished manuscript.

Deil-Amen, R., & Tevis, T. L. (2010). Circumscribed agency: The relevance of standardized college entrance exams for low SES high school students. *The Review of Higher Education, 33*(2), 141–175.

Engberg, M. E., & Wolniak, G. C. (2010). Examining the effects of high school contexts on postsecondary enrollment. *Research in Higher Education, 51*(2), 132–153.

Ewing, M., & Howell, J. (2015). *Is the relationship between AP participation and academic performance really meaningful?* (Research Brief 2015-1). New York, NY: The College Board. Retrieved from https://research.collegeboard.org/sites/default/files/publications/2015/9/relationship-between-ap-participation-academic-performance-really-meaningful.pdf

Holland, M. M. (2015). College for all and community college for none: Stigma in high-achieving high schools. *Teachers College Record, 117*(5), 1–51.

Holland, N. E. (2011). The power of peers: Influences on postsecondary education planning and experiences of African American students. *Urban Education, 46*(5), 1029–1055. http://dx.doi.org/10.1177/0042085911400339

Kim, J. K., & Gasman, M. (2011). In search of a "good college": Decisions and determinations behind Asian American students' college choice. *Journal of College Student Development, 52*(6), 706–728.

Lee, K. A., Almonte, J. L. J., & Youn, M-J. (2013). What to do next: An exploratory study of the post-secondary decisions of American students. *Higher Education, 66*, 1–16. http://dx.doi.org/10.10007/s10734-012-9576-6

Lillis, M. P., & Tian, R. G. (2008). The impact of cost on college choice: Beyond the mean of the economically disadvantaged. *Journal of College Admission, Summer, 200*, 4–14.

McNutt, M. I. (2014). There is value in liberal arts education, employers say: Return on investment may be less obvious, but hiring managers seek liberal arts-related skills. Retrieved from http://www.usnews.com/news/college-of-tomorrow/articles/2014/09/22/there-is-value-in-liberal-arts-education-employers-say

Mortenson, T. G. (2012). State funding: A race to the bottom. American Council on Education. Retrieved from http://www.acenet.edu/the-presidency/columns-and-features/Pages/state-funding-a-race-to-the-bottom.aspx

National Association for College Admission Counseling. (1999). *Statement on pre-college guidance and counseling and the role of the school counselor*. Retrieved from http://3fn72f6h8343uvxzx2v9bkc6-wpengine.netdna-ssl.com/wp-content/uploads/2014/07/NACACs-Role-of-School-Counselors.pdf

National Research Center for Career and Technical Education. (n.d.). Industry-recognized credentials. Retrieved from http://www.nrccte.org/core-issues/industry-recognized-credentials

Roderick, M., Nagaoka, J., Coca, V., & Moeller, E. (2008). *From high school to the future: Potholes on the road to college*. Chicago, IL: Consortium on Chicago Schools Research at the University of Chicago. Retrieved from http://consortium.uchicago.edu/downloads/1835ccsr_potholes_summary.pdf

Smith, J., Hurwitz, M., & Howell, J. (2014). Screening mechanisms and students responses in the college market. *Economics of Education Review, 44*, 17–28.

Smith, J., Pender, M., & Howell, J. (2013). The full extent of student-college academic undermatch. *Economics of Education Review, 32,* 247–261.

Sparks, D., & Malkus, N. (2013). First-year undergraduate remedial course taking: 1999–2000, 2003–2004, 2007–08. Statistics in brief. National Center for Education Statistics. Retrieved from ERIC database (ED538339).

The College Board. (2015). 2015 College Board program and results: Access and participation. Retrieved from https://www.collegeboard.org/program-results/participation

The College Board. (2016a). College admission glossary: Learn the lingo. Retrieved from https://bigfuture.collegeboard.org/get-in/applying-101/college-admission-glossary

The College Board. (2016b). Meet the new SAT. Retrieved from https://collegereadiness.collegeboard.org/sat?navId=gh-sat

The College Board. (2016c). *Performance and success: 2015 program results.* New York, NY: Author.

The Economist. (2015, August). College debt: More is less. Retrieved from http://www.economist.com/news/united-states/21661008-more-less

The Institute for College Access & Success. (2015). Project on student debt. Retrieved from http://ticas.org/posd/map-state-data-2015

The Pell Institute. (2009). *National studies find TRIO programs effective at increasing college enrollment and graduation.* Washington, DC: The Pell Institute for the Study of Higher Education.

U.S. Bureau of Labor Statistics. (2015). *Persons with a disability: Labor force characteristics summary.* Washington, DC: U.S. Department of Labor. Retrieved from http://www.bls.gov/news.release/disabl.nr0.htm

U.S. Department of Education. (2016). Federal TRIO programs. Retrieved from http://www2.ed.gov/about/offices/list/ope/trio/index.html

U.S. Department of Labor. (n.d.). *Occupational outlook handbook.* Retrieved from https://www.bls.gov/ooh

U.S. News and World Report. (2015, June 8). The Hechinger Report: Heaviest debt burdens fall on 3 types of students: The typical undergraduate borrower isn't suffering from college loans. Retrieved from http://www.usnews.com/news/articles/2015/06/08/heaviest-college-debt-burdens-fall-on-3-types-of-students

Wilcox, D. (2006). The role of industry-based certifications in career and technical education. *Techniques: Connecting Education and Careers, 81*(1), 21–23.

Wood, J. L., & Harrison, J. D. (2014). College choice for Black males in the community college: Factors influencing institutional selection. *The Negro Educational Review, 65,* 1–4, 87–97.

Wyatt, J. N., Patterson, B. F., & Di Giacomo, F. T. (2015). *A comparison of the college outcomes of AP and dual enrollment students.* (Research Report 2015-3). New York, NY: The College Board. Retrieved from http://research.collegeboard.org/sites/default/files/publications/2015/10/a-comparison-of-the-college-outcomes-of-ap-and-dual-enrollment-students.pdf.pdf

THREE

P–12 Career and College Readiness: Professional Preparation

In any profession, basic knowledge and skills are requisite for an individual to competently engage in the tasks and responsibilities of that profession. Fortunately, for those individuals who wish to engage in career and college readiness counseling in schools, a number of documents are available to clarify what constitutes competent and ethical practice. In this chapter, we review competencies that school counselors need in order to effectively provide career and college readiness services in P–12 school settings.

Before we review specific competencies, we provide a brief overview of five documents that serve as the basis for subsequent information.

1. *National Career Development Association Minimum Competencies for Multicultural Career Counseling and Development* (NCDA, 2009). This document provides an overview of nine general competency areas for career counseling. It also emphasizes that career counseling must be provided to all individuals, regardless of their background, and that services should take into consideration the unique needs of individual clients. This document is available in Appendix A and the Guidelines section of the NCDA website (www.ncda.org).

2. *Career Counselor Assessment and Evaluation Competencies* (Krieshok & Black, 2009). This document was developed because of the importance of assessment and evaluation in effective career counseling. Competencies in eight areas are reviewed. A current version of this document is available in Appendix B and the Guidelines section of the NCDA website (www .ncda.org).

3. *ASCA Mindsets & Behaviors for Student Success: K–12 College- and Career-Readiness Standards for Every Student* (American School Counselor Association, 2014). The ASCA Mindsets & Behaviors are a set of research-based standards that target students' (a) mindsets, or psychosocial attitudes and beliefs, and (b) behaviors as evidenced through learning strategies, self-management skills, and social skills (Appendix C).

4. *ASCA Ethical Standards for School Counselors* (2016). ASCA's Ethical Standards provide guidelines for school counselors when they are faced with ethical concerns that might arise during career and college

planning, academic advisement, parent–student academic conferences, and assessment related to career and college readiness (Appendix D).

5. *Council for Accreditation of Counseling and Related Educational Programs Standards* (CACREP, 2016). CACREP provides guidance for content to be covered in counselor education programs. Ten core content area standards in career development are outlined as are other standards in areas that have relevance to career and college counseling (e.g., assessment, diversity). Additionally, the school counseling specialty area contains numerous standards directly related to school counselor roles in connection to careers and college. This document is available on the CACREP website (www.cacrep.org).

CAREER AND COLLEGE READINESS COUNSELING COMPETENCIES

This section contains information about numerous content and skills areas important for school counselors who will be providing career and college readiness interventions in P–12 schools. When applicable, we articulate some considerations that exist beyond the general competency area that are related to working specifically with a P–12 student population.

Knowledge of Career Theories

Just as counselors learn about a variety of general counseling and human development theories early in their graduate programs to help them conceptualize the issues their clients bring to them, they also should learn career counseling theories (CACREP, 2016; NCDA, 2009). Career counseling theories help to explain career-related thoughts and behaviors, and provide a framework for understanding students and developing interventions. Many career theories provide a life span perspective, which provides insight into how childhood career growth impacts lifelong career development. Further, knowledge of a variety of career counseling theories as well as the research related to those theories enables counselors and educators to design interventions based on the theories that best fit the populations they serve. Operating from a theoretical framework allows school counselors and educators to be intentional in their work and to anticipate potential outcomes. It also allows them to identify and choose assessments that measure factors consistent with those theories. Throughout this chapter, we review a variety of career counseling theories and discuss the ways in which they are applicable to students at various grade levels. We also review interventions and assessments that complement many of these theories.

Career and College Readiness Counseling Skills

Skills specific to career and college readiness counseling have been deemed important enough to be included in the documents we mentioned previously (CACREP, 2016; NCDA, 2009). But what exactly are career and college readiness counseling skills and how do they differ from basic counseling skills? Most counselors learn basic skills in individual and group counseling and consultation, collaboration, and referral, as well as skills related to working with diverse populations (see the discussion later in this chapter). They also learn skills in assessment and research (which we also discuss in more detail later). Further, graduate students in school counseling programs develop skills in classroom instruction, curriculum development, and lesson planning (see Chapter 6). All of these basic skills are relevant to career and college readiness counseling. Specifically, it isn't that different skills are needed for career and college readiness counseling; it is that counselors must be sure to develop and use all of those skills in their career- and college-related work.

For example, a school counselor who feels very comfortable engaging in individual career and college advising sessions (or *individual planning* activities as ASCA [2012] would describe them) might slowly work her way through her caseload seeing one student at a time. If she felt more confident in her psychoeducational group counseling or classroom skills, she could approach her meetings on a larger scale via small-group or classroom-based interventions, allowing her to be more efficient in reaching all of her students. Similarly, the same school counselor might feel very comfortable consulting and collaborating with teachers and parents, but doesn't typically reach out to individuals or organizations in the community. Given the importance of connecting with businesses and educational institutions that ensure career and postsecondary educational opportunities and connections are made available to students, this counselor ideally should work on developing her consultation skills.

Legal and Ethical Issues

What legal and ethical issues do counselors engaging in career- and college-related work encounter that are different from those they experience doing any kind of school counseling? Honestly, probably none in particular; they might encounter the same legal and ethical issues as they would with any kind of counseling with P–12 students. Again, it is more a function of making sure that counselors think about legal and ethical issues when providing career- and college-related services in P–12 schools. As with other school counseling issues, school counselors should rely on ASCA's (2016) *Ethical Standards* when considering ethical issues related to career and college counseling issues.

For example, issues related to confidentiality and not imposing one's values are very important to consider in career and college counseling. In an effort to be encouraging, a school counselor might be tempted to persuade a student to pursue college or might express an opinion about a student's occupational aspirations—the counselor is frustrated that the student is limiting his options, and tells the student to aim higher because the student has strong potential to do well in college. The counselor also might say something to the student's science teacher, asking that teacher to encourage the student to consider science careers. Although well-intentioned, these kinds of interactions do not align with ethical expectations related to confidentiality, promoting autonomy, and not imposing one's own values and beliefs.

Don't meddle — Focus on best interest of student

Another ethical problem arises when parents and students have conflicting views about what students should be doing in the future. For example, the first author worked with a family that owned a hair salon and the parents wanted their only child to work at the salon after high school. The parents enrolled the child in a cosmetology program (a technical program offered at the high school) and the student became very distressed because she wanted to attend college and become a teacher. The school principal insisted that the child be registered for cosmetology in spite of her career interests because it was required that parents approve the student's course work and they would not approve college-bound courses.

On the surface, career- and college-related legal and ethical issues may not seem as volatile in comparison to some of the more serious mental health concerns that counselors in schools encounter, but they may find themselves unintentionally loosening up on their professional obligation to treat the interactions as formal counseling sessions. That is, school counselors might believe it is acceptable to share information about career and college planning obtained during a session with a student with the parent or a teacher without the student's consent. They also might feel more comfortable "giving advice" to that student about future plans. It is somewhat amazing how quickly counselors can disregard the beliefs and values of students and their families in these ways without even realizing they are doing it—basic counseling skills seem to go out the window. Despite good intentions to be helpful, counselors must remember that ethical and legal obligations apply as much to their use of interventions and services to address career development as they do to any other counseling services.

Similar to the ethical codes of other counseling organizations such as the American Counseling Association (2014) or the ASCA (2016), which target, respectively, counselors in general and school counselors, the *NCDA Code of Ethics* (2015) serves as a guide for career practitioners, addressing ethical expectations related to career counseling. Technically, ethical codes can only be enforced for people who are members of the organizations that developed them, and it is unlikely that everyone who provides career-related services in P–12 schools will become members of all of these organizations. Still, school counselors should rely on the ASCA's (2016) *Ethical Standards*. Further, we recommend following an ethical decision-making model when faced with precarious ethical decisions.

Ethical decision making. One way to make an ethical decision is to follow an ethical decision-making model. As is noted in the *ASCA's* (2016) *Ethical Standards*, one such model was proposed for school counselors by Stone (2001). The Solutions To Ethical Problems in Schools (STEPS) model has nine steps:

1. Define the problem emotionally and intellectually
2. Apply the ASCA *Ethical Standards for School Counselors* and the law
3. Consider the students' chronological and developmental levels
4. Consider the setting, parental rights, and minors' rights
5. Apply the ethical principles of beneficence, autonomy, nonmaleficence, loyalty, and justice

6. Determine potential courses of action and their consequences
7. Evaluate the selected action
8. Consult
9. Implement the course of action

Based on the STEPS model, school counselors facing an ethical dilemma related to career and college readiness counseling should work through each of these steps sequentially.

Advocate for Student In sum, to competently practice career and college counseling in schools, counselors have to be able to accurately identify ethical dilemmas and respond in a conscientious manner that honors the rights of all parties involved. Keeping this balance in mind, and being vigilant to ensure that students' career goals are the focus for career and college counseling, positive outcomes are likely. Even with all of these safeguards in place, legal and ethical issues may still arise and counselors will need to exercise their best professional judgment.

Ability to Effectively Serve Diverse Populations

Picking up on the issue we just highlighted, school counselors providing career and college readiness interventions must be able to appropriately and effectively provide services to all individuals, no matter who they are (ASCA, 2016; CACREP, 2016; NCDA, 2009). Not only does doing so involve using skills and applying theories effectively with diverse populations, it also includes things such as choosing appropriate assessments (more information is given later in this chapter), having relevant resources, knowing when to make referrals, and using data to evaluate and identify students' needs broadly (including engaging in efforts to monitor access and achievement gaps across subgroups of students). In that vein, a major imperative of the ASCA's (2016) *Ethical Standards*, as indicated in code A.4.a., states that school counselors create a culture of postsecondary readiness and proactively analyze student data to identify trends that reveal a narrowing or expanding of student gaps in college and career access and the implication of such data for addressing both intentional and unintentional biases related to college and career counseling.

School counselors learn the importance of collecting and disaggregating school data in order to identify similarities and differences among various populations. For example, they might track postsecondary school attendance data to examine the percentage of students who pursue 4-year versus 2-year colleges, breaking down the data by factors such as gender, ethnic groups, disability status, or students who would be first-generation college students. Other data they might examine could include choice of career cluster or results of ability or aptitude tests. Once they know the status of various subpopulations in their schools, they can then develop targeted interventions to try to ensure that everyone has access to the same resources, information, and opportunities to learn about themselves, careers, and colleges, as well as to develop skills and knowledge in various areas.

It is important that school counselors be aware of specialized resources or services for diverse populations and have them available. For example, many students with disabilities need accommodations in order to fully participate in activities, complete school work, or take assessments, and school counselors cannot be expected to know how to address every student's need. They should, however, be able to identify others in the school or community who could become involved in facilitating the career and college readiness for these students. By partnering with special education teachers and vocational rehabilitation counselors, school counselors have a better chance of ensuring that the unique needs of students with disabilities are being considered during career and college planning. Also, by familiarizing themselves with the array of options available for students seeking postsecondary education (e.g., application fee waivers, summer orientation programs, supportive services designed for specific populations), school counselors can disseminate information and encourage involvement in these types of opportunities designed to help eliminate barriers.

General Knowledge of Assessment

Assessment is a critical component of career and college readiness work with P–12 students. Before they develop interventions, counselors and educators must identify the student needs, and assessment may help in that regard. Further, assessment is an activity that informs students' self-knowledge; students learn about themselves in relation to others and the world of work. In general, a basic working knowledge of assessment is necessary for school counselors and educators who are involved in some capacity with making decisions about which assessments to use or who are working directly with assessment data in schools (CACREP, 2016; Krieshok & Black, 2009; NCDA, 2009). In the following, we describe in more detail some important aspects of assessment that inform the knowledge and skills needed by school counselors and educators involved in career and college readiness assessment in schools.

Knowledge of Factors Important for Choosing Assessment Methods
School counselors and educators must possess knowledge that will enable them to make informed decisions about which types of assessments would be most appropriate for any given situation (Krieshok & Black, 2009). This knowledge would include an awareness of the different types of assessment approaches that are available (e.g., formal vs. informal), as well as the purposes, pros, and cons of using different approaches.

Knowledge of Assessments Instruments
Once school counselors and educators determine the types of assessments they want to use, they must narrow down their options. To do so, counselors must familiarize themselves with the array of career- and college-related assessments available (Krieshok & Black, 2009; NCDA, 2009). Knowledge of the factors that can be assessed (e.g., interests, values) as well as the different formats that are available (e.g., online, nonverbal) allows for comparison of the

assessment tools against both student needs and school resources. Further, an understanding of aspects such as norm groups and language, reading, or developmental level is critical for identifying assessments that match the needs of students. In order to choose assessments that will provide meaningful data, school counselors and educators need to be able to understand and evaluate the psychometric properties (e.g., reliability, validity) of assessments. Finally, professionals involved in career- and college-related assessment in schools must be able to identify assessments that they or others in their school are qualified to administer and interpret. In Chapter 5, we provide information about a variety of career- and college-related assessment tools commonly used with P–12 students.

Knowledge to Administer and Oversee School-Based Assessment

In a P–12 school, someone is responsible for ensuring that anyone involved in the administration of an assessment is prepared to administer the assessment, is aware of any standardized instructions that must be followed, and adheres to any protocol or policies regarding administration and confidentiality of assessment materials. The same importance should be placed on administering career- and college-related assessments (Krieshok & Black, 2009). School counselors or educators responsible for overseeing the administration of career- and college-related assessments, whether they are completed individually or in large groups, must be familiar with administration requirements and procedures so that they can enforce and monitor others who might be involved. They also should be familiar with policies and procedures for accommodating different learning styles and second language learners, and adhere to legal protections for students with Individualized Education Programs (IEPs) and 504 plans.

Skills to Interpret and Summarize Assessment Data

As we discuss in Chapter 5, assessment without interpretation is meaningless; it is important to ensure that people know how to make sense of assessing the results. As such, interpretation is an important competency area for school counselors and educators involved in career- and college-related assessment (Krieshok & Black, 2009). Not only should these professionals possess skills to explain assessment results to various groups (e.g., students, parents, teachers, or other stakeholders), they also should be able to adjust their explanations to accommodate language or other differences. The majority of individuals who will receive score reports will be unfamiliar with the terminology commonly used in career- and college-related assessment. It is the responsibility of school counselors and educators to avoid professional jargon, to use developmentally appropriate language, and to provide specific examples when possible to help ensure understanding.

Use common language

In addition to being able to generally interpret and explain assessment results to others, school counselors and educators must be able to compile and analyze statistical summary data (Krieshok & Black, 2009). This involves being able to explain the school summary data that are provided along with individual student score reports and/or calculating and generating summary data. These types of data could include frequency distributions, measures of central tendency (e.g., mean, median), and variability (e.g., standard deviation), and might include the use of graphs and charts.

Evaluating Assessment Data

A final competency area that is important for school counselors and educators involved in career- and college-related assessment is evaluation (Krieshok & Black, 2009). Evaluation practices might involve helping a student make sense of what a number of different assessment results mean in relation to his or her future plans or choices. They also might involve the professional appreciating that results from a single assessment most likely are not sufficient for decision making as thorough, comprehensive evaluation really requires multiple and different data points. On a broader level, evaluation also can refer to the ability to examine summary data and make decisions about programs and services.

Career, Educational, and Labor Market Information

In order to ensure that students and their families are provided with the most current and accurate information, school counselors and educators must themselves stay abreast of career, educational, and labor market information (CACREP, 2016; NCDA, 2009). They also must ensure that they can provide this information to students in developmentally and culturally responsive ways. In order to do this, school counselors should examine a variety of available online and print resources (e.g., O*Net, Occupational Outlook Handbook, U.S. Bureau of Labor Statistics) and make a determination about which would be most useful and relevant to their populations. Similar to helping students and others interpret assessment results, school counselors and educators have a responsibility to make sure that career, educational, and labor market information are understandable to everyone; they should proactively reach out to share and clarify information and resources in these areas, ensuring that everyone has access to this information in some format.

Career and College Planning and Placement

CACREP (2016) identifies the importance of education and career planning and placement in relation to career and college readiness. This refers to the implementation of activities and services to assist students in developing future career and postsecondary educational goals and to engage in activities to achieve those goals. The ability to educate students about decision making and goal setting is requisite for being able to help students figure out how to achieve their goals.

To assist with the latter, school counselors and educators must possess knowledge to help students navigate these areas—what is or is not required to achieve success in these different areas. Knowledge relevant to helping students navigate a number of educational milestones is important and includes: (a) the skills students need to succeed in high school and college, and how they can develop those skills; (b) the requirements for entering the career/vocational training program at the local high school; (c) high school graduation requirements; and (d) different college entrance requirements. It also would require that school counselors and educators possess knowledge of how to enter certain occupations—apprenticeship programs, job-shadowing opportunities, qualities desired by local business and industry, military options, and other training programs.

Collaboration skills are important since school and community connections are critical to successful career and college planning and placement (CACREP, 2016). School counselors and educators must rely on a number of other individuals to assist students in gathering information and navigating various systems outside of the school setting. School personnel ideally would work closely with military recruiters, college admissions representatives, and human resources personnel from local businesses. They also might collaborate with local service providers who can assist with the unique needs of students with disabilities, undocumented students, and homeless students, to name a few special populations. All of these community-based individuals can share information directly with students or can serve as sources of information for counselors and educators. By frequently touching base with contacts in various educational and occupational settings, school counselors and educators can ensure they keep current about requirements and expectations that students should be aware of as they transition from grade to grade and from school to postsecondary settings.

Career and College Program Planning, Implementation, and Evaluation

Skills in program planning, implementation, and evaluation are the final competency area we will highlight, but by no means are these skills the least important. Endorsed by both CACREP (2016) and NCDA (2009), these skills actually encompass many of the competencies we have already discussed. Someone in a school or school district will be responsible for overseeing the career and college readiness services that all P–12 students receive and someone needs to be in charge of the big picture. Often the only "experts" in the school system when it comes to career and college readiness, school counselors might be very involved in overseeing those services in their school or district, or might serve in an advisory capacity.

In any event, the individual responsible for career and college readiness planning must be able to generate a plan, which involves two major components: (a) conceptualizing the career and college readiness needs of the students at a particular school from a specific theoretical framework and (b) choosing assessments and interventions that are both developmentally and culturally appropriate, but that also match the theoretical framework. Collaboration with and input from others will be important, so here again, collaboration and consultation skills are critical. Although implementation of the programs and services will most likely involve more than one person, someone must be responsible for and capable of overseeing the implementation and management of services offered.

Finally, evaluation of career and college readiness programming and services is important in terms of monitoring the quality and effectiveness of those services. School counselors who receive training in the ASCA National Model (2012) learn to examine process, perception, and outcome data when they evaluate their work. Regarding process data, counselors might track the number of students who participated in a specific intervention (e.g., the number of students who attended a college fair) or who completed an assessment. They would examine those data by disaggregating it to examine across different groups. Next, counselors would gather and examine perception data. Perhaps they implement an opinion survey for parents or students, gathering feedback about how useful those groups thought a certain intervention was or how important an assessment was in helping them make future decisions. Finally, counselors would examine outcome data—graduation rates, the percentage of students who applied to or are starting a 4-year college, and so forth. Again, they would disaggregate these data to examine differences across various groups.

Program planning, implementation, and evaluation should be viewed as a cycle by school counselors and educators (Figure 3.1). Program planning, which includes the development of program goals, directs the implementation and evaluation of services provided. Feedback gathered during the implementation of services may influence decisions about which services to provide as well as how they were implemented, leading to potential changes to future program planning. Further, the experience of implementing the services might inform the direction or type of evaluation that occurs, either directly or indirectly, perhaps by opening up future program planning discussions. Similarly, overall evaluation data may inform decisions about program planning, such as determinations about which services will continue to be offered, new services that might be needed, or changes to the evaluation component. School counselors and educators involved in career and college readiness programming should be capable of participating fully in this type of process. See Exhibit 3.1 for a case study.

FIGURE 3.1   Career and College Program Planning, Implementation, and Evaluation Cycle

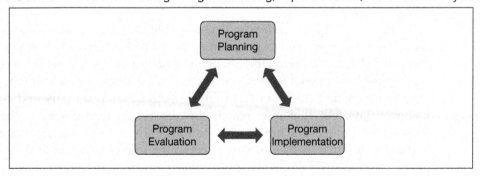

EXHIBIT 3.1
Professional Competency and Ethical Dilemma Case Study

Devin Johnson is an 11th-grade student at Cedar Crest High School. He is scheduled to meet with his parents and the school counselor, Merhoff, for a career and college planning session. Merhoff has a planned agenda: to review Devin's stated career choice (athletic trainer), review his current grade point average (GPA) and ACT® scores, develop a college application timeline, and plan his remaining high school course work. When they arrive, Devin is with his father, Johnson, who proceeds to dominate the conversation. Devin's father tells Merhoff that he and Devin's mom are recently divorced and that he received the call about this meeting and did not tell her because "she is not very educated and really doesn't need to have input on the boy's college decision." Devin's father proceeds to let Merhoff know that being an athletic trainer is not an acceptable career path and that Devin is going to major in prelaw so he can become an attorney. Merhoff knows that Devin is very committed to a career in athletic training as he has volunteered with his high school's athletic training coordinator for 2 years and has taken an extra biology course to prepare. He has even talked to Merhoff about the possibility of pursuing a doctorate in sports medicine after getting his bachelor's degree. Merhoff asks Devin's father what reservations he has about athletic training as a career and he says, "They are just dumb jocks. A bunch of guys that are gym rats. That's not a real job." Merhoff realizes that Devin's father likely does not understand how athletic trainers work during sporting events to respond to injuries through sport triage and by providing injury rehabilitation for athletes.

1. What ethical or legal issues do you possibly see arising from this scenario?
2. Using the STEPS (Stone, 2001) model, what are some possible courses of action for Merhoff?
3. What career development competencies might be beneficial to Merhoff in this situation?
4. What information or knowledge might be important to share with Devin's father to help him better understand Devin's career choice?

PREPARATION FOR PROVIDING CAREER AND COLLEGE READINESS INTERVENTIONS IN SCHOOLS

By virtue of their educational backgrounds and training, school counselors generally possess the qualifications needed to develop, implement, and evaluate career- and college-related counseling services in schools. In addition to numerous other courses, they usually have completed course work in general counseling skills, career counseling, assessment, research/statistics, and multicultural counseling. Ongoing professional development in the area of career development and college readiness is important to ensure that school counselors stay abreast of current trends in career and postsecondary transition counseling, assessment instruments, and resources that are available.

The backgrounds of other educators who are involved in career- and college-related programs vary greatly. The authors have worked with individuals from a variety of backgrounds, including one administrator who completed a 3-day career workshop and was placed in charge of an entire school district's career-related programming; someone with a bachelor's degree in science who completed Career Development Facilitator training and who was hired to provide career and college readiness interventions to students and their parents; and an individual who completed a graduate program in career counseling and served as a career counselor in a high school.

Each school or school district will differ in the types and qualifications of individuals available to provide career- and college-related services to P–12 students. No matter their backgrounds, all of these individuals could seek opportunities to enhance their career- and college-related knowledge and skills. They might do this through participating in professional development opportunities such as attending workshops or conferences, or they might pursue career-specific credentials. We discuss these two options in the following.

Professional Development and Credentials

Most professional positions within a school require the completion of renewal or continuing education credits in order to maintain eligibility to serve in that position. Fortunately for school employees, school districts typically offer, at no cost to their employees, various professional development seminars throughout the school year or during the summer. Sometimes school personnel can sign up for topics that interest them; other times everyone must attend a specific training session. Savvy school counselors and educators who are responsible for career- and college-related programming will advocate for schools to provide professional development opportunities related to career and postsecondary educational planning.

When opportunities are not available in-house, school counselors and educators can seek local or regional workshops. Colleges and universities occasionally offer workshops for counselors and educational consultants related to college admissions, choosing majors, or related topics. Local businesses, if asked, also may be willing to sponsor a speaker or offer seminars related to job trends or employability skills.

State and national conferences are always a good source of information. Although anyone can attend these conferences, registration rates tend to be higher for individuals who are not members of the organization sponsoring the conference. The ASCA and its individual state divisions hold annual conferences and one can always find career- and college-related sessions at those conferences. Labor market trends, career assessments, career interventions, and online resources are frequent session topics, usually presented by representatives of the organizations or companies that publish the resources, but often by school counselors who have tried-and-true programs to share. The NCDA also holds an annual conference, as do many of its state divisions. Although the focus of these conferences goes beyond P–12 career development, school counselors and educators would likely find them beneficial for professional development purposes.

A number of other professional organizations also sponsor conferences that could offer relevant information for school-based career professionals. For example, the Association for Career and Technical Education is an organization focused on preparing people for careers, as its name suggests. Also, the National Association for College Admissions Counseling is an organization that focuses on sharing information to help professionals help students successfully transition to postsecondary education. Finally, the Council for Exceptional Children's Division on Career Development and Transition provides information and resources to individuals who want to help persons with disabilities successfully transition to careers and college. Most of these professional organizations offer numerous professional development opportunities beyond conferences, including informational resources on their websites, webinars, and special opportunities for members.

School counselors may choose to acquire specific career counseling credentials. As mentioned earlier in this chapter, a school counseling credential (i.e., certificate or license, depending on the state) typically reflects that someone has completed a graduate program that prepared him or her to engage in career and college readiness-related work in schools. Although school counseling degree programs prepare graduates to address more than just career and college issues, one can feel confident in the preparation of someone who is certified or licensed as a school counselor.

Nevertheless, someone might choose or be encouraged to acquire a credential such as the Global Career Development Facilitator (GCDF). A person who holds the GCDF credential has completed a minimum of 120 hours of training in career development and is qualified to provide career-related services in a variety of settings. Depending on the level of education a person has completed (ranging from high school diploma to graduate degree), he or she can receive the GCDF credential after accumulating varying levels of experience in career work. Offered by the Center for Credentialing in Education (CCE), individuals can seek training through online or in-person formats through a number of approved providers. Although the GCDF is typically a voluntary credential, some schools require it for individuals without a school counseling credential who are hired to provide career-counseling services in schools.

SUMMARY

In this chapter, we discussed numerous issues related to the professional preparation of counselors who wish to provide career and college readiness counseling in P–12 schools. We referenced a number of documents, reviewed a variety of competencies, and discussed options for professional development. Ethically, counselors are responsible for developing the skills and knowledge to effectively provide career development and college readiness counseling services to diverse populations.

···❯ Test Your Knowledge

1. Provide one example of how easily a counselor could impose his or her values during a career or college counseling session.
2. Name at least three professional organizations where a school counselor could seek professional development related to career or college readiness counseling.

REFERENCES

American Counseling Association. (2014). *2014 ACA code of ethics.* Retrieved from https://www.counseling.org/resources/aca-code-of-ethics.pdf

American School Counselor Association. (2012). *The ASCA national model: A framework for school counseling programs* (3rd ed.). Alexandria, VA: Author.

American School Counselor Association. (2014). *ASCA mindsets & behaviors for student success: K-12 college- and career-readiness standards for every student.* Alexandria, VA: Author.

American School Counselor Association. (2016). *ASCA ethical standards for school counselors.* Alexandria, VA: Author.

Council for Accreditation of Counseling and Related Educational Programs. (2016). *2016 CACREP standards.* Alexandria, VA: Author.

Krieshok, T. S., & Black, M. D. (2009). Assessment and counseling competencies and responsibilities: A checklist for counselors. In E. A. Whitfield, R. W. Feller, & C. Wood (Eds.), *A counselor's guide to career assessment instruments* (5th ed., pp. 61–68). Broken Arrow, OK: National Career Development Association.

National Career Development Association. (2009). The National Career Development Association minimum competencies for multicultural career counseling and development. Retrieved from http://ncda.org/aws/NCDA/pt/sp/guidelines

National Career Development Association. (2015). *2015 NCDA code of ethics.* Retrieved from http://ncda.org/aws/NCDA/asset_manager/get_file/3395

Stone, C. (2001). *School counseling principles: Ethics and law.* Alexandria, VA: American School Counselor Association.

FOUR

P–12 Career and College Readiness: Cultural Considerations

Although all students need career and college exploration, it is important to understand that some populations are more vulnerable to inequities in access to careers and college. Although the demographic landscape of the U.S. educational system has changed dramatically and will continue to do so, the disparities in educational and career success among various groups of students persist. Moreover, many national trends have affected the job market for 21st-century students. For example, college affordability has decreased as the costs of tuition and fees have increased nearly 30% in the past 10 years, after adjusting for inflation (The College Board, 2015). Increases were reported at 29% and 26% for 2-year colleges and private 4-year colleges, respectively.

Because of the need to work for financial reasons and the fact that people are living longer and therefore are able to maintain full-time employment longer, many older Americans are not retiring at age 65. According to Ellis (2011), a reported 75% of Americans plan to work through retirement and 25% plan to work at least until the age of 80. These percentages are consistent with data from the U.S. Census Bureau's 2015 American Community Survey, which showed an estimated 25.3% of the U.S. population ages 65 to 74 were still working (U.S. Census Bureau, 2015a). That number is expected to nearly double (to 11.1 million) by 2018 as the baby boomer generation reaches retirement age. With fewer positions opening up, getting quality, high-paying jobs becomes more competitive than it was for previous generations, so the future workforce must be well prepared with employability skills and requisite education experiences.

These concerns, coupled with slow job growth, make postsecondary preparation a priority for school counselors. In this chapter, we explore issues of inequity and barriers to postsecondary access and success for specific populations as well as cultural competencies for school counselors in promoting career and college readiness. We caution readers that the specific populations highlighted here are by no means exhaustive of the subgroups school counselors need to consider. Further, we cannot comprehensively address all of these concerns; therefore, this chapter is meant to serve as an introduction to cultural considerations in career and college readiness. Finally, school counselors should consider the role of culture, ethnicity, race, gender, religion, socioeconomic status, sexual orientation, and other factors when designing career and college readiness interventions. The concept of intersectionality will be important to keep in mind—the fact that categories such as gender, race, disability, and sexual orientation, to name a few, interact on many levels. As such, the experiences of any student will be complex, and school counselors should strive to consider the multiple biological, social, and cultural factors that play a role in their career and college readiness rather than viewing them through a single lens.

SPECIAL POPULATION CONSIDERATIONS

Hispanics/Latinos

The terms *Hispanic* and *Latino* are often used interchangeably; however, understanding the differences between them is important, as many educators and counselors are unsure of which term should be used. In general, the term *Hispanic* refers to a region of origin, specifically regions that tend to be geographical locations that were historically occupied by, or conquered by, Spaniards; it is a term related to heritage, nationality, or lineage. *Hispanic* is the term most often used in federal documents (such as education and census data). However, some people prefer the term *Latino*, which refers to cultures of Latin America and is a term that may also encompass language and traditions. In this chapter, we use both terms based on the language chosen by authors and researchers in the literature reviewed.

An important consideration for school counselors is that the Hispanic populations served in U.S. schools are vastly diverse. For example, a student from Venezuela who is first generation in the United States and an English language learner is very different culturally from a student who is second generation, originating from Puerto Rico, and has always spoken English. The potential differences among students are highly complex, so although we present data for Hispanic students as a whole in order to examine these populations in depth, we encourage school counselors to assess their school community and make an effort to examine and understand the within-group differences of the specific populations they serve. To provide a general overview of trends, however, we present aggregate data on Hispanic student achievement and career and college readiness.

Projections of growth in the Hispanic population are predominant. Specifically, the percent of the U.S. population that is Hispanic is currently estimated at 17%, but is expected to increase dramatically to over 28.6% by 2060 (U.S. Census Bureau, 2014). Additionally, the percentage of Hispanic students in P–12 schools increased between 2003 and 2013—from 19% to 25%, with projections it will reach 28% by 2025 (NCES, 2015).

In spite of population growth, Hispanics continue to make markedly less reported income than their Asian and White counterparts, but slightly more than African Americans. Data from the U.S. Census Bureau reported the average annual income for Asians at $74,297 and Whites (non-Hispanic) at $60,256, while Hispanics earned an average of $42,491 and African Americans earned only $35,398 (DeNavas-Walt & Proctor, 2015). Furthermore, poverty appears to be a pervasive and ubiquitous problem, with more than 32% of Hispanic children under the age of 18 below the poverty level (DeNavas-Walt & Proctor, 2015). In addition to low family income, the Center on Education Policy (2010) concluded that limited English proficiency and low parental education levels compound educational difficulties faced by Hispanic students and become barriers to education and career success. These types of barriers often are reflected in the communities where Hispanic students live and the P–12 schools they attend. In particular, according to Hoover (2007), Latino students often attend P–12 education in districts with "limited rigorous course offerings, dilapidated school facilities, poverty . . ." (p. 33).

Because of these and other challenges, a large number of Hispanic students are not successful in their pursuit of postsecondary education. As noted by Dolan (2008), many Hispanic students are first-generation students, and the majority that do go to college attend 2-year community colleges. Concerns enumerated by Dolan include Hispanic students having lower college persistence rates, limited preparation for college course work necessitating remedial courses, and inadequate information about financial planning, effective study skills, college admission requirements, or career preparation. Further, in a qualitative inquiry of Latino students' college experiences, Taningco (2008) found that Latinos had difficulty adjusting to college life and the academic demands of higher education.

Hoover (2007) contended that many Latino students feel underprepared and are uninformed about postsecondary options and college entrance requirements. However, in a qualitative study, Boden (2011) found different results. In the study, Latino first-generation university students were interviewed about their perceptions of their own college preparedness. These participants reported feeling prepared and cited their understanding of academic skills, educational planning, guidance from a mentor, and their personal characteristics as precursors of successful college entrance and matriculation. Boden's (2011) sample size was extremely small, and while participants felt prepared for college, research demonstrates that many Hispanic students are not. Indeed, it is possible that participants in Boden's sample felt prepared because they had no way to gauge their preparation against other students.

As highlighted by Hoover (2007), however, admission to college and acquisition of scholarships largely depends on academic performance measured through grade point averages (GPAs) and SAT® or ACT® scores. Based on these academic requirements, Hispanic students applying to college are at a pervasive disadvantage. For example, in regard to the ACT, national statistics indicate an average ACT score of 22.4 for Whites and an average ACT score of 18.9 for Hispanics (ACT, Inc., 2015). This difference in ACT scores may reduce Hispanic students' ability to compete for early admission and academic scholarships.

In 2006, the Tomás Rivera Policy Institute provided an educational report on the current trends of access and achievement for education and career pathways for Latinos, particularly in advanced technology (Tornatzky, Macias, Jenkins, & Solis, 2006). The research was funded through a grant by the National Science Foundation (NSF) to investigate research and policy analysis pertaining to Latino students and technical careers. Given the importance and projected growth of science, technology, engineering, and mathematics (STEM) careers (see Chapter 1), it is critical that barriers to these careers are examined and that suggestions are made to improve educational practices that support Latino students' postsecondary success. When examining the types of occupations in which Hispanics work, the U.S. Census Bureau (2010) found that Hispanic males were largely employed in construction and maintenance, production and transportation, and service areas. Hispanic women were largely in sales and office occupations, followed by professional occupations, and then production and transportation.

In considering the career and college readiness of Hispanic students, Durodoye and Bodley (1997) suggested that counselors must understand that there are traditional cultural values (e.g., strong allegiance to family) that may influence Hispanic students' career and college decisions. Moreover, according to Taningco (2008), family members may not always support a Latino student's decision to go to college for a variety of reasons, including misconceptions or biases about the following: gender stereotypes related to career goals, negative views of education loans, use of family money prioritized for things other than education, and pressure on students to earn an income immediately after high school. Other factors, such as oppression, discrimination, and prejudice, may have psychological consequences for Latino students, including lower self-esteem and self-efficacy, which in turn affect career aspirations and decision making (Durodoye & Bodley, 1997).

Given the unique cultural characteristics of Hispanic populations and the ongoing disparity in educational achievement, career development, and college readiness, school counselors need to continue to examine ways to promote Hispanic students' access to postsecondary options. Ivers, Milsom, and Newsome (2012) conceptualized the academic and career needs of Latino students using Gottfredson's *Theory of Circumscription and Compromise* (1981) and offered suggestions for intervention to help improve school success. Target areas included identifying and involving Latino role models and mentors, providing information to students and parents about educational and career pathways, and increased communication between schools and families (including the use of translators).

African Americans

School counselors should be aware of the career- and college-related achievement gaps that exist for African American students For example, only 59% of African American males graduate high school on time compared to 80% of White males (Schott Foundation for Public Education, 2015). Additionally, by age 20, approximately 25% of African American males and 24% of African American females are high school dropouts, compared to 16% of White males and 9% of White females (Levin, Belfield, Muennig, & Rouse, 2007). Although they still lag slightly behind White students, interestingly the percentages of African American students enrolling in postsecondary school right out of high school have increased in recent years. This increase from 49% in 1990 to 63% in

2014 suggests that the achievement gap might be closing; while 63% of White students were enrolled in 1990, that percentage only increased slightly, to 68%, in 2014 (NCES, 2016).

Although many factors contribute to between-group differences in achievement, West-Olatunji, Baker, and Brooks (2006) noted that African Americans are expelled, suspended, or receive corporal punishment at rates far higher than other groups of students. The same authors observed that African American students, males in particular, are overrepresented in special education, are inordinately identified as emotionally disturbed, are underrepresented in gifted education, and are exposed to microaggressions, cultural hostility, and discriminatory practices in education settings that may be psychologically damaging. Goodman and West-Olatunji (2010) contended that many of the behaviors displayed by African Americans are misinterpreted as emotional disturbance or academic deficiency and may actually be the result of traumatic stress from living in systems of oppression and a hegemonic academy.

All of these factors may instill in African Americans a sense of inadequacy or low self-efficacy that, in turn, might lead to the exclusion or lack of equitable access to postsecondary success. For African Americans, not graduating from high school is compounded by subsequent social problems: significantly lower wages and yearly income throughout the life span, poorer health and higher mortality, higher stress, and greater risk of incarceration than their White counterparts (Levin et al., 2007; Muennig & Fahs, 2001; Raphael, 2004). According to Carty (2010), these differences are pervasive throughout the lives of African Americans, particularly African American males. Of the experiences of African American men, Carty stated:

> They have more trouble purchasing a home, have lower home values, have lower median incomes, own fewer businesses, and are less likely to be invested in a 401(k) retirement plan. Moreover, Black males are less likely than the general population to be employed, live above the poverty line, have a home computer with Internet access, or own a car. Health outcomes take into account death rates and life expectancy, lifetime health issues, and neonatal care and related issues. The prevalence of diabetes, homicide, and HIV are all higher among Blacks than Whites, and contribute to a difference in the age-adjusted death rate. Social justice factors highlight the heavy toll of incarceration and other interactions with the legal and criminal justice system. Black males are more likely to be murdered and/or to be the victim of a violent crime. (pp. 4–5)

Furthermore, African American students who graduate from high school and pursue a college degree often encounter challenges. For example, the national average for African American students on the ACT is 17.1, while it is 22.4 for White students (ACT, Inc., 2015). Lower ACT scores may limit students' access to early admissions and scholarships. Nevertheless, in a study of African American graduation rates in U.S. colleges and universities, Wright (2010) found that colleges and universities with Black cultural centers, high first-year retention rates, and a high number of student organizations were more likely to retain and graduate African American students.

Walker, Pearson, and Murrell (2010) studied differences between African American and White community college students and found that African American students relied more heavily on accessibility to faculty as a way of garnering academic support, learning about careers, and receiving career guidance and mentorship. Additionally, Walker et al. found that counseling was critical for African American students who chose to talk to their community college counselors and advisors about topics like course registration, careers and majors, vocational interests, abilities, and aspirations. Walker et al. surmised that career exploration is a major task for African American community college students. Similarly, Lucas (1993) found that African American college students reported worrying about grades, time management, study habits, lack of information about careers, lack of knowledge regarding personal interests and skills related to careers, and poor career decision-making skills.

In addition to challenges related to postsecondary school attendance, African Americans tend to be underrepresented in careers high in prestige that command higher salaries (e.g., STEM careers; see Chapter 1). Potential reasons for African Americans not entering STEM careers include lack of exposure to STEM careers and a lack of access to rigorous high school courses (e.g., Calculus, Trigonometry, Advanced Placement [AP] Chemistry) that prepare them for college course work. Also, compared to their White, middle-class peers, African American students also may lack financial resources to support activities such as attending summer space camp, participating in engineering clubs, or buying home chemistry sets where they could explore or develop interest in STEM areas.

A few researchers have examined factors that affect the educational and career experiences of African American students. Through a qualitative study, West-Olatunji et al. (2010) found that school counselors may lack the cultural competence to identify and utilize African American students' strengths and, therefore, view African American students' behaviors and academic potential through a deficit framework that could result in advising them toward less rigorous academic paths and lower career aspirations. Even when African American students are identified as gifted, it appears that their career aspirations are often lower than their White counterparts (Parris, Owens, Johnson, Grbevski, & Holbert-Quince, 2010). These researchers suggested that in order to support African American students in gifted programs, counselors need to assist them by acknowledging feelings of isolation, and address fears of being viewed as "acting White" or being different, heightened peer pressure, concerns about career access, and the need for career assessment and planning.

In addition to these types of systemic factors that affect African American students' educational and career decisions, cultural values also play a role. Specifically, Walker and Tracey (2012) found that Holland Codes for social and enterprising careers (e.g., teacher, clergy, business leader) are given high prestige in African American communities, whereas in other cultural groups (Caucasian, Asian), careers that are investigative in nature (such as STEM) have higher social prestige. Walker and Tracey noted that African Americans tend to value careers that have social impact and promote community well-being (e.g., social or enterprising jobs). Further, Walker and Tracy believed that Afrocentric values (such as cooperation) may influence the status that an individual places on a specific career (e.g., teaching may be viewed as a career that promotes community growth and development).

Improving African American Students' Access to Careers and College

To improve high school graduation rates and postsecondary success for African American students, many things may be done. To begin, counselors might use teacher in-service training opportunities to assist teachers in developing culturally responsive teaching practices (West-Olatunji et al., 2010). Curry (2010) suggested that counselors need to become aware of their own biases, and should consider how their language may be discriminatory or reflect cultural insensitivity (i.e., microinsults, microinvalidations). Ponec (1997) recommended that school counselors provide comprehensive college information, including presenting information about historically Black colleges and universities (HBCUs), incorporating collaborative and community activities with peers such as small-group programs for career and college readiness, and providing mentorship opportunities between African American students and successful adult African Americans in various careers and postsecondary educational backgrounds. For example, a school counselor at an all African American school in New Orleans takes eighth-grade students on a yearly tour of HBCUs (e.g., Spellman, Moorehouse, Fisk) and the Alabama civil rights museum. African American leaders from the New Orleans community are invited to attend the trip with the students and to facilitate group discussions on African American college opportunities.

Another strategy for promoting African American students' success is the use of Rite of Passage programs (West-Olatunji, Shure, Garrett, Conwill, & Rivera, 2008). These programs focus on the strengths of minority youth, emphasize involvement in the community through service and leadership, and promote self-control, creativity, moral development, problem solving, and academic skills. Other researchers have noted that including parents in career and college readiness opportunities (examples of how to do this are given throughout this book) is crucial to increasing African American adolescents' career self-efficacy (Alliman-Brissett, Turner, & Skovholt, 2004). However, more research needs to be conducted to find programs that are efficacious in serving the career and college readiness needs of African American youth.

Native Americans

It is difficult to make many assumptions about Native American students, as the term *Native American* refers to many populations. For example, the number of federally recognized Indian tribes in 2015 was 566 (U.S. Census Bureau, 2015b). Each of these tribal entities is vastly different and geographically diverse from the others (tribal groups are from Alaska, Hawaii, and the continental United States). Each has its own unique customs, language, and traditions; therefore, making definitive conclusions about all populations is impossible. However, some definite patterns exist.

Income and education gaps exist for Native Americans. For example, the percentage of American Indians and Alaska Natives who were in poverty in 2014 was 28.3%, the highest rate of any racial group. For the nation as a whole, the poverty rate was 15.5% (U.S. Census Bureau, 2015b). Additionally, only 67% of the American Indian/Alaskan Native youth graduated high school in 2014, compared to a national average of 80% (The White House, 2014). Students at Bureau of Indian Education (BIE) schools are less successful, with a graduation rate of 53%.

In spite of poor high school and college matriculation rates, Brown and Lavish (2006) found that Native American students valued and ranked career and work as valuable and important. Additionally, they reported that community and home/family hold more salience for Native American youth than do work or career, an indication of the collectivist nature of many Native American cultures. Indeed, Long (1999) underscored how important it is for school counselors to understand that assisting a Native American student in career or college preparation may need to involve multiple family members, as postsecondary decisions may be made by the whole family for the individual. Moreover, the connection between the family, school, community, and tribe may be important to consider, particularly for students living on reservations. Though Long's assertion may be true for many Native American youth, the degree to which family and tribe need to be consulted will be largely determined by individual characteristics such as the individual's degree of acculturation. Acculturation with tribal culture, or dominant White culture, may impact how much a Native American individual commits to tribal beliefs, values, and customs (Reynolds, Sodano, Ecklund, & Guyker, 2012).

Based on their qualitative study of Native American youth living on four different reservations, Hoffman, Jackson, and Smith (2005) noted that Native American students living on reservations experience common career-related concerns. Specifically, the students in their study experienced a limited range of possible careers, academic difficulties, financial concerns, and family and peer pressure to remain on the reservation. More complex themes also emerged from their study, including the misperception by many males that jobs were plentiful and easy to attain and a lack of awareness, knowledge, or expressed concern about academic and career barriers.

In addition to general career concerns, transitions from high school to college may be significantly difficult for Native Americans, especially if they have to leave behind existing support systems. Moreover, many Native American students may not be equipped with the skills necessary to achieve in college. Assisting Native Americans in finding colleges and universities that provide physical space where Native American students can meet with other Native American students and discuss and reflect upon their challenges, procure resources, and provide support for each other is crucial (Mihesuah, 2004).

Turner et al. (2006) asserted that an Integrative Contextual Model (ICM) of career development may be particularly salient with Native American adolescents. The authors contended that such a model provides a proactive approach that promotes positive adaptability and resilience. Specifically, they believed that utilizing an ICM can help Native American adolescents develop six vocational outcomes: (a) academic achievement, (b) positive self-efficacy expectations, (c) positive self-attributional styles, (d) vocational identity, (e) understanding of one's personally valued career interests, and (f) pursuit of one's life goals. In order to promote these outcomes, Turner et al. identified skills in six areas that must be taught to Native American youth: (a) career exploration, (b) person–environment fit, (c) goal-setting, (d) social and work-readiness, (e) self-regulation, and (f) utilization of social support.

Girls and Women

In a report issued by the Council of Graduate Schools, Allum and Okahana (2015) noted that women are achieving at greater levels than ever before, surpassing men in graduate and doctoral degree admissions and matriculation. Lewin (2006) observed that women are graduating from college with more honors (i.e., cum laude, magna, summa), have higher GPAs, are more likely to make the Dean's list, and spend more time studying and preparing for class than their male counterparts. Yet, in spite of these gains in achievement, women continue to earn less than their male counterparts and men are still overrepresented in math and science careers. In particular, only 25% of engineering jobs and 32.5% of mathematics and computer science areas are filled by women (Allum & Okahana, 2015) in spite of the fact that women in those careers earn 30% more than women in non-STEM professions (Koebler, 2012).

Girls and STEM

In a survey conducted by the Society of Women Engineers, 75% of girls reported having no interest in science careers and generally expressed interest in entertainment, fashion, and helping fields (Roach, 2006). The disconnect between girls and STEM may be largely based on social factors including cultural stereotyping of careers and social media's promotion of limited, sexualized female identities (Choate & Curry, 2009). Diekman, Brown, Johnston, and Clark (2010) found that when women opt out of science careers, it is often due to perceived incongruence of STEM majors and the communal goals that are socially promoted for women (i.e., working with and helping others). In their study, Diekman, Clark, Johnston, Brown, and Steinberg (2011) reported that participants who held high communal goal beliefs were more likely to perceive STEM careers as self-promoting, individualistic, and success-driven careers. Further, the lack of an integrated belief system (e.g., "I can have a STEM career and reach my communal goals") was absent for many of the participating women. However, effective career exploration might have helped women reach that type of integration (e.g., "By becoming a civil engineer I can work with a team to help make my community safe by providing a sound infrastructure for us") and may actually improve girls' attitudes toward STEM pursuits.

Stout, Dasgupta, Hunsinger, and McManus (2011) proposed that the stereotypes of STEM professions as male-dominated creates barriers for women entering those professions. Stout et al. proposed a stereotype inoculation model to promote STEM self-concepts for girls. One method they suggested was to expose girls to successful female role models in STEM professions. Additionally, the authors proposed that researchers and educators focus more on improving girls' STEM self-concepts than on improving test scores in the STEM domains.

Beyond a lack of role models and social reinforcement of communal goals for girls, research indicates that many girls are discouraged from pursuing STEM careers. For example, in the Bayer Facts survey (Bayer Corporation, 2012), 4 out of 10 females and underrepresented minorities with careers as chemists or chemical engineers reported that they had been discouraged from pursing STEM studies or STEM careers at some point in their lives. Similarly, in a qualitative study, researchers found that school counselors had advised African American females to take lower-rigor math and science classes in spite of their academic potential and interest in math and science (West-Olatunji et al., 2010). Further, women who enter college as STEM majors have lower persistence rates compared to males in STEM majors and are more likely to change majors (Griffith, 2010).

Researchers and scholars have proposed that there are many reasons why women may not pursue STEM careers, including self-efficacy, social encouragement to enter humanitarian and helping professions (i.e., psychology, teaching, counseling), and gender and cultural stereotypes that promote limited career aspirations (Diekman et al., 2010). Indeed, for women to fully commit to STEM careers and matriculate through postsecondary training, it is critical that they possess high career decision-making self-efficacy (CDMSE). In particular, CDMSE is affected by career maturity; that is, the degree to which an individual understands her career choice, including realistically understanding a typical day's work associated with an occupation, expected remuneration, training and education requirements, and personal values, aptitudes, and interests related to a given career choice. Interventions targeting those areas could help increase girls' self-efficacy beliefs.

Students With Disabilities

Currently, approximately 5.83 million students between the ages of 6 and 21 are eligible for and receive special education services in the United States (Education Week, 2016). Students are eligible for special education services if they meet criteria established under the Individuals with Disabilities Education Act (IDEA) and have an emotional, mental, or physical disability. The 14 categories of disabilities recognized in IDEA legislation are: autism, deafness, deaf–blindness, developmental delay, emotional disturbance, hearing impairment, mental retardation, orthopedic impairment, specific learning disability, speech and language impairment, traumatic brain injury, visual impairment, multiple disabilities, and other health impairments (The Center for Public Education,

2009). Education Week reports that the number of students diagnosed with autism and other health impairments has increased significantly in the past 10 years (165% increase for autism and 51% increase for other health impairments). In addition, notable decreases are evident for emotional disturbance (–27%), intellectual disabilities (–23%), learning disabilities (–17%), and speech and language impairments (–11%).

It is beyond the scope of this chapter to cover all of the educational needs and disparities among students with identified disabilities or the challenges faced by these populations in educational environments. Additionally, although it is out of our purview here to highlight the special education process (i.e., identification, screening, notification and consent, assessment, eligibility determination, Individualized Education Program [IEP] development), we encourage readers to review this process to more fully understand the role of the school counselor in special education (Rock & Leff, 2011). Rather, our focus here is on career and college readiness for students with identified disabilities.

Postsecondary School

Indicating that many students with learning disabilities end up working in low-paying jobs with few benefits and little job security. Dickinson and Verbeek (2002) suggested that completing postsecondary education could lead to greater career success for individuals with learning disabilities. Completion of a postsecondary degree can open up a vast array of options for students with disabilities. In college, students with disabilities experience the same challenges that students without disabilities face: academic demands, financial stress, balancing social life and work, and experiencing the transition to college life. However, Madriaga et al. (2010) reported that students with disabilities also face unique struggles in college related to their specific disabilities, including difficulty taking notes, hearing the instructor, reading and comprehending course materials, and gaining access to buildings/classrooms.

Since the passage of the Americans with Disabilities Act (ADA) in 1990 (PL 101-336), colleges and universities have experienced increasing enrollments of students with disabilities (Henderson, 1999). The implementation of college support services that arose as a result of the ADA is believed to have contributed to those increasing numbers (Flexer, Simmons, Luft, & Baer, 2005). Students with identified disabilities now can receive any number of accommodations (e.g., extended time or distraction-free tests, scribes) from postsecondary institutions in order to level the playing field.

Nevertheless, similar to the other populations we have highlighted so far, postsecondary educational achievement gaps also exist for students with disabilities. Specifically, looking at data for 4 years out of high school, in 2011 only 45.6% of students with disabilities were enrolled in college, compared to 62.6% of the general population (College and Career Readiness and Success Center, 2013). They also attend different types of colleges, with only 7.6% of students with disabilities attending 4-year universities compared to 29.2% of general population students (Newman, Wagner, Cameto, & Knokey, 2009). Finally, college completion rates are lower for students with disabilities (40.7% vs. 52.4%), and they were more likely to complete 2-year and technical school degrees than they were 4-year degrees.

Through her research, Milsom (Milsom & Deitz, 2009; Milsom & Hartley, 2005) identified a number of factors relevant to college success for students with disabilities. In addition to the career and college readiness skills relevant for all students (see Chapter 1), other important factors include (a) knowledge of one's disability, or disability self-awareness; (b) knowledge of the ADA of 1990, specifically regarding personal rights and responsibilities as well as postsecondary school responsibilities for providing accommodations; and (c) self-advocacy skills. Limited research, however, has specifically examined these factors in relation to college success. In one somewhat dated study, Dalke (1993) found that disability self-awareness was a characteristic of students with disabilities who were successful in college.

Little research exists connecting specific skills to college success for students with disabilities; likewise, research regarding effective interventions targeting the areas listed previously is limited and dated. Further, most of the empirically supported interventions were conducted with students after they graduated high school. Three interventions with high school students worth examining (Aune, 1991; Milsom, Akos, & Thompson, 2004; Phillips, 1990) all included strong psychoeducational components focused on the students' developing self and college awareness.

Career Preparation

Career outcomes for students with disabilities also tend to be of concern, in comparison to their peers without disabilities. In 2015, the unemployment rate for individuals with disabilities was around 10.7%, double that of individuals without disabilities (U.S. Bureau of Labor Statistics, 2015). Also, students with disabilities earn an average lower salary and tend to obtain fewer competitive employment opportunities than their peers without disabilities (Newman et al., 2011).

For students with disabilities who are not planning to pursue college, other postsecondary preparation is necessary and should be considered a priority. Such preparation may include filling out a job application, writing cover letters and resumes, developing interviewing skills, and participating in life skills training (i.e., creating a budget, balancing a checkbook, learning to navigate public transportation, securing housing)—skills relevant to any students who will be seeking employment right after high school. For many students with disabilities, this preparation also might involve connecting them to vocational rehabilitation personnel who can help them secure competitive employment and provide job skills training.

Research shows that in many instances, career development interventions designed for students who have more severe disabilities tend to focus on occupational choice rather than on broad career development issues like career and self-exploration (Rumrill & Roessler, 1999). Wadsworth, Milsom, and Cocco (2004) emphasized the importance of helping students with disabilities make meaningful career choices, which means involving students with disabilities and their families in all of the career development interventions provided to other students. Although the way career development activities are approached might vary depending on the cognitive or physical abilities of students with disabilities, every student in school deserves the opportunity to choose his or her future: "Having a career does not mean being placed in a job but having the opportunity to make choices" (Hagner & Salomone, 1989, p. 154).

Lesbian, Gay, Bisexual, and Transgender Students

Estimating the number of individuals who identify as lesbian, gay, bisexual, or transgender (LGBT) is challenging, mainly because population surveys do not always include items that allow for accurate identification of those subgroups. Estimates suggest that combined, approximately 4% of individuals in the United States identify as LGBT (Gates, 2011). Data from the 2013 National School Climate Survey (Gay, Lesbian, and Straight Education Network [GLSEN], 2014) revealed that over half of LGBT students felt unsafe at school because of their sexual orientation. Nearly three-fourths reported being verbally harassed in some way and over one-third reported being physically assaulted. Further, over half experienced some sort of discrimination from the school (e.g., a gay student being prohibited from attending a dance with a same-sex partner or a transgender student not being permitted to use a preferred name).

Why do these statistics matter? The school climate survey data (GLSEN, 2014) revealed that students who felt victimized at school had lower grade point averages than their less frequently victimized peers (2.8 vs. 3.3, respectively), were less likely to want to pursue any sort of postsecondary education, and were more likely to miss school. These behavioral and attitudinal outcomes have a direct impact on students' future career success. Also, LGBT students reported being more interested in pursuing STEM careers if the relevant courses contained positive LGBT content.

Career decision making is an important focus area for LGBT students, and a combination of internal and external factors play a role in their career development. Schmidt and Nilsson (2006) suggested that one reason many LGBT adolescents have difficulty making career decisions is because their psychological resources are being spent on their sexual identity, leaving little emotional energy for other things. In their study of LGBT youth, Schmidt and Nilsson found that higher levels of inner sexual identity conflict was associated with lower levels of career maturity and higher levels of career indecision. Interestingly, they also found similar results among students who reported lower levels of social support—those students also had lower career maturity and high career indecision. Other research shows that LGBT students perceived receiving limited support and guidance related to academic and career decision making (Nauta, Saucier, & Woodard, 2001).

Studies of college students reveal that nearly one-third of LGBT students experience harassment on campus (Rankin, 2003). Because of fears for their safety, many students choose to hide their sexual orientation in college. In their study of undergraduate students, Schmidt, Miles, and Welsh (2011) found that high levels of social support served as a buffer to discrimination—students who self-reported high levels of social support (friends or family) and high levels of perceived discrimination still had low levels of career indecision. Presumably their ability to talk with others about their discriminatory experiences helped them work through concerns and make resulting decisions. Thus, interventions focused on identifying possible supports both in personal life and at school seem warranted.

Schmidt et al. (2011) addressed the importance of considering the social, contextual, and environmental factors that might be at play in terms of how students make career and college decisions. Important factors related to career and college decisions for LGBT students relate to perceived barriers. For example, Schneider and Dimito (2010) found that identifying as LGBT influenced academic and career choices. Their participants discussed how important it was to make career and college decisions with their identity in mind. For example, some participants mentioned perceiving that working in any occupation that involved children might be off limits because of fears others might have about them interacting with kids.

Counseling Considerations

Numerous suggestions have been offered for counselors working with LGBT students in relation to career and college exploration. Regarding the decision-making process in general, Pope et al. (2004) highlighted the importance of exploring real and perceived barriers with students. Through open conversation, inaccurate perceptions can be challenged and discussions can occur about if and how to address realistic barriers. Pope et al. also indicated that a conversation about whether or not a student wants to come out or not could influence their decisions. Finally, Schneider and Dimito (2010) indicated that students looked for universities that appeared to be more open (e.g., visibility of groups for LGBT students or those that were not affiliated with conservative religions). They also reported that some students selected universities farther away from home so that they could come out more easily. These factors might be brought up for consideration with students who are exploring colleges.

In relation to career choices, LGBT students may not be aware that many occupations are available to them—they might have ruled them out based on barriers or on their perceptions of masculinity or femininity. Gottfredson's (1981) Theory of Circumscription and Compromise may be useful in conceptualizing the career development needs of LGBT students in this regard. Interventions to help break through stereotypes will be important in opening up career possibilities. Similarly, Pope et al. (2004) emphasized the importance of role models and mentors. As some students may not have had opportunities to interact with LGBT adults, school counselors can make efforts to identify individuals in the community who might be willing to serve as mentors. Involving people from diverse occupations, and especially those in nontraditional occupations, could help LGBT students challenge their preconceptions and become aware that more possibilities exist.

Undocumented Students

Undocumented students represent a growing population in the United States. The term refers to students 18 and younger who are foreign born or who were born in the United States to immigrant parents. An estimated one-fourth of school-age students meet these criteria, but it is estimated that they will comprise one-third of the school-age population by 2050 (Passel, 2011). The majority of the 1.1 million undocumented school-age students have lived in the United States for most of their lives, speak English, and want to attend college (Educators for Fair Consideration, 2012). In fact, undocumented students have been described as resilient, optimistic, and leaders in their schools (Perez, 2010). According to a report by Hoefer, Rytina, and Baker (2010), the states with the largest percentages of undocumented students are Texas and California, but these students reside in every state in the nation. Additionally, their data show that approximately 70% of undocumented students are Mexican, but undocumented students have connections to countries throughout the world.

Federal legislation plays an important role for undocumented students. *Plyler v. Doe* (1982) was an important Supreme Court case that prevented K–12 schools from discriminating against undocumented students based on their immigrant status. The court ruled that denying undocumented children the right to attend public school violates the Equal Protection Clause of the Fourteenth Amendment. While approximately 65,000 undocumented students graduate high school every year, it is estimated that between 7,000 and 13,000 attend some sort of postsecondary school. This low percentage seeking postsecondary education is in part because legal protections end when they graduate.

One of the biggest challenges for undocumented students is that they are not legal citizens and therefore have many barriers to careers and college. The Obama Administration made strides toward remedying this via the Deferred Action for Childhood Arrivals (DACA) program in 2012 (although as we write this the future of this controversial program is unknown). DACA outlined a way for individuals who meet conditional eligibility criteria (i.e., entered the United States before age 16 and lived here for at least 5 years, have a high school diploma or pass the general education development (GED) tests, and pass a background check) to eventually pursue permanent U.S. resident status if they complete a postsecondary degree or served in the military. We do not have space to describe that process in detail, but the important part for school counselors to be aware of relates to the pathway to postsecondary education. During the conditional status period, DACA-approved individuals would be eligible to apply for federal student loans and work study funding, something not available to undocumented students and one of the biggest barriers to college attendance. They also would be eligible to receive temporary social security numbers and work permits. Gonzales, Roth, Brant, Lee, and Valdivia (2016) reported that since its implementation, approximately 700,000 individuals have qualified for DACA status. They also found that DACA recipients have experienced increased educational and work opportunities, including access to scholarships as well as to more stable and better paying jobs. For many, DACA helped increase their hope that they could achieve their educational and career dreams.

Nevertheless, many states have laws that prevent undocumented students, and even DACA recipients, from attending public postsecondary schools, receiving state-based financial aid, being eligible for in-state tuition, or being eligible to receive a professional license to work in various fields. The variation in laws and policies across states coupled with the difficulty in finding information about this topic makes understanding and navigating the process of applying for DACA challenging. Gonzales et al. (2016) indicated that recipients felt their teachers and counselors were supportive and encouraging in relation to them pursuing postsecondary education, but many of those individuals had limited knowledge of the laws and often offered inaccurate information. Imagine a student spending time and money completing a degree only to find out that his state would not allow him to seek a license to practice. Further, many college personnel are equally uninformed and/or specific policies and processes for undocumented students are not always readily available on college websites (Perez, 2014).

Legally, school personnel are not permitted to ask about the immigration status of students and their parents. Although they might find out directly or indirectly, they may not know if they have students in their school who potentially could benefit from interventions or information. Students might be reluctant to disclose their immigrant status, and some students might not even be aware of their immigrant status (Perez, 2014). Assuming that every school counselor could have at least one undocumented student in his or her school, it is important that they become aware of laws and policies. Additionally, school counselors should be aware that many undocumented students assume they will not be able to attend college. Interventions to help explore and navigate real and perceived barriers include providing information, connecting students to mentors, and helping them identify ways to maximize their finances. These kinds of interventions could include encouraging students to explore targeted scholarship opportunities, consider dual enrollment options, earn college credit in high school, or take AP exams in an effort to test out of college course work (Perez, 2010).

Students Living in Foster Care or Who Are Homeless

Foster students refer to students placed, temporarily, in the care of a person or family (sometimes a relative, but most often not), or in group homes or institutional settings. Approximately 238,000 children entered foster care in 2014, and an estimated 415,000 were in foster care placements (U.S. Department of Health and Human Services, 2015). These students included a similar number of males and females, had an average age of 8 (age range 1–20), and mainly included students who were White (42%), African American (24%), and Hispanic (22%). Their time in foster care averaged 20 months but ranged from less than 1 month to over 5 years. In 2014, approximately 22,000 youth exited the foster care system without a permanent family, and Courtney et al. (2011) indicated that these students in particular were more likely to be homeless, unemployed, or incarcerated.

According to the McKinney–Vento Homeless Assistance Act (42 U.S.C. 11431 et seq.), homeless students are those who "lack a fixed, regular, and adequate nighttime residence" (Sec. 725). This includes students who share housing with other families and those who live in campgrounds, motels, cars, transitional shelters, or any other location not typically used for sleeping. It also includes students who are awaiting foster placement and those classified as migratory. School personnel might not be aware of a student's homeless status, but they should expect that probably some students in their schools meet those criteria. Because of the frequency of changes in their living situations, it is challenging to get an accurate count of homeless students. Data for the school year 2013–2014 show that approximately 1.3 million homeless youth enrolled in public schools, with the highest numbers in California, New York, and Texas (U.S. Department of Education, 2015). This reflects a 50% increase since 2006–2007; homelessness rates continue to rise, but those rates only include youth who are enrolled in schools (it is likely that many more youth are homeless and not attending school). Homeless students reflect all segments of the population.

Although being in foster care and being homeless are not exactly the same, a number of similarities exist among students who fit into these categories in relation to planning for careers and college. The first similarity is school instability. Foster students may or may not be placed in their current school zone, and in many instances they end up changing schools or districts. Homeless students also end up moving frequently due to things like limited lengths of time they can be at a shelter or the need to move for affordable housing or employment opportunities. Because of frequent changes in living situations (often multiple times per year), these students often fall behind in school, repeat grades, drop out of school at higher rates, and both attend and graduate from postsecondary schools at lower rates (Dworsky & Perez, 2010; Kirk & Day, 2011).

Another similarity between these two groups of students is financial concerns. In addition to limited resources available among families affiliated with foster care or homeless situations, students in foster care who age out without finding a permanent family and unaccompanied homeless students (i.e., on their own, without parents) face extreme challenges once on their own. Some of these students have difficulty finding jobs after high school because they lack important documentation like birth certificates, Social Security cards, or driver's licenses. Additionally, it can be so daunting to think about how they will support themselves and where they might live that many of these students view college as completely unrealistic. For those who hope to attend college, paying for school (including admissions exam fees, application fees, and housing deposits), finding transportation to and from school, and figuring out how to work and attend school become potential barriers to attendance and completion (Dukes, 2013; Unrau, Font, & Rawls, 2012).

School counselors can help these students in various ways—focusing on academics, college awareness, financial concerns, and college choice. In addition to the challenges noted previously, research suggests that homeless and foster students often are not academically prepared for college (Unrau et al., 2012) and lack information about college (Dworsky & Perez, 2010). Those two things go hand in hand many times, and since many of these students also are first-generation college students (FGCS) (Unrau et al., 2012), the suggestions discussed later related to FGCS would apply here as well. Additionally, foster and homeless students need help figuring out how to pay for college, so information about financial aid, work study, and scholarships will be critical. School counselors should be sure to gather information about scholarships and government funding specific to these populations (e.g., educational training vouchers available through the Chafee Foster Care Independence Act; unaccompanied homeless youth are granted independent status for federal financial aid through the College Cost Reduction and Access Act). With all of these things in mind, school counselors can help students identify colleges that offer targeted supports such as housing options during semester breaks, year round employment options, and free transportation (Dukes, 2013; Kirk & Day, 2011).

A final area of focus for school counselors relates to emotional and social support. Foster and homeless students often come from families or situations where they experienced or witnessed domestic abuse and violence, substance abuse, or other environmental stressors. Many of these students have mental health needs that have never been addressed (Dukes, 2013). Also, likely due to having limited family stability, some students have expressed a desire for general support at college—they want to know that they have someone on campus who they can turn to for support and someone who is on their side (Dworsky & Perez, 2010). Foster and homeless students tend to be highly motivated (Unrau et al., 2012) and school counselors can help them identify their own personal strengths and proactively explore colleges to identify potential sources of support (individuals or services).

First-Generation College Students

The term *FGCS* refers to students who would be the first in their family to attend college. Definitions of this term vary, however, and have referred to students whose parents have never attended any postsecondary school to those with parents whose highest level of education is anything less than a 4-year college degree (Tate et al., 2015). No matter what definition is used, these students tend to be overrepresented among low-income families and minority groups. Given that they comprise nearly one-third of all school-age students (Aud et al., 2012), it is important to explore the unique needs to this population.

In their review of literature, Balemian and Feng (2013) reported some important trends among FGCS in comparison to non-FGCS. Regarding their postsecondary school attendance, FGCS are more likely to pursue degrees at 2-year schools over 4-year schools, to attend public versus private colleges, to attend schools closer to home, and to live at home during college. In terms of academic preparation, smaller percentages of FGCS enroll in rigorous core academic subjects (e.g., two-thirds of FGCS took advanced math courses versus three quarters of non-FGCS). Additionally, FGCS tend to enroll in fewer AP courses, take fewer AP exams, score lower on AP exams, and score lower on the SAT. Finally, more FGCS end up needing remedial course work in college, and higher percentages of those students drop out of college. Financially, more FGCS used fee waivers for AP tests and college entrance exams, plan to apply for financial aid, and plan to work during college.

These outcomes highlight a clear achievement gap between FGCS and non-FGCS. School counselors should consider important external and internal factors that affect college outcomes. One of the most obvious external factors relates to social capital; because their parents did not attend college and have limited knowledge, FGCS students lack access to the resources and information that many non-FCGS receive from their families (Atherton, 2014). Although their families are generally very supportive of their interest in seeking higher education, FGCS students cannot rely on their families when it comes to navigating the college admissions process (Tate et al., 2015). Examples of how this could play out are that students do not recognize the importance of enrolling in advanced courses, and by the time they do realize it, they are behind their peers. Another example could be that they do not know how to navigate the college admissions or financial aid process, so they either do not consider college at all because it is too overwhelming, or they pursue college but miss out on opportunities that are obvious to other students.

For these reasons, schools play an incredibly important role in ensuring FGCS and their families receive information early and support throughout the process. Bordieu's (1977) theory and the Krumboltz's (2009) "Happenstance Learning Theory" (see Chapter 1) offer useful frameworks for conceptualizing the needs of FGCS. Counselors should consider the importance of early intervention via information disseminated to students and parents (e.g., paying for college or curricular requirements). They also can provide exposure opportunities and consider the ways that programs such as GEAR UP and TRIO could be helpful to these students.

Regarding internal factors, research has shown that FGCS tend to have lower self-efficacy related to succeeding in college and perceive more barriers to college success (Gibbons & Borders, 2010). Nevertheless, in their qualitative study, Tate et al. (2015) found their participating FGCS students to be motivated, persistent, and adaptable. They also reported that these students appreciated their postsecondary educational opportunities rather than feeling entitled to them. Additionally, FGCS students had a sense of personal responsibility and self-reliance, which possibly resulted from them having to navigate much of the college process on their own. These strengths will be important when considering the types of interventions that might be helpful to these students. Early exploration of their career and college aspirations can serve as a starting point for addressing any unrealistic concerns as well as developing plans for combating realistic barriers. By connecting them to mentors who have successfully navigated the college process, these students might come to realize how their strengths can become important assets to their future success.

ADVOCACY AND EQUITY IN P–12 CAREER AND COLLEGE READINESS

Examining Personal Biases

To develop critical consciousness and become a stronger advocate for equity for all students in the areas of career and college readiness, it is important first to consider one's own biases (Bailey, Getch, & Chen-Hayes, 2007; Durodoye & Bodley, 1997; Gibson & Mitchell, 2008; Holcomb-McCoy & Chen-Hayes, 2011; Remley & Herlihy, 2007). Thinking about personal biases and limitations will allow counselors to be more open to understanding the perspectives of others and the barriers that exist within the school and community context for certain groups of students. It is recommended that all school counselors continue to receive supervision and feedback throughout their careers, and that supervision should include personal reflection, an examination of one's own values, and an honest self-appraisal of areas where cultural sensitivity and growth need to be cultivated.

Understanding Patterns in School Data

Consistent with the American School Counselor Association's National Model (2012), school counselors should use data to identify inequities in educational achievement and should work collaboratively with other professionals to improve student outcomes. Exhibit 4.1 includes a list of critical data elements that a school counselor could review in order to identify educational disparities between groups of students, as well as potential barriers to success for specific groups. This list is not meant to be exhaustive, as school counselors are encouraged to use databases that exist in their school districts and to actively collect data to drive curriculum changes and student success.

EXHIBIT 4.1

Critical Data Elements for School Counselors to Review and Disaggregate

ACT scores
AP course enrollment
Attendance records
Curriculum track (e.g., general, college prep)
Disciplinary reports
Dropout rates
End of course test results
Extracurricular activity participation
Gifted education enrollment
Grade level retention and promotion data
Grades and GPAs
Parent education/income data
SAT scores
Special education and 504 eligibility
Standardized test scores

Best Practices for Supporting College Preparation Options for At-Risk Students

Multiple strategies have demonstrated evidence for supporting college prepara-tion and academic achievement for low socioeconomic status, first-generation, and minority students. Some school-based practices that school counselors can promote include (a) providing adequate and diverse course offerings, (b) providing teacher in-service (i.e., cultural competence training, postsecond-ary preparation and options), (c) creating professional learning communities for faculty to research and discuss cultural concerns, (d) developing engaging and intense course curricula, and (e) increasing rigorous course offerings such as college preparatory, accelerated, honors, AP, and dual enrollment oppor-tunities (Center for the Study of Education Policy, 2005). When school coun-selors lack information about certain diverse populations, they should seek additional training and supervision when possible, and also should locate local experts or *cultural brokers* (i.e., individuals who, based on their knowl-edge and understanding of the culture of the families, can help to bridge the gap between family and school) who can help them develop knowledge and skills to effectively assist these groups of students. Exhibit 4.2 illustrates how a school counselor took the initiative to gather and share information about an unfamiliar cultural group at her school.

EXHIBIT 4.2
Example of a School Counselor Using Data to Identify a Concern and
Learning About an Unfamiliar Culture Before Intervening

Mrs. Chandler, a new ninth-grade school counselor at Burlington High School, ran grade reports during the first 9 weeks of the school year in order to identify any students who were falling behind in their course work and were at risk of failing. After compiling and reviewing data, she noticed that nearly all of the Kurdish girls in ninth grade had low to failing grades in the majority of their courses (the Kurdish are a group of Iranian people, pre-dominantly Muslim, who fled Iraq during Saddam Hussein's regime due to persecution). Mrs. Chandler's school had a significant population of Kurdish students (15% of the school's overall population) because the city in which she lived had a nonprofit organization that had assisted the Kurdish in political exile from Iraq.

Mrs. Chandler decided to consult with Mrs. Stewart, the ninth-grade algebra teacher, to find out why this group of students had such low grades. Mrs. Stewart stated that, in general, the Kurdish girls were not turning in any of their homework. At the ninth-grade team meeting, it was confirmed that this was true in other courses as well; yet, the Kurdish boys *were* turning in their work. One teacher, Mr. Simms, noted that he had asked a particu-larly bright female Kurdish student why her homework was not completed, and stated that she replied, "I can't do it at home. I have to cook and watch

(continued)

EXHIBIT 4.2 (continued)

Example of a School Counselor Using Data to Identify a Concern and Learning About an Unfamiliar Culture Before Intervening

my little sisters." Before assuming that this one student's statement indicated anything about this pattern among all of the girls, Mrs. Chandler requested that Mr. Huertas, the 10th-grade counselor, investigate to see if there was a similar pattern in 10th-grade report data, and there was.

Deciding that having a better understanding of Kurdish culture might be important, Mrs. Chandler and Mr. Huertas contacted the local Islamic center and were granted a meeting with the imam, a local Muslim leader. At their meeting, the imam explained that for some Islamic groups, their beliefs exclude girls from education. He explained that because they are legally obligated in the United States to register and enroll their daughters in school, they do so, but culturally, these families believe that girls need to learn domestic responsibilities to fulfill their future duties as wives. So, when the daughters come home each day from school, their domestic responsibilities and domestic training are the priority. He also noted that Kurdish families most likely are not preparing their daughters for postsecondary options, but they are generally okay with their daughters receiving career and college information as part of their U.S. education. The imam also cautioned the school counselors that Kurdish Muslims are distinctly different from other groups of Muslims.

After meeting with the imam, Mrs. Chandler and Mr. Huertas delivered a faculty in-service where they discussed what they had learned and had teachers brainstorm different ways to assess work in class rather than using homework as the primary assessment of student knowledge. The teachers decided to use more collaborative in-class projects and in-class writing assignments in lieu of homework grades for the Kurdish girls. Additionally, the administration scheduled a time to have the imam come speak with the faculty and answer questions about how to better serve Muslim students and families in the Burlington High School community. Although the counselors in this case example found some answers for how to work with the Kurdish population in their school, they were left with many questions such as: What type of career education is culturally appropriate for the Kurdish girls in our school? How do you work with the family of a Kurdish female who wants to go to college?

Designing Targeted Intervention Programs

Durodoye and Bodley (1997) encouraged systemic, small group, and one-on-one interventions to promote career and college readiness for high risk groups. They encouraged counselors to disseminate accurate and consistent information about STEM careers, assist students with resume-building and interviewing skills, provide students with mentors and role models, and promote culturally sensitive teaching practices. Although it may not be possible to always find adult role models or mentors within the community, seeking role models who inspire students in their respective interests is important.

For example, in a qualitative study of Latinos in STEM careers conducted by the Tomás Rivera Policy Institute (2008), one successful Latino engineer noted that his interest in science began when he learned about the first Latino astronaut who had traveled in space, Dr. Franklin Chang-Diaz.

SUMMARY

In this chapter, we highlighted some of the cultural considerations that school counselors must make when implementing career and college readiness interventions. Although the information covered here is not exhaustive, it is meant to illustrate some of the systems issues affecting the academic and career development of specific populations. School counselors are encouraged to (a) become aware of their biases, (b) use data to identify group differences, (c) develop professional learning communities about culturally relevant practice within their school communities, and (d) consult with experts on culturally sensitive practices with specific groups.

··❯ Test Your Knowledge

1. Consider a population in your community that you don't know much about. How could you learn more about the customs, traditions, and values of that group? How could you learn about the unique needs of those individuals?
2. Explain the relationship between historical racial oppression and the current trends in career and college readiness for African American youth.
3. In what ways can school counselors increase STEM opportunities for students from low socioeconomic families?

REFERENCES

ACT, Inc. (2015). *Profile report-national: Graduating class 2015.* Iowa City, IA: Author.

Alliman-Brissett, A. E., Turner, S. L., & Skovholt, T. M. (2004). Parent support and African American adolescents' career self-efficacy. *Professional School Counseling, 7*(3), 124–132.

Allum, J., & Okahana, H. (2015). *Graduate enrollment and degrees: 2004 to 2014.* Washington, DC: Council of Graduate Schools.

American School Counselor Association. (2012). *The ASCA national model: A framework for school counseling programs* (3rd ed.). Alexandria, VA: Author.

Atherton, M. C. (2014). Academic preparedness of first-generation college students: Different perspectives. *Journal of College Student Development, 55*(8), 824–829. http://dx.doi.org/10.1353/csd.2014.0081

Aud, S., Hussar, W., Johnson, F., Kena, G., Roth, E., Manning, E., & Zhang, J. (2012). *The condition of education 2012* (NCES 2012-045). Washington, DC: U.S. Department of Education, National Center for Education Statistics. Retrieved from http://nces.ed.gov/pubs2012/2012045.pdf

Aune, E. (1991). A transition model for postsecondary-bound students with learning disabilities. *Learning-Disabilities Research & Practice, 6*, 177–187.

Bailey, D. F., Getch, Y. Q., & Chen-Hayes, S. F. (2007). *Achievement advocacy for all students through transformative school counseling programs.* In B. T. Erford (Ed.), *Transforming the school counseling profession* (2nd ed., pp. 98–120). Upper Saddle River, NJ: Pearson.

Balemian, K., & Feng, J. (2013). *First generation students: College aspirations, preparedness and challenges.* Retrieved from https://research.collegeboard.org/publications/first-generation-students-college-aspirations-preparedness-and-challenges

Bayer Corporation. (2012). Bayer facts of science education XV: A view from the gatekeepers—STEM department chairs at America's Top 200 research universities on female and underrepresented minority undergraduate STEM students. *Journal of Science Education Technology, 21,* 317–324. http://dx.doi.org/10.1007/s10956-012-9364-1

Boden, K. (2011). Perceived academic preparedness of first-generation Latino college students. *Journal of Hispanic Higher Education, 10*(2), 96–106. http://dx.doi.org/10.1177/1538192711402211

Bourdieu, P. (1977). *Outline of a theory of practice.* Cambridge, UK: Cambridge University Press. http://dx.doi.org/10.1017/CBO9780511812507

Brown, C., & Lavish, L. A. (2006). Career assessment with Native Americans: Role salience, and career decision-making self-efficacy. *Journal of Career Assessment, 14,* 116–129. http://dx.doi.org/10.1177/1069072705281368

Carty, K. (2010). *Trajectories of Black men from baccalaureate degree attainment through career transition.* Doctoral dissertation. Retrieved from ProQuest Dissertations and Theses database (UMI No. 3410469; http://gradworks.umi.com/34/10/3410469.html).

Center for the Study of Education Policy, Illinois State University. (2005). Improving chances for college success for low income and minority high school students. Retrieved from http://centereducationpolicy.illinoisstate.edu/initiatives/college success/finalreport.pdf

Center on Education Policy. (2010). *Improving achievement for the growing Latino population is critical to the nation's future* (Student Achievement Policy Brief #3: Latino Students). Washington, DC: Author.

Choate, L. H., & Curry, J. (2009). Addressing the sexualization of girls through comprehensive programs, advocacy and systemic change: Implications for professional school counselors. *Professional School Counseling, 12*(3), 213–221. http://dx.doi.org/10.5330/PSC.n.2010-12.213

College and Career Readiness and Success Center. (2013). *Improving college and career readiness for students with disabilities.* Washington, DC: American Institutes for Research.

Courtney, M., Dworsky, A., Brown, A., Cary, C., Love, K., & Vorhies, V. (2011). *Midwest evaluation of the adult functioning of former foster youth: Outcomes at age 26.* Chicago, IL: Chapin Hall at the University of Chicago.

Curry, J. (2010). Addressing the spiritual needs of African American students: Implications for school counselors. *Journal of Negro Education, 79*(3), 405–415.

Dalke, C. (1993). *Making a successful transition from high school to college: A model program.* In S. A. Vogel & P. B. Adelman (Eds.), *Success for college students with disabilities* (pp. 57–80). New York, NY: Springer Verlag.

DeNavas-Walt, C., & Proctor, B. D. (2015). *U.S. Census Bureau, current population reports, P60-252, income and poverty in the United States: 2014.* Washington, DC: U.S. Government Printing Office.

Dickinson, D. L., & Verbeek, R. L. (2002). Wage differentials between college graduates with and without LD. *Journal of Learning Disabilities, 35,* 175–185.

Diekman, A. B., Brown, E. R., Johnston, A. M., & Clark, E. K. (2010). Seeking congruity between goals and roles: A new look at why women opt out of science, technology, engineering and mathematics careers. *Psychological Science, 21,* 1051–1057. http://dx.doi.org/10.11777/0956797610377342

Diekman, A. B., Clark, E. K., Johnston, A. M., Brown, E. R., & Steinberg, M. (2011). Malleability in communal goals and beliefs influences attraction to STEM careers: Evidence for a goal congruity perspective. *Journal of Personality and Social Psychology, 101*(5), 902–918. http://dx.doi.org/10.1037/a0025199

Dolan, T. G. (2008). Minority students and college success: Challenges and solutions. *Education Digest: Essential Readings Condensed for Quick Review, 73*(7), 27–30.

Dukes, C. (2013). *College access and success for students experiencing homelessness: A toolkit for educators and service providers.* Minneapolis, MN: National Association for the Education and Homeless Children and Youth. Retrieved from http://www.naehcy.org/sites/default/files/dl/toolkit.pdf

Durodoye, B. A., & Bodley, G. (1997). Career development issues for ethnic minority college students. *College Student Journal, 31*(1), 27–32.

Dworsky, A., & Perez, A. (2010). Helping former foster youth graduate from college through campus support programs. *Children and Youth Services Review, 32,* 255–263. http://dx.doi.org/10.1016/j.childyouth.2009.09.004

Education Week. (2016). U.S. special education enrollment. Retrieved from http://www.edweek.org/ew/section/multimedia/chart-us-special-education-enrollment.html

Educators for Fair Consideration. (2012). Fact sheet: An overview of college-bound undocumented students. Retrieved from http://www.e4fc.org/images/Fact_Sheet.pdf

Ellis, B. (2011, November 16). Delaying retirement: 80 is the new 65. Retrieved from http://money.cnn.com/2011/11/16/retirement/age/index.htm

Flexer, R. W., Simmons, T. J., Luft, P., & Baer, R. M. (2005). *Transition planning for secondary students with disabilities* (2nd ed.). Upper Saddle River, NJ: Pearson.

Gates, G. J. (2011). *How many people are lesbian, gay, bisexual, and transgender?* Los Angeles, CA: The Williams Institute.

Gay, Lesbian, and Straight Education Network. (2014). *The 2013 national school climate survey: Executive summary.* New York, NY: Author. Retrieved from https://www.glsen.org/sites/default/files/GLSEN_2013_NSCS_Executive_Summary.pdf

Gibbons, M. M., & Borders, L. D. (2010). A measure of college-going self-efficacy for middle school students. *Professional School Counseling, 13,* 234–243.

Gibson, R. L., & Mitchell, M. H. (2008). *Introduction to counseling and guidance* (7th ed.). Upper Saddle River, NJ: Pearson.

Gonzales, R. G., Roth, B., Brant, K., Lee, J., & Valdivia, C. (2016). *DACA at year three: Challenges and opportunities in accessing higher education and employment. New evidence from the National UnDACAmented Research Project.* Washington, DC: American Immigration Council. Retrieved from https://www.americanimmigrationcouncil.org/sites/default/files/research/daca_at_year_three.pdf

Goodman, R. D., & West-Olatunji, C. A. (2010). Educational hegemony, traumatic stress, and African American and Latino American students. *Journal of Multicultural Counseling and Development, 38*(3), 176–186. http://dx.doi.org/10.1002/j.2161-1912.2010.tb00125.x

Gottfredson, L. S. (1981). Circumscription and compromise: A developmental theory of occupational aspirations. *Journal of Counseling Psychology, 28*(6), 545–579. http://dx.doi.org/10.1037/0022-0167.28.6.545

Griffith, A. L. (2010). Persistence of women and minorities in STEM field majors: Is it the school that matters? *Economics of Education Review, 29,* 911–922. http://dx.doi.org/10.1016/j.econedurev.2010.06.010

Hagner, D., & Salomone, P. R. (1989). Issues in career decision making for workers with developmental disabilities. *Career Development Quarterly, 38,* 148–159.

Henderson, C. (1999). *1999 college freshmen with disabilities, statistical year 1998: A biennial statistical profile.* Washington, DC: American Council on Education, HEATH Resource Center. Retrieved from ERIC database (ED436900).

Hoefer, M., Rytina, N., & Baker, B. C. (2010). Estimates of the unauthorized immigrant population residing in the United States: January 2010. Retrieved from https://www.dhs.gov/xlibrary/assets/statistics/publications/ois_ill_pe_2010.pdf

Hoffman, L. L., Jackson, A. P., & Smith, S. A. (2005). Career barriers among Native American students living on reservations. *Journal of Career Development, 32*(1), 31–45. http://dx.doi.org/10.1177/0894845305277038

Holcomb-McCoy, C., & Chen-Hayes, S. F. (2011). *Culturally competent school counselors: Affirming diversity by challenging oppression.* In B. T. Erford (Ed.), *Transforming the school counseling profession* (3rd ed., pp. 90–109). Upper Saddle River, NJ: Pearson.

Hoover, N. (2007). *Cultural disparities of SAT scores and the influence on higher education opportunities for African American and Latino students* (Master's thesis). Retrieved from ERIC database (ED499158).

Ivers, N. N., Milsom, A., & Newsome, D. W. (2012). Using Gottfredson's theory of circumscription and compromise to improve Latino students' school success. *Career Development Quarterly, 60,* 231–242.

Kirk, R., & Day, A. (2011). Increasing college access for youth aging out of foster care: Evaluation of a summer camp program for foster youth transitioning from high school to college. *Children and Youth Services Review, 33,* 1173–1180. http://dx.doi.org/10.1016/j.childyouth.2011.02.018

Koebler, J. (2012, April 11). White house report: More women need to study STEM. *U.S. News.* Retrieved from http://www.usnews.com/news/blogs/stem-education/2012/04/11/white-house-report-more-women-need-to-study-stem

Krumboltz, J. D. (2009). The happenstance learning theory. *Journal of Career Assessment, 17*(2), 135–154. http://dx.doi.org/10.1177/1069072708328861

Levin, H., Belfield, C., Muennig, P., & Rouse, C. (2007). The costs and benefits of an excellent education for all of America's children. Retrieved from http://www.all4ed.org/publication_material/research/costsbenefits_exed

Lewin, T. (2006, July 9). At colleges, women are leaving men in the dust. *New York Times.* Retrieved from http://www.nytimes.com/2006/07/09/education/09college.html?pagewanted=all

Long, J. (1999). *School-to-work transitions with Native American Indians: Implications for counselors.* Retrieved from ERIC database (ED444787).

Lucas, M. S. (1993). Personal, social, academic, and career problems expressed by minority college students. *Journal of Multicultural Counseling & Development, 21*(1), 2–13. http://dx.doi.org/10.1002/j.2161-1912.1993.tb00578.x

Madriaga, M., Hanson, K., Heaton, C., Kay, H., Newitt, S., & Walker, A. (2010). Confronting similar challenges? Disabled and non-disabled students' learning and assessment experiences. *Studies in Higher Education, 35*(6), 647–658. http://dx.doi.org/10.1080/03075070903222633

Mihesuah, J. K. (2004). *Graduating indigenous students by confronting the academic environment.* In D. A. Mihesuah & A. C. Wilson (Eds.), *Indigenizing the academy: Transforming scholarship and empowering communities* (pp. 191–199). Lincoln, NE: University of Nebraska.

Milsom, A., Akos, P., & Thompson, M. (2004). A psychoeducational group approach to postsecondary transition planning for students with learning disabilities. *Journal for Specialists in Group Work, 29,* 395–411.

Milsom, A., & Dietz, L. (2009). Defining college readiness for students with learning disabilities: A Delphi study. *Professional School Counseling, 12,* 315–323.

Milsom, A., & Hartley, M. T. (2005). Assisting students with learning disabilities transitioning to college: What school counselors should know. *Professional School Counseling, 8,* 436–441.

Muennig, P. A., & Fahs, M. (2001). The cost-effectiveness of public postsecondary education subsidies. *Preventive Medicine, 32,* 156–162. http://dx.doi.org/10.7916/D8SB4612

National Center for Education Statistics. (2015). *Enrollment and percentage distribution of enrollment in public elementary and secondary schools, by race/ethnicity and region: Selected years, fall 1995 through fall 2025.* Washington, DC: U.S. Department of Education. Retrieved from http://nces.ed.gov/programs/digest/d15/tables/dt15_203.50.asp

National Center for Education Statistics. (2016). *Immediate college enrollment rates.* Washington, DC: U.S. Department of Education. Retrieved from http://nces.ed.gov/programs/coe/indicator_cpa.asp

Nauta, M. M., Saucier, A. M., & Woodard, L. E. (2001). Interpersonal influences on students' academic and career decisions: The impact of sexual orientation. *Career Development Quarterly, 49,* 352–362.

Newman L., Wagner, M., Cameto, R., & Knokey, A.-M. (2009). *The post-high school outcomes of youth with disabilities up to 4 years after high school.* A report from the National Longitudinal Transition Study-2 (NLTS-2). Washington, DC: National Center for Special Education Research. Retrieved from http://www.ies.ed.gov/ncser/pdf/20093017.pdf

Parris, G. P., Owens, D., Johnson, T., Grbevski, S., & Holbert-Quince, J. (2010). Addressing the career development needs of high-achieving African American high school students: Implications for counselors. *Journal for the Education of the Gifted, 33*(3), 417–436.

Passel, J. (2011). Demography of immigrant youth: Past, present, and future. *Future of Children, 21*(1), 19–41.

Perez, W. (2010). Higher education access for undocumented students: Recommendations for counseling professionals. *Journal of College Admission, n206,* 32–35. Retrieved from www.nacacnet.org

Perez, Z. J. (2014). Removing barriers to higher education for undocumented students. Retrieved from https://www.luminafoundation.org/files/resources/removing-barriers-for-undocumented-students.pdf

Phillips, P. (1990). A self-advocacy plan for high school students with learning disabilities: A comparative case study analysis of students', teachers', and parents' perceptions of program effects. *Journal of Learning Disabilities, 23,* 466–471.

Plyler v. Doe, 457 U.S. 202 (1982).

Ponec, D. L. (1997). *African-American females: A theory of educational aspiration.* Paper presented at Symposium on African Americans and Their Great Plains Experiences, Lincoln, NE, February 1997. Retrieved from ERIC database (ED415457).

Pope, M., Barret, B., Szymanski, D. M., Chung, Y. B., Singaravelu, H., McLean, R., & Sanabria, S. (2004). Culturally appropriate career counseling with gay and lesbian clients. *Career Development Quarterly, 53,* 158–177.

Rankin, S. (2003). *Campus climate for LGBT people: A national perspective.* New York, NY: National Gay and Lesbian Task Force Policy Institute.

Raphael, S. (2004). *The socioeconomic status of Black males: The increasing importance of incarceration* (Unpublished manuscript). Berkley, CA: Goldman School of Public Policy, University of California.

Remley, T. P., & Herlihy, B. (2007). *Ethical, legal, and professional issues in counseling* (2nd ed.). Upper Saddle River, NJ: Pearson.

Reynolds, A. L., Sodano, S. M., Ecklund, T. R., & Guyker, W. (2012). Dimensions of acculturation in Native American college students. *Measurement and Evaluation in Counseling and Development, 45*(2), 101–112. http://dx.doi.org/10.1177/0748175611428330

Roach, R. (2006). Survey: American girls aren't interested in STEM careers. *Diverse Issues in Higher Education, 23*(4), 54.

Rock, E., & Leff, E. H. (2011). *The professional school counselor and students with disabilities.* In B. T. Erford (Ed.), *Transforming the school counseling profession* (3rd ed., pp. 314–341). Upper Saddle River, NJ: Pearson.

Rumrill, P. D., & Roessler, R. T. (1999). New directions in vocational rehabilitation: A "career development" perspective on "closure." *Journal of Rehabilitation, 65,* 26–30.

Schmidt, C. K., Miles, J. R., & Welsh, A. C. (2011). Perceived discrimination and social support: The influences on career development and college adjustment of LGBT college students. *Journal of Career Development, 38*(4), 293–309. http://dx.doi.org 10.1177/0894845310372615

Schmidt, C. K., & Nilsson, J. E. (2006). The effects of simultaneous developmental processes: Factors relating to the career development of lesbian, gay, and bisexual youth. *Career Development Quarterly, 55,* 22–37.

Schneider, M. S., & Dimito, A. (2010). Factors influencing the career and academic choices of lesbian, gay, bisexual, and transgender people. *Journal of Homosexuality, 57,* 1355–1369. http://dx.doi.org/10.1080/0091839.2010.517080

Schott Foundation for Public Education. (2015). *Black lives matter: The Schott 50 state report on public education and Black males.* Retrieved from http://blackboysreport.org/ national-summary

Stout, J. G., Dasgupta, N., Hunsinger, M., & McManus, M. A. (2011). STEMing the tide: Using ingroup experts to inoculate women's self-concept in science, technology, engineering, and mathematics (STEM). *Journal of Personality and Social Psychology, 100*(2), 255–270. http://dx.doi.org/10.1037/a0021385

Taningco, M. T. (2008). *Latinos in STEM professions: Understanding challenges and opportunities for next steps. A qualitative study using stakeholder interviews.* Washington, DC: The Tomas River Policy Institute. Retrieved from the Education Resources Information Center online (ED502064).

Tate, K. A., Caperton, W., Dakota, K., Pruitt, N. T., White, H., & Hall, E. (2015). An exploration of first-generation college students' career development beliefs and experiences. *Journal of Career Development, 42*(4), 294–310. http://dx.doi .org/10.1177/0042085911400339

The Center for Public Education. (2009). *Special education: A better perspective.* Retrieved from http://www.centerforpubliceducation.org/Main-Menu /Evaluating-performance/Special-education-At-a-glance/Special-education-A -better-perspective-full-report.html

The College Board. (2015). Trends in college pricing 2015. Retrieved from http://trends .collegeboard.org/sites/default/files/2015-trends-college-pricing-final-508.pdf

The White House. (2014). *2014 native youth report.* Washington, DC: Author. Retrieved from https://www.whitehouse.gov/sites/default/files/docs /20141129nativeyouth report_final.pdf

Tomás Rivera Policy Institute. (2008). Latinos in STEM professions: Understanding challenges and opportunities for next steps. University of Southern California: Author. Retrieved from http://www.exploringcs.org/wp-content /uploads/2010/09/latinos.pdf

Tornatzky, L. G., Macias, E. E., Jenkins, D., & Solis, C. (2006). *Access and achievement: Building educational and career pathways for Latinos in advanced technology. Report on a national study of Latino access to postsecondary education and careers in information technology.* Los Angeles, CA: The Tomás Rivera Policy Institute, University of Southern California. Retrieved from ERIC database (ED502061).

Turner, S. L., Trotter, M. J., Lapan, R. T., Czajka, K. A., Yang, P., & Brissett, A. E. A. (2006). Vocational skills and outcomes among Native American adolescents: A test of the integrative contextual model of career development. *Career Development Quarterly, 54*(3), 216–226. http://dx.doi.org/10.1002/j.2161-0045.2006.tb00153.x

U.S. Bureau of Labor Statistics. (2015). *Persons with a disability: Labor force characteristics summary.* Washington, DC: U.S. Department of Labor. Retrieved from http://www .bls.gov/news.release/disabl.nr0.htm

U.S. Census Bureau. (2014). *Percent distribution of the projected population by Hispanic origin and race for the United States: 2015 to 2060.* Washington, DC: Author. Retrieved from http://www.census.gov/population/projections/data/national/2014/ summarytables.html

U.S. Census Bureau. (2015a). Employment status: 2015 American Community Survey 1-year estimates. Retrieved from https://factfinder.census.gov/faces/tableservices/ jsf/pages/productview.xhtml?pid=ACS_15_1YR_S2301&prodType=table

U.S. Census Bureau. (2015b). *Profile American facts for features: CB15-FF.22. American Indian and Alaska Native heritage month: November 2015.* Washington, DC: Author. Retrieved from http://www.census.gov/newsroom/facts-for-features/2015/cb15-ff22.html

U.S. Department of Education. (2015). *Total number of homeless students enrolled in LEAs with or without McKinney-Vento -total: 2013-14.* Washington, DC: Author. Retrieved from http://eddataexpress.ed.gov/data-element-explorer.cfm/tab/data/deid/5353/sort/idown

U.S. Department of Health and Human Services. (2015). *The AFCARS report. Preliminary FY 2014 estimates as of July 2015.* Washington, DC: Author. Retrieved from http://www.acf.hhs.gov/sites/default/files/cb/afcarsreport22.pdf

Unrau, Y. A., Font. S. A., & Rawls, G. (2012). Readiness for college engagement among students who have aged out of foster care. *Child and Youth Services Review, 34,* 76–83. http://dx.doi.org/10.1016/j.childyouth.2011.09.002

Wadsworth, J., Milsom, A., & Cocco, K. (2004). Career development for adolescents and young adults with mental retardation. *Professional School Counseling, 8,* 141–147.

Walker, T., Pearson, F., & Murrell, P. (2010). Quality of effort and career preparation differences between African American and White community college students. *Community College Journal of Research and Practice, 34*(9), 738–754. http://dx.doi.org/10.1080/10668920902917450

Walker, T. L., & Tracey, T. J. G. (2012). Perceptions of occupational prestige: Differences between African American and White college students. *Journal of Vocational Behavior, 80,* 76–81. http://dx.doi.org/10.1016/j.jvb.2011.06.003

West-Olatunji, C. A., Baker, J. C., & Brooks, M. (2006). African American adolescent males: Giving voice to their educational experiences. *Multicultural Perspectives, 8*(4), 3–9. http://dx.doi.org/10.1207/s15327892mcp0804_2

West-Olatunji, C., Shure, L., Garrett, M. T., Conwill, W., & Rivera, E. T. (2008). Rite of passage programs as effective tools for fostering resilience among low-income African American male adolescents. *Journal of Humanistic Counseling, Education and Development, 47*(2), 131–143. http://dx.doi.org/10.1002/j.2161-1939.2008.tb00053.x

West-Olatunji, C., Shure, L., Pringle, R., Adams, T., Lewis, D., & Cholewa, B. (2010). Exploring how school counselors position low-income African American girls as mathematics and science learners. *Professional School Counseling, 13*(3), 184–195. http://dx.doi.org/10.5330/PSC.n.2010-13.184

Wright, L. L. (2010). *Social, demographic, and institutional effects on African American graduation rates in U.S. colleges and universities.* Doctoral dissertation. Retrieved from ProQuest Dissertations and Theses database (UMI No. 3417790).

FIVE

P–12 Career and College Readiness: Assessment and Evaluation

What is assessment? Why is it important? What does it look like for students across P–12 grades? In this chapter, we review the purpose of assessment in relation to P–12 career and college readiness, as well as important considerations for choosing and interpreting assessments. We also review various types of assessments relevant to career and college readiness in P–12 schools. Before we jump in, however, we set the stage by clarifying these two important terms. The National Career Development Association (NCDA, 2009) defines *assessment* as:

> the systematic gathering of information for decision making about individuals, groups, programs, or processes. Assessment targets include abilities, achievements, personality variables, aptitudes, attitudes, preferences, interests, values, demographics, beliefs, and other characteristics. Assessment procedures include, but are not limited to, standardized and nonstandardized tests, questionnaires, inventories, checklists, observations, portfolios, performance assessments, rating scales, surveys, interviews, card sorts, and other measurement techniques. (p. 2)

Evaluation refers to "the collection and interpretation of information to make judgments about individuals, programs, or processes that lead to decisions and future actions" (NCDA, 2009, p. 2).

Assessment and evaluation are both important in the counseling process, and they complement each other. Assessment is critical to evaluation; without assessment data, counselors would have nothing to evaluate. Further, assessment without evaluation is meaningless. Why gather information only to do nothing with it? Schools sometimes get caught in the trap of collecting assessment data, but not always using that data to transform education and counseling practices. For example, a school counselor may collect data that show that only 25% of graduating seniors at the school are taking the ACT® before their senior year. In order to increase that percentage, the counselor may need to inform parents and students about the benefits of taking the ACT earlier in high school.

Another example occurred when the second author worked in a high school that encouraged all students to take the Armed Services Vocational

Aptitude Battery (ASVAB) because it was offered at no cost. But, the school had no plans for formally using the results and the school counselors did not have time to meet with all students regarding their results. Although the ASVAB results were used by military personnel in making decisions about possible occupations for those students who were going to enter the military, the school counselors only occasionally were able to engage other students in discussions about their results and how they might inform career decision making. Was it worthwhile for students to take that test?

School counselors often are the only professionals in schools who have knowledge and skills related to career and college readiness. School districts usually employ administrative personnel with expertise in assessment and evaluation, but their focus often is on school accountability and accreditation with an emphasis on academics. School counselors should work closely with these individuals to make decisions about district-wide career and college readiness assessments. In Chapter 3, we reviewed a number of important career and college readiness counseling competencies. With regard to assessment, school counselors also should remember their roles as leaders and advocates and take a proactive approach to ensuring that school-wide assessment is meaningful and purposeful.

PURPOSE OF CAREER AND COLLEGE READINESS ASSESSMENT

For over 100 years, guidance workers and counselors have engaged in career assessment. Parsons (1909) introduced the *trait-and-factor* approach that serves as a basis for much career counseling and assessment today. A number of career counseling theories were developed based on this approach, but today, the most widely used trait-and-factor approach is that of Holland (1973, 1997). We introduced Holland's theory briefly in Chapter 1 and review it further in some of the grade-level chapters in this book. We also cover various assessment tools based on Holland's approach later in this chapter and some grade-level chapters.

The main goal of a trait-and-factor approach is to help people identify possible future occupations—a very relevant goal for students in P–12 schools. In general, a trait-and-factor approach suggests that by knowing oneself and knowing occupational requirements and characteristics, a person can make an informed decision by looking for a match between self and occupation. Such assessment data are critical to gaining self and occupational awareness. Parsons' three-part trait-and-factor approach involves (a) gathering information about self, (b) gathering information about the world of work, and (c) applying a decision-making process to make an occupational choice. Common target areas for self-assessment include abilities, interests, values, and personality styles; we present assessments related to these target areas later in this chapter. Results from these kinds of assessments can be used to help students identify occupations that might or might not match their personal characteristics or colleges that match their interests and values. For example, for a student whose aptitude test results show strengths in math and spatial skills, a counselor might suggest that student explore occupations in Holland's realistic personality type. For a student who values his Jewish faith, a counselor might help him identify colleges that have active Jewish student organizations.

Other career counseling theories provide guidance to help school counselors identify specific P–12 student career development needs, design relevant interventions, and determine appropriate target areas for assessment. Based on *developmental career counseling theories* such as those of Super (1980) or Gottfredson (1981, 2002, 2005), school counselors might examine how ready an individual is to engage in various career counseling tasks or identify what factors are informing his or her career interests and behaviors. With this in mind, assessment results can be used as a foundation for determining what types of interventions might or might not be relevant for a particular student. For example, a counselor might want to start by implementing activities to help a student whose assessment results indicate limited knowledge of occupations develop a greater awareness of the world of work.

School counselors adhering to *learning-based career counseling theories* like those of Krumboltz, Mitchell, and Jones (1976), Lent, Brown, and Hackett (1994), or Peterson, Sampson, and Reardon (1991) would assess things such as beliefs, self-efficacy, and perceived barriers in order to better understand how career- and college-related decisions are being made. Results from assessments targeting these areas can be used to identify where to focus career and college readiness intervention. For example, if a student's assessment results showed that she was not very motivated to explore careers or that she did not believe she could succeed in college, then a counselor could develop interventions to explore those issues or challenge faulty thinking. Throughout this book we discuss many of these theories as they relate to P–12 students, and assessments relevant to these theories are presented later in this chapter.

Career assessment is particularly important during the initial process of choosing an occupation or career path, as it can help counselors identify occupations that students might like or in which they might excel. Assessment data may also help explain why some students struggle with career decision making or why they limit their college options. Because the focus of this book is to help school counselors and educators working with students who will be making initial career and college decisions, we are limiting our discussion of assessment to issues most relevant to working with P–12 students. In the section that follows, we discuss factors that school counselors and educators should consider when choosing career and college readiness assessments.

CHOOSING CAREER AND COLLEGE READINESS ASSESSMENTS

In Chapter 3, we discussed important competencies related to career and college readiness assessment and evaluation, and we want to emphasize the importance of having qualified individuals making decisions about assessments and administering and/or interpreting assessments. Resources such as *A Counselor's Guide to Career Assessment Instruments* (Wood & Hayes, 2013) that contain information about and critiques of a variety of career assessments can be useful to school counselors. In this section, we review factors that should be considered when choosing career and college readiness assessments.

Reliability and Validity

Reliability and validity arguably are two of the most important things to consider when choosing an assessment. *Reliability* refers to how stable or consistent the assessment is in measuring a construct, and *validity* indicates whether or not an assessment measures what it intends to. Information about the psychometric properties of an assessment, including reliability and validity data, generally can be found in the technical manual or user's guide that accompanies the assessment. We do not have space in this book to review psychometric properties of assessments in detail, and most readers should have or will cover these topics in a graduate-level assessment course. Needless to say, school counselors and educators want to feel confident that the time and money they put into purchasing, administering, and interpreting assessments are well spent. They need to be able to guarantee that the results will be meaningful, and using assessments that have proven reliability and validity is a good way to start.

Norms

Norms help school counselors determine whether or not a particular assessment is appropriate for their students, and information about norm groups should be included in an assessment's technical manual and/or the assessment summary reports the school receives. The norm group reflects the individuals who participated in the early development, or piloting, of an instrument. It also includes the group(s) for whom an assessment has been determined valid through additional research.

For example, an assessment instrument might initially be piloted with a group of 10th-grade students from a suburban area outside a large city in the Northeastern part of the United States. The initial norm group would reflect the characteristics of this specific population: Let's say it included males and females, students with a variety of disabilities, and a majority of White students from middle to upper-middle class families. This group of students is not representative of most places in the United States, so an assessment that is normed on this group would have limited applicability to most schools. Over time, the individual who developed the instrument piloted it with other populations, including students from rural and urban areas, from low socioeconomic status families, from diverse racial and ethnic groups, and from different grade levels. Information was now available regarding the applicability of the assessment to a much broader group of students. Assuming no major differences or concerns were noted regarding its use, the assessment would now be appropriate for a larger set of schools throughout the United States because the norm group is representative of their populations.

School counselors and educators should be mindful about choosing assessments in relation to norm groups, especially as school populations change over time. If a particular school's population shifts dramatically over the course of a few years, an assessment instrument that the school has successfully used for many years may become relevant only for a specific subgroup of the school. Further, as more and more research is conducted with assessments, information about their norms changes. It is important that someone in the school keeps abreast not only of changes in the school's population, but also of the information that is available about the assessments they are using.

Usefulness for Diverse Populations

Choosing an assessment that is appropriate for diverse populations means examining information about a number of factors, including norm groups (see the preceding), age level, reading level, and other factors. Some instruments have different versions designed for use with different age groups, and others have versions in multiple languages. With the growing population of second language learners in the United States, especially students who speak Spanish, ideally school counselors and educators should be looking for career and college readiness materials that are available in English, as well as Spanish, or other languages as needed. Students will not always tell the counselor when they don't understand a question; they often just fill in answers to avoid drawing attention to themselves. If students have difficulty reading or understanding assessment materials, but do not express these concerns, then counselors have no way of knowing if their scores or results are valid.

Considering the content of an assessment is important in determining its relevance for various populations. To do this, school counselors and educators should try to make sure that they choose instruments for which cultural bias is not evident, and examining norms data is a useful way to do this. Further, school counselors might review any pictures that are used to ensure that they are representative across diverse groups as well as represent individuals in nontraditional careers. They also can review sample test items to determine if bias in language use or terminology is present. Additionally, reading reviews and critiques of assessments specifically in relation to their appropriateness with diverse populations is an important way to gather information about an instrument's appropriateness for various groups.

Finally, some instruments offer alternative formats to accommodate different learning styles. Although most assessments require reading and answering questions by hand or on a computer, a few of the assessments we list later in this chapter involve the use of pictures or videos, which is useful for students with low reading or comprehension levels. Other assessments permit accommodations for individuals with disabilities, such as responding verbally, having unlimited time, or using a scribe or test reader. School counselors and educators want to ensure that all students have an opportunity to be accurately assessed via whatever instruments are used, and consideration of these kinds of factors is important.

Cost, Time, and Ease of Administration

Assessment is a common practice in schools, especially as it relates to academics. Achievement tests, end of course or end of grade tests, aptitude tests, Advanced Placement tests, and other assessments are used to help monitor student academic progress and allow schools to show how they are, or are not, meeting various standards. Given the amount of time that students spend in school taking tests, and the money and time it takes faculty to administer and interpret them, school counselors and educators absolutely need to take cost and time into consideration when choosing career and college readiness assessments. Fortunately, a variety of options exist for assessing constructs related to career and college readiness.

Regarding cost, some of the comprehensive, online systems that we describe later in this chapter can be the most cost-effective for schools, as they include multiple assessments as well as access to supplemental information. A school district can sometimes purchase access to those kinds of systems at a lower cost than if they purchased individual assessment instruments. Further, some states supplement the cost of online systems or have their own (e.g., South Carolina Occupational Information System [SCOIS]), which allows anyone in the state to access at no cost via a username and password.

Online career guidance systems may not be the most appropriate choice for every school. In some instances, schools might want to assess factors that are not covered in those online systems (e.g., career beliefs, self-efficacy), or they might prefer to use assessments that have known psychometric properties. In those instances, school counselors and educators must weigh their options and prioritize based on availability of resources, student needs, and other factors. Availability of space and staff to administer assessments are important considerations as well.

Purpose

As we discussed earlier in this chapter, there are multiple potential purposes of career- and college-related assessments. School counselors and educators must consider their main goal in working with students on career and college readiness. Do they want to focus on students' self-exploration or self-awareness? If so, then assessments that focus on interests, abilities, personalities, or values might be most useful. Do they want to identify student needs, readiness for change, or figure out where students are developmentally? If any of those areas reflect their goal, then assessments that focus on factors like beliefs, attitudes, or self-efficacy would be most appropriate. In the next section, we review a variety of career and college readiness assessment instruments that can be used with school-age students, broken down by target areas.

CAREER AND COLLEGE READINESS ASSESSMENTS

Assessments can be either formal or informal, and both types can be of benefit to school counselors and educators. In this section, we present formal assessments by categories focusing on different target areas and review some common informal assessments. The career and college readiness assessments presented in this section are listed alphabetically within each category.

Formal Assessments

Formal assessments are considered *formal* because they have been developed through a scientifically rigorous process. These kinds of assessments are standardized; they rely on consistency by having specific instructions for administration, scoring, and interpretation. Formal assessments also have reliability and validity data, and usually a norm reference group for results comparison. These assessments range in price, type of administration, and scoring, but most are designed for large group administration.

Ability, Achievement, and Aptitude Assessments

ACT Aspire. Published by ACT, Inc. (2016a), this assessment is designed to help schools monitor students' readiness for college by measuring achievement in five content areas: English, reading, writing, science, and math. It can be administered to students in grades 3 to 10, with summative reports showing student progress over time. Score reports also provide an indicator of college readiness and a predicted ACT score.

ACT WorkKeys. Published by ACT, Inc. (2016b), this assessment is available in English and Spanish. WorkKeys is an assessment measuring basic and soft skills in a variety of areas—focusing on skills that employers have identified as being important in the workplace. Test-takers receive scores in the form of levels, with higher levels representing acquisition of more advanced skills. A National Career Readiness Certificate can be earned based on scores from the Applied Mathematics, Locating Information, and Reading for Information subscales, with each subtest requiring just under 1 hour to complete.

Armed Services Vocational Aptitude Battery (ASVAB). Published by the U.S. Department of Defense (2004), this assessment is used to determine which types of military occupations individuals are eligible to pursue. The ASVAB is a multi-aptitude test with eight subscales (arithmetic, auto and shop information, general science, electronics information, math knowledge, mechanical comprehension, paragraph comprehension, and word knowledge). The battery takes approximately 3 hours to complete either in person or online. It is appropriate for students in grades 10 to 12.

Campbell Interest and Skill Survey (CISS). Published by Pearson Assessments (Campbell, Hyne, & Nilsen, 1992), the CISS is an assessment that measures self-reported interests and skills in seven broad scales (adventuring, analyzing, creating, helping, influencing, organizing, and producing) that are broken down further into 25 categories. The survey takes approximately 30 minutes to complete and can be administered individually or in a large group. It is appropriate for use with adolescents ages 15 and up.

Differential Aptitude Test (DAT). Published by Pearson Assessments (Bennet, Seashore, & Wesman, 1990), the DAT is an assessment that measures eight types of aptitudes grouped in three broad categories: cognitive skills (verbal reasoning and numerical ability), perceptual skills (abstract reasoning, mechanical reasoning, and space relations), and language and clerical skills (spelling, language usage, and clerical speed/accuracy). The test takes approximately 3 hours and is usually administered in large groups. Different forms of the assessment target students in grades 7 to 9 or in grades 10 to 12.

Self-Directed Search (SDS). Published by Psychological Assessment Resources, Inc. (Holland, 1994), the SDS is an assessment that measures self-reported interests and skills and presents results in the form of Holland Codes. The self-assessment takes approximately 20 minutes to complete, can be self-scored, and can be administered individually or in a large group as well as online. Different forms of the assessment target students in middle and high school.

Attitudes, Beliefs, and Readiness Instruments

Career Beliefs Inventory (CBI). Published by Mind Garden, Inc. (Krumboltz, 1994), the CBI is an assessment consisting of 96 items that are rated on a Likert scale. A total of 25 subscales are reported under five main categories: (a) Changes I am willing to make, (b) efforts I am willing to initiate, (c) factors that influence my decisions, (d) my current career situation, and (e) what seems necessary for my happiness. The CBI can be administered individually or in groups and it is appropriate for use with students in grades 8 to 12.

Career Decision Making Self-Efficacy Scale (CDSE). Published by Mind Garden, Inc. (Taylor & Betz, 1983), the CDSE includes items that address how confident someone is to make career decisions. Items reflect five broad areas: (a) self-appraisal, (b) gathering occupational information, (c) selecting goals, (d) making plans, and (e) solving problems. Long (50 item) and short (25 item) versions are available. The instrument can be administered individually or in groups and is appropriate for high school students.

Career Development Inventory (CDI). Published by Consulting Psychologists Press (Super, Thompson, Lindeman, Jordan, & Myers, 1984), the CDI is an 80-item assessment that identifies four aspects of career maturity: career planning, career exploration, decision making, and world of work information. The assessment takes approximately 1 hour to complete and can be administered individually or in groups. It is appropriate for use with high school students.

Career Thoughts Inventory (CTI). Published by Psychological Assessment Resources, Inc. (Sampson, Peterson, Lenz, Reardon, & Saunders, 1996), the CTI is an assessment consisting of 48 items, with results presented in three scales: commitment anxiety, decision-making confusion, and external conflict. The assessment takes approximately 15 minutes and is usually administered individually. It is appropriate for use with high school students.

College-Going Self-Efficacy Scale (CGSES) (Gibbons & Borders, 2010). The CGSES measures beliefs about college attendance and persistence. The instrument consists of 30 items and can be administered individually or in groups. It is designed for use with middle school students.

My Vocational Situation (MVS). Published by Consulting Psychologists Press (Holland, Daiger, & Power, 1980), the MVS is an assessment that identifies factors that affect career decision making. The three main factors assessed via the 18 items of this scale are (a) lack of vocational identity, (b) lack of information or training, and (c) barriers. The assessment can be administered individually or in groups, and it is appropriate for use with high school students.

Interest Inventories

CISS. See the description in the Ability and Aptitude Assessments section.

Pictorial Inventory of Careers (PIC). Published by Talent Assessment, Inc. (2000), the PIC requires students to rate how much they like certain occupations after watching short video segments of people at work. The 17 subscales include agricultural, business (data processing, marketing/sales, and secretarial), communications–art/graphics, electrical/electronics, engineering technology, environmental services, food services, health services, protective services, science and laboratory, service–barber/cosmetology, service–personal and industrial (construction, mechanical, and metal trades). The PIC takes approximately 22 minutes to complete and can be administered individually or in groups. It is designed for use with middle and high school students as well as individuals with disabilities. The PIC also can be used with individuals who have limited English speaking skills.

Reading-Free Vocational Interest Inventory-2 (R-FVII:2). Published by Elbern Publications (Becker, 2000), the R-FVII:2 requires students to indicate how much they like certain occupations by circling pictures of individuals in different work settings. The 11 interest areas measured are animal care, automotive, building trades, clerical, food service, horticulture, housekeeping, laundry service, materials handling, patient care, and personal service. The R-FVII:2 takes approximately 20 minutes to complete and can be administered individually or in groups. It is designed for use with students ages 13 and up who have a diagnosis of mental retardation or learning disability, but it can be used with any students who might benefit from a nonverbal assessment.

SDS. See the description in the Ability and Aptitude Assessments section.

Strong Interest Inventory (SII). Published by Consulting Psychologists Press (Harmon, Hansen, Borgen, & Hammer, 1994), the SII is an assessment that measures self-reported interests. Results are present in relation to six occupational themes (realistic, investigative, artistic, social, enterprising, and conventional) as well as by basic interest scales, occupational scales, and personal style scales. The test takes approximately 45 minutes to complete, and can be administered individually or in large groups as well as online. The SSI is designed for students ages 14 and up.

Personality Assessment

The Myers–Briggs Type Indicator (MBTI). Published by Consulting Psychologists Press (Briggs & Briggs Myers, 2004), the MBTI is an assessment that measures personality traits across four dimensions: extraversion/introversion, sensing/intuition, thinking/feeling, and judging/perceiving. The assessment takes approximately 30 minutes to complete, and can be administered individually or in a large group as well as online. The MBTI is appropriate for use with high school students.

Comprehensive, Online Systems

Career Key (Jones, 2009). This system is appropriate for use with students in middle and high school and is based on Holland's theory. Students complete the online interest inventory and receive ratings by Holland Type (RIASEC). Within the system they can explore occupations, career clusters, and college majors. Information is also available regarding how to choose a career and a college major.

DISCOVER. Published by ACT, Inc. (2011), the DISCOVER system is appropriate for use with middle and high school students. It offers ACT's UNIACT interest inventory as well as skill and values assessment—all self-report. After completing all or some of the inventories, students receive results related to career clusters and the World-of-Work Map. Within the system students can search occupational information and college majors.

EXPLORE. Published by ACT, Inc. (2012), *EXPLORE* is designed for students in grades 8 and 9. It offers assessments in English, math, reading, and science, as well as a career exploration component. Results are provided in relation to how scores on the assessments align with benchmarks for college readiness. Students also are provided information about possible careers related to interest areas they identified.

Kuder® Career Planning System. The Kuder system (2006) offers options for elementary (Kuder Galaxy—career exploration) and middle and high school students (Kuder Navigator—interest, skills and values assessments). The Kuder Navigator assessments produce results in the form of percentile ranks for each of the 16 National Career Clusters (National Association of State Directors of Career and Technical Education consortium, 2012): (a) agriculture, food, and natural resources; (b) architecture and construction; (c) arts, audio/visual technology, and communication; (d) business management and administration; (e) education and training; (f) finance; (g) government and public administration; (h) health science; (i) hospitality and tourism; (j) human services; (k) information technology; (l) law, public safety, corrections, and security; (m) manufacturing; (n) marketing; (o) science, technology, engineering, and mathematics; and (p) transportation, distribution, and logistics. The Kuder interest and skills assessments can be completed in approximately 20 minutes and are appropriate for use with students in grades 7 to 12. With the Kuder system, students can create portfolios and explore career and college information.

Naviance. Published by Hobsons (2016), this comprehensive system can be used in all grade levels. It offers counselors a platform for students to engage in self- and career exploration (e.g., interest inventories, career and college exploration), monitor their academic plans, and engage in college preparation activities. Additional functions enable counselors to send secure transcripts to colleges and track student data.

Informal Assessments

Informal assessments are just that—informal. They usually do not have reliability or validity data to support their use, they do not come with comparison norms, there are no specific ways that results must be interpreted, and they usually allow for flexibility in use, administration, and scoring.

These types of assessments can be desirable to schools because they tend to be free or inexpensive, do not require assessment booklets to be purchased, require limited materials, and can be used creatively. In the following we discuss some of the more common informal assessments used in schools.

Card Sorts. Card sorts may be used in career or college counseling to help students identify occupational or college major interests (e.g., *Missouri Occupational Card Sort*—Hansen, Johnston, Krieshok, & Wong, 2012), values (e.g., *Career Values Card Sort*—Knowdell, 2005), or other areas. Just as the name suggests, card sorts rely on a set of cards with words or pictures on one side and a longer description or related information on the other side. In counseling, students would be asked to organize the cards in some manner, often into piles labeled Like, Dislike, and Unsure, or Like Me, Not Like Me, or Not Sure. Because card sorts are informal assessments, there is no right or wrong way to use them. Counselors can be creative in how they have students organize the cards.

Typically, once piles are sorted, students are asked to go through and further sort each pile however they want or based on some suggestion made by the counselor. For example, a student might say that she wants to sort cards with college majors she likes based on how much she knows about them. The counselor might encourage her to sort the majors she says she dislikes in the same manner, and could follow up with discussion about majors she ruled out but didn't really know much about. A follow-up activity could be having the student research some of the unfamiliar majors from all of her main categories.

Options for using card sorts are unlimited, and most card sort sets come with suggestions for use. An important aspect of using card sorts is examining the process—how students feel as they are sorting or what they are thinking as they are sorting. Students can use card sorts independently, but while it might be less stressful for them to sort without someone watching, they may miss out on processing their experience. Counselors who ask students to use card sorts on their own should consider providing a worksheet, like the one in Exhibit 5.1, that the student could complete (with instructions provided in advance) and bring in for discussion later. Additionally, some of these card sorts (e.g., Knowdell's) actually come with worksheets so students have a copy of their value rankings to store in a portfolio.

Career Genograms. Career genograms are commonly used in counseling to explore family relationships, composition, and patterns. Genograms or family tree activities can be useful tools for examining career and educational trends throughout a person's family (Gibson, 2012). Typically, students would be asked to start by listing themselves, then adding relatives to the extent the counselor deems relevant. For example, elementary students might just include parents and grandparents, where high school students might include aunts and uncles, great grandparents, cousins, and so on. Then they would be asked to indicate the occupations represented by each person and also the level of education those individuals completed. This kind of activity can easily be adapted to meet the needs of all students—using pictures and templates for younger students or those with cognitive deficits, and perhaps allowing older students to create their own formats.

EXHIBIT 5.1
Card Sort Worksheet

1. Which main categories did you use to sort your cards?
   Like/Dislike/Unsure
   Very Important/Not Important/Not Sure
   Like Me/Not Like Me/Not Sure
   Definitely/Absolutely Not/Not Sure
   Other . . . please list your categories

2. Explain how you sorted within each main category.
   _____
   _____

3. In the following space, list the cards that were easy for you to sort. What made them easy? What were you thinking or feeling at the time? How did you finally decide?
   _____
   _____

4. In the following space, list the cards that were difficult for you to sort. What made them difficult? What were you thinking or feeling at the time? How did you finally decide?
   _____
   _____

5. In the following space, list the cards you ended up with as your final choices, and indicate why you kept them. How certain are you about your final choices?
   _____
   _____

6. What next steps do you plan to take based on completing this activity?
   _____
   _____

7. Why is it important to consider your values when choosing a career or college?
   _____
   _____

In reviewing career genograms, counselors have the flexibility to focus on whatever seems relevant for the student. When used as part of a classroom activity, school counselors might have a specific set of questions to help students make sense of what they learned; it could be as simple as asking, "How similar are your career and educational goals to those of your family?" It is important to remember that P–12 students may or may not feel comfortable sharing their family work or educational history with their peers, so if used in large group settings, school counselors and educators should find ways to help all students benefit without making them share aloud. An easy solution is to use worksheets that can be collected, so students who want to share in class can do so, but others can have private follow-up sessions later as relevant.

Career genograms often require the involvement of families, as many students may not be familiar with the employment or educational history of their relatives. We see this as one of the benefits of this kind of activity, although it is important to realize that some students will have difficulty gathering information from their families. The authors have found it helpful to send a letter home to parents/guardians explaining the purpose of the activity and providing suggestions for how they can discuss with their child/adolescent their family work and educational history. For example, counselors might encourage families to share what they know about how decisions were made by different people, what expectations family members did or did not have for them, whether or not people worked in occupations that they truly enjoyed, or what barriers might have existed for them to pursue certain occupations or types of education.

Sometimes family involvement leads to unplanned information that benefits students. The second author worked with a 10th-grade student who discovered through this activity that one of his distant family members had attended college and everyone else found work with high school degrees. He said that when his mother helped him complete the genogram and pointed this out, she told him that she really hoped he could be the next one to go to college. Until that point, he had not been aware that she felt that way—they never really talked about school or work. He had wanted to go to college but didn't think his family cared, so he wasn't planning to go.

Follow-up activities are important when using genograms, and they will depend on why the genogram was initially used and what information was gathered. For example, with elementary students who might be asked to simply identify what their parents and grandparents do, a follow-up activity might be for them to learn more about the occupations of their family members by interviewing at least one person about his or her job. The high school student in the previous example might be encouraged to explore occupations that require a college degree given that he had not considered them before. School counselors and educators can think of endless possibilities for taking students beyond the information they put into their genograms.

To help young students who are not familiar with some of the occupations held by family members, a relevant activity is to create a paper doll that goes to work with the family member. The doll is designed and decorated by the child. The child then gives the paper doll to the family member who takes the doll to work and takes pictures of the doll engaging in work tasks. For example, a parent who is an auto mechanic would take a picture of the paper doll in the auto shop, possibly pretending to work on a car. Similarly, a student who has a parent who is a nurse may have pictures of the paper doll in the hospital taking someone's blood pressure. The teacher could make a video montage of all of the paper dolls in the class at "work" and the class gets to see many different work environments and what types of work occur in each.

Career Style Interview (CSI). The CSI (Savickas, 2005) is grounded in the *Career Construction Theory* (see Chapter 14). Savickas believes that while objective data obtained from formal assessments are important, subjective data that reflect personal experiences are equally important, as they help to explain how students make sense of things in their lives. The CSI allows counselors to examine students' experiences and to help them identify patterns and themes that might suggest possible future career paths.

The CSI is an informal assessment, meaning that it does not need to be completed in a specific or consistent manner. Nevertheless, Savickas (2005) provides a structure for gathering and making sense of the information gleaned from the interview. Ideally, in completing the interview, students provide information about the following: role models, favorite books and magazines, favorite hobbies, favorite and least favorite school subjects, favorite quote or motto, ambitions and parent's ambitions for them, and an important choice or decision they made and how they made it. Information gathered is used to collaboratively identify themes or patterns (see Chapter 14 for an example of what this "interpretation" looks like).

As with other informal assessments, counselors using the CSI should take advantage of opportunities to process information with students and expand their discussion and insight. For example, Savickas (2005) suggested that when identifying role models, counselors ask follow-up questions such as "What do you like or respect about this person?" or "Why did you identify his or her as your role model?" Follow-up questions related to school subjects might help to examine aspects of those subjects or classes that the student enjoys or does not enjoy. The main goal for such processing is to better understand the student's choices and decisions, as that information will inform the interpretation and identification of themes.

In addition to costing nothing and being very flexible (the interview can be completed over a number of sessions or all at once—there is no time frame), another benefit of the CSI is its adaptability. It can be completed in numerous ways, verbally or by using pictures. The second author has successfully used the CSI by having students create collages in which they represent each topic area, or by drawing or bringing in pictures to reflect some of their responses. Follow-up discussion of the collage items can be done the same way as in an interview. This author also has successfully approached the process by having students complete the interview during a session or by having them take a worksheet home and then meeting with them later to review responses. School counselors should consider the developmental needs and personal styles of students when determining the most effective format and time frame for completing the CSI.

USING ASSESSMENT RESULTS: EVALUATION

Choosing and administering career and college readiness assessments is only half the picture—what is done with the assessment data is what really matters. This is not an assessment textbook, so we want to just briefly address a few important considerations for interpreting and using assessment data.

Considerations for Interpreting Assessment Data

1. *Examine Data from Multiple Assessment Tools.* No one single assessment tool should be used to make a determination about a student's future. On any given day in any given situation, a student may or may not have been at her best. Further, some students respond better to one type of assessment versus another. Data collected over a number of different instruments will likely be more reliable in reflecting that student.

2. *Consider the Benefits of Using Different Types of Assessments.* A combination of formal and informal instruments assessing the same factor can be useful in comparing and contrasting results and looking for themes or patterns. Also, assessments targeting different areas (e.g., interests, skills) can be combined in order to more comprehensively assess a student.

3. *Interpret Results Accurately.* Each assessment has its own unique score report or instructions for interpretation, and school counselors and educators must ensure that they are accurately making sense of results. Given the variety of ways that assessment data are reported, it is imperative that the individuals reviewing and explaining the results understand concepts such as correlations, standard scores, percentile ranks, stanine scores, and grade or age equivalents. Further, in order to help make meaning of the results, school counselors and educators need to understand how to read norm tables and expectancy tables.

4. *Ensure that Students Understand their Results.* Do not leave students on their own to make sense of the results. Both of the authors have had experience working with students who jump to conclusions about what their results "are telling them" to be or do. Often, students want tests to give them answers. It is up to us to help them realize that assessment results are helpful in identifying factors such as strengths, weaknesses, or things to consider, and that future plans and decisions should be made with that information in mind. Handing students their assessment results without explanation or follow up can quickly lead to misperceptions and inaccurate assumptions on their part. Just because instructions and interpretations might be included as part of an individual student's summary report doesn't mean that the student will understand them or read them carefully. Verbal explanations and follow-up discussions can be very important to ensure accurate understanding by students as well as their parents or guardians.

Using Assessment Data for Program Planning

While individual student assessment results are beneficial to students, school counselors and educators should consider the benefits of examining student data for the purposes of informing program planning. For example, if a school counselor administered an interest inventory and, through summary data, learned that the majority of student interests fell into five specific career clusters, perhaps the counselor could initiate a discussion about the possibility of offering elective courses or supplemental learning opportunities related to those clusters. Or, if through an assessment the counselor learned that students do not feel confident in their abilities to access college information, supplemental educational or information sessions could be implemented in order to better prepare students and their families to engage in college exploration activities.

An important skill for school counselors (ASCA, 2012) is to examine data, and specifically to disaggregate data. By breaking results down into various groups (e.g., ethnicity, disabilities, first-generation college students), school counselors can identify any populations that might need more support. Efforts to close the achievement gap can be facilitated by evaluating assessment data—without knowing what differences exist or in what areas they exist, school counselors and educators cannot effect change.

Subsequent to student assessment and results interpretation, school counselors should be prepared to share their findings. By reporting findings to the counseling advisory council, administration, parents, or other stakeholders, school counselors can garner support for program planning in response to student outcomes. To use an example from the beginning of the chapter, if a school counselor learns that only 25% of students at the school take the ACT before their senior year, the counselor may choose to design an intervention to increase the number of students taking the ACT in their sophomore and junior years and may report this information to the school principal and the counseling advisory council. Together they may decide that a classroom lesson plan highlighting the benefits of early ACT participation is necessary and that they should send out a letter to parents explaining the importance of taking the ACT early. In this way, data are being used to drive decision making and interventions. Following these interventions, the school counselor would continue to monitor ACT participation for sophomores and juniors to determine if there is an increase or not.

SUMMARY

In this chapter, we discussed the importance of assessment and evaluation in relation to P–12 career and college readiness. When considering which assessment instruments to choose for their schools, counselors should be familiar with psychometric properties (e.g., validity, reliability), normed populations, potential content, and language biases, as well as how the assessment can be administered or modified to appeal to various learning styles or students with learning disabilities. We also cautioned readers to comprehensively consider the time, cost, and purpose of assessments given to students to ensure that the assessment is worthwhile. We reviewed numerous formal and informal assessments that can be used in P–12 settings and offered tips on interpreting results and using assessment and evaluation data for program planning. In the grade-level chapters that follow, we refer to many of the assessments listed in this chapter.

···❯ Test Your Knowledge

1. Name at least one assessment that you could use to assess each of the following: (a) interests, (b) abilities, and (c) beliefs.
2. Explain why counselors would want to consider using a combination of formal and informal assessments.
3. Why are norm groups important?
4. Clarify the difference between reliability and validity.

REFERENCES

ACT, Inc. (2011). *DISCOVER career planning program.* Iowa City, IA: Author.

ACT, Inc. (2012). *EXPLORE.* Iowa City, IA: Author.

ACT, Inc. (2016a). *Aspire.* Iowa City, IA: Author.

ACT, Inc. (2016b). *WorkKeys.* Iowa City, IA: Author.

American School Counselor Association. (2012). *The ASCA national model: A framework for school counseling programs* (3rd ed.). Alexandria, VA: Author.

Becker, R. L. (2000). *Reading-free vocational interest inventory-2 (R-FVII:2).* Columbus, OH: Elbern Publications.

Bennet, G. K., Seashore, H. G., & Wesman, A. G. (1990). *Differential aptitude test.* San Antonio, TX: Pearson Assessments.

Briggs, K. C., & Briggs Myers, I. (2004). *The Myers-Briggs type indicator.* Palo Alto, CA: Consulting Psychologists Press.

Campbell, D. P., Hyne, S. A., & Nilsen, D. L. (1992). *Manual for the Campbell interest and skill survey.* Minneapolis, MN: National Computer Systems.

Department of Defense. (2004). *Armed services vocational aptitude battery.* Washington, DC: Author.

Gibson, D. M. (2012). Using career genograms in K-12 settings. Retrieved from http://associationdatabase.com/aws/NCDA/pt/sd/news_article/5473/_PARENT/layout_details/false

Gibbons, M. M., & Borders, L. D. (2010). A measure of college-going self-efficacy for middle school students. *Professional School Counseling, 13,* 234–243.

Gottfredson, L. S. (1981). Circumscription and compromise: A developmental theory of occupational aspirations. *Journal of Counseling Psychology, 28*(6), 545–579. http://dx.doi.org/10.1037/0022-0167.28.6.545

Gottfredson, L. S. (2002). Gottfredson's theory of circumscription, compromise, and self-creation. In D. Brown (Ed.), *Career choice and development* (4th ed., pp. 85–148). San Francisco, CA: Jossey-Bass.

Gottfredson, L. S. (2005). Applying Gottfredson's theory of circumscription and compromise in career guidance and counseling. In S. D. Brown & R. W. Lent (Eds.), *Career development and counseling: Putting theory and research to work* (pp. 71–100). Hoboken, NJ: John Wiley & Sons.

Hansen, R., Johnston, J., Krieshok, T., & Wong, S. C. (2012). *Missouri Occupational Card Sort.* Columbia, MO: University of Missouri.

Harmon, L. W., Hansen, J. C., Borgen, F. H., & Hammer, A. L. (1994). *Strong interest inventory applications and technical guide.* Palo Alto, CA: Consulting Psychologists Press.

Hobsons. (2016). *Naviance.* Cincinnati, OH: Author.

Holland, J. L. (1973). *Making vocational choices: A theory of careers.* Englewood Cliffs, NJ: Prentice Hall.

Holland, J. L. (1994). *Self-directed search.* Lutz, FL: Psychological Assessment Resources.

Holland, J. L. (1997). *Making vocational choices: A theory of vocational personalities and work environments* (3rd ed.). Odessa, FL: Psychological Assessment Resources.

Holland, J. L., Daiger, D. C., & Power, P. G. (1980). *My vocational situation.* Palo Alto, CA: Consulting Psychologists Press.

Jones, L. K. (2009). *The career key.* Hood River, OR: Career Key, Inc.

Knowdell, R. L. (2005). *Career values card sort.* San Jose, CA: Career Research & Testing, Inc.

Krumboltz, J. D. (1994). *Career beliefs inventory.* Menlo Park, CA: Mind Garden, Inc.

Krumboltz, J. D., Mitchell, A. M., & Jones, G. B. (1976). A social learning theory of career selection. *The Counseling Psychologist, 6,* 71–81.

Kuder, F. (2006). *Kuder career planning system.* Adel, IA: Kuder, Inc.

Lent, R. W., Brown, S. D., & Hackett, G. (1994). Toward a unifying social cognitive theory of career and academic interest, choice, and performance. *Journal of Vocational Behavior, 45,* 79–122.

National Association of State Directors of Career and Technical Education consortium. (2012). The 16 career clusters. Retrieved from https://www.careertech.org/career-clusters

National Career Development Association. (2009). The National Career Development Association minimum competencies for multicultural career counseling and development. Retrieved from http://ncda.org/aws/NCDA/pt/sp/guidelines

Parsons, F. (1909). *Choosing a vocation.* Boston, MA: Houghton Mifflin.

Peterson, G. W., Sampson, J. P., Jr., & Reardon, R. (1991). *Career development and services: A cognitive approach.* Pacific Grove, CA: Brooks/Cole.

Sampson, J. P., Jr., Peterson, G. W., Lenz, J. G., Reardon, R. C., & Saunders, D. E. (1996). *Career thoughts inventory.* Odessa, FL: Psychological Assessment Resources.

Savickas, M. L. (2005). *The theory and practice of career construction.* In S. D. Brown & R. W. Lent (Eds.), *Career development and counseling: Putting theory and research to work* (pp. 42–70). Hoboken, NJ: John Wiley & Sons.

Super, D. E. (1980). A life-span, life-space approach to career development. *Journal of Vocational Behavior, 16*(3), 282–298. http://dx.doi.org/10.1016/0001-8791(80)90056-1

Super, D. E., Thompson, A. S., Lindeman, R. H., Jordan, J. P., & Myers, R. A. (1984). *Career development inventory.* Palo Alto, CA: Consulting Psychologists Press.

Talent Assessment, Inc. (2000). *Pictorial inventory of careers.* Jacksonville, FL: Author.

Taylor, K. M., & Betz, N. E. (1983). *Career decision making self-efficacy scale.* Menlo Park, CA: Mind Garden, Inc.

Wood, C., & Hayes, D. (Eds.). (2013). *A counselor's guide to career assessment instruments* (6th ed.). Broken Arrow, OK: National Career Development Association.

SIX

P–12 Career and College Readiness: Curriculum Development

Developing and delivering a core counseling curriculum are essential tasks for school counselors and a direct service component of the American School Counselor Association's (ASCA) National Model (2012). Jalongo and Isenberg (2004) defined *curriculum* as "the pathway of education; it is what children actually experience in schools from arrival to departure and reflects the philosophy, goals, and objectives of the program, classroom, or school district" (p. 185). According to Graves (1996), a curriculum that is well designed engages students through active learning, a process that involves both *action* and *reflection*. *Action* occurs through directly interacting with "people, materials, events, and ideas" (p. 4) and *reflection* occurs when students are asked to construct knowledge about those interaction experiences in a way that is relevant and meaningful. Curriculum should be rigorous, establishing high expectations for all students, while also being culturally relevant (Jalongo & Isenberg, 2004).

With all of this in mind, curriculum development can be a daunting task for new school counselors who may be unsure of how to design or write curricula. A further concern is that stakeholders may question the need for career or college readiness activities, especially if those activities take time away from the core academic curriculum, particularly for elementary students, since many adults may not understand the need for career and college interventions in primary grades (Niles & Harris-Bowlsbey, 2009). In this chapter, we explore critical issues in curriculum development including curriculum foundations, developing objectives, choosing interventions and writing lesson plans, implementing the curriculum, and evaluating outcomes.

CHOOSING A CURRICULUM FOUNDATION

As noted by Niles and Harris-Bowlsbey (2009), one major barrier to successful career and college readiness interventions is that the curriculum is often patched together rather than being a cohesive, systematic program throughout P–12 grades. For example, at a conference one middle school counselor recently told the first author how difficult it is for her to know what the sixth-grade students in her school understand about careers and college, as she had no idea what career and college interventions they were given in elementary

No sequential program for CC-planning curricula

school. This lack of cohesive, formal planning across school levels (elementary, middle, and high) means that students may be given duplicate information (i.e., learning the same information about career clusters in both elementary and middle school) or miss information at one level that they are expected to know (i.e., being asked to choose a college in their junior year when they haven't had any career exploration and therefore don't know what postsecondary training they need). These types of dilemmas underscore the rationale for having a developmental and sequential approach to career and college readiness and for collaboration across grade levels.

In essence, to avoid some of these problems, it is important that school counselors within districts and school clusters coplan curricula. Further, Brown (2012) noted that school counselors will want to gain administrative support before designing and implementing a career and college readiness curriculum in order to allocate time for coplanning curricula across schools and to ensure that teachers will support time away from core academics. Additionally, school counselors should garner input from their advisory council and base curricular decisions on school and district data, national and state standards, and the ASCA (2014) Mindsets and Behaviors (see Appendix C) in order to provide a foundation for success. In this chapter, we provide an overview of how school counselors begin the process of designing career and college readiness curricula.

Creating a Standards-Based Curriculum

The ASCA (2014) *Mindsets and Behaviors for Student Success: College and Career Readiness Standards for Every Student* provides school counselors a framework for identifying the mind-sets or attitudes, thoughts, and behaviors that P–12 students need to develop in personal, social, career, and academic domains (see Appendix C). It is up to individual schools to determine which of these standards are most relevant for students in their buildings. Some standards might be covered and assessed multiple times and in different ways across grade levels. Other standards might be addressed only once. In some instances, states have developed a set of standards for student learning they would like school counselors to follow when developing curriculum. These are known as grade level expectations (GLEs).

In order to effectively use standards for curriculum development, we suggest that school counselors should: (a) read all of the standards thoroughly, (b) identify, by grade, what students need to know, (c) write curriculum objectives, (d) design assessments to measure student learning, (e) design lesson plans, (f) deliver lesson plans and assess student learning, (g) share assessment results with the school counseling advisory council, and (h) use assessment results to plan future core counseling instruction.

WRITING CURRICULUM OBJECTIVES

After reviewing standards and determining which are wanted or needed as a foundation for their curriculum, school counselors should develop learning objectives, by grade, for the career and college readiness curriculum.

It is important to understand that these objectives need to be developmental and sequential. In other words, the exact same objective should not be written for kindergarten, first, and second grade. Rather, each grade would have a distinct set of learning objectives for career and college readiness. Moreover, objectives should be written such that outcomes are specific and measurable. In this section, we review key concepts for writing effective curriculum objectives.

Bloom's Taxonomy

Benjamin Bloom's *Taxonomy of Educational Objectives* (i.e., Bloom's taxonomy) is a seminal work that has been informative to education practitioners in constructing curricula (Bloom, Engelhart, Furst, Hill, & Krathwohl, 1956). Based on the psychology of learning and developmental theories, Bloom's taxonomy is designed to help educators make conscious choices about how the educative process unfolds and challenges students' thinking. That is, educators should expect that students will be able to engage in more advanced ways of thinking about various concepts as they develop and, therefore, activities and assessments should match where students are developmentally.

According to Bloom et al. (1956, p. 25), the following four questions should be considered and used as a guide in developing curricula:

1. What educational purposes or objectives should the school or course seek to attain?
2. What learning experiences can be provided, which are likely to bring about the attainment of these purposes?
3. How can these learning experiences be effectively organized to help provide continuity and sequence for the learner and to help the learner to integrate what might otherwise appear as isolated learning experiences?
4. How can the effectiveness of learning experiences be evaluated by the use of tests and other systematic evidence-gathering procedures?

Bloom's taxonomy is meant to help educators to organize, developmentally, a curriculum that addresses the aforementioned questions by graduating learning experiences in a systematic, hierarchical order. The original taxonomy objectives were revised by a group of cognitive psychologists to reflect modern learning. The most current Bloom's taxonomy learning objectives are: (a) remembering, (b) understanding, (c) applying, (d) analyzing, (e) evaluating, and (f) creating. An explanation of each objective is provided in Table 6.1, and the hierarchical nature of Bloom's revised taxonomy is represented in Figure 6.1.

Writing Measurable Objectives

Curriculum objectives should be established for the school counseling program at the beginning of each year and developed based on data (e.g., from needs assessments, from previous year's assessments). These objectives ideally should cover all three of the ASCA (2012) domains—career, personal/social,

6.1 Taxonomy of Educational Objectives and a Description of Each for the Revised Taxonomy

Objectives and Descriptions From the Revised Bloom's Taxonomy
Remembering: Remembering is the ability to recall, recognize, and retrieve information that has been previously learned. Defining, memorizing, and repeating information are all included in this objective.
Understanding: Understanding is the construction of meaning from graphs, data, charts, and written and oral language. Students demonstrate understanding by interpreting, summarizing, comparing, and explaining information.
Applying: Applying a theory to a problem, particularly in a new way, or implementing a procedure.
Analyzing: Breaking information into parts; developing an understanding of how each part works, how it works compared to other parts, and how each part contributes to the whole; differentiating; and organizing information.
Evaluating: Reviewing and critiquing information based on standards or specific criteria.
Creating: Putting together or reorganizing elements into a new pattern to create a functional whole, generating, and producing.

FIGURE 6.1 Taxonomy of Revised Education Objectives From Most Concrete to Most Abstract

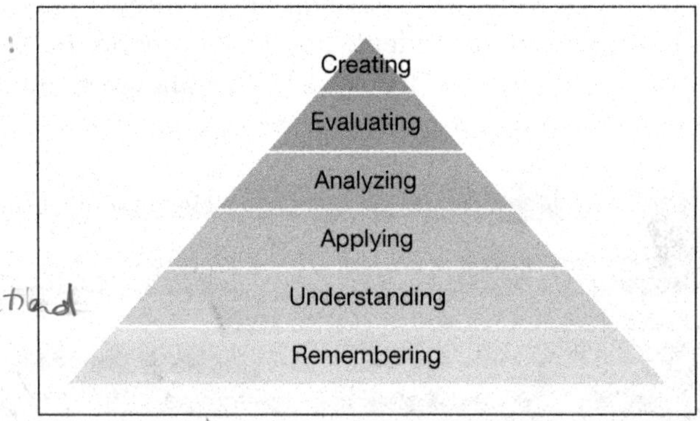

Career Maturity:
1 Orientation to vocational choice
2 Specific info re: preferred occupation
3 Consistency
4 Crystallization of traits
5 Wisdom of vocational preference

and academic. Educators at state and district levels often refer to objectives by a variety of terms (e.g., student learning targets), but all of those terms refer to what we want students to know or be able to do in relation to a specific content area.

When writing career and college readiness curriculum objectives, it is important that school counselors be as specific as possible. By doing so, the objectives provide an indication of what the school counselor will do and what outcomes are expected as a result. In order to have developmentally appropriate objectives, counselors should write separate objectives for each grade level. We recommend the ABCD method of writing objectives proposed by Heinrich, Molenda, Russell, and Smaldino (1996). The ABCD method consists of including the following elements in each objective: (a) The *audience* element denotes who is the intended learner; (b) the *behavior* element indicates what you expect the learner to be able to do, and it should be observable; (c) the *condition* element describes the specific circumstances or context in which the learning will occur; and (d) the *degree* is the amount of mastery the learner will achieve.

Table 6.2 provides examples of career and college readiness curriculum objectives written with the ABCD method for elementary, middle, and high school. Objectives are most easily measured when they have only one behavior

TABLE 6.2 Sample Career and College Readiness Curriculum Objectives for School Counseling Programs

Grade Level	Sample Curriculum Objective
Third grade	At the conclusion of a unit on career clusters, third-grade students will be able to identify the career clusters that specific careers belong to 80% of the time.
Seventh grade	At the conclusion of a classroom lesson on career values, 85% of seventh-grade students will be able to list five personal values they have related to careers.
Eleventh grade	At the completion of two classroom lessons on writing effective scholarship essays, 80% of 11th-grade students will be able to identify four components of a well-written college scholarship essay.

associated with them (as in the examples in Table 6.2). Including two separate objectives in a lesson rather than writing one complex objective can help to ensure each unique behavioral component stands out and is not overlooked.

CHOOSING INTERVENTIONS AND WRITING LESSON PLANS

As previously mentioned, prior to designing and delivering lesson plans, school counselors should review state and national standards, determine what students need to know by grade level, write curriculum objectives, and choose assessment methods. After engaging in these curriculum planning activities, school counselors can begin to design lesson units and plans. In this section, we describe how the choice of interventions and activities may help to increase student maturity, and we provide the reader with considerations for creating student learning experiences.

Increasing Career Maturity

One of the most important and desired outcomes of career and college education and counseling is that students gain career maturity throughout their time in P–12 education. The concept of career maturity came from Super (1980) and is described by Sharf (2006, p. 180) as having five distinct components:

1. Orientation to vocational choice, which deals with concern about career choice and using occupational information.
2. Information and planning about a preferred occupation; that is, the specific information that the individual has about the occupation he or she intends to enter.
3. Consistency of vocational preference, concerned not only with stability of an occupational choice over time, but also with its consistency within occupational fields and levels.
4. Crystallization of traits, including seven indices of attitudes toward work.
5. The wisdom of vocational preference, which refers to the relationship between choice and abilities and activities and interests.

To comprehensively increase students' career maturity, it is essential that the counseling curriculum reflect an underlying theoretical framework.

Lessons should be developmentally appropriate, culturally responsive, and appeal to a variety of learning styles. Furthermore, school counselors should choose interventions that are theory- and evidence-based and ensure that they evaluate the effectiveness of their lessons by formally measuring whether or not their objectives were met. We discuss each of these in this section.

Grounded in Theory and Developmentally Appropriate

In order to design meaningful and relevant career and college readiness lessons, school counselors should have in-depth knowledge of theories of child and adolescent development. In the subsequent chapters, we provide an overview of holistic development related to career growth including socioemotional, cognitive, physical, and cultural development concepts, and continue to connect career and college readiness activities to developmental and career theories. Proposed grade-level interventions are based on the work of various theorists, including Bourdieu (1977), Gottfredson (1981), Holland (1997), Bandura (1977), and Super (1980), to name a few.

Culturally Responsive Curriculum

Effective and appropriate curriculum is culturally relevant, supporting students' home culture and language while also assisting students in navigating the culture of the school (Jalongo & Isenberg, 2004). A culturally relevant curriculum supports diverse learners in three ways: (a) by accepting, valuing, and welcoming all students *and their families*, (b) accommodating different learning styles through varied teaching strategies, and (c) encouraging students to have personal pride in their culture and to use cultural knowledge to motivate students by increasing self-esteem, self-knowledge, and an appreciation for others (Jalongo & Isenberg, 2004). Further, a culturally responsive curriculum promotes cultural understanding, awareness, acceptance of other cultures, and sensitivity to others.

When designing a culturally responsive curriculum, school counselors should choose culturally relevant materials (e.g., books, pictures, music) that reflect and value the unique cultural lives, languages, and abilities of all students (Utley, Obiakor, & Bakken, 2011). A truly culturally responsive career and college readiness curriculum includes much more than lesson plans that reflect an appreciation of diversity. Indeed, school counselors should remember that students have the knowledge to help transform school environments, and culturally responsive teaching practices pull on the strengths of all groups to enhance curriculum and improve pedagogy (Utley et al., 2011). In order to encourage all students, it is critical that students are given access to a counseling curriculum consistently throughout P–12 education and that diverse academic courses are offered in every school environment that are both rigorous and challenging to students.

Addressing Learning Styles and Multiple Intelligences

Alexander (2000) noted that each individual receives information in particular ways. Specifically, Alexander organized learning styles into three major categories that can be considered when developing an instructional or training plan: (a) visual learners, who prefer seeing pictures, graphs, charts, PowerPoints, props, and videos; (b) auditory learners, who prefer hearing instructions and explanations; and (c) kinesthetic learners, who prefer hands-on opportunities to learn, such as role-plays, science experiments, and math labs. Howard Gardner is credited with expanding Alexander's work through the development of the concept of multiple intelligences. In his seminal work, *Frames of Mind: The Theory of Multiple Intelligences,* Gardner (1983) explained that individuals have different learning styles and that instruction should reflect these multiple styles in order to engage all students. Table 6.3 contains a list of intelligences and provides a description of each.

TABLE 6.3 Gardner's Multiple Intelligences

Type of Intelligence	Characteristics
Linguistic Intelligence	These individuals have natural mastery or expertise in language. Individuals with linguistic intelligence use language for communicative and expressive purposes; for example, an individual with a natural ability to understand words and use them, such as writing poetry. Students with this learning style may enjoy activities like writing career stories.
Logical– Mathematical Intelligence	Individuals with this learning style enjoy learning information through reasoning, abstraction, mathematics, and scientific investigation. Students with this learning style may enjoy exploring careers through technology.
Musical Intelligence	Gardner noted that musical talent is the first type of intelligence to emerge. Individuals with this type of intelligence may use songs or rhythm to remember information, and have a propensity toward playing musical instruments, singing, or composing music. Students with this learning style may enjoy careers in the music industry and may enjoy alternative learning techniques, such as writing a career rap song.
Bodily Kinesthetic Intelligence	Individuals with this learning style enjoy movement such as sports, dance, and other physical activities. Students with this learning style learn better when they are moving and may enjoy career exploration games that involve physical activity (i.e., career baseball, career safari).
Spatial Intelligence	Individuals with this learning style have strong visual observation skills and are often artistic. Students with this learning style may like career exploration activities that include drawing careers, creating career genograms, mapping career clusters, and other artistic/visual activities.
Interpersonal Intelligence	Individuals with this learning style generally enjoy social pursuits and collaborative and teamwork activities. Students in this category may enjoy creating career skits, interviewing people, and classroom career discussions.
Intrapersonal Intelligence	Individuals with this learning style are very reflective and introspective. They may prefer working alone and enjoy analyzing their own thoughts and perceptions as they are effective contemplators. Students in this category might enjoy reading career information, taking assessments and reflecting on the results, and doing individualized exploration activities.
Naturalistic Intelligence	Individuals with this learning style enjoy learning in natural environments, such as growing and nurturing animals and plants. Students in this learning category may enjoy career exploration with natural elements. For example, students with this type of intelligence might enjoy activities like learning about agricultural careers if they get an opportunity to actually interact with elements (i.e., taking a field trip to a farm and feeding animals).

Adapted from Gardner (1983).

The Well-Written Lesson Plan

After completing a review of standards, writing the counseling program's curriculum objectives, choosing assessments, and considering culture, developmental level, and theory, the school counselor is ready to write (or choose) lesson plans. A wealth of free and downloadable lesson plans are available online (e.g., see Missouri Center for Career Education, www.missouricareereducation .org). However, before acquiring lesson plans written by others, school counselors should ensure that the selected lesson plans adequately address the standards and objectives of their specific school counseling program. We recommend that school counselors plan to make some modifications to any lesson plans they find to ensure relevance for their specific students (e.g., grade level, cultural characteristics, and learning styles).

handwritten margin note: Free Lesson Plans →

Components of a Well-Written Lesson Plan. A well-written lesson plan includes, at minimum, six core components: (a) standards, (b) objectives, (c) materials, (d) detailed instructions, (e) summary, and (f) evaluation. At the beginning of the written lesson plan, school counselors should indicate the *standards* they are addressing through the lesson. As previously mentioned, we strongly recommend the ASCA (2014) Mindsets and Behaviors as a foundation (see Appendix C). The *objectives* for the lesson plan should also be listed; these specific objectives should align in some way with the school counseling program objectives and should articulate what skills or knowledge students should acquire at the completion of the lesson or learning unit. The *materials* section includes any supplies necessary for delivering the lesson plan, including items like markers, paper, worksheets, puppets, and so forth. In the *detailed instructions* section of the lesson plan, the school counselor provides step-by-step directions for delivering the lesson to students. The *summary* section denotes how the school counselor will wrap up the lesson and provides closure instructions such as reflection questions, follow-up activities for the teacher to implement, and suggestions for practicing newly acquired skills or knowledge. Finally, the *evaluation* component includes assessments that measure whether or not the specific objectives of the lesson plan have been met. ASCA (2012) recommends addressing process, perception, and outcome data in the evaluation section. For an example of a lesson plan containing these six key components, see Exhibit 6.1.

handwritten margin note: 1. Review Standards 2. Write objectives 3. Choose assessments 4. Consider Culture 5. Write/Choose LP 6. Implement 7. Evaluate outcomes

IMPLEMENTING THE CURRICULUM

Prior to implementing the curriculum and classroom lesson plans, Brown (2012) suggested that school counselors consider the following: (a) What types of materials and resources are needed to effectively deliver the lessons (e.g., games, assessments, experiential components)? (b) How might technology be used to deliver or enhance the curriculum? (c) What aspects of the career and college readiness curriculum might be integrated with classroom academic content? (d) How might parents be included in the curriculum?

The answers to these questions will be school specific and, as is evidenced throughout this book, it is not necessary for school counselors to buy a lot of expensive curricular books and materials. However, if counselors have a budget and can buy some materials, they should do so with intentionality. For example, expensive career exploration software programs can be purchased, but many free technology resources may serve similar purposes (e.g., *Occupational Outlook Handbook* online, Drive of Your Life, *O*Net*, California Career Zone).

Classroom Curriculum Integration

Although school counselors deliver career and college readiness curriculum, teachers may also integrate related activities into the core curriculum to enhance students' understanding of how P–12 academics relate to the world of work and postsecondary education. According to Jalongo and Isenberg (2004), an integrated curriculum joins together multiple content areas and "teaches skills and concepts from the different subject areas based on the study of a broad concept or theme, and on the developmental needs of the learners" (p. 203). For example, given the federal focus on science, technology, engineering, and mathematics (STEM) careers, school counselors and teachers can discuss opportunities to include career and college information in science, math, and technology classrooms through collaboratively planned projects. Throughout the grade-level chapters of this book (Chapters 7–15), we provide examples of classroom integration of career and college readiness. Exhibit 6.1 is an example of how one school counselor worked in collaboration with social studies teachers at her high school to codevelop curriculum for students' future career and college success.

Other School Counseling Program Components

Beyond providing classroom lesson plans, school counselors also coordinate whole school activities (i.e., career and college fairs), grade-level activities (i.e., a visit to the space center that includes career speakers such as astronauts and aeronautical engineers), and parent activities such as workshops on career and college readiness topics. Throughout this book, we share examples of these additional career and college readiness curriculum activities.

EVALUATING OUTCOMES

As noted by Carter and Curtis (1994), ongoing evaluation (i.e., at the end of individual lessons or curricular units), as opposed to end of year evaluation, allows for more immediate feedback. By evaluating student performance on curriculum objectives, school counselors can determine which career and college readiness knowledge areas and skills students are learning through the counseling curriculum. Second, if evaluations are thoughtfully created, then the act of providing evaluation feedback can be a learning and reflection experience for students (Carter & Curtis, 1994). Finally, student outcome evaluation data are important for determining the success of program objectives and for determining future plans of action.

Choosing Evaluation Methods

The method that is used to evaluate a lesson will depend on a number of factors, including the developmental level of the students as well as their learning styles. In Table 6.4, we revisit the curriculum objectives we presented earlier in this chapter. Beside each objective, we offer a couple of ways that it could be evaluated. In the first example for third grade, you can see two different methods for assessing the same *remembering* objective—the picture option could be beneficial for individuals with lower reading skills or for students who are visual learners. The idea of having multiple ways of evaluating objectives could be used for learning objectives at any grade level—to accommodate different learner needs.

Sharing Results and Making Decisions

Evaluation data collected should be shared with major stakeholders annually. The school counseling advisory council, composed of community members and school personnel, should agree upon the objectives of the career and college readiness curriculum at the beginning of the school year. If the evaluation data reflect that students did not meet the expectations set by the objectives,

TABLE 6.4 Sample Career Curriculum Objectives and Evaluation Methods

Grade	Sample Curriculum Objective	Sample Evaluation Methods
Third grade	At the conclusion of a unit on career clusters, third-grade students will be able to identify the career clusters that specific careers belong to 80% of the time	1. Students will complete a test in which they match a list of careers to a list of clusters or students place pictures of individuals in careers under the appropriate cluster headings (Bloom's *remembering* objective). 2. Students will create a collage in which they visually place career cards in clusters and demonstrate an understanding of how those careers fit together (Bloom's *understanding* objective).
Seventh grade	At the conclusion of a classroom lesson on career values, 85% of seventh-grade students will be able to list five personal values they have related to careers	1. Students will create a picture in which they represent the five personal values that arose as strongest influences based on their assessment results (Bloom's *understanding* objective). 2. Students will submit a written list of their personal values, including a brief explanation of how they might influence their career choices (Bloom's *applying* objective).
Eleventh grade	At the completion of two classroom lessons on writing effective scholarship essays, 80% of 11th-grade students will be able to identify four components of a well-written scholarship essay	1. Students will produce a scholarship essay that contains the four components (Bloom's *applying* objective). 2. Students will critique an essay based on the four components (Bloom's *evaluating* objective).

the advisory council can be helpful in determining why outcome targets were not reached and how the program plan might be altered in the future to meet objectives. Conversely, if projected outcomes were met, then the advisory council can celebrate these findings and begin to plan new objectives for the following year (ASCA, 2012).

Other ways that the school counselor can make outcomes known is through marketing within the school and in the larger community. For example, one school counselor at an inner city school shared with the first author that she includes outcomes of the school counseling program in the morning announcements at her school when it seems appropriate to do so. She offered the example of the results of a career fair that she reported over 90% of the ninth-grade class attended (process data). After the fair, nearly 100% of attendees were able to write down three careers that they had learned about during the fair that they would like to know more about (perception data). She also shared that increases in college admissions and commitment to colleges for seniors, increases in the number of students taking honors courses, and number of scholarships attained are things she reported to the local paper for publication each spring (outcome data). School counselors may also want to share results in administrative team meetings, at parent workshops, and during faculty in-service days.

EXHIBIT 6.1
Voices From the Field: Sample Lesson Plan

Jodi Manton, PLPC, NCC, EdS

School Counselor, Private, Parochial

As noted in the ASCA Mindsets and Behaviors (2014), students need to be able to lead and apply teamwork skills within diverse groups in order to be successful in career and college settings. As a high school counselor at a predominantly White, private college preparatory school in the southeastern United States, I recognize the importance of increasing my students' multicultural awareness and sensitivity in order to promote their future success.

As my students enter a higher education system and workforce with a growing diversity and globalization, their limited exposure to individuals from different racial and ethnic backgrounds might inhibit their social, academic, and career development. As school counselors, we are in a position to help all of our students obtain the knowledge and skills they need to develop their multicultural awareness and build relationships with individuals from backgrounds different than their own. Therefore, I collaborated with the social studies faculty at my school to develop a unit on diversity conjunctive with a social studies class. My school is offering a course entitled *Southern History: The Long Civil Rights Movement* to juniors and seniors, who will spend a semester exploring the U.S. civil rights movement beginning

(continued)

EXHIBIT 6.1 (continued)
Voices From the Field: Sample Lesson Plan

with emancipation and the Great Compromise in the late 19th century and concluding with an analysis of the Black Lives Matter movement. I designed a Civil Rights Field Trip for the students enrolled in this course to increase (a) students' awareness of and (b) empathy for the experience of marginalized racial groups by providing an experiential opportunity to reinforce the historical context they are receiving during the course. In addition, I designed lesson plans to promote awareness of interpersonal communication and diversity. The following lesson is designed for a block schedule class, but could be broken up into multiple lessons if class sessions are shorter.

Assessment and Outcome Measures

Student Learning Outcome 1

Students will explain the influence of various historical events leading up to and during the civil rights movement on American history and society.

Assessment Plan: Student Learning Outcome 1

- Students will write a minimum three-page reflection paper addressing the following:
    1. Their understanding of the actions and motives of civil rights activists
    2. Their perspective on the status of racial and ethnic minorities in America today
    3. How this trip has impacted both their academic and personal experiences in this course
    4. What their role is in social justice and how they can impact oppressive systems

Their papers will be assessed by their teacher according to the Association of American Colleges and Universities' *"Critical Thinking VALUE Rubric"* (2010). Students will also deliver a brief presentation about their experience on the trip and how it impacted them personally to the upper school during announcements upon their return describing their experience.

Student Learning Outcome 2

Students will develop greater **empathy** for the struggles of racial and ethnic minorities throughout American history as well as within our current society.

Assessment Plan: Student Learning Outcome 2
- Prior to the delivery of classroom lessons and the field trips, students will complete the Scale of Ethnocultural Empathy (SEE), a self-report instrument designed to measure an individual's "empathy toward people from racial and ethnic backgrounds different from one's own" (Wang et al., 2003). They will complete this assessment again after the field trip to measure any change to their empathy level.

(continued)

EXHIBIT 6.1 (*continued*)

Activities

Field Trip Itinerary

The field trip includes a 4-day trip. On the first day, students will visit Birmingham, Alabama, and tour the Civil Rights Institute, the Historic Sixteenth Street Baptist Church, and Kelly Ingram Park. On the second day, students will visit Selma, Alabama, and tour the National Voting Rights Museum and participate in the "Footprints to Freedom Tour." On the third day of the field trip, students will visit Montgomery, Alabama, and follow the Selma-to-Montgomery Trail across the Edmund Pettis Bridge, visit the Rosa Parks Museum, tour the Dexter Avenue King Memorial Baptist Church and Dexter Parsonage Museum, and tour the Alabama State Capitol. Students will return home on day four of the trip. Time is built into each day for group and individual process and reflection of the day's events.

Core Counseling Curriculum Unit

For this unit, I deliver three core counseling curriculum lessons over 3 weeks during the class period. The lessons are (I) Multicultural Awareness, (II) Equity and Diversity, and (III) Racial Disparities Presentations. Following is a sample lesson from the unit.

Lesson I: Multicultural Awareness
　　Grade Levels: 11th and 12th grades
　　Domain: Social emotional
　　Objective: Students will identify five unique aspects of their identities.

Mindsets and Behaviors

Mindsets
　　A. Belief in development of whole self, including a healthy balance of mental, socioemotional, and physical well-being
　　B. Sense of belonging in school environment

Behaviors
　　A. Demonstrate critical-thinking skills to make informed decisions
　　B. Gather evidence and consider multiple perspectives to make informed decisions
　　C. Use effective oral and written communication skills and listening skills
　　D. Demonstrate ethical decision making and social responsibility
　　E. Use leadership and teamwork skills to work effectively in diverse teams
　　F. Demonstrate social maturity and behaviors appropriate to the situation and environment

(continued)

EXHIBIT 6.1 (*continued*)
Voices From the Field: Sample Lesson Plan

Materials: "My Multicultural Self" handouts (18 copies), "Definition of Culture" (electronic display on SMART Board), "Microaggressions in Everyday Life" video, "Visualizing Microaggressions Photos" (electronic display on SMART Board), computer, SMART Board, Internet access

Class Activities

A. *My Multicultural Self*: (*Source*: Teaching Tolerance, Retrieved from www.tolerance.org/lesson/my-multicultural-self)—**10 to 15 minutes**

   a. *1 to 2 minutes*: The following definition of *culture* will be displayed on the SMART Board. Ask one student to read this definition aloud for the class:
   "What is culture? It is a shared system of meanings, beliefs, values, and behaviors through which we interpret our experiences. Culture is learned, collective, and changes over time. Culture is generally understood to be 'what we know that everyone like us knows'" (Teaching Tolerance, n.d.).

   b. *3 to 5 minutes*: Next, distribute the "My Multicultural Self" handouts to students. The counselor will display and briefly review one she has completed as a model. Ask students to write their name on the center line. Then, they will use the identity bubbles to name aspects of themselves that are important in defining who they are. Ask students to do this quietly to ensure everyone is able to reflect.

   c. *6 to 8 minutes*: Ask students to reflect on and share how each individual identity colors and shapes the way they view and interact with the world. Use the following prompts to guide the discussion:

      i.   How would you feel if someone ignored one of your multicultural identity bubbles?

      ii. Can you see how ignoring one of your identity bubbles could cause miscommunication? Can anyone give an example?

      iii. Do you have more than these five identities?

   d. Conclude by reminding students that identity is not static but rather is ever evolving and changing based on how we grow and change. "What we once knew to be true about ourselves and others can change over time. For this reason, we should always try to suspend judgment, ask questions of others, and talk with those different from us as much as possible" (Teaching Tolerance, n.d.).

B. *Microaggressions* (*Source*: Anti-Defamation League, Retrieved from www.adl.org/assets/pdf/education-outreach/microaggressions-in-our-lives.pdf)—**30 to 35 minutes**

   a. *10 to 15 minutes*: Play the video "Microaggressions in Everday Life" (4:24 minutes; www.youtube.com/watch?v=BJL2P0JsAS4), featuring

(continued)

EXHIBIT 6.1 (*continued*)

Dr. Derald Wing Sue. Ask students to reflect upon the information in the video using the following discussion prompts:

    i.   What are some examples of microaggression that were revealed in the video?

    ii.   What is the impact of microaggression?

    iii.   How are microaggressions communicated nonverbally?

    iv.   What groups or groups of people are microaggressions directed toward?

    v.   What can we do to combat microaggressions, according to Dr. Sue?

    vi.   What does it mean to "make the invisible visible"?

b. *20 to 25 minutes*:

    i.   Display the six "Visualizing Microaggressions Photos" on the SMART Board, explaining that the photos are from a larger photo exhibit created by a photographer named Kiyun who asked her friends to write down instances of racial microaggression they have encountered and create a series of images of the students holding up placards with their microaggressions. Use the following questions to facilitate a discussion:

    1.   What did you observe in the photos?

    2.   How did you feel looking at these examples of microaggressions?

    3.   Did any of the photos resonate with you? If so, which ones and why?

    4.   Did seeing the photos make you think about microaggressions you have experienced or witnessed?

    5.   Identify the hidden messages or underlying assumptions behind each microaggression. Use the following examples if necessary:

        a.   *Microaggression*—"No, where are you really from?"; *Message*—"You are not American."

        b.   *Microaggression*—"You are so articulate." *Message*—"It is unusual for someone of your race to be intelligent and well-spoken."

    6.   Ask students to consider Dr. Sue's advice for combating microaggressions and think of responses to these microaggressions.

Management of Class: The counselor and teacher will cofacilitate class and discussions. Prior to each lesson, the counselor will remind students of the importance of class participation while also maintaining respect for one another.

Evaluation of the Lesson: Students' completion of the "My Multicultural Self" handouts will be used to evaluate this lesson.

SUMMARY

In this chapter, we highlighted key aspects of career and college readiness curriculum development. Creating curriculum interventions can be a complicated process for beginning school counselors and involves understanding and managing many pieces of information. Specifically, to effectively design a career and college readiness curriculum, school counselors should review state and national standards, write measurable and specific objectives, choose assessment methods, develop and deliver classroom lesson plans and other program activities, and evaluate student outcomes.

···❯ Test Your Knowledge

1. Pretend to be an elementary school counselor. Write a rationale for why you should implement a grades P–5 career and college readiness curriculum for your school.
2. Imagine you are a middle school counselor in a very diverse school. Your school is 35% African American, 35% Hispanic, 20% Asian, and 10% Caucasian. How might you include diversity considerations in a classroom unit on personal values related to career and college exploration?
3. Explain how you might evaluate the following career objective for ninth grade: "At the completion of a career exploration unit, 80% of ninth-grade students will be able to write a five-paragraph research essay on a career of their choice."

REFERENCES

Alexander, N. P. (2000). *Early childhood workshops that work! The essential guide to successful training and workshops.* Beltsville, MD: Gryphon House.

American School Counselor Association. (2012). *The ASCA national model: A framework for school counseling programs* (3rd ed.). Alexandria, VA: Author.

American School Counselor Association (ASCA). (2014). *ASCA mindsets & behaviors for student success: K-12 college- and career-readiness standards for every student.* Alexandria, VA: Author.

Association of American Colleges and Universities. (2010). Critical thinking value rubric. Retrieved from https://www.aacu.org/value/rubrics/critical-thinking

Bandura, A. (1977). *Social learning theory.* Englewood Cliffs, NJ: Prentice Hall.

Bloom, B. S., Engelhart, M. D., Furst, E. J., Hill, W. H., & Krathwohl, D. R. (1956). *Taxonomy of educational objectives: The classification of educational goals.* New York, NY: David McKay Company.

Bourdieu, P. (1977). *Outline of a theory of practice.* Cambridge, United Kingdom: Cambridge University Press.

Brown, D. (2012). *Career information, career counseling, and career development* (10th ed.). Boston, MA: Pearson.

Carter, M., & Curtis, D. (1994). *Training teachers: A harvest of theory and practice.* St. Paul, MN: Redleaf Press.

Gardner, H. (1983). *Frames of mind: The theory of multiple intelligences.* New York, NY: Basic Books.

Gottfredson, L. S. (1981). Circumscription and compromise: A developmental theory of occupational aspirations. *Journal of Counseling Psychology, 28*(6), 545–579. http:// dx.doi.org/10.1037/0022-0167.28.6.545

Graves, M. (1996). *Planning around children's interests: The teacher's idea book 2.* Ypsilanti, MI: High/Scope Press.

Heinrich, R., Molenda, M., Russell, J. D., & Smaldino, S. E. (1996). *Instructional media and technologies for learning.* Englewood Cliffs, NJ: Merrill.

Holland, J. L. (1997). *Making vocational choices: A theory of vocational personalities and work environments* (3rd ed.). Odessa, FL: Psychological Assessment Resources.

Jalongo, M. R., & Isenberg, J. P. (2004). *Exploring your role: A practitioner's introduction to early childhood education* (2nd ed.). Upper Saddle River, NJ: Pearson.

Niles, S. G., & Harris-Bowlesbey, J. (2009). *Career development interventions in the 21st century* (3rd ed.). Upper Saddle River, NJ: Merrill.

Sharf, R. S. (2006). *Applying career development theory to counseling* (4th ed.). Belmont, CA: Thomson.

Super, D. E. (1980). A life-span, life-space approach to career development. *Journal of Vocational Behavior, 16*(3), 282–298. http://dx.doi.org/10.1016/0001-8791(80)90056-1

Teaching Tolerance. (n.d.). My multicultural self. Retrieved from http://www.tolerance .org/lesson/my-multicultural-self

Utley, C. A., Obiakor, F. E., & Bakken, J. P. (2011). Culturally responsive practices for culturally and linguistically diverse students with learning disabilities. *Learning Disabilities: A Contemporary Journal, 1*, 5–18.

Wang, Y., Davidson, M. M., Yakushko, O. F., Savoy, H. B., Tan, J. A., & Bleier, J. K. (2003). The scale of ethnocultural empathy: Development, validation, and reliability. *Journal of Counseling Psychology, 50*(2), 221–234.

SEVEN

Career and College Readiness for Grades P–1: Exposure and Awareness

At a research university, in a graduate-level research course in education, students were asked by a guest lecturer, "At what age should career counseling and education begin?" The students (who represented a wide range of fields including higher education, curriculum and instruction, and education leadership) voted and overwhelmingly said either late high school (junior and senior year) or in the first year of college. Out of a class of 23, only two of the graduate students indicated that elementary school was the appropriate time to begin such exploration. It was apparent that the majority of graduate students in the course knew little about the developmental nature of career and college readiness for P–12 students. In this chapter, we explore the early elementary years and how career and college education can positively impact academic success and open postsecondary options, even for very young students.

CAREER AND COLLEGE READINESS FOR PreK, KINDERGARTEN, AND FIRST GRADE

The American School Counselor Association's (ASCA's) National Model (2012), ASCA Mindsets and Behaviors (2014), and federal initiatives such as the National Math and Science Initiative (2017) and the Every Student Succeeds Act (Executive Office of the President, 2015) all underscore the importance of career and college readiness for all students. Historically, attention to career and college readiness for students in PreK, kindergarten, and first grade has been limited, as schools have concentrated mainly on late adolescence and high school, yet studies show that young children can realistically understand careers and need career education in order to connect academics to the world of work. Development of career and college readiness skills such as critical thinking and problem solving begins early in life as well. In this chapter, readers will note that we focus more on career development than on college exploration. Young children need to have a foundation for understanding what careers are and how the school day and workday are alike, an understanding of their interests, and a connection between what they are learning in school and world of work before making links to postsecondary expectations. We advocate building that base in P–1 and allowing students to familiarize themselves with the language of careers before introducing how careers relate to postsecondary training options.

In this chapter, we use Gottfredson's career theory and Young's (1983) eco-systemic career development concepts to illustrate how school counselors can design practical and fun career and college readiness activities for PreK, K, and first-grade students. Additionally, we explore stakeholder education related to career and college readiness for parents, teachers, and community partners. Using developmentally appropriate play techniques and student competencies, we examine how to effectively design and implement PreK, K, and first-grade career and college readiness activities for classroom counseling as well as grade-level activities.

DEVELOPMENTAL OVERVIEW

In order to effectively implement career and college readiness education and counseling in PreK, K, and grade 1, it is important to consider the overall development of children at those grade levels. What follows is a general overview of child development and how each area of development connects to career growth. Please note that this overview is general and may not apply to every child.

Psychosocial and Socioemotional Development

According to Erikson (1963), children between the ages of 3 and 5 are in the psychosocial stage known as *initiative versus guilt*. During this time, the main psychosocial task is to actively explore one's environment and to develop a sense of control over physical surroundings. Therefore, children in this age group are very active, inquisitive, and, because of their natural curiosity (Sharf, 2006), love to play in the world of fantasy. They are beginning to engage with other children, although much of their play is still side-to-side rather than face-to-face play (particularly in PreK), and the major influence in the life of children in this age group is predominantly the family unit.

Around the transition period from kindergarten to first grade, children begin to enter the stage of *industry versus inferiority* (Erikson, 1963). The focus in this stage is on children learning and mastering academic tasks; students are continually learning new information and, particularly in today's educational environment, are tested to demonstrate their competence. Students who excel at tasks gain self-confidence while those who do not often develop feelings of inferiority (e.g., poor self-concept). These positive and negative feelings might affect future career and college outcomes as well as overall self-esteem. Teachers and counselors may begin to notice some children in PreK, K, and first grade starting to have negative thoughts about themselves, having doubts about their likability or attractiveness, or worrying that they are not smart enough. Self-esteem may be built through helping children have success experiences and assisting them in recognizing their unique strengths.

During the early elementary years, two major feelings develop that contribute to socioemotional development: shame and guilt. Shame comes from feeling humiliated, while guilt comes from feeling badly about hurting another person (Belsky, 2007). While shame can foster unhealthy socioemotional development, guilt may be essential to ensuring that children learn that other peoples' feelings matter. Learning to care about the feelings of others, but not be consumed by focusing on others, is an important skill. Further, Belsky identified an orientation toward prosocial tendencies as an important part of socioemotional development. Prosocial behavior is described as "behavior intended to benefit another" (Eisenberg et al., 1999, p. 1360). Prosocial behaviors may include comforting others, using manners, sharing, engaging in cooperative work or play, exhibiting kindness, and displaying empathy for others (Belsky, 2007; Simmons & Sands-Dudelczyk, 1983) and are largely formed during early elementary years. In the context of career and college readiness, socioemotional maturity is a critical element for developing effective relationships in college and in the workplace.

One final socioemotional skill that is critical during this developmental period is emotional regulation (Belsky, 2007). Emotional regulation becomes possible as children gain self-awareness and self-control. According to Belsky, emotional regulation includes learning to manage feelings and deal appropriately with emotions—neither having externalizing (e.g., inappropriate outbursts, fighting, demanding, controlling behaviors, or acting out aggressively toward others) nor internalizing (e.g., timidity, self-consciousness, unmanageable anxiety) tendencies. Children with emotional regulatory capacities display balanced emotion that is appropriately expressed given their circumstances. So, a child with positive emotional regulation skills who falls down may cry but is consolable and, once comforted, resumes normal activities. Conversely, a child with poor emotional regulation skills who falls down may cry but may also get up and, in a fit of rage, hit others who are nearby or blame others for falling down. Emotional self-regulation is important for success in both career and college because of the need to get along with others in collaborative group work as well as deal with stress, anxiety, and conflict.

Cognitive Development

According to Piaget (1977), children in PreK, K, and first grade are generally in the cognitive stage of development known as *preoperational thought*. During this stage, children have difficulty conceptualizing time (such as the future) and, therefore, may have difficulty projecting what their future lives may be like, including considering what careers they may want. This does not mean, however, that they can't think about and learn about careers and college.

Children in this stage generally do not display logical, linear thought and are often very egocentric. *Egocentrism* in regard to preoperational thought refers to the child's lack of understanding that other people have worldviews or perspectives that differ from their own (Belsky, 2007). Children at this age may display thought influenced by fantasy, or magical thinking, and can have some difficulty discerning what is real or not; children in preoperational thought literally believe that what they see is real (Belsky, 2007).

Learning for children at this stage of cognitive development requires that adults delivering instruction are excellent scaffolders, meaning that they break down content into smaller, more manageable pieces of information, give students lots of opportunities to practice what is learned in order to achieve mastery, and give students autonomy to direct some learning activities (Belsky, 2007). According to Vygotsky (1978), children use a working memory where they actively process information based on prior learning or discard information that is not necessary to remember. Adults may help children improve their memory capacities by incorporating activities that involve repetition and practice. These skills are highly necessary for future academic success.

Children can begin problem-based learning at this age and their natural curiosity lends to this type of learning. For example, students in one preschool class had a garden where they were growing carrots. A number of the students and a teacher noticed that some of the carrots had been eaten. The teacher had the class think about what kind of animal might eat carrots and how they could find out for sure what was eating the carrots. The class hypothesized that a rabbit was eating their carrots. They also had a parent agree to install a motion video camera that could film the culprit eating the carrots. They later discovered it was a raccoon! This kind of hands-on learning is ideal for young children.

Other considerations for addressing the learning needs of young children include using contextual learning strategies (e.g., using examples that are familiar to students) and providing interactive and experiential learning opportunities where students can manipulate and interact with objects and tap into their need for fantasy and creative play. Counselors can be most effective when they meet students where they are developmentally, starting with familiar concepts, then exposing them to new ideas through activities that allow them to discover. Overall, students at this age are very active learners. Career play is very appropriate and can easily be integrated in classroom career instruction. We explore play techniques later in this chapter.

Moral Development

According to Kohlberg (1981) most children in PreK, K, and first grade are in the preoperational stage of moral development and, therefore, judge actions as either right or wrong based on the consequences of the action. In short, if the person committing the action gets punished, then students in this stage of development would believe the action was wrong. Two forces of thought are predominant in preoperational moral development: (a) obedience and punishment characterized by deference and respect to authorities, and (b) self-interest–driven behavior characterized by behavior that benefits the self. For this reason, students at this age are impressionable and may show interest mainly in careers held by their parents, teachers, and other adults they want to please rather than based on career knowledge or exploration.

Students in grades PreK to grade 1 also are vulnerable to integrating judgments about careers and college based on the perspectives of family or other adults. Indeed, according to Kohlberg (1981), children in this developmental period have an orientation to obedience and make choices based on what is denoted as right and wrong from the authorities in their lives. It is very common for students at this age to tattle on their peers if they see them breaking a rule. Likewise, they may have very rigid beliefs about which careers and postsecondary educational options are acceptable and which are not. They also might categorize careers as "good" or "bad"—for example, being a police officer may be perceived as a "good" career and being a sanitation worker may be perceived as a "bad" career based on judgments the students have internalized from their family or from gender and social status socialization.

Gender

In early elementary school, children's preoperational cognitive development leads to a tendency to categorize pesople, including by gender. In PreK, K, and grade 1, students have very concrete views of what men and women should look like, how they should act, and what roles are appropriate. Much of this comes from socialization in the family where children are often given sex-typed toys and their parents or guardians treat them in sex-typed ways. For example, girls may be given play dishes, a kitchen set, and a doll for gifts, whereas boys may receive tools, cars or trucks, and building blocks. This type of gender socialization can have a lasting impact throughout the life span (Ivey, Ivey, Myers, & Sweeney, 2005).

According to Belsky (2007), "once children understand which basic category (girl or boy) they belong in, they selectively attend to the activities of their own sex" (p. 193). By early elementary school, many students have begun to play with same-sex friends primarily, have received gender-type reinforcement from family members, and understand that their sex is a permanent characteristic (can't be changed by chance). These differences manifest in play and school through common behavior patterns; in general, girls are more collaborative while boys are more competitive, girls are usually calmer while boys experience greater excitability, and boys seek group dominance in play while girls display nurturance (Belsky, 2007). Finally, gender matters in career decision making for early elementary students. In the next section we review Gottfredson's theory and just how predominant sex typing is in the career development of children.

RELEVANT CAREER THEORY FOR PreK, K, AND FIRST-GRADE STUDENTS: GOTTFREDSON (1981) AND YOUNG (1983)

Gottfredson's Theory of Circumscription and Compromise

Historically, school systems have introduced career and college readiness activities for students in high school. This approach is incredibly problematic, according to Gottfredson's (1981) theory, because children and adolescents have already been circumscribing (i.e., narrowing) their career options since early elementary school. Recent support for Gottfredson's theory came from a study of elementary children conducted by Auger, Blackhurst, and Wahl (2005), where they found that by fifth grade, many students had already circumscribed their career aspirations and self-limited their career options. Indeed, it appears that circumscription begins around the age of 6. This finding underscores the need to continually work on broadening students' understanding of career and existing postsecondary options throughout P–12 education. In this chapter, we focus on Stage 1: *Orientation to Size and Power* and Stage 2: *Orientation to Sex Roles,* as these are the predominant stages of career development for children in grades PreK–1.

According to Sharf (2006), Gottfredson's Stage 1: *Orientation to Size and Power* refers to how children begin to understand that their world is different from the world of adults. They realize that there are limits to what they can do because of their size and power; for example, a child may see that his father owns a lawn care company where he has to run lawn equipment such as mowers, weed eaters, and edgers. The child realizes that the work his father does takes strength and height that the child does not have. So, although the child understands that the tools used for lawn care are part of the father's work, the child also believes that he is too small or weak to do that type of work.

As children get chronologically older (around the age of 6), they enter Stage 2: *Orientation to Sex Roles.* Once this occurs, they begin to develop a strong sense of sex-typing, which dictates which careers are tolerable for girls and which are tolerable for boys. This boundary can be very definitive, and adults must be intentional and deliberate in order to challenge sex-type assumptions. We explore this stage more fully in Chapter 8 as it affects second and third graders comprehensively.

In spite of children's career assumptions, there is reason for optimism, according to Gottfredson (1981, 2002). Specifically, she notes that children can be encouraged to reconsider their career choices by being given formative new experiences that challenge career sex types. When school counselors understand how to do this effectively, they may increase student perceptions of possible career options.

Young's Career Concepts

As previously mentioned in Chapter 1, and according to the National Poverty Center (2011), in the United States one in five children under the age of 18 lives in poverty. With this in mind, school counselors have to consider how the systems in which children live may affect their understanding of careers and college. Students living in poverty may have fewer opportunities for exploring academic interests or exposure to events and places that stimulate future career and college decision-making processes. For example, students living in poverty may not have access to museums, galleries, or travel. Young (1983) asserted that an ecosystemic approach to career development was critical, and this may be especially true for elementary school students, as their parents and teachers are so influential in their lives. Additionally, teachers and parents may not have received career or college education as young children and may be unsure of how or why they should help their early elementary school-aged

TABLE 7.1 ASCA Mindsets and Behaviors for Preschool Through First-Grade Curriculum Planning Focus

CATEGORY 1: MINDSETS STANDARDS		
Belief in development of whole self, including a healthy balance of mental, socioemotional, and physical well-being Self-confidence in ability to succeed Sense of belonging in the school environment Positive attitude toward work and learning		
CATEGORY 2: BEHAVIOR STANDARDS		
Learning Strategies	**Self-Management Skills**	**Social Skills**
Demonstrate creativity	Demonstrate self-discipline and self-control	Use effective collaboration and cooperation skills
Apply self-motivation and self-direction to learning	Demonstrate personal safety skills	Use effective collaboration and cooperation skills

children explore careers or colleges. Thus, considering how to engage teachers and parents within the scope of a comprehensive school counseling program to promote career and college readiness is important, and we address this concern more fully later in this chapter. Beyond considering Gottfredson's and Young's work with small children, school counselors must also have an understanding of how to integrate play techniques in career and college education for elementary students as part of the fun in the career and college readiness curriculum. Further, the curriculum should align with the ASCA National Model (2012) and the Mindsets and Behaviors (2014). Although school counselors will need to consider adjusting the curriculum to the unique needs of their own school populations, we suggest concentrating on the following ASCA Mindsets and Behaviors when planning career and college readiness interventions for P–1 students (see Table 7.1).

Through curriculum that supports students in becoming good classroom citizens, using study, homework, and test-taking skills to be academically successful, and promoting creativity, safety and motivation, school counselors can encourage students to build their efficacy to become strong leaders and learners. The school counseling curriculum should be broad, energizing, and fun for P–1 students, and school counselors need to remember the incredible value of play for the experience of learning with this age group.

PLAY TECHNIQUES AND CAREER AND COLLEGE EXPOSURE FOR P–1 STUDENTS

Play is the natural language of children and is the manner in which children communicate (Landreth, 1982). Play is used by children to explore and experiment; therefore, it is a critical learning tool and part of the process by which children can understand their own thoughts, feelings, ideas, and behaviors (Frank, 1982; McMahon, 1992). Play is a means for promoting formative cognitive development (Yawkey & Diantoniis, 1984). Further, McMahon (1992) contended that play may be one of the best learning mediums for children with learning difficulties or disabilities. Through the manipulation of play materials, children resolve conflicts, practice new behaviors, and engage the world around them. Additionally, children use play to understand the functions of things in their environment (Caster, 1984). For instance, when playing with building blocks (such as Legos, Tinker Toys, or Lincoln Logs) children learn about building and construction. Similarly, children playing with tools and a tool bench become oriented to the use of those tools as they begin to explore how they are used in the real world (e.g., a hammer is used for pounding). Using play techniques to engage children might help adults in schools develop relationships through establishing mutual positive affect, reacting with warmth and empathy, conveying caring and nurturance, and developing rapport through eye contact and verbal and nonverbal behaviors (Wettig, Franke, & Fjordbak, 2006). Therefore, play is a very functional approach for school counselors to use in teaching young children, particularly PreK, K, and first-grade students, about career, college, and real world success skills.

Some might ask if play therapy should be used by school counselors. And if so, what kinds of play? Structured? Guided? Unstructured? According to Nelson (1982), there are many uses of play in therapy, yet not all types of play therapy may be appropriate for elementary school settings due to the nature of the environment and the intended use in learning. For example, play therapy has been used in the treatment of severe sexual abuse for young children, but this type of counseling is most likely out of the scope of competence of school counselors and an inappropriate use of service delivery time; therefore, this type of play therapy should be referred to a specialist (ASCA, 2012). For the purposes of this chapter we are focusing on large-group, structured, and directed play in PreK to first-grade classrooms for the purpose of engaging students in learning about careers. Although many elementary school counselors may have received some training in play techniques in their graduate programs, they are not required to be registered play therapists and most do not have advanced training in play therapy techniques. Thus, the interventions we discuss in the following require little specific training and could be reasonably and ethically initiated by most school counselors. We review some basic principles of play as they relate to career exploration.

The Nature of Play and Learning

According to McMahon (1992), play allows children to take risks through imagination, a key benefit of the fantasy nature of play. In terms of careers and college, children are allowed to explore possibilities through the creativity and autonomy afforded in play in spite of the realities in which they live. Applied to careers, children may choose to explore the world of an astronaut (space toys), an archeologist (dinosaurs and digging), or a safari guide (toy animals and vehicles) even if these opportunities are not accessible through their home or immediate surroundings. Equally important, during play children might choose to step out of expected gender roles; girls may be construction workers and boys may be cooks and caregivers. This exact realm of play, fantasy and exploration, might be the initial way in which career circumscription (Gottfredson, 1981) can be combatted for very young children (grades PreK–1). McMahon (1992) also pointed out that play comes without the risks associated with the real world; in terms of play and career exploration in schools, children may be or do anything without being told "You are not capable of that." They may play the role of a doctor, a scientist, or the president without the reminders of social stigma, gender roles, or low social expectations. Truly, children may be free to explore the careers they wish to explore if school counselors and teachers create the expectation that play is autonomous. Explorative play can be integrated in the classroom through the use of career centers where students have access to dress-up and play items associated with careers. Students may visit these centers when they have completed their classwork and during structured breaks.

Play may also be integrated in the core counseling curriculum. Ericksonian play therapy (named after Milton Erickson) uses an approach that may be particularly helpful in schools due to the limited amount of time the school counselor has in each classroom. In the Ericksonian approach, two layers of communication are occurring, known as parallel communication or *refraction* (Marvasti, 1997). We will use puppets as the medium to illustrate the concept. In this type of play, the counselor introduces children to a metaphorical problem similar to the child's own problem or issue needing resolution. In regard to career, in order to promote career awareness and decision-making self-efficacy, a school counselor may introduce a puppet to children during a classroom lesson. In the following case, this activity is used at the culmination of a classroom unit on careers to help students with application of prior knowledge. The puppet's dilemma is that she doesn't know about careers and so the students will be teaching the puppet what they have learned and will help the puppet make career decisions. In doing so, the students' learning will be reinforced, resolving confusion about careers and career decision making. Exhibit 7.1 gives an example of the use of puppets as a play technique with a group of kindergarten students.

EXHIBIT 7.1
An Example of Refraction in a Kindergarten Classroom Career Lesson

Counselor: Okay, students, today I have a very special guest for you to meet. Her name is Sally. (Counselor holds up puppet.) Oh, no! Sally looks sad. (Puppet is slouching, looking down.) Sally, what's wrong?

Puppet: In my class, my teacher said we are going to be learning about careers, but I don't know what a career is.

Counselor: Sally, the students in this class have also been learning about careers. Maybe the students would like to help you. Students, would you like to help Sally? (Students say yes—loudly.)

Puppet: Oh, thank you so much. (Sally looks up.)

Counselor: Great. Okay, who can tell Sally what a career is?

Student 1: It's like something you want to do when you grow up. Kind of like work only you plan to do it.

(continued)

EXHIBIT 7.1 (continued)
An Example of Refraction in a Kindergarten Classroom Career Lesson

Counselor: Thank you, something you do when you grow up, something planned.

Student 2: And you are trained to do something. You might go to college or be trained by someone to do a career.

Student 3: Ummm . . . my dad . . . works in an office. And my mom works at a school as a teacher. Those are their careers.

Student 4: It's work you like to do.

Counselor: Thank you all. Sally, does that help?

Sally: I think I understand that career is something that a person chooses and plans to do, it requires training beyond school, and it is something that a person likes and wants to do. Is that right?

Students: Yes!

Sally: But I don't know what I want to be when I grow up! I don't even know what choices I have!

Counselor: Well, Sally, that's okay. Many girls and boys are unsure of what they want to be when they grow up. Students, how many of you are unsure of what you want to be? (Some students raise hands.)

Puppet: Golly! I thought I was the only one!

Counselor: Students, what have we discussed about careers that might help Sally?

Student Responses: Careers in your neighborhood.

Counselor: Good answer! Yes, we talked about community helpers. What were some examples of community helpers?

Student Responses: Mail carrier, firefighter, police officer, day-care worker.

Counselor: Well, these students are great listeners, Sally, because we did talk about all of those. What other types of career things have we talked about this year?

Students: Your family's careers. What your mom or your granny or your uncles and people like that do . . . what their career is. We also talked about our likes and dislikes.

Counselor: Oh my! I can tell you all have been really listening. I definitely think we can help. Sally, let's start by talking about the careers you see in your neighborhood. . . .

By helping the puppet (Sally), students are integrating and applying prior career learning and are also beginning to use the career language they are developing (Pellegrini, 1984). The material the students suggest to the counselor to help Sally solidifies salient information they have acquired and demonstrates that they are internally thinking through developmentally appropriate strategies for career decision making, a skill they are just starting to learn and a key piece of developing career maturity. Through a fun and engaging activity, the counselor is helping the students use what they know to resolve a parallel conflict.

Counselors may also use play in early childhood education to allow students to explore a career. An example of this happened when a group of PreK teachers and the school counselor took PreK students to the local fire department for a tour and fire safety tips at the end of a unit on community helpers. The students were all given plastic fire safety helmets and honorary firefighter badges. The children were given 20 minutes of playtime in the field area beside the firehouse to play firefighters with the real firefighters. Through the use of an obstacle course and their new gear, the students were guided through a simulated fire field where they got the chance to experience the role of a firefighter, regardless of gender. A digital photograph of each child was taken and printed at school on a sheet of paper that said: "What I learned about firefighters." Each child was assisted by his or her teacher and teacher's aide in writing a sentence about what he or she learned at the firehouse. In this way, students were integrating imitative role-play (playing the firefighter) and symbolic meaning (words to describe what they learned) in order to continue to develop a lexicon for career with a conscious understanding of career roles (Pellegrini, 1984). At the end of the day each child was sent home with a fire safety coloring and workbook for their families with instructions for parents about talking to their child about fire safety in their home, how to call 911, and community helper careers.

THE SCHOOL COUNSELOR AND THE CORE COUNSELING CURRICULUM

During PreK, K, and first grade there are some essential career, academic, and personal social skills that are vital for postsecondary success. Most importantly, many students may not know anything about what careers or college are or even have a language to discuss careers or college in PreK. The core counseling curriculum should focus on the major tasks of beginning to understand career. Specific to careers, by the end of first grade, students should be able to (a) recognize careers and how they are different from jobs, (b) identify community helpers, (c) use career language, (d) demonstrate positive attitudes toward self, others, school opportunities, and feelings of competence, and (e) articulate likes and dislikes (Missouri Center for Career Education, 2006). Additionally, when students have been given opportunities to learn about careers in PreK and kindergarten, they are often ready to learn about tools of the trade for careers. For example, students may start to recognize that doctors use stethoscopes, firefighters use a water hose, musicians use instruments and sheet music, and carpenters use hammers and saws. By the end of first grade they may be able to understand that people use different tools to perform specific work, that work occurs in a variety of locations, and that various types of occupations require different clothes (i.e., a nurse wears scrubs). They also might be introduced to the idea that people might need to spend more time in school in order to become a doctor or a firefighter or a musician—introducing the concept of college.

In developing the career and college readiness curriculum, school counselors should consider several pieces of information including the ASCA National Model (2012), ASCA Mindsets and Behaviors (2014) (see Appendix C), and needs assessment and critical data for the population at the specific school where they work. To begin, ASCA (2014) delineates the standards for student competence in the area of career and college readiness in terms of the attitudes, beliefs, and behaviors that students will need to be successful in exploring and making career and college decisions. We reviewed these and other resources in Chapter 6.

Helping students achieve these competencies is critical to early academic and career development and should be guided by the school counselor who has expertise in these areas. As noted in Chapter 6, curriculum development is an essential role for school counselors and writing lesson plans is an important task. School counselors need to be strategic given that their time in the classroom is limited. Each lesson should be methodically planned, evidence based, goal-oriented, and designed with specific outcomes in mind. In P–1, much of the career and college exposure is done in the classroom setting or through the creation and cultivation of a career- and college-bound culture. Moreover, an effective school counseling program has data to demonstrate that these things are happening.

In order to demonstrate program effectiveness, it is important that school counselors consider how they will assess student learning outcomes and they will need to be flexible when choosing methods for assessment with P–1 learners because of early elementary students' disparate levels of reading comprehension. Often counselors must be creative to ensure that they are accurately assessing student knowledge in a developmentally appropriate way. With early elementary students, counselors may want to use matching and other recognition activities. For instance, as previously mentioned, by the end of first grade students can realistically understand the tools that go with specific occupations. Imagine that a school counselor had written the following outcome objective for a lesson on "Tools of the Trade" using the ABCD method highlighted in Chapter 6: *At the completion of this lesson, 80% of first-grade students will be able to accurately match tools to specific occupations four out of five times.* For the lesson, the school counselor has 30 toy tools (e.g., plastic hammer). After explaining tools of the trade, the school counselor hangs pictures of careers around the room. Students are placed in dyads and are given two or three "tools" per dyad. They are asked to place their tools by the careers they match. Next, the school counselor and the students discuss each picture, which tools match each picture, and how the tools are used in each specific career. Examples might include a hairdryer for a hairstylist, a rolling pin for a baker, a stethoscope for a doctor, and so on. After the lesson the school counselor could give the students a worksheet with five pictures of occupations being performed (i.e., teacher, firefighter, doctor, construction worker, and artist). Opposite of the occupations are pictures of five instruments (i.e., hammer, water hose, paint palette, stethoscope, and chalk). Students are asked to draw a line from the "tool" to the matching career. The school counselor is assessing whether or not 80% of students can get four out of five correct to assess student learning for this activity. Again, the point is not to grade the students' individual work as right or wrong. The school counselor may collect the students' assessments and calculate the percent of correct answers. The data gathered is meant to help the school counselor assess whether or not students understood the lesson content rather than to give a score, or grade, to students' work. The school counselor is simply assessing whether or not, as a whole, students were able to match tools and careers. Exhibit 7.2 gives an example of one school counselor's career curriculum development for kindergarten and first grade.

EXHIBIT 7.2
Voices From the Field: Early Elementary Career Exposure

Meghan Birch, PLPC

School Counselor, Dorseyville Elementary School

I am a school counselor at an elementary school in a low socioeconomic, rural area. There are 377 students from PreK–sixth grade that attend my school. The demographics are 92% African American, 7% White, and 1% Hispanic, and 100% of our students are on free lunch. Because my students are from a low socioeconomic background, most have limited exposure to career options. With the support of my administration, I am able to implement a comprehensive career and college readiness program in grades K–6. Although there are benefits to teaching career lessons in each grade, I especially enjoy working with the lower grades because of the opportunity to broaden the range of career options these students consider. I will give an overview here of typical career lessons in my kindergarten and first-grade classes.

A good starting point with kindergarten is simply to expose them to a variety of careers. I am often surprised by their limited knowledge of career options. I usually begin the first lesson by asking students to name different careers they have seen in their families. Student responses typically vary between local fast-food restaurants and convenience stores in the area, which seem to indicate a limited exposure to careers or misunderstanding of the definition of career. I want to begin in kindergarten to expand their understanding of a career and how they can decide which career paths interest them.

All students seem to love puppets, especially the younger ones (although I am always surprised at how excited my fifth and sixth graders get about puppets!). I introduce my kindergarten classroom lessons using an entertaining pair of puppets representing a police officer and chef. The puppets keep the children engaged and add an extra element of fun. From the carpet, students interact with the puppets as they discuss their careers with each other and the class. The puppets ask the class questions about their classroom jobs and start to help students define "career" as a combination of what you

(continued)

EXHIBIT 7.2 (continued)
Voices From the Field: Early Elementary Career Exposure

enjoy doing (interest) and what you are good at (skill/aptitude). Each puppet talks about his career and how his interests and skills match his career. At the kindergarten level, I wrestle with whether students are ready to understand these complex topics, but I have found value in introducing this concept early. Knowing that some students may not be ready to grasp this abstract definition, I revisit this topic in my first-grade lessons.

Kindergarten students often have the misconception that a person should not have dislikes. I want students to understand that it is important to be aware of likes, as well as dislikes, in exploring career options. Many kindergartners think that you must like, or pretend to like, every activity. The puppets help me to address this misconception through their dialogue. One puppet will say he doesn't like something—usually eliciting a gasp or laugh from the students—and the other puppet will explain that it is okay to have likes and dislikes. I use the puppets to explain the importance of knowing what you dislike in order to decide what careers are best for you.

After our time on the carpet, students complete a worksheet with four quadrants on which they draw pictures of their favorite activities at school and at home and their least favorite activities at school and at home. In reviewing students' work samples, I am looking for student work that represents likes and dislikes appropriately and reveals a beginning understanding of these preferences.

In subsequent lessons with kindergarten students we discuss how careers are different, but all important. I use a book such as the *LMNO Peas*, a career read-aloud, to talk about a variety of careers and how they are useful. There are many follow-up activity sheets from this book involving letters of the alphabet and careers that begin with each letter. In these work samples I reinforce students who choose to include previously unfamiliar careers in their responses. The career learning goals for the series of kindergarten lesson are: (a) to understand that the word *career* refers to activities that combine skills and interests, (b) to identify likes, dislikes, and skills that can help you choose a career, and (c) to understand that all careers are important in some way. I am also reinforcing classroom literacy skills (academics) through the use of reading and writing.

With first graders, I start to introduce the idea of career clusters. I use a simplified four career cluster approach: careers outside/working with animals, careers working with technology, careers making things, and careers working with people. In second grade, the clusters are narrowed into six categories, and then by third grade I begin to introduce the full 16 career clusters. Ideally, I like to come to each first-grade class for three lessons. In the first lesson I introduce the concept of a career as being more than a job, involving training, skills, and interests. Defining and identifying skills and interests can be an entire lesson in itself depending on the level of the students. Next, I introduce the four career clusters, usually through a presentation with

(continued)

EXHIBIT 7.2 (*continued*)

plenty of pictures and a handout to go along. We discuss examples of careers in each cluster and I ask them to think about the clusters that best fit their skills and interests.

Once the students seem to have an understanding of the career clusters, we play a matching game using a poster at the front of the room, divided into four quadrants containing each of the four career clusters. Using cards with the names of different careers, I call on students one at a time to place a career card in the correct cluster. Students love participating in the activity and helping their classmates choose the correct cluster. The activity also provides an extra incentive for students to stay engaged during the presentation in order to participate in the activity afterwards. The learning goals of my first-grade career lessons are: (a) to define *career* (as a combination of skills, interests, and training), (b) identify the four broad career clusters, and (c) to categorize careers within those clusters. I typically use a short assessment at the end of the series of lessons in which students are asked to place careers from a word bank into one of the four career clusters. By the end of the first-grade career lessons, typically 80% to 90% of the students are able to match careers with the appropriate cluster.

As you see from Exhibit 7.2, a lot of thought, planning, organization, and assessment is done when developing and providing classroom lessons. From the onset, the school counselor must have lesson objectives, some ideas about what students in her school know based on culture and geography, a sense of the students' developmental abilities, and some creative ideas for engaging students during classroom presentations. So far, she has been able to demonstrate some impressive outcomes. However, implementing the career and college readiness curriculum in P–12 schools is not the sole responsibility of the school counselor. Following, we discuss the important roles that various stakeholders play in students' career and college readiness development even as early as PreK.

IMPORTANCE OF STAKEHOLDERS

Parents/guardians, extended family members, and other adults are highly influential in the lives of PreK, K, and first-grade students. Helping stakeholders develop awareness and knowledge of careers can foster positive communication and interaction about careers between adults and kids. Through collaboration and consultation, providing faculty in-service training, offering parent workshops, and developing a comprehensive career and college readiness curriculum, school counselors are well positioned to assist stakeholders in becoming more aware of the needs of their children/students as well as the roles they all can play in helping students become exposed to and more aware of careers and college.

Stopping the Dream Squasher

Adults often have the inclination to promote what they perceive to be realistic career and college options for children rather than allowing kids to simply explore. In other words, they may intervene to stop students from imagining or discussing careers or postsecondary educational options that they perceive as being difficult to attain or undesirable in some way. For example, the first author was at a family's home when their 6-year-old son brought out a play guitar and began strumming and screaming "I'm a rock star!!! Yeah, yeah, yeah . . . I'm a rock star!!!" The father laughed and said, "I hope not, that means you'll be starving or eating cans of ravioli for the rest of your life." Most of the adults in the room laughed at the father's joking cliché about the starving artist. However, it is important for parents to realize that a natural interest their child may have could be linked to many careers, and that within career clusters there may be many lucrative careers and opportunities for gainful employment. Although the child in this example may not have had a true aspiration to be a rock star (he was simply playing at the time), there is room to discuss careers even in the context of ordinary play. For example, careers in the music industry go well beyond rock star to include music producers, technicians, talent scouts, signing agents for record labels, videographers, promoters, and disc jockeys, among others. Helping parents expand their vocabulary and understanding of careers gives them a common language to discuss careers with their children. Also, providing concrete examples of the subtle and not-so-subtle ways they might squash their children's dreams may encourage them to monitor their reactions.

A similar scenario happened with the first author (an elementary school counselor at the time) and a first-grade teacher. The teacher had students in her classroom write down on a piece of paper what they wanted to be when they grew up. Five of the boys in the class wrote down "football player" (it may be contextually important to note that this occurred the week of the Super Bowl). The teacher was frustrated and began to tell the class what a poor career choice football is and how most people don't become professional athletes. The teacher came to the counselor later and shared her frustration and exasperation about what she perceived to be poor choices. The first author then encouraged the teacher to help students explore related areas of work to professional sports, including sports journalists, reporters, physical therapists, marketers, trainers, coaches, sports agents, and others. By assisting the teacher in understanding how to link students' interests with a broader range of career opportunities, the author was hopefully able to intervene against future incidents of dream squashing!

Working With Teachers to Integrate Career and College Information in Classroom Curriculum

Teachers play an integral role in student academic and career development. To begin, teachers influence students' understanding of how classroom instruction relates to careers and the world of work, provide meaningful learning opportunities for students both in and out of the classroom, and influence the positive work habits and attitudes students develop (Curry, Belser, & Binns, 2013). Yet, many teachers may not have received training in how to integrate career or college content into their existing curriculum, so we begin by discussing career and college faculty in service for early elementary teachers.

Faculty in Service for Early Elementary Teachers

When teachers are asked to integrate career and college information in the education curriculum, they may feel hesitant due to the overwhelming demands placed on them already from high-stakes testing and other measures of accountability. However, when school counselors demonstrate that integrating career and college information is a natural adjunct to the existing curriculum and does not require an extraordinary amount of time, teachers may be more open. Illustrating the infusion of career and college content for teachers is critical and may be done through faculty in-service programs, team meetings, or one-on-one consultations. Sample faculty in-service activities might include: how to find quality guest speakers for career or college topics, finding out about careers and colleges through technology (e.g., demonstrating *O*Net* and the *Occupational Outlook Handbook* online), connecting classroom content to the world of work or college majors, or providing information about science, technology, engineering, and mathematics (STEM) careers and STEM content, and so forth.

Developing Positive Work Habits and Work Attitudes

Beyond assisting teachers with how to integrate career and college information within the academic curriculum, school counselors may also help teachers emphasize workplace (and academic) success skills. Work habits and work attitudes begin to develop very early in life. These habits include organization, community and social responsibility, cooperation, sharing, appropriate participation, and emotional self-regulation. Students can learn to enjoy and appreciate the importance of work and community through classroom interactions. One kindergarten teacher described how she worked to promote community and social responsibility in her classroom. She stated that she had weekly assignments for each child (such as being line leader, pushing chairs in under desks, collecting papers, and organizing materials) and that these responsibilities allowed each child to try a different role each week while always contributing to the organization of the classroom.

Creating a College-Going Culture

It is never too early to promote a college-going culture, and students need to hear consistent messages from the adults around them about high expectations. Creating a college-going culture does not have to be through large scale events; it may take place through subtle, intentional means on a daily basis. One example came from an elementary school that purposely calls each of its entering kindergarten classes by their intended date of college graduation. Thus, students entering kindergarten in 2020 would be called the class of 2036 as this would be their intended date of 4-year college completion. Once every 6 weeks, teachers, parents, and students wear the colors of a favorite college or university. Another elementary school does a "daily career highlight" in their morning announcements. This highlight features a different classroom each week so a different teacher takes responsibility each time and the segment only lasts a few seconds. Although the teacher and school counselor collaborate to develop the features, a different student reads the feature for the morning announcement, which includes telling about a career (what the person in the career does) and what kind of training you would need to get the career. Other ways to create a college-going culture include having "college talking points" as a feature each month in the school newsletter or on each teacher's webpage with tips for parents on talking to their children about college—making sure to inform parents of the many postsecondary educational options available to their children.

Meaningful Academic Opportunities That Promote Careers

Beginning early in their school careers, students need to understand how the content they are learning is related to the world of work. By giving students opportunities to practice hands-on learning, teachers promote student understanding of what they can do with what they are learning. School counselors should encourage teachers to do this and explain why it is helpful. One important way to do this is to develop community partnerships so that students have career development support from professionals and workers in the community. For example, at one elementary school, the school counselor and first-grade teaching team collaborated on a science unit on weather. The students learned about weather patterns, seasonal changes, temperature readings, and precipitation. At the end of the unit the school counselor arranged for a field trip to the local news channel (community partner) where students met a meteorologist and learned about hurricanes. Later, when they came back to school, they drew weather pictures and set up their own weather lab in the classroom where they did daily precipitation and temperature readings, noted the weather patterns and changes, and used the Internet to record the 3-day weather outlook. Each morning, one student played weather reporter and gave the results to the class, giving each child a chance to practice the role of meteorologist. Exhibit 7.3 gives another example of an activity that links academic content and career education.

Parent Engagement Activities

As previously mentioned, parents play a critical role in students' exposure to careers and college. Fortunately, there are many ways to engage parents in career- and college-related activities in the early elementary years. In this

---

EXHIBIT 7.3
Sample Activity to Connect Academic Content and Career
Learning Opportunity

During a health sciences unit, the kindergarten classes at Great Oaks Primary were given information on personal hygiene (e.g., the importance of proper handwashing). As one of the unit lessons, the kindergarten teachers and school counselor collaborated to have a dentist and a dental hygienist (community partners) come to the school to talk about the importance of brushing and flossing teeth. The dentist brought models of human teeth and demonstrated the correct way to brush teeth and the students practiced brushing the models' teeth using toothbrushes provided by the dentist. During the presentation the dentist and dental hygienist explained what they do each day at work. They described how they work together and what their individual roles are when a patient comes for a visit; additionally, they showed the students the types of tools they use to do their jobs. They also told the students what they can expect if they come to the dentist to get their teeth cleaned. At the end of the day each student was given a bag containing a coloring book about going to the dentist, a letter home to parents about what they had learned about oral hygiene and dental careers, a small tube of toothpaste, a child-size toothbrush, and a sample of dental floss.

section, we focus on practical strategies for including parents and assisting them in career and college education and curriculum, including communicating with parents about careers and college, financial literacy training, and school-based activities that promote learning and career.

Communicating With Parents About Careers and College

Developing a culture of career and college readiness in the school begins with including parents. Communicating about careers and college and suggesting home-based strategies for career and college exploration (e.g., pull out pictures of where you went to college and share stories with your children) is a crucial role for school counselors. A comprehensive approach to disseminating this type of information may be best for communicating with parents. For example, many school counselors have websites, but given the current poverty and unemployment rates in the country, a substantial number of parents may not have a computer or Internet access. Those who don't may miss out on important information if it is only disseminated online. Therefore, including a career and college corner in the school's newsletter, asking local newspapers and news reporters to highlight career and college readiness events, and advertising through parent–teacher associations and parent–teacher conferences are all helpful ways of reaching out to ensure information is accessible to all parents. School counselors should not underestimate the power of using news media; indeed, the local news and newspaper often enjoy running stories about positive things happening in the community.

Financial Literacy Training

Financial literacy is crucial for children's postsecondary success, whether they attend college or not. Learning to manage a budget, save money, and plan for financial difficulties are crucial skills to lifelong financial health and stability. Many parents may be in need of information either to manage their own finances, to help teach their children how to manage money, or to know what options they have to save for their children's future. As an outreach activity, schools can partner with a local bank or credit union to offer free educational workshops on all of those topics.

At one elementary school, the school counselor has an account manager from a local credit union speak at a parent night once a year. The account manager also comes to the school once per semester and parents can schedule time to talk one-on-one during that time about long-term college savings plans. By conveying the importance of thinking and planning ahead, school counselors may help families realize their children can have more opportunities than they initially thought. During one such meeting, a family shared a unique strategy for saving money. The family was going through a lot of financial difficulty (father lost his job) and the family was living on just the mother's income. So, each week, the parents had their children cut coupons from the newspaper, and for each coupon used, the family put the saved money into a college fund. Opportunities such as parent workshops can allow families to share their creative ideas for saving.

Including Parents in School-Based Career and College Awareness Activities. Just as students need a common language to discuss careers and college, helping parents develop the language of careers and college can promote communication at home. Offering a workshop on the importance of career and college awareness for young children would allow school counselors to provide parents with relevant information and language. Moreover, by creating opportunities for parents to participate in learning activities with their children, school counselors and teachers can model how to integrate career and college information into learning activities and can deliver important career and college concepts to both children and their parents. Exhibit 7.4 provides a sample parent–student activity that illustrates a way to promote student learning and career awareness.

EXHIBIT 7.4
Sample First Grader–Parent Activity

At Windy Hills Elementary, the first-grade teaching team developed a classroom unit on plant science. Students learned about the differences between flowers, plants, vegetables, and trees. They also learned about the conditions plants need to live: soil with nutrients, water, and sunlight.

At the end of the unit, parents were invited to participate with their children in a plant science night at the school. Funding for the night was provided

(continued)

EXHIBIT 7.4 (*continued*)

by a local Lowe's Home Improvement store (community partner) and the Parent–Teacher Association at Windy Hills. Parents and children first met in their child's classroom for a 10-minute review on plant science. Afterward, each family was asked to go out into the school yard and pick five different leaves. They brought the leaves to the gym where tables were set up so that the leaves could be sorted by categories: oak, palm, maple, grass, and so on. Students learned that all trees have unique leaves. At each table a teacher or teacher's aide helped them categorize their leaves and talked about what the tree does for the leaf and what the leaf does for the tree.

After the leaf collection and category activity, parents and students sat in the bleachers as the school counselor showed a quick video with pictures and descriptions of careers related to plants (gardener, lawn care worker, greens keeper, farmer, and horticulturist). Parents and children then went to the cafeteria where displays were set up. The displays were designed by and set up by fifth-grade students. Each display had a picture of a type of plant and a career. For example, one display had a picture of a farmer with a wheat crop. Each child who visited that display received a wheat cracker. The next display had a farmer with an orchard, and each child visiting received a slice of apple. The next was a picture of farm hands picking walnuts (students each got a walnut to taste). In all, 30 displays that demonstrated a plant and a plant career were set up. Not all had food; for example, the greens keeper display had a miniature golf hole (borrowed from a local mini golf course!).

At the end of the night, courtesy of Lowe's Home Improvement store, each student and parent were given a small pack of flower seeds and a small plastic pot. Instructions were given on how to grow them, and families were sent home to begin their own plant science experiment. This family science night did not cost the school or families any money and was well received by all who attended.

SUMMARY

In this chapter, we have highlighted career and college awareness opportunities specifically for PreK, K, and first-grade students. As elaborated, students in this age group are beginning to explore the world around them through play and interaction with other students, teachers, parents, and counselors. This is an essential time to intervene, as students are influenced by their social environments and are developing their own conceptions of their strengths and limitations applied to careers and college. In particular, we reviewed Gottfredson's first two career development stages and examined the integration of play techniques in career and college curriculum. We continue to look at the role of the school counselor and the development of students' career and college awareness in Chapter 8 with a focus on second and third grade.

···❯ Test Your Knowledge

1. What is refraction?
2. In what ways have you seen children play out careers?
3. What keeps parents or teachers from helping PreK to grade 1 children explore careers or colleges?

REFERENCES

American School Counselor Association. (2012). *The ASCA national model: A framework for school counseling programs* (3rd ed.). Alexandria, VA: Author.

American School Counselor Association. (2014). *ASCA mindsets & behaviors for student success: K-12 college- and career-readiness standards for every student.* Alexandria, VA: Author.

Auger, R. W., Blackhurst, A. E., & Wahl, K. H. (2005). The development of elementary aged children's career aspirations and expectations. *Professional School Counseling, 8*(4), 322–329.

Belsky, J. (2007). *Experiencing the lifespan.* New York, NY: Worth Publishers.

Caster, T. R. (1984). The young child's play and social and emotional development. In T. D. Yawkey & A. D. Pellegrini (Eds.), *Child's play and play therapy* (pp. 17–29). Lancaster, PA: Technomic Publishing.

Curry, J., Belser, C. T., & Binns, I. C. (2013). Integrating post-secondary college and career options in the middle school curriculum: Considerations for teachers. *Middle School Journal, 44*(3), 26–32.

Eisenberg, N., Guthrie, I. K., Murphy, B. C., Shepard, S. A., Cumberland, A., & Carlo, G. (1999). Consistency and development of prosocial dispositions: A longitudinal study. *Child Development, 70*(6), 1360–1372. http://dx.doi.org/10.1111/1467-8624.00100

Erikson, E. H. (1963). *Childhood and society* (2nd ed.). New York, NY: W. W. Norton.

Executive Office of the President. (December, 2015). *Every student succeeds act: A progress report on elementary and secondary education.* Executive Summary. Retrieved from https://www.whitehouse.gov/sites/whitehouse.gov/files/documents/ESSA_Progress_Report.pdf

Frank, L. K. (1982). Play in personality development. In G. L. Landreth (Ed.), *Play therapy: Dynamics of the process of counseling with children* (pp. 19–32). Springfield, IL: Charles C Thomas.

Gottfredson, L. S. (1981). Circumscription and compromise: A developmental theory of occupational aspirations. *Journal of Counseling Psychology, 28*(6), 545–579. http://dx.doi.org/10.1037/0022-0167.28.6.545

Gottfredson, L. S. (2002). Gottfredson's theory of circumscription, compromise, and self-creation. In D. Brown (Ed.), *Career choice and development* (4th ed., pp. 85–148). San Francisco, CA: Jossey-Bass.

Ivey, A., Ivey, M., Myers, J., & Sweeney, T. (2005). *Developmental counseling and therapy: Promoting wellness over the lifespan.* Boston, MA: Lahaska Press.

Kohlberg, L. (1981). *The philosophy of moral development.* San Francisco, CA: Harper & Row.

Landreth, G. L. (1982). Children communicate through play. In G. L Landreth (Ed.), *Play therapy: Dynamics of the process of counseling with children* (pp. 45–46). Springfield, IL: Charles C Thomas.

Marvasti, J. A. (1997). Ericksonian play therapy. In K. O'Connor & L. M. Braverman (Eds.), *Play therapy theory and practice: A comparative presentation* (pp. 285–305). New York, NY: John Wiley & Sons.

McMahon, L. (1992). *The handbook of play therapy.* New York, NY: Routledge.

Missouri Center for Career Education. (2006). Missouri comprehensive guidance program content standards grade level expectations (GLE). Retrieved from http://www.missouricareereducation.org/project/guidegle

National Math and Science Initiative. (2017). Do the math. Retrieved from https://www.nms.org/Home.aspx

National Poverty Center. (2011). Poverty in the United States: Frequently asked questions. Retrieved from http://npc.umich.edu/poverty

Nelson, R. C. (1982). Elementary school counseling with unstructured play media. In G. L. Landreth (Ed.), *Play therapy: Dynamics of the process of counseling with children* (pp. 259–264). Springfield, IL: Charles C Thomas.

Pellegrini, A. D. (1984). Children's play and language: Infancy through early childhood. In T. D. Yawkey & A. D. Pellegrini (Eds.), *Child's play and play therapy* (pp. 45–58). Lancaster, PA: Technomic Publishing.

Piaget, J. (1977). *The development of thought: Equilibration of cognitive structure.* New York, NY: Viking Press.

Sharf, R. S. (2006). *Applying career development theory to counseling* (4th ed.). Belmont, CA: Thomson.

Simmons, C. H., & Sands-Dudelczyk, K. (1983). Children helping peers: Altruism and preschool environment. *Journal of Psychology, 115*(2), 203–207. http://dx.doi.org/10.1080/00223980.1983.9915437

Vygotsky, L. S. (1978). *Mind in society: The development of higher mental processes.* Cambridge, MA: Harvard University Press.

Wettig, H. H. G., Franke, U., & Fjordbak, B. S. (2006). Evaluating the effectiveness of theraplay. In C. E. Schaefer & H. G. Kaduson (Eds.), *Contemporary play therapy* (pp. 103–135). New York, NY: Guilford Press.

Yawkey, T. D., & Diantoniis, J. M. (1984). Relationships between child's play and cognitive development and learning in infancy birth through age eight. In T. D. Yawkey & A. D. Pellegrini (Eds.), *Child's play and play therapy* (pp. 31–44). Lancaster, PA: Technomic Publishing.

Young, R. A. (1983). Career development of adolescents: An ecological perspective. *Journal of Youth and Adolescence, 12*(5), 401–417. http://dx.doi.org/10.1007/BF02088723

EIGHT

Career and College Readiness for Grades 2 and 3: Career Play and Exploration

Students in second and third grade are naturally inquisitive, energetic, and are developing their own unique personalities, interests, and attitudes. However, school counselors may be unsure of how to help students at this age develop career-related skills and connect academics to the world of work. Therefore, it is critical to remember that the objective of career and college exploration in elementary schools is to expand students' options rather than to push students to make forgone conclusions that limit their future options (Herr, Cramer, & Niles, 2004). We begin this chapter by highlighting unique developmental aspects of middle childhood.

DEVELOPMENTAL OVERVIEW

The areas of physical, psychosocial, social, cognitive, and cultural development have a large impact on students' career development, understanding of the world of work, and postsecondary preparation. As with early childhood development, in middle childhood context matters, and systems influences should be taken into consideration. Specifically, the family continues to play a primary role in influencing the exploration of options for both careers and college (Herr et al., 2004). In this section, we explore developmental milestones of middle childhood as they influence career and college readiness, but wish to note that although there are general patterns of development, children progress at their own pace. We also acknowledge that many factors that are beyond the scope of this chapter (e.g., chronic anxiety, learning disabilities, mental health concerns) could emerge that would affect students' development.

Physical Development

Children in second and third grade are generally between the ages of 7 and 9, and these are unique ages in regard to physical development, particularly as it relates to self-concept. Specifically, by the time children reach second grade, they generally have highly developed motor skills. There are two types of motor skills: gross and fine. *Gross motor skills* involve large muscle movements

163

(e.g., running, jumping, climbing) and are necessary for athletic success in most sports. *Fine motor skills* involve small, coordinated movements necessary for painting, coloring within lines, printing, and writing in cursive (Belsky, 2007), and lend to artistic endeavors. These skills become important to self-concept because they affect student success in sports and art, two socially valued skill sets. Because students in this age group can compare and contrast their skills with other children, they may feel insufficient or insecure when they assess their skills to be below those of their peers, especially if the lack of skill has a social consequence. For example, students with poor motor skills may lack athletic talent and may not be chosen (or may be chosen last) to participate in sports teams.

Moreover, differences in physical development and skills become apparent in relation to academic course work as well as in ancillary classes such as physical education and art. Students who excel in these areas may experience significant gains in academic self-concept while those who fall behind may suffer from lower self-concept. Their self-concept, in turn, may impact students' willingness to put forth effort in related future endeavors. Thus, a student who is unsuccessful at climbing a rope in gym class may also feel anxious about trying other activities that involve arm strength (pull-ups, push-ups, etc.) due to self-consciousness at the prospect of failing the physical task in front of others.

Although this may not seem like a significant concern to adults, it is crucial to consider how these types of day-to-day accomplishments, or lack thereof, impact students' self-concept, particularly with regard to psychosocial development (see more on this in the Psychosocial and Social Development section). Further, students may receive affirmation or support from adults for various skills that may then influence their self-concept related to tasks where those skills are utilized. For instance, a second grader told the first author, "I'm really good at art." I asked the student, "What does it mean to be 'really good at art'?" The student replied, "My mom says I'm good at it and she hangs up my pictures at home."

Psychosocial and Social Development

Students in second and third grade are most likely in Erikson's (1963) stage of psychosocial development known as *industry versus inferiority*, which generally begins around the age of 6 and ends around the age of 12. During this stage, the main task is for the children to develop a sense of accomplishment through competence in academics and other socially valued activities. Students who are successful gain confidence, positive academic self-concept, and the support and encouragement of adults. As a result, they may be more open and curious about career and college exploration, as future options may seem more attainable (Niles & Harris-Bowlsbey, 2009). Children who don't develop competence in valued activities begin to have a sense of inferiority and feelings of doubt about their abilities. They may also experience social humiliation, alienation, and lower academic self-concept.

Two critical developments can occur at this stage. The first development is *task attempt.* Students who experience a sense of accomplishment and industry may continue to attempt new tasks, including tasks they are unfamiliar with or those they fear they may not successfully complete. The opposite may occur for students who don't have a sense of accomplishment or an expectation of being successful. For example, a second-grade teacher was frustrated by a student who sat day after day without doing any work in class. No matter how much encouragement the teacher provided, the student didn't try. The teacher referred the student to the school counselor. When asked why he didn't do his class work, the student shrugged and stated, "I'm dumb. I don't know how." The student believed that he could not be successful and, therefore, it was pointless to even try; he had resigned himself to failure.

Children who internalize their failures can develop learned helplessness, a condition where they believe that they are absolutely helpless to overcome a situation (such as academic difficulties). Learned helplessness leads to low task attempt, as students believe there is no point in even trying (Belsky, 2007). The primary way to combat learned helplessness is to give children opportunities for efficacy building through small, planned accomplishments (Bandura, 1986).

The second key development at this age is *internal motivation.* As students begin to develop positive feelings of personal accomplishment and competence, they require fewer external motivators. Although many schools have incentive programs, such as Accelerated Reader programs, where students can earn prizes for reading books, students actually need fewer incentives as they become successful and gain confidence in their abilities.

Social tasks second and third graders are developing include (a) an understanding of social norms, (b) complex, collaborative play, (c) friendships based on trust and emotional support, and (d) an understanding of how to navigate conflict. All of these tasks are critical to building a foundation of future workplace social skills such as collaboration, conflict resolution, and appropriate boundaries for social versus workplace conduct. In addition, children ages 7 to 9 need to be able to pick up on social cues (e.g., when it is appropriate to laugh, the normal cadence of a conversation, sharing, taking turns). Students who have trouble with social norms may act immature for their age, use inappropriate humor, monopolize conversation or play, and be bossy or overly aggressive.

Regarding future career, college, and workplace relationships, the middle childhood tasks of developing friendships based on trust and support and learning to deal with conflict are critical. Children in second and third grade often form secret clubs or groups where they have a password or a secret handshake and club information. These kinds of activities are attempts to socially organize, share secrets, build trust, and foster support; all of these skills are essential to navigating workplace social structures. However, although developmentally appropriate, these kinds of activities can cause hurt feelings and negative self-worth for children who are excluded. Additionally, complex play may lead to more conflicts and arguments as children have to learn to navigate roles within the social structure of playgroups. Although it is tempting for adults to become involved in resolving these issues, it is important to note that students need the opportunity to develop and practice conflict resolution skills that they will put to use in their future roles in the workplace. We explore these in depth later in this chapter.

Finally, play also changes at this time as children become more collaborative and their play begins to resemble complex social functions. One example is that children need to learn to lose games with grace. Children who cannot do this may become aggressive (sore loser) or may begin to cheat in order to win. Learning to lose without compromising one's self-esteem or blaming others is an important social development. More so, students need to be able to learn from their mistakes and improve in future endeavors, and this is an important aspect of future career and college success (e.g., how to accept and integrate feedback).

Cognitive Development

Although students in second and third grade may still be in the stage known as *preoperations* (see Chapter 7), they are likely transitioning to the *concrete operations* stage of cognitive development (Piaget, 1977). Students may still exhibit egocentrism and may continue to display thought that is largely influenced by fantasy and magical thinking (Belsky, 2007). However, in second or third grade, concrete thinking begins to emerge as children develop a more realistic understanding of the world. One task that children can perform in the concrete operations stage is *reversibility*, or an understanding that the stages of the problem-solving process can be worked backward, or in the opposite direction. For example, during a maze activity with a third-grade class, the first author noticed that some of the children worked the maze from the end point backward to the beginning point. This skill is an essential foundation of future problem-solving work. When it comes to tasks of conservation, children in concrete operations can *decenter,* or focus on the whole picture and multiple aspects of a problem, rather than focusing on one small detail at a time (Belsky, 2007). This ability sets the stage for students to develop more complex skills needed in the workforce.

Other important cognitive skills that students begin to develop include *class inclusion*, the ability to understand that a category can include multiple subcategories, and *seriation*, or the ability to group objects based on some type of principle or characteristic (Piaget, 1965). For example, a second-grade child might group a bunch of toy animals by places where these animals would live in the wild (e.g., ocean, jungle, the desert). These two cognitive skills are especially useful in career education in middle childhood as students begin to understand the relationships between specific careers and the common characteristics of careers in a career cluster.

Students in the early stages of concrete operations are becoming more complex in their understanding of patterns, measurements, and the transformation of various materials (liquids, solids, and gases). For example, in middle childhood, most children understand that water is a liquid, ice is a solid, and steam is a gas, but that the chemical properties of the substance are the same (H_2O).

Additionally, during the emergence of the concrete operations stage, students begin to practice new behaviors for academic success, including the use of executive functions—actions used to promote memory. Examples include (a) rehearsing information (children may repeat material in order to retain it) such as through the use of flash cards or via oral recitation of vocabulary words and songs to remember facts, (b) demonstrating selective attention or a focus on relevant detail, (c) practicing self-control, such as controlling the impulse to shout out an answer in class, and (d) organizing through anticipation (e.g., a student determining what materials he will need for a class project) (Belsky, 2007). All of these skills are critical for academic success, even in postsecondary institutions.

Most importantly, children in concrete operations (Piaget, 1977) gain self-awareness (Harter, 1999), which affects how they perceive themselves in relation to others and the ideals set by society. This self-awareness greatly contributes to psychosocial development in the stage of *industry versus inferiority* (Erikson, 1963), as they compare their successes, or lack thereof, with their peers. The development of all of these skills is critical for academic success and, subsequently, career and college success, as these skills will be useful for understanding and completing job- and academic-related tasks in the future. Students who struggle to develop these skills may need to receive remediation through the school counselor or teachers through services such as study skills groups.

Gender and Culture

Gender and culture begin to exert a stronger influence in middle childhood as children begin taking greater notice of things like media, social class, and race. These influences begin to shape and impact students' career growth and development. Consequently, students in second and third grade may circumscribe their career and college aspirations and expectations based on cultural contexts and restrictive, negative stereotypes (Herr et al., 2004). We covered culture and gender in Chapter 4 but wish to reiterate that influences from both highly impact students in middle childhood in regard to career development and perceived college options. Specifically, even when barriers to postsecondary success are removed for marginalized groups, the internalization of discriminatory and prejudicial realities might manifest as self-limiting, a condition the theorist Bourdieu termed "habitus" (Connolly, 1998, p. 17). In other words, negative, lived experiences shape our future expectations and behaviors even when circumstances of our social world change and permit more positive outcomes (Connolly, 1998).

RELEVANT CAREER AND SYSTEMS THEORY: BOURDIEU (1977) AND GOTTFREDSON (1981)

As previously mentioned in Chapters 1 and 7, an ecological perspective (Bronfenbrenner, 1979) of children's career and college readiness takes into consideration the developing individual within multiple contexts. In this section, we review theoretical concepts that are relevant to career and college readiness interventions for second- and third-grade students. Both theories we review herein propound significant ecological frameworks.

Bourdieu

In middle childhood, the impact of culture greatly influences career development and college readiness. The theorist Bourdieu (1977) highlights three major concepts that should be considered when conceptualizing student career growth and development within systems contexts: habitus, field, and capital. As previously mentioned, *habitus* refers to the internalization of experiences that shape our future beliefs and actions. In regard to culture, habitus can refer to the internalization of social discourse, prejudice, discrimination, and oppression about race, gender, sexual orientation, religion, and other individual characteristics. Specifically, these internalized experiences become habitualized thoughts and behaviors (Connolly, 1998). When it comes to careers and college, children can habituate low social expectations for academic, career and college success.

The term *capital* is used by Bourdieu to describe the limited goods and resources of a society and how they are distributed based on social status, social relationships, and dominant discourse (Connolly, 1998). Bourdieu (1977) described four types of capital: (a) economic or financial, (b) cultural, referring to the legitimacy of a person's knowledge or behavior, (c) social, referring to resources gained through significant connections with others, and (d) symbolic, referring to a person's prestige. All four types of capital relate to career development and college readiness. For example, social capital can influence an individual's ability to gain entrance into prestigious postsecondary schools or programs, or to gain highly competitive employment through networking (i.e., it's not what you know, it's who you know). Although capital largely is a result of the culture and family to which an individual is born, some capital may be attributed to certain individual characteristics. For example, females who fit social ideals for beauty (e.g., thin, attractive) may gain capital. Likewise, males who fit social ideas for athleticism might also gain capital. In terms of career and college settings, characteristics like self-initiating behavior and high motivation may be forms of capital. Children begin early in life to recognize signs that they do or do not have capital, and they begin to attempt and struggle to gain capital—part of the habitus process.

The term *field* is used by Bourdieu (1977) to describe the contexts in which capital occurs. Specifically, something that is highly socially valued in one context may not be in another. For example, traditional and socially valued feminine characteristics (e.g., having a sense of style) may make a girl popular among other girls. However, boys displaying the same characteristic, stylishness, may become ostracized by other boys. Another example of an attribute that may be context specific is a personal sense of humor.

These three terms—habitus, capital, and field—are important for understanding academic development as well as career, and college readiness. Connolly (1998) noted that schools are a type of field and that what constitutes capital within different school fields varies, particularly in regard to masculine and feminine characteristics. So while in one school field it may be highly socially valued for individuals to be able to read music and play an instrument, in other school fields individuals may not gain, or could even lose, capital for such skills.

It can be difficult for students to appreciate that the academic or career activities they are engaging in will only increase their capital if those activities are within the realm of what is deemed socially desirable in the contexts in which they live. What is most notable in regard to student development in second and third grade is that much of the focus on capital comes from meeting the requirements of socialized gender roles (see the following discussion of Gottfredson's theory). Therefore, combatting gendered notions for careers and college options should be a primary focus in designing curriculum as well as career college readiness interventions for second and third graders. Specifically, helping students to recognize that there are many ways to be successful, and that different contexts demand different skills, is important to the task of broadening their interests.

Gottfredson's Theory of Circumscription and Compromise

Gottfredson's Stage 2: *Orientation to Sex Roles* occurs from about ages 6 to 8, and according to Sharf (2006), children in this stage often believe they are a member of the superior gender (e.g., girls rule!). Because children in middle childhood are concrete thinkers, they are often very dualistic in their thinking. As such, they begin to develop a tolerable sex-type boundary of occupations that are acceptable for girls and those that are acceptable for boys. For example, a boy may perceive that nurses should be girls and, therefore, that occupation is not a tolerable consideration for him. During this time, it is important to have role models and examples of individuals in nontraditional roles. For example, teachers can be provided with coloring sheets representing people in nontraditional careers to use on occasions when students have extra time in class before the next academic activity. By intentionally displaying the colored pages around the classroom, teachers can provide subtle reminders that people can work in nontraditional careers.

THE SCHOOL COUNSELOR AND CORE COUNSELING CURRICULUM

The career and college counseling curriculum is an essential component of a comprehensive program (ASCA, 2012). In order to provide the best possible career development curriculum, school counselors should consider the academic and personal skills that students will need to be successful after high school. An overarching focus in these grades should be career and college exploration. Moreover, school counselors should use the ASCA Mindsets and Behaviors (2014) to determine age-appropriate career and college competencies for second- and third-grade students. See Table 8.1 for our recommendation

TABLE 8.1 ASCA Mindsets and Behaviors for Second- and Third-Grade Curriculum Planning Focus

CATEGORY 1: MINDSETS STANDARDS		
Belief in development of whole self, including a healthy balance of mental, socioemotional, and physical well-being Self-confidence in ability to succeed Positive attitude toward work and learning		
CATEGORY 2:BEHAVIOR STANDARDS		
Learning Strategies	**Self-Management Skills**	**Social Skills**
Demonstrate creativity	Demonstrate ability to assume responsibility	Create positive and supportive relationships with other students
Apply self-motivation and self-direction to learning	Demonstrate ability to work independently	Demonstrate empathy
Actively engage in challenging course work	Demonstrate ability to overcome barriers to learning	Demonstrate social maturity and behaviors appropriate to the situation and environment

for which of the ASCA Mindsets and Behaviors could be used for second- and third-grade curriculum planning focus. However, we recommend that school counselors consider the populations in their schools and modify their curriculum planning focus as needed.

SCHOOL COUNSELING INTERVENTIONS

Findings from a qualitative study by Blackhurst, Auger, and Wahl (2003) revealed that by fifth grade, most of the participants in their study had an inaccurate understanding of the preparation needed for particular jobs. They also found that fifth-grade students had a limited ability to distinguish among postsecondary options (technical school, community college, 4-year university). These results support the need to help students in middle elementary grades (second and third) to explore careers, learn about preparation requirements for careers (including college or vocational and technical training), and be exposed to postsecondary educational options.

School counselors should focus on ways to engage students in the career and college readiness curriculum by making activities fun, engaging, and meaningful. Given their developmental level, the activities should provide opportunities for students to gain feelings of confidence in their abilities and to challenge their preconceived ideas. We provide numerous examples in the following.

Career Exploration Activities

To engage students and explore careers, I, the first author—an elementary school counselor at the time—used a lot of games. One example was at the end of a career exploration unit; I worked with the art teacher to create a lake in the middle of a classroom. I designed a lake using blue butcher paper and the art teacher had students use time in art class to create fish using construction paper, glitter, markers, and glue. The fish were laminated and a paper clip was added to each one. I then created fishing poles using dow rods, yarn, and a magnet. The game was called "Fishing for Careers" and as students caught a fish they had to answer career-related questions. If they were successful, they were able to place the fish in a bucket. The goal was to get all of the fish in the bucket by the end of the game. Here are a few sample questions:

1. Name three careers from the hospitality and tourism cluster.
2. Name two types of scientists.
3. How much education is required to be a teacher?
4. What does an architect do?
5. True or False? A woman can be a construction manager.
6. True or False? A man can be a ballet dancer.
7. Name a career where workers use math.
8. Name two careers where workers do a lot of writing.
9. List two work habits a farmer needs.

When students didn't know answers, they were allowed to use one lifeline (other students in the class). In this way, it promoted collaboration over competition. At the end of the game, the entire class got a stamp, a pencil, or a sticker. This game was very popular, and kids, teachers, and parents all asked for the return of "Fishing for Careers" each year. Once the materials were designed and the questions were created, the game was very easy to use each year. This type of activity is appropriate because it is creative, engaging for students, and helps them gain confidence in their career knowledge. Further, the questions can be created to challenge students' gender and cultural stereotypes, increase career knowledge, and help them to better understand the relationships between careers and academics. School counselors can tailor the questions for different age groups (PreK, kindergarten, grades 1, 2, 3, 4, and 5) and use the same materials.

Based on student cognitive development in middle childhood (e.g., seriation, the ability to categorize and subcategorize), students in second and third grade are ready to be introduced to career clusters. Students' natural curiosity lends to career exploration, and students in second and third grade love to use multiple types of media to play through career exploration. Using puzzles or art activities to draw and include careers that are within clusters is a fun way to help students visually map the relationships among careers.

For example, I, the first author, provided students with a graphic organizer worksheet that had 20 careers illustrated. The students would use crayons to draw lines connecting the careers in the same cluster. On the worksheet were illustrations of careers that were in the information technology cluster (i.e., web designer, graphic designer, network administrator, 3D animator, computer game programmer). Students would use a designated color, such as blue, to circle the information technology careers on their sheet and then draw a line connecting those careers together. Then, using a different color, like yellow, students would circle all of the careers in agriculture, food, and natural resources and draw a line connecting those careers together. Where older students might be capable of articulating or discussing in detail the different career clusters, having younger students recognize and match careers based on similar characteristics using active strategies is a developmentally appropriate way of engaging them.

Developing Career and College Language

Popular media for teaching the career curriculum to elementary students include storytelling and role-playing (Herr et al., 2004), both of which are excellent for building career and college vocabulary and beginning to explore careers and colleges. Truly, school counselors can choose many creative games and should work to make learning fun and engaging. The more students are exposed to careers and college information, the more of that language they will use. Increasing students' vocabulary related to careers and college can start with breaking down broad career areas into specific occupations (e.g., science careers, like doctor, can be broken down into specifics such as cardiologist and dentist). Other career terms and postsecondary terms that could be introduced include career clusters, college, university, and technical school. Exhibit 8.1 demonstrates how one elementary school counselor works with second- and third-grade students to explore careers and develops lessons that promote career and college mindsets, language, and behaviors.

EXHIBIT 8.1
Voices From the Field: Expanding Career and College Exploration in Middle Elementary Grades

Elizabeth Singletary, MEd

School Counselor, St. James Episcopal Day School

I am a school counselor at a private elementary school in a rural area. There are 291 students at the school ranging from PreK through third to fifth grade, with 18 classrooms total. The majority of our students come from high socioeconomic status families and have a lot of exposure to career options, which gives me a step ahead in what I am able to teach. Over the years, I have created a comprehensive counseling program, including career development at every grade level. I enjoy teaching every grade, but especially second- and third-grade students, because they have a grasp of career concepts and can really start to narrow down their likes and dislikes into future career options.

Second- and third-grade students know about a variety of occupations, and they have been exposed to a handful of the career clusters. This allows

(continued)

EXHIBIT 8.1 (*continued*)

them to begin placing themselves into certain career paths. I start off the first lesson refreshing their memory about the six career paths/clusters they have been exposed to in previous years: (a) business (Business, Management, & Technology), (b) creative (Arts & Communications), (c) nature (Natural Resources/Agriculture), (d) fixing and building and technology (Industrial and Engineering Technology), (e) helping (Human Services), and (f) health (Health Services). Once they have been reintroduced to the paths, we begin to dig deeper into the many different options within those paths using technology and writing skills.

Technology plays a strong part in all students' daily education, and understanding how to use basic technology is an important skill for students to have when moving forward throughout school and into college and careers. Students need to understand the basics of research, especially research using the Internet to acquire information. My career lessons starting in second and third grade do have technology aspects to them in order to teach beginning research skills. Students use the *O*Net* and *Occupational Outlook Handbook* websites to learn about careers. Students are asked to find various information about certain careers based on the information available on the websites. For example, as a class, we search for *Elementary Teacher* in the *Occupational Outlook Handbook* website to find information about that occupation. We find information about the occupation, such as (a) median pay, (b) education needed, (c) on-the-job training, (d) what do they do, (e) job outlook, and (f) similar occupations. It is always interesting, and kind of funny, to hear how surprised the students are when they find out how much additional education can be involved in obtaining a degree as an elementary teacher as well as the average amount of money teachers make each year. They always expect it to be much more!

After our time working together, students are able to search for information about an occupation they think they are interested in, using the same six points we looked for earlier together. They also recall their stated dislikes and likes from earlier years to help narrow their search. Some students search through many occupations before they find one that truly suits their interests. The students compose a short paper compiling the information and are welcomed to share their papers with the class if they would like to do so. Usually, the students that chose a career in the Creative Path are the first to raise their hands to present, sharing information about their future career in performing arts, journalism, or communications. It's always fun to see the personalities of the students match the careers! During this chapter, I assess student research abilities with a simple checklist. By the end of the unit, 80% of students will be able to find career information using the Internet without the help of a teacher/counselor.

In future lessons, students are asked to match careers with the corresponding career clusters/paths they have been introduced to thus far. I call out a career that is written on an index card and one student at a

(*continued*)

EXHIBIT 8.1 (continued)

Voices From the Field: Expanding Career and College Exploration in Middle Elementary Grades

time volunteers to sort the index card into one of the six career cluster envelopes available. Their classmates say "agree" or "disagree" when the student places the index card into the folder. After a few rounds of this sorting activity, students begin to easily see which careers fall into which cluster. Once the students match careers to clusters, they create skits choosing one occupation from each cluster. The goal of the skits is for the students to show how different people can work together for one common goal, and that a strength in one person may be a weakness in another, and vice versa. It is a great way for students to cooperate as a group to see that individuals need to work together to be successful, and that one occupation is not more important than another.

The career learning goals for these lessons are (a) to be able to use research and information resources to obtain career information, (b) to learn to use the Internet to access career-planning information, (c) to know the various ways in which occupations can be classified, and (d) to learn how to interact and work cooperatively in teams. Career development has always been about more than just teaching the material to a group of students. Having the students work individually, and as a group, to find information, collaborate with each other while working toward a common goal, and sharing information with others are all necessary skills needed for the future. Our students need to learn how to model these skills in their everyday lives to be ready for career and college.

Interpersonal Skills and Career and College Readiness

As noted in Chapter 1, changes to the U.S. economy have necessitated changes to how the future workforce is trained. According to a study by Barker and Satcher (2000), school counselors recognize the need to consistently provide skills training that promotes career competency equitably among college-bound and work-bound students. Indeed, the skills needed for both may be more similar than disparate. Specifically, beginning in elementary school, students should be comprehensively prepared for all potential postsecondary options through the development of academic, social, and work-related skills.

According to Greene (2006), technical skills and education are no longer sufficient for career success, as many employers now seek individuals with more advanced "soft skills" that may include communication skills, being a team player, generating solutions and problem solving, and demonstrating self-understanding and awareness, cultural sensitivity, positive manners, and workplace etiquette. As discussed previously, these are all things that students in grades 2 and 3 are capable of working on. Therefore, we review opportunities for promoting social skills that will allow students to be successful in postsecondary life.

Collaborative Groups and Team Building

Within classrooms during counseling activities or in small-group counseling, students can learn the skills of working as a team. Giving students the opportunity to set goals in small groups and to work together to achieve those goals is an excellent start toward workplace camaraderie and collective efforts for success. Activities that involve problem solving and a whole-group effort are especially helpful. An example of this occurred in a third-grade classroom where a school counselor and classroom teacher put students into groups of four. Groups were given Tinkertoys and building blocks and instructed to create the highest tower they could. After the activity, the teacher and school counselor processed with the students what teamwork skills they used (listening to each other, trying multiple ways of completing the task) and discussed careers related to the activity (e.g., architecture, construction, and engineering).

Conflict Resolution

Any elementary school counselor can testify to the difficulty experienced by students in middle childhood who are learning to navigate play in groups. Friendship conflicts are frequent as children learn to handle disagreements in everyday discussions. Conflict resolution, cultural sensitivity and awareness, and communication and active listening skills are necessary for future workplace success and should be introduced by second grade. School counselors can do this through the provision of classroom lessons addressing these skills, and many different curricula are available for this type of activity. However, we suggest school counselors consider best practices for implementing these types of pro-social skills and conflict resolution curricula. For example, the *Enhancing Relationships in School Communities* project (Wertheim, Freeman, & Trinder, 2012) was formulated with the following principles in mind: (a) administrator support and buy-in are critical to the success of any program or initiative, (b) teachers must take ownership in order to help students use the conflict resolution skills after they learn them, (c) there should be professional development available to teachers and staff on conflict resolution strategies being taught to students, and (d) sufficient time has to be given to students to learn and practice the conflict resolution skills. School counselors can visit the ASCA website to view the catalog of resources (curriculum, games) available for purchase for teaching the skills mentioned here.

IMPORTANCE OF STAKEHOLDERS

As mentioned in previous chapters, engaging stakeholders in students' career and college readiness development is critical to ensure that students get a comprehensive introduction to career and college exploration. As is noted in the ASCA *National Model* (2012), collaboration is a key theme of school counseling and is vital to the implementation of a successful career and college readiness curriculum. Although we have discussed integrating career education within the classroom curriculum through collaboration with classroom teachers in previous chapters, we have not explored the role of specialty faculty in promoting careers and college. In this section, we focus on ways in which specialty faculty can be included in a comprehensive school counseling program's career and college readiness curriculum.

Specialty Faculty

Specialty, or related arts, faculty in elementary schools generally teach ancillary classes that are meant to enrich student learning in the areas of physical education, library and media studies, art, music, and foreign languages. The curriculum offered by specialty faculty can be particularly useful to assist children in learning about diverse career and college opportunities. However, like classroom teachers, specialty faculty may have had very little training in career education and development and may need support and encouragement from the school counselor in order to effectively integrate career and college information. Moreover, students who have fantasy occupational aspirations (e.g., professional athlete, rock star, model, actor/actress) may benefit from a more realistic understanding of related careers. This is especially true given that students, boys in particular, who have fantasy occupation aspirations as professional athletes in third grade continue to have the same aspirations by sixth grade (Helwig, 1998). See Exhibit 8.2 for an example.

EXHIBIT 8.2
Third-Grade Sport Careers Unit

Mrs. Callahan, an elementary school counselor, was conducting a career and college exploration unit with third-grade students and was concerned about the number of students (particularly males) who were displaying an interest in becoming professional athletes. During a third-grade classroom lesson, students were asked to draw a career that they were interested in and over half the boys in the class drew a picture of a football player. Mrs. Callahan was concerned that focusing on athletics was self-limiting and an unrealistic career choice for most students. Indeed, she knew that the majority of students would not become professional athletes and she wanted them to embrace other options; however, she did not want to discourage student interest in athletics. Therefore, she decided to collaborate with the physical education (PE) teacher, Mr. Jackson, to develop a sports careers and college unit.

Mrs. Callahan and Mr. Jackson worked collaboratively to develop a unit on sports careers, relying on Mrs. Callahan's knowledge of careers and Mr. Jackson's knowledge of sports. In the first lesson, students were introduced

EXHIBIT 8.2 (*continued*)

to the many careers related to professional athletics, including athletic trainers, coaches, physical therapists, medical staff, sports managers/administrators, ticket sales, photographers/camera and film technicians, marketing staff, retail sales, sports reporters, and facilities management. Students were put in small groups where they discussed and wrote a list of responsibilities and skills for each of these careers.

In the second lesson, Mrs. Callahan and Mr. Jackson set up five centers and the students rotated through in small groups of five, spending 10 minutes at each center. At the centers, they learned more about careers, including required education for the career, and completed a related activity. The centers were staffed by volunteers and teacher's aides. See Table 8.2 for a list of the centers, careers included at each center, and activities students completed at each center.

For the third and final lesson, the students, under the direction of Mrs. Callahan and Mr. Jackson, were randomly assigned one of the careers they had learned about in the last few weeks. Role-plays included helping an injured athlete (sports medicine), training the team (coaching), selling merchandise and tickets, photography and reporting, and statistics. As the final activity, students selected three careers related to professional athletics that they found interesting and wrote two sentences about each.

TABLE 8.2 Third-Grade Sports Career Unit Centers

Center	Careers Covered	Activities
Center 1: Sports Training	Sports trainers and coaches	A sports trainer was at this center and did a demonstration with volunteers of strength-training activities and regular workouts.
Center 2: Sports Medicine	Physical therapy, injury prevention/treatment, sports improvement, and fitness	A sports therapist was there with a model of a human leg and students practiced wrapping a sprained ankle.
Center 3: Sports Marketing	Ticket sales, retail, branding, public relations	A speaker from the local NFL retail store talked about merchandise and team branding. Students were given a paper with the outline of a jacket. Students were able to design a jacket with their favorite team logo.
Center 4: Sports Reporting	Photo journalism, televised reporting, film technicians	A member of the sports reporting team at a local news station was the speaker at this center. Students watched a 30-second clip of a sports play and practiced reporting the play in a microphone. Their reports were recorded on video and they viewed them later.
Center 5: Sport Administration	Facilities management, accounting, team management, statistics, scouts	One of the statistics keepers from a local university basketball team was the speaker for this center. Students practiced watching a 2-minute basketball clip and using a spreadsheet to record attempted baskets, scored points, fouls, and foul shots.

In the example, the school counselor used students' natural and socially constructed interest in athletics to foster career exploration; the collaboration with Mr. Jackson allowed both professionals to use their strengths to promote student career understanding beyond professional athletics.

Academic Subject Teachers

Teachers have an opportunity to exact a strong influence on student career and college readiness in second and third grade, particularly in the areas of academic and social skills development. School counselors should work collaboratively with all teachers to design classroom lessons that encourage career and college exploration opportunities.

Academic Growth

School counselors can provide students with developmentally appropriate academic skills instruction, and teachers can reinforce these skills in the classroom. Using the ASCA (2014) Mindsets and Behaviors as a foundation, students in second and third grades should learn to write academic goals and monitor their progress toward those goals (initiating self-regulatory behavior). Students in these grades also need to learn personal organization skills, use a planner, manage homework and supply materials, and develop homework, test-taking, and study-skills strategies. These skills are essential to career and college readiness in that organization, planning, and goal setting are critical to success in higher education and the workplace. School counselors can develop lesson plans that address these skills and cofacilitate instruction with classroom teachers. Classroom teachers, in turn, will be able to reinforce the skills in the classroom on an ongoing basis.

Social Growth

To promote the development of prosocial skills, school counselors should encourage teachers to include collaborative and group work assignments for second- and third-grade students. Further, school counselors can provide classroom lessons on conflict resolution strategies and communication skills, and teachers can reinforce these skills in day-to-day interactions with students. School counselors also can foster social development through the collaborative implementation of positive behavior programs and character education throughout the school, which support personal responsibility as well as civic and social interest.

Career Growth

As mentioned in Chapter 7, school counselors can work with teachers to integrate career information in the classroom. Because students in second and third grade can understand career clusters, it can be fun and engaging to include clusters with academic content (see Exhibit 8.3). During classroom lessons, school counselors can introduce all of the career clusters and help students understand the relationships between careers. Most importantly, school counselors need to continually help teachers infuse career and college in their curriculum.

Create a college-going culture. There are so many ways for teachers to create a positive and truly inspiring college-going culture that is engaging and fun for students. The most important thing that can be done is to ensure that college is a constant mention in the day-to-day operation of the school. It must be a clear expectation that every student will pursue a postsecondary educational option and that expectation must be consistently conveyed with enthusiasm. Teachers can begin by talking about their own college learning experiences. Field trips to local universities are a wonderful opportunity to connect classroom learning to larger academic concepts. For example, in one town, the local elementary students are invited to visit a land grant university as part of extension programs for an annual Agriculture Exposition. Students learn about forestry, livestock, local farming techniques, planting and harvesting, and more. They interact with college students and faculty, and learn about research through exhibits provided by faculty and staff. They also get ice cream made at the dairy store made on campus. These types of activities are fun, educational, and expose students to the college environment in an engaging, age-appropriate manner.

Other suggestions include inviting members of the college community to the elementary school. One elementary school principal set a fund raising goal for the year. When her school achieved the goal, they had a 20-minute afternoon pep rally with the local high school band (next door) coming over and playing music and a local university's beloved football coach and mascot coming by to congratulate the students. Obviously, this would not happen for every school, but this was a very special and exciting event for the students at that particular elementary school. However, a more lasting impression might be created through more sustained relationship-building opportunities. To accomplish this, some schools have implemented Adopt-a-College programs for every elementary classroom. Teachers adopt a university or college for the year and reach out to the university president or provost and request a partnership. Students in the class research the institution and learn about the programs offered and they may also interview, via Skype or Adobe Connect, members of the college community such as administrators, faculty, and students. They also write letters about their career and college aspirations. The college in return often sends items such as T-shirts, water bottles, and so on, to the students. Each year, students get the opportunity to learn all about a new university or college.

Parent Engagement Activities

As noted in Chapter 7, parents can have the greatest influence on student career and college readiness in early and middle childhood; therefore, including parents is a necessary and desirable way to promote student career and college growth (ASCA, 2012; Herr et al., 2004). Evidence of this comes from findings of a longitudinal study of students, beginning in second grade (Helwig, 1998).

According to Helwig, parents were a major influence on students' career development throughout childhood, adolescence, and early adulthood. Therefore, he suggested that parents should be included in career and college preparation activities and given the tools and resources to assist their children in career growth and college decision making. Specifically, students from low socioeconomic status (SES) families (a determination based on family income, prestige of parents' occupations, and parent education level) are more likely to have lower educational attainment and lower occupational status than their higher SES peers; this is a generational problem that may be in part due to the fact that the parents of low SES students may be unable to offer career guidance due to a lack of knowledge about career development or how to guide their children through career and college readiness tasks (Shaffer, 2009). By including parents, school counselors can help them develop skills necessary to support and guide their children. It is important to note that regardless of a family's SES, all parents should be invited to participate in career and college readiness activities.

According to Amundson and Penner (1998), parents who aren't given a rationale for exploring careers and college with their child or don't possess the skills to assist their child's career and college readiness may be prone to

---

EXHIBIT 8.3

Second-Grade Health and Safety Unit With Careers and College

Mr. Denton, an elementary school counselor, worked with Mrs. Norton, a second-grade teacher, to design a career clusters game to go with a health and safety unit. In the unit, Mrs. Norton covered topics such as food safety, nutrition, food groups, personal hygiene, illness, and injuries. Mr. Denton and Mrs. Norton collaborated to design one career and college assignment for the unit. Students were given a homework assignment that included reading a paragraph about the health sciences career cluster and a link to a list of careers in health sciences (www.worldwidelearn.com/career-planning -education/health-sciences/index.html). Each student was asked to choose a career from the list of health science careers. With their parents' help, students were asked to do the following:

1. Choose a career from the health sciences career cluster list.
2. Describe what people with this career do in two sentences.
3. Write one sentence about the kind of training or education that is necessary for this career.
4. Write one sentence about how people with this career help others to be healthy.
5. Write one sentence about why you might or why you might not like this career.

Although this was a short homework assignment, it helped students connect what they were learning in their academic unit with the world of work and reinforced technology, research, and writing skills.

push their own personal preferences for their child (e.g., parents deciding the child needs to be a doctor or others pushing their child into manual labor jobs). As noted by Amundson and Penner, increasing parental involvement in career development activities promotes a positive parent–child relationship and greater family communication. Parents may wonder how to help students connect academic instruction and careers, a skill they can be taught by school counselors and teachers. Moreover, given the current federal initiatives for science, technology, engineering, and mathematics (STEM) careers, it is important to recognize the role of parents for encouraging student interest in the STEM areas. Because many parents may not possess knowledge of STEM careers or may not feel confident about their math or science skills, an educational approach is warranted (see Exhibit 8.4 for an example).

As illustrated in the math night example, including parents is an important way to improve student STEM performance and to help families connect academics and the world of work. It is also a great way to help parents think about ways to integrate math at home (e.g., baking, measuring things at home, and

EXHIBIT 8.4
Third-Grade Parent and Student Math Night

Once a month at Norcross Elementary School, the school counselor, Miss Sanchez, would meet with each grade-level team to discuss any student concerns such as academics and behavior and to coordinate and plan grade-level activities. During one such meeting with the third-grade team, the teachers disclosed that students were struggling with understanding many of the math concepts being taught in a new unit on metric to fraction conversions. One of the teachers, Mr. Nelson, stated that he asked the students when they might use fractions at home and none of them had an answer. Another teacher suggested that they could have a math day at school and focus on math activities. Miss Sanchez suggested instead that they have a parent and student math night so that parents could learn ways to integrate math at home. The team decided to do this and the parent–teacher association (PTA) agreed to sponsor the event.

The math night was scheduled for a Thursday evening and a local pizza parlor supplied a pizza dinner for the families. Parents and children ate in the cafeteria where they were introduced to the evening's activities. The counselor did a short presentation on math-related careers and college programs (engineering, accounting, actuary) and then each family was given a ruler, a worksheet, and a conversion sheet. Families took measurements and then worked on converting (e.g., inches to centimeters). For the culminating activity, all of the students and parents got to play the role of bakers. Each family was given a calculator and instructions on how to convert decimals to fractions to get the measurements needed to make no-bake cookies. Teachers were available to answer questions and found that many parents revealed that they had forgotten some of the math skills reviewed. At the end, all of the families enjoyed a tasty treat.

(continued)

EXHIBIT 8.4 (continued)
Third-Grade Parent and Student Math Night

As a result of the math night, teachers reported that students were more enthusiastic about fractions and measurements. Several of the teachers noted that students appeared to be turning in more homework and that math homework scores seemed to be higher. The teachers attributed this to parents feeling more efficacious to help students with math conversions and students feeling more excited about math.

doing conversions). Other ways to include parents are to conduct workshops that focus on labor market information, training requirements for a diversity of careers, and how to access current career information using up-to-date technology (Amundson & Penner, 1998). Other family night activities for second and third graders could include financial literacy (how to help your child understand money and develop a simple budget), educational planning and goal setting, and how to provide academic enrichment for children.

The latter, academic enrichment, is an important topic to cover before long breaks (such as summer vacation). A presentation or workshop on this topic ideally should include a focus on local, community-based opportunities such as public library reading programs, sports camps, summer learning programs through zoos or museums, or camps or programs for specialty training such as music, art, and theater, to name a few. If it is possible, having local donors and business partners support scholarship funds for enrichment programs is a great way to ensure all students have equitable access to such programs.

SUMMARY

In this chapter, we discussed the developmental milestones of middle childhood in relation to career and college readiness. We highlighted relevant career theory with a special emphasis on Bourdieu and Gottfredson in regard to the influence of culture and gender. We reviewed the importance of a multisystemic approach to career and college readiness counseling in comprehensive school counseling programs and focused attention on specialty faculty, classroom integration, and parent engagement activities.

···❯ Test Your Knowledge

1. How does lack of success in elementary school academics impact students' career and college development?
2. What career and college topics are important to share with parents of second- and third-grade students?
3. What gendered messages do students receive in schools that may increase their propensity for *Orientation to Sex Roles* (Gottfredson's Stage 2) based on stereotypes?

REFERENCES

American School Counselor Association. (2012). *The ASCA national model: A framework for school counseling programs* (3rd ed.). Alexandria, VA: Author.

American School Counselor Association. (2014). *ASCA mindsets & behaviors for student success: K-12 college- and career-readiness standards for every student.* Alexandria, VA: Author.

Amundson, N. E., & Penner, K. (1998). Parent involved career exploration. *Career Development Quarterly, 47*(2), 135–144. http://dx.doi.org/10.1002/j.2161-0045.1998.tb00547.x

Bandura, A. (1986). *Social foundations of thought and action: A social cognitive theory.* Englewood Cliffs, NJ: Prentice Hall.

Barker, J., & Satcher, J. (2000). School counselors' perceptions of required workplace skills and career development competencies. *Professional School Counseling, 4*(2), 134–139.

Belsky, J. (2007). *Experiencing the lifespan.* New York, NY: Worth Publishers.

Blackhurst, A. E., Auger, R. W., & Wahl, K. H. (2003). Children's perceptions of vocational preparation requirements. *Professional School Counseling, 7*(2), 58–67.

Bourdieu, P. (1977). *Outline of a theory of practice.* Cambridge, UK: Cambridge University Press.

Bronfenbrenner, U. (1979). *The ecology of human development.* Cambridge, MA: Harvard University Press.

Connolly, P. (1998). *Racism, gender identities and young children: Social relations in a multiethnic inner-city primary school.* London, UK: Routledge.

Erikson, E. H. (1963). *Childhood and society* (2nd ed.). New York, NY: W. W. Norton.

Gottfredson, L. S. (1981). Circumscription and compromise: A developmental theory of occupational aspirations. *Journal of Counseling Psychology, 28*(6), 545–579. http://dx.doi.org/10.1037/0022-0167.28.6.545

Greene, M. J. (2006). Helping build lives: Career and life development of gifted and talented students. *Professional School Counseling, 10*(1), 34–42.

Harter, S. (1999). *The construction of the self: A developmental perspective.* New York, NY: Guilford Press.

Helwig, A. A. (1998). Occupational aspirations of a longitudinal sample from second to sixth grade. *Journal of Career Development, 24*(4), 247–266. http://dx.doi.org/10.1023/A:1025085830778

Herr, E. L., Cramer, S. H., & Niles, S. G. (2004). *Career guidance and counseling through the lifespan: Systematic approaches* (6th ed.). Boston, MA: Pearson.

Niles, S. G., & Harris-Bowlsbey, J. (2009). *Career development interventions in the 21st century* (3rd ed.). Upper Saddle River, NJ: Merrill.

Piaget, J. (1965). *The moral judgment of the child.* New York, NY: Free Press.

Piaget, J. (1977). *The development of thought: Equilibration of cognitive structure.* New York, NY: Viking Press.

Shaffer, D. R. (2009). *Social and personality development* (6th ed.). Belmont, CA: Wadsworth.

Sharf, R. S. (2006). *Applying career development theory to counseling* (4th ed.). Belmont, CA: Thomson.

Wertheim, E., Freeman, E., & Trinder, M. (2012). Enhancing relationships in school communities: Promoting cooperative conflict resolution and respect for cultural diversity in schools. In D. Bretherton & N. Balvin (Eds.), *Peace psychology in Australia* (pp. 139–146). New York, NY: Springer Science + Business Media. http://dx.doi.org/10.1007/978-1-4614-1403-2_9

4th & 5th grade (9-11yrs)

Erikson - Industry vs Inferiority
"Issues Re: competence; social acceptance vs development
of unique identity

Piaget - Concrete Operations
• Cognitive Tasks: Conservation, Decentering, Seriation
• Metacognition skills develop
• Rehearsal activities help develop understanding of
personal responsibility, how to keep track of what
they need to do → self-regulatory behavior

Gottfredson Stage 2: Orientation to Sex Roles
• Social pressures for gender ideals increase
• Girls begin to self-objectify
• When women & girls believe that gender will have academic
consequences, they perform worse
• STEM Stereotype Threat

Career Theories
— Bandura's Social Learning Theory - 3 Major Constructs
Re: to career efficacy development:
• Reciprocal Determinism - Cognitive, Behavioral, & Environmental
factors interact
• Self-Regulation - AKA Self-Management/Self-Monitoring = Ability to
plan & manage behavior to successfully reach a goal
• Efficacy Expectancy = The conviction that one can successfully
execute behavior required to produce outcomes
"4 Sources of Efficacy Expectancy
1- Performance Accomplishments = lived experiences (most dependable)
2- Vicarious Experience
3- Verbal Persuasion
4- Emotional Arousal
• Efficacy beliefs differ on 3 dimensions: Magnitude, Generality, Strength
— Gottfredson's Theory of Circumscription & Compromise
• Stage 3: Orientation to Social Valuation - Ss begin to notice how
they are viewed by peers; recognize social values of careers
— Young's Career Concepts - Influence of peer group
— Super's Life-Span, Life-Space Approach - 9 Concepts/Activities that -p.195
Foster career development via personal awareness & career decision-making
Nilesh Harris-Bowlsbey - Basic career development skills by end of elem school:
— Self-knowledge; skills for interacting w/ others; etc. (p.196)

Two most important cross-theoretical concepts: Self-Regulation & career
self-efficacy

Career and College Readiness for Grades 4 and 5: Preparing for the Middle School Transition

Throughout this book, we have maintained the critical importance of beginning career- and college-related counseling in early childhood and of consistently promoting career and college readiness throughout the P–12 years. Yet, as alleged by Watson and McMahon (2008), it is important to note that career development practices by elementary school counselors still largely lack a comprehensive, integrated, and holistic approach. As previously mentioned (Chapter 1), much of the career literature and education for school counselors is based on theories that address adolescent and adult career development, rather than that of children (Porfeli, Hartung, & Vondracek, 2008). Although research on children's career development has begun to emerge, there is often no theoretical framework consistently applied to practice (Schultheiss, 2008). For this reason, we have utilized Gottfredson, Young, and Bourdieu to frame middle childhood career development in this text. Noteworthy, similar to career education and counseling, little has been written on college preparation practices for students in elementary school. In this chapter, we add Bandura's social learning theory to expand the theoretical framework to tailor career and college counseling interventions for fourth- and fifth-grade students and give examples of activities being done by school counselors in the field that highlight unique aspects of school counselors' role in preparing students for the transition to middle school.

DEVELOPMENTAL OVERVIEW

Fourth and fifth graders (generally between the ages of 9 and 11) are at the end of childhood and are transitioning to early adolescence (preteens). According to Havighurst (1972), several developmental tasks should be achieved before the adolescent transition. Some of these tasks include developing the physical skills to successfully participate in sports and games, building a positive attitude toward self, developing interpersonal skills, becoming tolerant and accepting of others, developing academic skills in core areas, and achieving a sense of independence. The development of these tasks occurs within many contexts (e.g., family, school, church, community) and various factors affect individuals' growth. In this section, we cover physical, social, cognitive, and gender development. However, we again caution that not all students will move through developmental stages at the same pace, and it is outside the scope of this book to review all developmental trends and possibilities.

Physical Development

Physically, students in fourth and fifth grades are undergoing the initial changes associated with transitioning to early adolescence. Specifically, the development of secondary sexual characteristics may begin to emerge as pre-teens begin the physical changes associated with puberty. According to Belsky (2007), there appears to be a drop in the age of puberty, with girls beginning menarche younger than in previous generations, sometimes as early as late elementary school. This change in the onset of puberty and secondary sexual characteristics may be attributed to major changes in lifestyle; in particular, nutrition appears to be the principal underlying variable (Belsky, 2007).

As these physiological changes occur, preteens' brains also are changing because of the impact of hormones on the functioning of neurotransmitters. Changes in mood and increased emotionality often result. It is important for adults to recognize these changes and to help students develop strategies for emotional self-regulation and for reducing emotional reactivity—skills they will need for maintaining positive working relationships in their careers and throughout their schooling. It is also important to identify students who are having difficulty navigating these changes, as manifested by feelings of self-consciousness about their bodies and/or displaying embarrassment about changes in their appearance. Students struggling with body image concerns may need extra support (small group or individual counseling) in order to continue to have a positive self-concept, a critical dimension of positive career development.

Psychosocial and Socioemotional Development

In late childhood, children are most likely still in Erikson's stage of *industry versus inferiority*, and are continuing to resolve issues related to competence in academics, athletics, and other socially valued activities. By late childhood and early adolescence, social relationships, primarily peer friendships, are based on mutual interests, and the peer group becomes a socializing force for what is normal and acceptable. In particular, social acceptance and popularity are based on social characteristics, "such as friendliness, a moderate degree of assertiveness, a sense of humor, and competence in valued activities" (Ferguson, 1970, p. 143). Popularity and social acceptance can serve to bolster self-concept and this, in turn, can impact career development. Moreover, the development of meaningful and intimate friendships can promote empathy for others (Ferguson, 1970), which may lead to an increase in prosocial behaviors such as compassion, kindness, forgiveness, and gratitude (Shaffer, 2009). All of these characteristics and behaviors are important for developing future workplace relationships.

Cognitive Development

Fourth- and fifth-grade students most likely continue to be in Piaget's (1977) stage of *concrete operations,* as discussed in Chapter 7. The cognitive tasks of conservation, decentering, and seriation become more solidified and are used by children with greater consistency as they apply these skills to day-to-day learning. Additionally, children are being introduced to more complex functions; for example, in fourth and fifth grades, students are often introduced to the mathematical concepts of proportions, ratios, fractions, and decimals. These tasks require students to use more metacognition skills as they have to translate words into numbers or transform numbers. Students often learn creative ways of doing this; some students learn to use visual representations of math (consider the pie chart for the fraction two fifths), and others memorize patterns for solving equations. Either way, the growing complexity requires new strategies and skill development. Further, as previously noted in Chapter 7, students in middle childhood begin to use information processing to promote their own memory (i.e., use of rehearsal and selective attention).

By late childhood, the cognitive functions associated with memory require that students have opportunities to use multiple strategies, and, by doing so, will find strategies that are most helpful to them. Belsky (2007) asserted that parents can practice these strategies with children at home to help them identify responsibilities and expectations and remember what they need to do to meet those expectations. For example, parents might ask their children to articulate the daily tasks they need to complete (e.g., chores such as feeding the dog or washing dishes). Through using this type of rehearsal activity, children begin to develop an understanding of personal responsibility and how to keep track of what they need to do, an important step in developing self-regulatory behavior (see Bandura, discussed in the following), which is a necessary skill for workplace success. Further, in order to promote positive self-concept, it is important to help students at this age begin to understand that everyone has unique gifts and talents that they can use to become better learners and workers.

Gender

As fourth- and fifth-grade students become more immersed in popular culture, the influences of macrosystems become more pronounced. In Chapter 7, we highlighted Gottfredson's (1981) Stage 2: *Orientation to Sex Roles,* and it is important to underscore that the continued effects of gendered socialization are strong in the late elementary years. In many ways, social pressures for gender ideals increase as preteens view social media, listen to music, and begin to notice trends and patterns of how other males and females dress, act, respond, and which actions bring social value.

As proposed by Choate and Curry (2009), problems resulting from the sexualization of girlhood are noticeable in 21st-century schools. Girls begin to self-objectify in middle childhood, and there is an increased ruminative pattern of self-objectification in late elementary and early middle school. According to the American Psychological Association's *Report of the APA Task Force on the Sexualization of Girls* (2007), the negative mental health impact (e.g., anxiety, depression, negative self-concept) on girls based on sexualization may lead to lower academic achievement, career expectancy, and decreased career aspirations (Choate & Curry, 2009). This might be especially true when considering careers outside of typical gender roles. Research on stereotype threat has demonstrated that when women and girls believe that gender will have academic consequences, they perform worse. This was shown in a landmark study conducted by Spencer, Steele, and Quinn (1999), which has been frequently cited. In the study, men and women were given a math test. Approximately one-half of the women in the sample were told that gender differences had been shown by the test previously. The other half of the women participating were told gender differences had not been shown. For the women who were told there were no differences shown, they performed equal to men on the test. For those who were told there were differences by gender, they performed significantly lower than the men in the sample.

This notion of stereotype threat is so critical with fourth- and fifth-grade students because girls may be starting to feel the effects of stereotype threat in terms of career and college, especially in areas of math and science (i.e., "girls aren't good at math"). If this is internalized, it may lead to lower achievement in math and science and lack of career aspirations in science, technology, engineering, and mathematics (STEM) fields. Certainly, women are highly underrepresented in STEM professions and stereotype threat may play a large role in that fact. Overcoming this gender gap may be complicated but there have been successes. For example, an intervention designed for fourth- and fifth-grade girls known as Bringing Up Girls in Science (BUGS), with a focus on environmental sciences, used an afterschool, extracurricular approach to encourage girls to change their science career perceptions (Tyler-Wood, Ellison, Lim, & Periathiruvadi, 2012). Key aspects of the program included an after school outdoor science lab, assignment of formal high school mentors who assisted in science projects and weekly science activities, and a 2-week summer program. Multiple measures were collected including perceptions of science careers, interest in science careers, intent to major in science in college, and longitudinal data on student achievement, career outcomes, college major, and so forth. In sum, the major impact of the program, although the sample size was modest ($n = 32$), was that the participants had significant gains in science knowledge and science career perceptions compared to nonparticipant peers.

Although programs like this are costly and may be difficult to maintain, there are more cost-effective mechanisms for promoting girls' science and math self-concepts. Some ideas include reminding teachers to invite girls to lead math and science activities in the classroom and organizing a "Girls Science Club" or a "Girls Math Club" that meets monthly and has a different female professional in a math or science career serving as a guest speaker. It could be important to have that individual lead an activity and connect the career to postsecondary options (i.e., Ms. Roosevelt is an economist and she has a bachelor's degree in business and finance) as well as have her talk about what she does and how she was trained for her career.

Beyond issues related to girls and stereotype threat, there are gendered social inductions for males as well. According to Kimmel (2005), male bravado and overconfidence promoted in social media stereotypes for boys increase risk-taking behaviors, violent reactions, and inauthenticity as boys are forced to display emotions that are not congruent with their true feelings (i.e., appearing tough, aloof, uncaring). These behavior patterns lead boys to experience more disruptive behaviors in school, suspensions, grade-level retention, lower grades, referrals for psychological screenings, attention deficit hyperactivity disorder diagnoses, and other negative consequences (Kimmel, 2005). Indeed, Kimmel stated, "Boys see academic success itself as a disconfirmation of their masculinity" (2005, p. 241) based on traditional stereotypes that the ideal male has great athletic prowess and is unemotional and disinterested in academic pursuits.

This "boy code" as noted by Kimmel (2005) results in boys displaying more anger (as is socially promoted) and less compassion, empathy, and vulnerability (socially sanctioned). The consequences for long-term career development are that boys are left still needing to develop critical skills (e.g., academic, positive interpersonal communication, relationship building) for future workplace success. Therefore, school counselors need to be aware that gender socialization should be addressed throughout the school curriculum and career curriculum in particular, by challenging stereotypes and traditional roles with consistency and deliberation (Choate & Curry, 2009; Curry & Choate, 2010).

RELEVANT CAREER THEORY: BANDURA (1977), GOTTFREDSON (1981), YOUNG (1983), AND SUPER (1980)

In this section, we review career theories and concepts important to the future career success of fourth- and fifth-grade students. We introduce two of the most important cross-theoretical concepts: self-regulation and career self-efficacy. Our review starts with an in-depth look at social learning theory (Bandura, 1977).

Bandura's Social Learning Theory

Albert Bandura, the originator of social learning theory, has contributed greatly to how we conceptualize life tasks related to career development (Bandura, 1977). In his theory, Bandura propounds three major constructs pertinent to understand the development of career efficacy: reciprocal determinism, self-regulation, and efficacy expectancy.

Reciprocal Determinism
Bandura (1977) proposed that reciprocal determinism exists among cognitive, behavioral, and environmental factors. He contended that the interactions of this trifecta, not just one facet, impact the individual as variant sources of influence, depending on circumstances and context. Bandura further believed that the relationship among these factors was not a function of unidirectional operation, but rather, "interlocking determinants" (p. 10) (see Figure 9.1).

FIGURE 9.1   Behavior, Cognition, and Environment as Interlocking Determinants

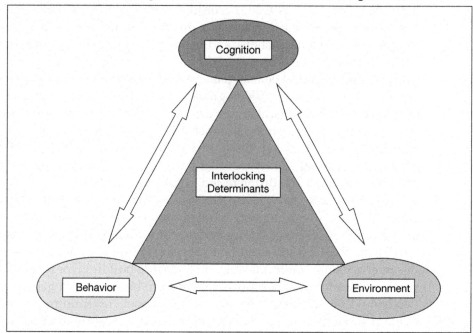

Adapted from Bandura (1977).

As noted by Bandura (1977), the environment may support positive growth for individuals or it may inhibit optimal development. The individual's behavior may reciprocally influence the environment through positive or negative impact. Further, characteristics of the individual (cognitive, affective, and physiological) also interact with the environment and behavior to shape circumstances (Bandura, 1977). In other words, students are influenced by the environments they are in (school, family, community) and also by the way they cognitively process information (person) and react to it (behavior). In this way, students influence the environment as well as the reactions other people have to them. For this reason, children must learn to regulate all of these aspects (thoughts, emotions, and behaviors) in order to move toward goals.

Self-Regulation

Based on the theoretical assumptions of social learning theory (Bandura, 1977), self-regulation (sometimes referred to in professional literature as self-management or self-monitoring) is an individual's ability to plan and manage his or her own behavior toward successfully reaching a goal. To fully comprehend self-regulation, it is critical to conceptualize how it is generated and maintained. Self-regulation stems from individuals envisioning potential courses of action, judging their ability to produce the actions necessary for desired outcomes, and then setting goals and taking action (Bandura, 1977). An example of this type of behavior comes from marathon runners who have to manage their behavior (nutrition intake, sleep/rest, consistent training) in order to successfully complete the task of running an endurance race.

Self-regulation is important for future career success, as students need to learn to set goals and engage in behaviors that will assist them in progressing toward those goals. In the workplace, employees may be expected to complete large-scale or long-term projects that require breaking the projects into small, manageable tasks and determining a timeline for completing tasks. Beyond project-based work, in the average workplace employees are expected to self-manage their behaviors to produce results in line with their employer's expectations. Self-regulation is a learned skill that can be taught in the day-to-day operations of fourth- and fifth-grade education, and we provide some examples later in this chapter of how teachers and parents can help students develop this skill.

Individuals with strong self-regulatory capacity also have the ability to regulate emotions appropriately and to cope effectively with stress. Coping by attempting to understand and acknowledge one's emotions during distressing events has been found to be significantly linked to lower trait anxiety, lower depressive symptoms, and positive adjustment (Stanton, Parsa, & Austenfeld, 2002). All of these positive outcomes of emotional self-regulation promote workplace success as they improve the mental health of individuals. School counselors can work with students through a personal/social curriculum to develop strategies to appropriately express emotions and learn how to accept support in overcoming stress (Stanton et al., 2002).

Efficacy Expectancy

Pivotal to regulating one's own behavior, individuals must be able to estimate outcomes of their actions. These expectations, referred to by Bandura as efficacy expectancies, include approximating consequences, identifying the action required for any behavior, and evaluating one's abilities to successfully complete a desired behavior (Bandura, 1977). An efficacy expectation is "the conviction that one can successfully execute the behavior required to produce the outcomes" (Bandura, 1977, p. 79). Competent mastery of any given task requires the minimal skills necessary to perform the task and feelings of efficacy in one's ability to effectively apply the skills (Bandura, 1986).

According to Bandura (1977), self-efficacy—a person's determination about his or her ability to be successful—affects the degree of effort an individual will put forth in overcoming difficult or arduous circumstances. When people believe they are competent, they are more likely to undertake challenging tasks. Evidence of this can be seen in any classroom as students who believe they cannot do a particular assignment may not even attempt to do the work assigned. According to Bandura (1977), "perceived self-efficacy not only reduces anticipatory fears and inhibitions but, through expectations of eventual success, it affects coping efforts once they are initiated" (p. 80). The relationship between efficacy and coping through stress was underscored by Fernandez-Ballesteros, Diez-Nicolas, Caprara, Barbaranelli, and Bandura (2002) when they suggested that, "unless people believe they can produce desired outcomes and forestall undesired ones through their actions, they have little incentive to act or to persevere in the face of difficulties" (p. 108). Consequently, a sense of efficacy about a given task promotes persistence toward meeting a goal.

Therefore, self-efficacy prompts people to proaction, and fosters the ability to endure stress for greater quantities of time in order to achieve some goal or to perform some desired behavior. Thus, students with greater academic and career efficacy may persist in school, even when they struggle, as they perceive they are capable of eventual success. Indeed, building the capacity to persevere through skill building to tolerate stress, manage time, and have effective study habits and organization can lead to college retention and success. Conversely, students who don't think they will be successful in career and college pursuits may see no reason to take more rigorous courses, and may show a decreased commitment to academics. Therefore, building student academic, career, and college efficacy is an important task for elementary school counselors to undertake before students transition to middle school.

Sources of Efficacy Expectancy. According to Bandura (1977), there are four main sources of efficacy expectations: (a) performance accomplishments, (b) vicarious experiences, (c) verbal persuasion, and (d) emotional arousal. Bandura labeled these hierarchically based on each source's dependability as an influence on efficacy. The strongest dependent contributor is performance accomplishments and the least is emotional arousal.

Performance accomplishments (Bandura, 1977) are the most dependable source of efficacy expectation because they are based on the lived experience of the individual. For example, for students to envision their ability to become a scientist, being able to partake in activities that scientists do (e.g., lab work, field experiences) is critical. The more success individuals experience in related activities and tasks, the greater will be their efficacy for mastery of increasingly difficult competencies. The converse is also true: If individuals experience repeated failure, then they are at risk of producing lower efficacy expectations.

Vicarious experience was the second most dependable producer of efficacy expectation. Bandura (1977) stated that "seeing others perform threatening activities without adverse consequences can create expectations in observers that they too will eventually succeed if they intensify and persist in their efforts" (p. 81). For this reason, career role models are important. When students see people similar to themselves (based on race, gender, socioeconomic background, religious affiliation, English-language learners, etc.) being successful in a given occupation or activities related to that occupation, they are more likely to assess that they also could be successful in that occupation.

Verbal persuasion (Bandura, 1977) includes encouragement or prompting, such as exhortation and suggestion; it is the third most dependable source of efficacy expectancy. Bandura ascertained that this type of efficacy would be short lived at best, especially if the individual experiences disconfirmation of competence. For example, some students internalize negative feedback much more easily than they do positive feedback. No matter how many people comment on their strengths or express confidence in their abilities, those students only recall the one person who said they had no chance of making it, and they make decisions with that one person's input in mind.

The last of the sources of efficacy expectancy is *emotional arousal*. Emotions are often perceived by individuals as indicators of the amount of stress they are able to endure or how capable they are of completing a task. For example, some people might interpret emotional reactions of fear, anxiety, and nervousness (normal emotions in new or stressful circumstances) as indicators that they cannot handle the task at hand. This negative labeling may spark a cyclical reaction according to Bandura (1977): "Because high arousal usually debilitates performance, individuals are more likely to expect success when they are not beset by aversive arousal than when they are tense, shaking, and viscerally agitated" (p. 82). For example, students undertaking a new academic task (such as fourth and fifth graders learning about ratios) may mistakenly attribute their anxiety about undertaking the task as an inability to successfully complete the task.

Finally, Bandura (1977, 1986) contended that efficacy beliefs differ on three dimensions. The first is *magnitude*, based on the simplicity versus the complexity/difficulty of the task being considered. The second dimension is *generality*. Generality is the degree to which efficacy beliefs are specific to given tasks or if they broadly encompass other life arenas or competencies. The third dimension is *strength*. The stronger an efficacy belief, the less impact disconfirming circumstances will have, and the greater effort one will exert to master challenges. Conversely, individuals with low self-efficacy discontinue or decline efforts if they are met with failure (Bandura, 1986).

While self-efficacy may be the impetus for the bridge from cognition to action, it may also serve other purposes. According to Masten and Reed (2002), self-efficacy is a personal characteristic predictive of "good adaptation in the context of risk" (p. 82); promoting self-efficacy may mitigate risk factors and improve resilience. Bandura, Barbaranelli, Caprara, and Pastorelli (1996) stated that self-efficacy may impact individual development and adaptation. Maddux (2002) maintained that self-efficacy beliefs are critical for psychological adjustment and physical health, as well as competency-based pursuit behaviors—such as those necessary for a successful work life. Maddux further enumerated many benefits of self-efficacy. To begin, strong self-efficacy beliefs promote and encourage exploration—a skill critical to one's sense of agency and career development. Also, self-efficacy beliefs have been found to assist in self-regulation toward goal attainment by influencing the types of goals an individual chooses. Self-efficacy beliefs also lead to more effective problem solving, better utilization of personal and cognitive resources, lower depression, increased coping strategies (Fernandez-Ballesteros et al., 2002; Maddux, 2002), and improved academic functioning (Bandura et al., 1996).

Gottfredson's Theory of Circumscription and Compromise

Students in fourth and fifth grades are in Gottfredson's (1981) Stage 3: *Orientation to Social Valuation*. Students in fourth grade begin to view themselves from a third-party perspective. This means they are noticing how valued they are by their peers who have social capital (Bourdieu, 1977) as manifested by popularity, prestige, and status symbols. According to Sharf (2006), students begin to notice the types of clothes their peers are wearing as well as the size and expense of their and others' homes, cars, and so on. For example, while working in an elementary school I (first author) would occasionally have older students ask me what kind of car I drove or what I lived in (i.e., a home, an apartment, a trailer?). These questions were all part of the situation, from the students' perspectives, of discovering what professional people garner in terms of material things. I never assumed that students were being nosy or inappropriate; rather, I believed that they were curious about how other people lived as they were beginning to compare their circumstances to others.

In fourth and fifth grades, students also begin to recognize the social value of the careers of family members, to understand which careers will be accepted by their families, and to circumscribe career choices that they perceive as above or below their own social position. One aspect of social valuation that is important for school counselors to pay attention to is that students begin to place a value on how hard certain occupations are (i.e., perceived difficulty). Generally, the harder the occupation is perceived to be, the more social value it is assigned. For example, students rate being a doctor as very hard and highly valued; therefore, students who don't view themselves as intelligent (self-concept) or don't believe they have the ability to learn what is needed to become a doctor (self-efficacy) may eliminate such a career choice as beyond their abilities. For this reason, students can benefit from opportunities to experience firsthand the activities related to highly valued or "difficult" careers so that they can experience success, build self-efficacy (performance accomplishment), and then envision themselves in these kinds of occupations.

Young's Career Concepts

By fourth and fifth grades, peers are beginning to gain prominence in their importance and influence on each other, and this is true even in relation to career and college readiness. For example, an elementary school counselor asked one fifth-grade classroom of students what careers they were interested in, and a popular young man raised his hand and said, "Sportscaster." Immediately following, about five other boys in the class raised their hands and gave the same answer. Students with prestige and social capital begin to gain leadership in the classroom and other students begin to follow.

Regarding careers, as was noted in Gottfredson's (1981) Stage 3, the social value assigned to careers by students can evolve largely based on their peer group in the classroom (Young, 1983), and that peer group is influenced in general by the larger community in which they all live. The same can occur for postsecondary education. One of my (second author) good friends has a daughter who is certain she will attend the Pennsylvania State University (Penn State). Many of her friends all want to go there too. My friend talks all the time about Penn State at home and his daughter has numerous T-shirts and watches football games. She doesn't know why she loves Penn State other than she knows it is something of value to her family and her friends. She hears her parents talking proudly about their alma mater and she internalizes those feelings, leading her to express to her friends and teachers, "I will go to Penn State when I graduate." In most instances, children in fourth and fifth grades have no clear understanding of what college entails, but the influence of others can be powerful.

For this reason it is important that school counselors continue to give students individual reflection time and activities that allow them to consider their own career interests and aptitudes. So, although working in small groups with peers during classroom instruction is desirable, school counselors should also ensure that students get some personal reflection time to think about careers. Further, Young (1983) underscored the ongoing importance of parents and family in career exploration and decision making. Thus, school counselors need to support parent–child activities to promote career and college development. Specifically, parents need to be offered opportunities to consistently engage in career and college conversations with their children through structured offerings that foster parent understanding of career and college exploration and parent–child engagement.

Super's Life-Span, Life-Space Approach

Although we discuss Super's theory in greater detail in subsequent chapters, we do wish to highlight Super's (1980) nine concepts or activities of childhood career development that foster career development through personal awareness and career decision making. These concepts are: (a) curiosity, (b) exploration of oneself or environment, (c) information that promotes awareness of the importance of career information, (d) key figures or career role models that play a meaningful role in a child's life, (e) a child's personal interests, (f) locus of control, (g) time perspective that aids in student awareness of the need to plan, (h) self-concept, and (i) planfulness or an understanding of the importance of planning.

Super's concepts were investigated through qualitative inquiry by Schultheiss, Palma, and Manzi (2005). Forty-nine urban elementary students participated in the study (writing assignments using open-ended career development questions as prompts) and data revealed that overwhelmingly, students' writings reflected the importance of Super's concepts in career development. The only one of the nine concepts missing from the data was curiosity. Schultheiss et al. reported that fourth- and fifth-grade students in their study described career exploration activities in the classroom, connected learning to work, and explored careers through play. Regarding self-concept, participants in the study were able to identify interests, abilities, and activities they found enjoyable. Further, students were able to express an internal locus of control (belief that they had control over their own behavior and future), key figures in their career development, conceptions of work, time perspective and the importance of planning, and decision-making processes.

These findings underscore the importance of understanding and identifying markers of career development and career maturity. School counselors should consider Super's concepts and ask themselves, "Are the students at my school displaying, consistently, that their career decision making and maturity include these concepts?"

THE MIDDLE SCHOOL TRANSITION

The transition to middle school can seem like a predominantly academic milestone for students, but the impact of this transition on career development is critical. Students prepared for the academic rigor of middle school are more likely to be academically successful in their middle grades education. Specifically, students and their parents/guardians need to be well informed of the available options for course work, encouraged to register for the most rigorous classes they are capable of taking, and prepared for the differences in their daily routine as they move from elementary to middle school. Most notably, it is important to prepare parents, guardians, and teachers to provide supportive guidance and to promote student academic and career efficacy (Hall, 2003) during this adjustment period. Although personal/social issues are also very important during this transition, our discussion focuses on academic and career interventions.

THE SCHOOL COUNSELOR AND THE CORE COUNSELING CURRICULUM

According to Niles and Harris-Bowlsbey (2009), by the end of elementary school, students should have gained several basic career development skills including: "self-knowledge, skills for interacting with others, basic skills in educational and occupational career exploration, awareness of the relationship between work and learning, basic skills to understand and use career information, awareness of the importance of personal responsibility and good work habits, and awareness of the career planning process" (p. 322). If school counselors approach career and college readiness intervention through a comprehensive, systematic approach, including multisystems stakeholders (ASCA, 2012), then by the time students reach the fourth and fifth grades, they should be equipped for deeper career and college exploration. To effectively design curriculum, school counselors should think developmentally about promoting time management and study skills and increasing self-discipline, self-control, leadership, and teamwork. Most importantly, students in fourth and fifth grades should be receiving less external motivators and becoming more internally motivated toward achievement. Table 9.1 features ASCA Mindsets and Behaviors (2014) that school counselors could focus on when developing fourth- and fifth-grade curriculum.

Career Exploration, Technology, and Interests

If students have been adequately introduced to career clusters and the relationships among careers in the second and third grades, then they will be ready by the fourth and fifth grades to learn the process of exploring individual careers. In order to develop career decision-making self-efficacy, that is, feeling that they can successfully engage in the tasks of exploring and deciding on a career, students have to gain relevant experience (performance accomplishment) in varied career exploration activities (Gushue, Scanlan, Pantzer, & Clarke, 2006). Utilizing technology for career exploration, students can be introduced to sources that will assist them in better understanding careers they are interested in and how to use these tools to explore careers on their own (e.g., *Occupational Outlook Handbook* online, *O*Net*). In Exhibit 9.1, we illustrate a culminating activity that a school counselor can use to help students explore careers and colleges and develop efficacy.

TABLE 9.1 ASCA Mindsets and Behaviors for Fourth- and Fifth-Grade Curriculum Planning Focus

CATEGORY 1: MINDSETS STANDARDS		
Belief in development of whole self, including a healthy balance of mental, socioemotional, and physical well-being Self-confidence in ability to succeed Positive attitude toward work and learning		
CATEGORY 2: BEHAVIOR STANDARDS		
Learning Strategies	**Self-Management Skills**	**Social Skills**
Use time management, organizational, and study skills	Demonstrate self-discipline and self-control	Use leadership and teamwork skills to work effectively in diverse teams
Apply self-motivation and self-direction to learning	Demonstrate ability to manage transitions and ability to adapt to changing situations and responsibilities	Demonstrate empathy
Actively engage in challenging course work	Demonstrate the ability to balance school, home, and community activities	

EXHIBIT 9.1
The Student Career and College Fair

Mr. Butler, an elementary school counselor in an inner city school, Westdale Elementary, had completed a five-lesson career and college unit with fifth-grade students. In the unit, students learned introductory career exploration skills using technology, the components of a resume, how to determine the postsecondary educational and training requirements for a career, and how to write a cover letter for a job that highlights personal characteristics and values related to a career. Although the students were at a beginning level in all of these skills, Mr. Butler wanted them to apply the skills to further solidify their knowledge and understanding. Mr. Butler considered hosting a career and college fair, but it was difficult to get community partners and parents to participate in these types of activities at his school.

Mr. Butler consulted with the fifth-grade team. They decided to have a student-led career and college fair. Students were allowed to choose a career and they were given 2 weeks to create cardboard trifolds to present their career and college findings to the rest of the fifth grade. Mr. Butler was able to get the trifolds and other materials necessary for the project through Office Depot, a local community partner with the school. Students mounted multiple career and college exploration artifacts on the trifold. Each trifold

(continued)

EXHIBIT 9.1 (continued)
The Student Career and College Fair

contained a picture of someone performing a work task associated with the career, a fact sheet about the daily responsibilities of the career, a sheet with education requirements including a list of three colleges that offered training for the career chosen, projected salary, and a student resume and cover letter designed for the career. Other artifacts included drawings or construction paper cutouts that represented tools of the trade. For example, one student, Clarissa, studied the career of a zookeeper. She had a picture of a zookeeper with a zebra, a fact sheet, a sheet with education requirements for a zookeeper and colleges where she could receive this education, and multiple artifacts attached to the trifold (cutouts of animals, a packet of bird seed for feeding birds, and pictures of animal habitats). Students set up their trifolds in the gym and each class took turns presenting their career and college trifolds to the entire fifth grade. Students and teachers love the career and college fair and Mr. Butler continues to host it each year.

As noted in Exhibit 9.1, Mr. Butler helped his students apply their career and college readiness knowledge (promoting career exploration efficacy through performance accomplishment) by having the students design and host their own career and college fair. The activity promoted student career exploration efficacy and self-regulation behaviors. Specifically, because students had to complete multiple tasks over time, as well as develop a way to present their projects using the trifold and other materials, self-regulation was necessary to successfully complete the task (setting a goal and breaking it down into smaller, manageable tasks). Although Mr. Butler didn't have the parent and community resources at his disposal for a more traditional career and college fair (adult speakers and demonstrations), he used the resources available in his school community to meet the comprehensive needs of his students.

IMPORTANCE OF STAKEHOLDERS

Parents and teachers continue to exert a large influence on fourth- and fifth-grade students and, therefore, should continue to be an integral part of a comprehensive career and college readiness curriculum.

Promoting Student Self-Regulation in the Classroom

It is important that, by fourth grade, students are able to keep their own daily agenda, write down tasks to complete for each day, and organize their materials in the classroom. Teachers can assist students by allotting 5 to 10 minutes at the beginning of each day to help them get their materials organized. Moreover, students need to learn the skills of effective note taking, outlining ideas before writing, and creating plans to follow for long-term projects. By doing so, the foundation is being laid for strong self-regulatory behavior. Further, students who accomplish these tasks will likely receive positive reinforcement through improvement in their grades, and this performance accomplishment may increase efficacy expectancies in future academic endeavors as they learn to implement success skills and strategies. By increasing student self-regulation and efficacy, teachers are effectively preparing students for future career and college success.

Collaborating With Teachers

Collaborating with teachers is critical to the successful integration of career and college information into the classroom curriculum (ASCA, 2012). Based on the ASCA Mindsets and Behaviors (2014), there are numerous student career and college readiness competencies that teachers could integrate into the education curriculum with the assistance of the school counselor. Specifically, in fourth and fifth grades, students need to be able to demonstrate self-confidence in their ability to succeed, have positive attitudes toward work and learning, demonstrate critical thinking skills, apply self-motivation and self-direction to learning, use leadership and teamwork skills for working with diverse groups of people, demonstrate self-discipline and self-control, and relate academic learning to career paths.

Moreover, teachers and counselors might consider alternative and creative methods for exposing students to opportunities to explore and experience careers and college. One way to do this is through peer and cross-age programs. Most often when people think of peer and cross-age programs they may imagine peer tutoring, mentoring, and conflict resolution. However, an example of an afterschool enrichment program for fifth-grade students (see Junior Engineers in Exhibit 9.2) exemplifies how teachers collaborated with the school counselor in a cross-age program to expose students to exploring the work (performance accomplishment) of the field of engineering.

EXHIBIT 9.2
The Junior Engineers Club

Mr. Thompkins, an elementary school counselor, was contacted by Mr. Donaldson, a high school physics teacher, who was the club sponsor for the Engineering Club at the high school. The Engineering Club met once a month at the high school and had recently decided that they wanted to develop a cross-age program to introduce younger students to engineering as a service learning project. They decided to provide the opportunity to fifth graders interested in engineering, and they decided to call the group the Junior Engineers Club. Mr. Thompkins agreed to cosponsor the club.

All fifth-grade students were invited and 18 decided to participate. A fifth-grade teacher, Mrs. Simmons, also attended in order to get ideas for

(continued)

EXHIBIT 9.2 (continued)
The Junior Engineers Club

integrating engineering in the future fifth-grade curriculum for all students. The group met once a month. For each meeting, a different structural design was introduced. For example, during the first meeting, high school students presented a PowerPoint of the structural components of pyramids and showed pictures of ancient and modern-day pyramids. High schoolers presented the strengths of the pyramid's design. Afterward, club members learned to sketch a design of a pyramid three dimensionally, and then used different materials to create pyramids using what they learned (wood blocks, Styrofoam blocks, and Legos). Other designs that were explored in subsequent months included columns (Roman design), arches, cubes, foundations, and supports.

Beyond exploring structures and engineering, Mr. Thompkins visited the group and they talked about careers and college. Some careers included engineering, architecture, and construction management. Mr. Thompkins decided that in the future one of the goals of the club would be a field trip (with their high school mentors and if funding could be secured) to a local university to visit these degree programs. This experience would allow the fifth-grade students to gain information about both the career side (architects, engineers, construction managers at work) and the training aspects through the college.

The high school Engineering Club enjoyed working with the fifth graders and the partnership continues today. Additionally, Mrs. Simmons was able to integrate some of the activities into the regular fifth-grade curriculum and eventually wrote a small grant ($1,200) to purchase the materials needed to develop engineering projects. Today, the Junior Engineers Club explores more complex engineering feats such as bridges, roads, and towers.

The example in Exhibit 9.2 demonstrates how a cross-age program was used to expose students to engineering. The Junior Engineers Club gave students specific content knowledge, engineering role models (the older students), and an opportunity to experience the work of engineers (performance accomplishment), all of which are important for developing feelings of efficacy in one's ability to successfully become an engineer. Infinite possibilities exist for the types of clubs that could be started in elementary school. Clearly, such clubs have existed at the high school level for a long time (e.g., Future Farmers of America); yet, based on the importance of developing career- and college-related efficacy (Bandura, 1977), teachers and counselors can consider creating these opportunities for younger students.

Although STEM careers have gained importance in recent years, there are many forums in which other types of careers can be examined, including those in fine arts (i.e., drama, music, visual arts, painting, writing, poetry, and dance). For example, in Exhibit 9.3 we review a fourth-grade project demonstrating how fine arts, business, and economics were combined to allow students to become exposed to a wide range of careers.

EXHIBIT 9.3
Fourth-Grade Coffee House and Fine Arts Night

At LaGrange Elementary School, the fourth-grade classes offer a quarterly (once every 9 weeks) Coffee House Night for parents, grandparents, and other special guests. For each quarter, a different fourth-grade class runs the coffee shop. Students take turns playing different roles in the coffee shop (cashier, server, marketing director, menu developer, pastry baker, coffee barista, dishwasher, purchasing manager, etc.) and they are responsible for all of the preparation necessary under the supervision of their teacher, teacher's aides, and a few parent volunteers. This preparation includes marketing through the development of materials (flyers/brochures) and communication (developing letters of invitation and business e-mails).

Parents come to the coffee shop and order from a simple menu (pastries, coffee, tea, water) while the fourth-grade classes perform entertainment. Parents can walk through a gallery with art produced by students in art class (pencil drawings, watercolors, oil pastels), and students read poetry, and short stories, perform short skits, dance, and play instruments. Income generated from the Coffee House funds materials and supplies needed for future Coffee House Nights and fourth-grade field trips.

Additionally, the Coffee House Nights give students a chance to learn about how a business is run. The students have to prepare the Coffee House (decorate the cafeteria), develop a purchasing list (purchases are made by a parent volunteer), take orders, give change, deduct expenses from money generated to fund future coffee nights, and serve parents. In addition, they get to practice displaying art, designing an "art gallery," and performing music and written arts. Students experience various roles hands-on. At the conclusion of each class's running of the Coffee House, they categorize the different jobs by career clusters and write a short essay on "What It's Like to Run a Coffee Shop." After completing the essay, the school counselor and teacher cofacilitated a classroom guidance follow-up where students discussed how they felt about the Coffee House Night. In small groups, students discussed what they liked or didn't like about running a coffee shop, what they learned from the activity, what skills or talents they had to contribute to running the coffee shop, and how confident they felt that they could run a coffee shop (or other business venture) in the future.

As illuminated in Exhibit 9.3, students were allowed to explore a variety of roles in entertainment and business. In this way, multiple intelligences (Gardner, 2004) were used and students were able to bring their own strengths and interests to the activity. By having students write their reflective essays and discuss their views on the project afterward, the school counselor and teachers promoted student awareness of their skills, interests, and feelings of efficacy related to the project (running a coffee shop). Additionally, by experiencing the various roles, the students were given an opportunity for performance accomplishment (Bandura, 1977) in managing a small business, the result of which may be increased efficacy expectancy for careers in business and marketing. Of additional importance, parents were invited to participate, an intentional strategy for increasing family involvement in career development.

Parent Engagement

As we discussed earlier in this chapter, by middle school, peers become a predominant influence in each other's lives (Young, 1983). However, for fourth- and fifth-grade students, parents continue to play a paramount role in career and college readiness and need to be included in ongoing career and college exploration opportunities. Based on Bandura's social learning theory (1977), one very important topic to cover with parents of fourth- and fifth-grade students is how to help their kids become better self-regulators. As the demands of homework increase and students become more involved in extracurricular activities, students need to become better organized, manage their time, and learn how to break projects down into doable tasks. Some fun ways to do this at home include letting kids co-plan family activities like vacations. Families do not have to start with a large project like a vacation; planning a family game night will also help children practice the same skill set.

After implementing a parent workshop that promoted ways for parents to help their middle school students develop self-regulatory skills, the first author received a call from a fifth-grade parent who implemented the suggestions. The parent, who had twin fifth graders, had her children plan the dinner menu for two nights per week. She had her kids write down what they wanted to serve for dinner, figure out the ingredients needed, and write a grocery list. She then issued a budget for each dinner and the kids had to shop and meet the budget (sometimes choosing generic options or making substitutions if necessary). When it came to cooking, the children prepared the food by following a recipe and if they didn't have a recipe they wrote out the steps to follow to create the dish they were making (e.g., the steps for making pizza). During the phone call, the first author suggested to the mother that she tie this activity to her children's career development by having the kids come up with a list of careers where they could use the skills they were learning. The kids did this activity at home and the mother was amazed by the variety of careers the kids thought of (bank teller, sports manager, chef, grocery manager, etc.). Some months later, the mother told this author that her children were up to planning dinner four nights per week, something they enjoyed and their mother was proud of! Many parents are not aware of the simple ways that they can facilitate their child's development. Simply by recognizing this need and following through with education as well as concrete ideas, school personnel can help parents become active partners in their child's career development.

THE FIFTH- TO SIXTH-GRADE TRANSITION

The fifth- to sixth-grade transition constitutes one of the most important academic transitions for P–12 students. Most often, students enter a new school building (middle school) often on a separate campus than previously attended for elementary school. Students may feel fearful and concerned about the social system they are entering and how their experiences will differ from what they have experienced in elementary school.

Partnering With Middle School Personnel

As an elementary school counselor, the first author compiled a portfolio of all academic, personal/social, and career activities students had completed in their K–5 experience (Curry & Lambie, 2007). This portfolio was given to the middle school counselor to ensure that the middle school counselor knew what kinds of ASCA Student Standards (2004) had been promoted and what competencies the students had demonstrated in elementary school. Because the middle school counselor met with the elementary counselor and received these materials, she was able to provide continuity in career education and counseling by not duplicating the same content and experiences. Besides communicating about the counseling curriculum, there are many ways that elementary and middle school counselors can collaborate to promote a successful transition for fifth-grade students moving to middle school.

The Middle School Field Trip

One great way to prepare students and introduce them to middle school is to have the school counselor and fifth-grade teachers take the students on a field trip to the middle school. During the visit, students can meet with a panel of middle school students for a question-and-answer session. The middle school students can serve as role models and can help to assuage many of the fifth-grade students' fears (e.g., fears about switching classes in the time between class periods, using lockers, homework). The middle school counselor can share suggestions for fifth-grade students about what types of skills they would need to be successful in middle school, being certain to highlight specific self-regulation skills (homework strategies, note taking, organizing homework materials), and the types of resources offered to assist students in being successful (e.g., before and after school tutoring, small group counseling, study skills summer institute).

Engaging Parents in the Fifth- to Sixth-Grade Transition

It is incumbent upon elementary school counselors to assist students and their parents in preparing for the fifth- to sixth-grade transition. As previously mentioned, classroom presentations aimed at preparing students for the ambiguity of adjusting to a new school and new expectations are very important. It is equally important to assist parents and one way of doing so is through parent workshops. The first author, while running a focus group for parents in a local school district, found that parents were shocked by the changes as their students moved from elementary to middle school. Things parents listed as surprising were the amount of homework, expectations for students to be self-directed and self-regulating, differences in how much communication they received from classroom teachers (they received significantly less as the students went from one teacher to six teachers), and the difficulty of assignments (parents felt unsure of how to help their children as they were unfamiliar with the content).

An optimal way to conduct workshops for parents regarding the fifth- to sixth-grade transition is to have the elementary and middle school counselor cofacilitate and answer questions. Potential topics for these workshops are listed in Table 9.2.

Using the ASCA Mindsets and Behaviors to Plan Transition Activities. When planning for the sixth-grade transition, beyond thinking about field trips and parent workshops, intentionally organizing curriculum and working with stakeholders with the ASCA (2014) Mindsets and Behaviors framework can help school counselors visualize what students need during the transition and beyond. This approach will help school counselors blend information needed for the transition with skill development for future career and college preparation. In Exhibit 9.4, one school counselor shares how she developed her transition program with the ASCA Mindsets and Behaviors as a guide.

TABLE 9.2 Potential Topics for Parent Workshops on Middle School Transitions

Title of Workshop	Material Covered
Helping your child prepare for middle school academics	Getting organized, study skills, and homework strategies
Helping your child connect career goals to middle school academics	Career clusters, paths, and the middle school education agenda
Talking to your child about difficult topics	Sex, drugs, etc.
Harder classes or straight As? Which should you choose?	Introduction to the importance of rigor as postsecondary and career preparation instead of the assured "A"
Increasing the middle schooler's responsibilities at home: How much should you expect?	Helping parents recognize chores that are appropriate and how to help students become increasingly responsible

EXHIBIT 9.4

Voices From the Field: Transition Planning for Fourth and Fifth Grades

Anne Perrone, NCC, LPC

School Counselor, Our Lady of Mercy School

As a school counselor in a large, faith-affiliated P–12 school with approximately 100 students in each grade, the developmental needs of my student

(continued)

EXHIBIT 9.4 (*continued*)

population are broad and seemingly overwhelming. I have learned that programs cannot simply be created, but must be developed over time. Consideration for program development should always be geared toward specific needs of your student population and, in doing so, creating vertical alignment along the P–12 timeline. In fourth and fifth grades, my goals are to help students with the necessary skills for solid executive functioning, responsibility, and independence. I typically see each grade once per month unless the curriculum requires a more frequent interaction. Each lesson is allotted 30 minutes of instruction time and can occur over two sessions or follow up with the teacher. When referencing ASCA Mindsets and Behaviors for lesson development, I have included acronyms and corresponding numbers with each lesson description.

Our focus in fourth grade has been taking control of our responsibilities primarily as a student and subsequently any other life roles in which they may engage. Students participate in a series of four lessons focused on establishing basic time management skills and individual goal setting using the SMART goal setting model (ASCA Mindset: 5, Behavior: LS1, S3, M4, M8).

For time management, students first learn about how to classify activities as required and/or optional. As students work through several vignettes of a typical fourth-grade student's schedule, they work individually to create a visual daily and weekly calendar for the student in the vignette. This gives students a better understanding of how to prioritize school work over video games and other leisure activities and helps them consider how to plan for projects instead of procrastinating. Once completing these vignettes, students plan out their current week for academic and extracurricular responsibilities and pair-share ways to plug in activities they want to do, but are not obligated to do, such as watch YouTube videos, play video games, and sleep over at a friend's house. The student pair-share encourages the students, with counselor support, to engage in peer mentoring. Time management lessons take three class periods to complete. As a result, 10% of students requested follow-up individual support from the counselor to establish a personalized time management routine.

SMART goal setting is regularly addressed following this lesson (particularly in individual sessions) to help students set realistic goals, specifically when referencing individual academic achievement. In this lesson, students understand each foundation element of the SMART model (goals should be Specific, Measurable, Achievable, Relevant, and Time-based). Once students understand the concept and examples given, students are challenged to create one SMART goal for the week, month, and academic year. These goals may be academic or personal and, upon completion, students are invited to share their goals with the class.

Our fifth-grade students, eagerly anticipating the transition to middle school, share a variety of positive and negative emotions related to changes in their perceived role as a student, including readiness for advanced math and

(*continued*)

EXHIBIT 9.4 (continued)
Voices From the Field: Transition Planning for Fourth and Fifth Grades

English language arts classes. We offer these students a variety of transitional activities to process their emotions and perceived goals, as well as establish a better understanding of their future roles as middle school students.

While part of the academic enrichment rotation at our school is a 9-week study skills class for fifth-grade students, they also participate in a counseling lesson on time management as a follow-up activity to those delivered in fourth grade (ASCA M5, BSM4&8).

As part of the transition to middle school activities, a self-reflection lesson focused on sixth grade steers the direction of subsequent transition activities based on the needs of the current fifth-grade class (M2&3, BLS4, BSM7&10, BSS1,3,6). Students work with the counselor through a series of prompts related to hopes, fears, and expectations of sixth grade. It is important that students feel heard in this moment in preparation for the second part of the lesson. Next, the students participate in a 3-minute relaxation activity to transition into a gallery walk with prompts related to topics such as what makes them excited, anxious, or fearful for sixth grade, and things they want their teachers or counselor to know about them. A gallery walk is where the students physically walk around the room to each of the prompts hanging on the wall. At the prompts students talk in dyads and disclose what they feel comfortable disclosing in the larger group. It is important to review any "red flag" statements from the gallery walk such as fears of bullying and any repetitive statements such as "excited about lockers." Similar to small group counseling, this gives your students an opportunity for last minute additions or explanations that they want the counselor or group to hear before concluding the lesson. It also promotes a sense of universality, as they recognize that others around them have similar concerns.

Once data from the gallery have been organized, questions are created for a sixth-grade transition panel, consisting of current sixth-grade students (ASCA M3&6, BLS9, BSM10, BSS2&9). Over the years, there has been a standard selection of questions, but there is some adjusting based on the responses from the gallery walk. This panel is chosen with the intention of a multiperspective approach (academic achievement and interpersonal skills) and panel cohesion is strongly considered. This panel might be adapted to include a teacher or older middle school student, but it is important for students to have their questions answered by their peers. In the past, this panel has occurred immediately following sixth-grade Drug Abuse Resistance Education (DARE) Graduation, which the fifth-grade class attends. In doing so, fifth-grade students learn about DARE, understand why the sixth-grade students are so excited, and observe grade-level cohesion.

In addition to the aforementioned grade-specific activities, grades 2 to 8 participate in "College Colors Day." This is a great opportunity for students to learn about a variety of postsecondary education opportunities from teacher-led presentations. At the beginning of each class, teachers share information

(continued)

EXHIBIT 9.4 (*continued*)

such as the location of the education institution, campus population, popular majors of study, academic and athletic accolades, famous alumni, and personal experiences with this institution, if applicable.

Because our students are regularly exposed to athletics of a local, major Southeastern Conference (SEC) university, teachers are encouraged to select an institution outside of our city to give students a broad scope of the different schools out there. Because enrichment teachers also participate in this activity, students were exposed to three to nine different education institutions nationwide, including large 4-year universities, rural 4-year universities, and liberal arts colleges, as well as postsecondary service opportunities such as the Peace Corps and Catholic Charities Service Corps. Additionally, administration and staff members joined in and led a presentation about their alma mater or university not chosen by a teacher.

These programs have been established for several years, but there are still opportunities each year for me to adjust and build upon them based on my current population needs. Being able to align these lessons with ASCA Mindsets and Behaviors allows me to create a map for my students, career and college readiness.

SUMMARY

In this chapter, we provided an overview of salient developmental milestones on student career development (physical, cognitive, social, and gender), and focused on career theory specific to fourth- and fifth-grade students. Of utmost importance, we took an in-depth look at Bandura's social learning theory (1977) as it pertains to the development of self-regulation behaviors and the promotion of efficacy expectancies for future career and college success. We underscored the importance of a multisystem approach to comprehensive career and college readiness counseling (parents, teachers) and expanded this to include the middle school counselor. Finally, we focused on the importance of the fifth-grade transition to middle school for future academic and career success.

⋯❯ Test Your Knowledge

1. Define career self-efficacy.
2. Define efficacy expectancy. What are the three dimensions of efficacy beliefs?
3. Give three to four examples of self-regulatory behaviors that are age appropriate for fourth- or fifth-grade students at home and at school.
4. How is self-regulatory behavior related to academic success? Future career and college success?

REFERENCES

American Psychological Association, Task Force on the Sexualization of Girls. (2007). *Report of the APA task force on the sexualization of girls.* Retrieved from www.apa.org/pi/wpo/sexualization.html

American School Counselor Association. (2004). *ASCA student standards.* Alexandria, VA: Author.

American School Counselor Association. (2012). *The ASCA national model: A framework for school counseling programs* (3rd ed.). Alexandria, VA: Author.

American School Counselor Association. (2014). *ASCA mindsets & behaviors for student success: K-12 college- and career-readiness standards for every student.* Alexandria, VA: Author.

Bandura, A. (1977). *Social learning theory.* Englewood Cliffs, NJ: Prentice Hall.

Bandura, A. (1986). *Social foundations of thought and action: A social cognitive theory.* Englewood Cliffs, NJ: Prentice Hall.

Bandura, A. (1997). *Self-efficacy: The exercise of control.* New York, NY: Freeman.

Bandura, A., Barbaranelli, C., Caprara, G. V., & Pastorelli, C. (1996). Multifaceted impact of self-efficacy beliefs on academic functioning. *Child Development, 67*(3), 1206–1222. http://dx.doi.org/10.2307/1131888

Belsky, J. (2007). *Experiencing the lifespan.* New York, NY: Worth Publishers.

Bourdieu, P. (1977). *Outline of a theory of practice.* Cambridge, UK: Cambridge University Press.

Choate, L. H., & Curry, J. (2009). Addressing the sexualization of girls through comprehensive programs, advocacy and systemic change: Implications for professional school counselors. *Professional School Counseling, 12*(3), 213–221. http://dx.doi.org/10.5330/PSC.n.2010-12.213

Curry, J., & Choate, L. (2010). The oversexualization of young adolescent girls: Implications for middle grades educators. *Middle School Journal, 42*(1), 6–15.

Curry, J., & Lambie, G. W. (2007). Enhancing school counselor accountability: The large group guidance portfolio. *Professional School Counseling, 11*(2), 145–148. http://dx.doi.org/10.5330/PSC.n.2010-11.145

Ferguson, L. R. (1970). *Personality development.* Belmont, CA: Brooks/Cole Publishing.

Fernandez-Ballesteros, R., Diez-Nicolas, J., Caprara, G. V., Barbaranelli, C., & Bandura, A. (2002). Determinants and structural relation of personal efficacy to collective efficacy. *Applied Psychology: An International Review, 51*(1), 107–125. http://dx.doi.org/10.1111/1464-0597.00081

Gardner, H. (2004). *Frames of mind: The theory of multiple intelligences.* New York, NY: Basic Books.

Gottfredson, L. S. (1981). Circumscription and compromise: A developmental theory of occupational aspirations. *Journal of Counseling Psychology, 28*(6), 545–579. http://dx.doi.org/10.1037/0022-0167.28.6.545

Gushue, G. V., Scanlan, K. R. L., Pantzer, K. M., & Clarke, C. P. (2006). The relationship of career decision-making self-efficacy, vocational identity, and career exploration behavior in African American high school students. *Journal of Career Development, 33*(1), 19–28. http://dx.doi.org/10.1177/0894845305283004

Hall, A. S. (2003). Expanding academic and career self-efficacy: A family systems framework. *Journal of Counseling & Development, 81*(1), 33–39. http://dx.doi.org/10.1002/j.1556-6678.2003.tb00222.x

Havighurst, R. J. (1972). *Developmental tasks and education* (3rd ed.). New York, NY: David McKay.

Kimmel, M. S. (2005). *Manhood in America: A cultural history* (2nd ed.). New York, NY: Oxford University Press.

Maddux, J. E. (2002). Self-efficacy: The power of believing you can. In C. R. Snyder & S. J. Lopez (Eds.), *Handbook of positive psychology* (pp. 277–287). New York, NY: Oxford University Press.

Masten, A. S., & Reed, M. J. (2002). Resilience in development. In C. R. Snyder & S. J. Lopez (Eds.), *Handbook of positive psychology* (pp. 74–88). New York, NY: Oxford University Press.

Niles, S. G., & Harris-Bowlsbey, J. (2009). *Career development interventions in the 21st century* (3rd ed.). Upper Saddle River, NJ: Merrill.

Piaget, J. (1977). *The development of thought: Equilibration of cognitive structure*. New York, NY: Viking Press.

Porfeli, E. J., Hartung, P. J., & Vondracek, F. W. (2008). Children's vocational development: A research rationale. *Career Development Quarterly, 57*(1), 25–37. http://dx.doi.org/10.1002/j.2161-0045.2008.tb00163.x

Schultheiss, D. E. P. (2008). Current status and future agenda for the theory, research, and practice of childhood career development. *Career Development Quarterly, 57*(1), 7–24. http://dx.doi.org/10.1002/j.2161-0045.2008.tb00162.x

Schultheiss, D. E., Palma, T. V., & Manzi, A. J. (2005). Career development in middle childhood: A qualitative inquiry. *Career Development Quarterly, 53*, 246–262.

Shaffer, D. R. (2009). *Social and personality development* (6th ed.). Belmont, CA: Wadsworth.

Sharf, R. S. (2006). *Applying career development theory to counseling* (4th ed.). Belmont, CA: Thomson.

Spencer, S. J., Steele, C. M., & Quinn, D. M. (1999). Stereotype threat and women's math performance. *Journal of Experimental Social Psychology, 35*, 4–28.

Stanton, A. L., Parsa, A., & Austenfeld, J. L. (2002). The adaptive potential of coping through emotional approach. In C. R. Snyder & S. J. Lopez (Eds.), *Handbook of positive psychology* (pp. 148–158). New York, NY: Oxford University Press.

Super, D. E. (1980). A life-span, life-space approach to career development. *Journal of Vocational Behavior, 16*(3), 282–298. http://dx.doi.org/10.1016/0001-8791(80)90056-1

Tyler-Wood, T., Ellison, A., Lim, O., & Periathiruvadi, S. (2012). Bringing up girls in science (BUGS): The effectiveness of an afterschool environmental science program for increasing female students' interest in science careers. *Journal of Science Education and Technology, 21*(1), 46–55. http://dx.doi.org/10.1007/s10956-011-9279-2

Watson, M., & McMahon, M. (2008). Children's career development: Metaphorical images of theory, research, and practice. *Career Development Quarterly, 57*(1), 75–83. http://dx.doi.org/10.1002/j.2161-0045.2008.tb00167.x

Young, R. A. (1983). Career development of adolescents: An ecological perspective. *Journal of Youth and Adolescence, 12*(5), 401–417. http://dx.doi.org/10.1007/BF02088723

TEN

Career and College Readiness for Grades 6 and 7: Promoting Self-Awareness

Adolescence was described by Hall (1904) as a time of storm and stress, a description that underscores the turbulent nature of vast changes experienced by youth in the transition from childhood to adulthood. Yet, Hindley (1983) asserted that much of the turmoil of the adolescent experience depends on prior learning, support, and environmental factors that either promote or inhibit an individual's ability to cope with the stressors brought about by growth, change, and development in the adolescent years. The ambiguity of adolescence—balancing the desires of childhood with the impending responsibilities of being an adult—helps to make adolescence an ideal time for exploration, contemplation, and hope for many life possibilities. Equally important, recent research suggests middle school may hold much of the key to future college success. Of note, Gaertner and McClarty (2015), using the National Educational Longitudinal Study (NELS) database, found that 69% of the variance in college readiness could be explained with middle school factors, with the most important two being motivation and behavior. School counselors play a critical role in fostering the positive development of both of these middle school factors. In this chapter we review developmental concepts, career theory, counseling curriculum, and the involvement of stakeholders in career and college readiness interventions for sixth- and seventh-grade students.

DEVELOPMENTAL OVERVIEW

Although there are notable patterns of development in adolescence, it is an incredibly complex period of growth (Hindley, 1983). In this section, we cover major changes in physical, cognitive, psychosocial, social, and cultural development in the adolescent years. As always, we caution readers to be aware that each student is unique and that characteristics and patterns discussed here may not apply to every individual.

Physical Development

Adolescence is a time of unparalleled physical changes, including the development of primary and secondary sexual characteristics, growth spurts (e.g., musculoskeletal changes, changes in body proportions, and strength),

211

physical coordination, hormonal and neurochemical changes, motor skills, and mechanical abilities (Ausubel, 1954). Most importantly, as noted in Chapter 9, these physical changes are important when considering career and college readiness and development as they may have a lasting impact on self-concept based on body image and evaluations of self from a social perspective. The impact on self-concept may be particularly salient during adolescence given the social capital credited to individuals based on physical attributes. An example given by Crow and Crow (1965) is that males who attained greater height and strength compared to their peers experienced greater social prestige (popularity) and personal adjustment.

Another important consideration for future career and college readiness is the effects of hormones and physical changes that influence personality, temperament, and other aspects of personal expression (e.g., self-consciousness). An example of this was noted by the first author during her work as a middle school counselor helping a seventh-grade male with anger management concerns. The student stated, "Nothing's really different at home or school, it's just me, I suddenly started feeling angry all the time." Although the anger experienced by the student may have been due to a variety of potential factors, the anger might have also been brought about by the introduction of increased hormones, such as testosterone, that were disrupting the student's normal affective responses to stressors.

As mentioned in Chapter 9, students learn to regulate their emotions and behaviors by gaining self-control. Doing so might be difficult for students in early adolescence, especially because they are going through a great magnitude of change that impacts every aspect of their lives, from sleep patterns to social interactions. Emotional self-regulation and the ability to express oneself appropriately is part of the preparation adolescents must have for the world of work, and this can be a challenging task as they undergo dramatic physical changes.

Cognitive Development

According to Crow and Crow (1965), numerous characteristics emerge in adolescence that create the composite of intelligence and are considered markers of mental maturation: verbal comprehension, word fluency, mathematical abilities, spatial relations, memory, perceptual abilities, and reasoning. During adolescence, successful students demonstrate the ability to adapt to the demands of the educational environment by developing skills to concentrate, utilize imagination and creativity, memorize, and solve problems (Crow & Crow, 1965). Piaget (1969) maintained that there are multiple intellectual transformations with salient characteristics in the stage of *formal abstract* thought, which begins around the age of 11 or 12 and reaches equilibrium around the age of 14 or 15. These characteristics include the ability to (a) manipulate thoughts rather than just objects, (b) project into the future (e.g., understand long-term consequences of behavior), (c) formally reason based on a hypothesis, propositional operations (based on logic), reversibility by inversion, or reciprocity (e.g., algebraic equations), (d) synthesize information, and (e) generate experimentally formulated hypotheses.

Hindley (1983) acknowledged that major changes in cognitive functioning have implications for how individuals conceptualize the world and social concerns as well as how moral thought, reasoning, and behavior are manifested. For example, the ability to empathize with others, demonstrate compassion, and develop altruistic thoughts and behavior are largely based on cognitive development (Eisenberg, Miller, Shell, McNalley, & Shea, 1991). In this way, social maturation and development of positive interpersonal relationships are related to cognitive development. Further, the development of these cognitive skills helps sixth- and seventh-grade students apply logic and reasoning to how they conceptualize careers, understand college options, and project future actions necessary for workplace success.

Psychosocial Development

According to Erikson (1963), students entering adolescence are transitioning from the stage of *industry versus inferiority* to the stage of *identity versus role confusion*. Many things go into identity formation, including a sense of awareness about one's interests, strengths, weaknesses, and beliefs. The *identity versus role confusion* stage can be a difficult time for students and their families as adolescents may begin to differentiate from the views and beliefs of their families, which may cause strain on the family system (Bowen, 1976). According to Bowen, when students have low differentiation from their family of origin, they are overly dependent on their family members' acceptance of their choices and, therefore, have difficulty making decisions based on their individual preferences, thoughts, and beliefs. During the *identity versus role confusion* stage, students also begin to view themselves through a third-party perspective and begin to evaluate their social status and capital (Bourdieu, 1977) based on their social interactions with others. Low social capital and status can injure young adolescents' self-concept as their perceived weakness, low status, and lack of popularity may become predominant in their view of self.

Havighurst (1972) expanded on Erikson's theory and reported that the stage of *identity versus role confusion* is a very active time for youth and has specific challenges that include planning for one's future. This planning requires an understanding of oneself, one's future goals, and the consequences of behavior as it applies to the future. Further, based on Havighurst's research (1972), conceptualization and positive identity formation in adolescence is dependent on the following tasks:

- Achieving new and more mature relations with age mates of both sexes
- Achieving a masculine or feminine social role
- Accepting one's physique and using the body effectively
- Achieving emotional independence from parents and other adults
- Preparing for intimate relationships and family life
- Preparing for an economic career
- Acquiring a set of values and an ethical system as a guide to behavior—developing an ideology
- Desiring and achieving socially responsible behavior

Students may vary in the amount of time it takes to master the tasks suggested by Havighurst, as individual development and system supports both play significant roles in how adolescents navigate these tasks.

Other theorists also have contributed to an expanded understanding of Erikson's stage of *identity versus role confusion*. Specifically, Marcia (1987) proposed identity statuses to describe how individuals explore the possibilities of their adult lives, including their future careers. Marcia (1987) concluded that there are two major tasks that comprise the achievement of identity: (a) actively exploring future options and (b) committing to an identity. Marcia identified four *identity statuses* that comprise the relationship between these two tasks.

The first identity status is *identity diffusion*, where adolescents neither have explored future options nor committed to an identity. Adolescents in this status often seem withdrawn, resigned, and unmotivated; they are without a plan, and may seem as though they are drifting through life with no future goals. The second identity status is *identity foreclosure*. In this status, adolescents have committed to an identity, but did so without exploration, which may result in unhappiness later in life. For example, a school counselor asked a middle school student what type of career she was interested in exploring. The student said, "I think I'll be an orthodontist like my dad." Her dad then interrupted and said, "It would be crazy for her to do anything else. I am an orthodontist, my father was an orthodontist. She can be one and inherit our practice." Although the student may be happy with other possible future careers, she has committed to being an orthodontist before taking the time to explore other options. The third status Marcia (1987) proposed is *moratorium*. In this status, students are actively exploring options but have not committed to a career. This is an ideal status for sixth and seventh graders as they might be thinking critically about their future and keeping their options open. The fourth status, *identity achievement*, occurs after students have fully and critically considered their future options and then committed to an identity.

Beyond the stage of *identity versus role confusion* (Erikson, 1963), other social and emotional changes begin to occur in early adolescence. According to Crow and Crow (1965), changes to adolescent physical and cognitive development lead to greater ability to understand self and personal feelings, and adolescents are more expressive of a wide range of emotions including anxiety, worry, jealousy, and fear. Adolescents also may appear to be moody; for example, students who have been previously happy and well adjusted may seem melancholic or display a lack of interest in other people and activities. It is important for middle school counselors to recognize emotional reactivity and heightened behavioral changes that accompany the physical maturation of adolescents and how it may become problematic in the classroom. Helping adolescents to develop self-control and other self-regulatory behaviors rather than having emotional outbursts is important for their future workplace success.

As adolescents begin to develop a sense of understanding about others and relationships with others, they may become more open to self-exploration and defining "who am I" (Hindley, 1983, p. 40). Indeed, the ability to understand other people and to understand others' perspectives helps students become more aware of their own interests, dispositions, and aptitudes related to careers and college.

Gender/Culture

Havighurst (1972) proposed that many developmental tasks, such as sexual maturation, occur across cultures; however, he also noted that many developmental tasks are culture specific. Yet Havighurst (1972) pointed out that the complexity of career growth and development is based on social expectation and opportunity. For example, in more primitive and agrarian societies, youth might only have one career option (farming). Within the contemporary U.S. culture, there are myriad differences based on community and environmental factors for what is expected of adolescents. Likewise, tremendous variations in the opportunities perceived to be available by youth exist.

Most importantly, in middle school, students generally want to fit in and feel accepted. However, during this time, cultural differences (e.g., being Muslim in a primarily Christian community) and individual differences (e.g., sexual orientation or gender expression, disability) may cause students to stand out and gain negative attention from peers. Helping students feel comfortable with who they are and encouraging students to be welcoming of diversity are critical to their future career development as they will need to work successfully with others different from themselves (American School Counselor Association [ASCA], 2014).

CAREER THEORY AND DEVELOPMENT: GOTTFREDSON (1981), HOLLAND (1973), AND YOUNG (1983)

A focus on career development is crucial in early adolescence. As noted by Ausubel (1954), although each adolescent may have an "apparent preoccupation with the immediate and often esoteric activities of his interim peer culture, the adolescent's primary goals are really predicated upon inclusion in the adult world" (p. 437). Ausubel (1954) contended that as adolescents develop formal abstract thought and patterns of thinking about issues with greater complexity and depth, they develop an initial understanding of the dynamic relationship between career choice and multiple factors such as personal economic needs, social status (prestige) of specific occupations, special talents and abilities, perceived intelligence, interests, and economic urgency (i.e., financial considerations of college or technical training versus immediate income). Interest, motivation, and maturity also become largely influential in early adolescents' career aspirations and expectancies. Therefore, previous aspirations may not be stable over time (Ausubel, 1954), as many emerging factors substantially persuade the individual's career choices. Most importantly, career and college readiness in early adolescence is largely influenced by self-concept and an awareness of one's own interests, abilities, values, and aptitudes. In short, knowing oneself is the key to early adolescent career growth. In this section, we review theories that speak specifically to the career needs of early adolescents.

Gottfredson's Theory of Circumscription and Compromise

Similar to students in fourth and fifth grades, students in grades 6 and 7 are most likely in Gottfredson's career development Stage 3: *Orientation to Social Valuation*.

As stated in Chapter 9, students in this stage begin to consider which careers are within or outside of their tolerable level boundary. In other words, students will circumscribe careers that are, in their evaluation, either socially beneath or socially above them. Adolescents also may have heightened preoccupation with status and status symbols, a developmental milestone of understanding their own social capital and positionality. This can be exemplified in daily activities at school (e.g., students paying attention to the brand names of each other's clothing).

Although a focus on material things may seem unrelated to career development, this focus is a sign that students are considering the social value of things and people—a definitive measure that they are entrenched in Gottfredson's Stage 3. The important thing for school counselors to remember is that students in the stage of orientation to social valuation need opportunities to challenge, through exploration, their tolerable level boundary. In other words, career exploration may decrease self-circumscription of career and college options. It is important to remember that students circumscribe college choice as well, which often leads to over- and undermatching as their choices are made based on perceptions of what is tolerable rather than on aspirations that relate to their true abilities.

Holland's Theory of Vocational Choice

Holland's career theory (1973, 1997), known as *Theory of Types*, encompasses six different categories that represent individuals' self-perceived competencies and interests. The six types created by Holland (1973) are an amalgamation of the interaction among a person's heredity (or biological traits), interests, self-perceived competencies, and dispositions (personality traits, sensitivity to environmental influences, values, perceptions of self and world, and self-concept). Holland himself acknowledged that many factors influence the expression of a person's type: ethnicity, race, religion, sexual orientation, socioeconomic status (SES), and more. Therefore, the types provide a guide, not absolutes, for career exploration.

As mentioned in Chapter 1, the six Holland types are: realistic, investigative, artistic, social, enterprising, and conventional. A description of the six different Holland types can be found in Table 10.1. By having students complete one of Holland's assessments (e.g., the self-directed search [SDS]; see Chapter 5), school counselors can help students narrow down career exploration to sets of careers that may fit them as individuals.

Because Holland's theory begins with an assessment of a person's interests and aptitudes, it is ideal for middle school students because they love learning about themselves. Moreover, Holland's theory is very useful in helping students to critique how they might enjoy certain work environments and daily tasks. As noted by Sharf (2006), most individuals will have more than one Holland type (generally a combination of up to three); this may be particularly true for individuals exposed to a variety of environments and activities (e.g., extracurricular activities, hobbies, athletics, and travel).

In a study of middle school students, Turner, Conkel, Starkey, and Landgraf (2010) found that males tended to have greater realistic interests and females had greater artistic and social interests. More gender differences emerged in the study, including females capitalizing on their skills and abilities and more actively preparing for their future career plans than males. Males, on the other hand, were more assertive and desired to create their own career opportunities and were more apt to use instrumental, or tangible, support (i.e., assistance creating a resume). These findings suggest that continuing career exploration, increasing self-awareness, and increasing students' perceptions of career options that are not rigidly bound by gender are critical in elementary and middle school career counseling programming.

Young's Career Concepts

As discussed in previous chapters, Young (1983) highlighted the vital role of parents in adolescent career development. He particularly highlighted the dynamics of the parent–child relationship including: parent–child interaction, identification with parents, adolescents' perception of parental influence, and amount of contact with parents. Because of these relationship dynamics, intentional inclusion of parents in career and postsecondary exploration is an important component of the school counselor's career curriculum. According to Young, Paseluikho, and Valach (1997), parents need to co-construct career goals with their children through meaningful dialogue that promotes shared interests, values, and emotions.

TABLE 10.1 Holland Types

Type	Description	Possible Occupations
Realistic	Prefer activities that are practical in nature including manipulation of tools, machinery, objects, and animals. Some careers in this field require physical strength. Does not enjoy therapeutic or educational activities.	Farmer, surveyor, electrician, roofer, auto mechanic, and painter
Investigative	Prefer to investigate physical, biological, and cultural phenomenon through observation, symbolism, and systematic processes with strong scientific and mathematical competence. Does not enjoy selling, leadership, or persuading people or repetitive activities.	Chemist, biologist, anthropologist, medical technologist, and geologist
Artistic	Prefers creative activities such as fine arts (e.g., sculpting), performing arts (e.g., drama, music), dance, and creative writing. Does not enjoy repetitive activities or highly structured, ordered activities.	Stage director, choreographer, actor/actress, interior decorator, and musician
Social	Prefers activities that encompass working with others to train, educate, develop, enlighten, or cure in order to help others reach a goal. Does not enjoy mechanical or scientific activities.	Nurse, counselor, teacher, speech therapist, social worker, and religious worker
Enterprising	Prefers activities that include manipulating others to attain economic gain or organizational change. Does not enjoy observational, symbolic activities.	Producer, sports promoter, salesperson, manager, business leader, and buyer
Conventional	Prefer activities that include interpretation of data, record keeping, filing materials, and organizing written and numerical data. Does not enjoy ambiguous, unstructured, and exploratory activities.	Bookkeeper, accountant, financial analyst, cost estimator, and banker

Source: Adapted from Holland (1973, 1997), Jones (2011), and Niles and Harris-Bowlsbey (2009).

Young et al. (1997) contended that emotions in career conversations are demonstrative of the level of adolescent career motivation and cognitive appraisal of self (i.e., self-concept related to career). Specifically, they found that emotion in parent–adolescent career conversations promoted career action. It is presumed that this connection exists because language (in this case, conversation) provides a primary medium for adolescents to conceptualize and negotiate career goals, construct personal meanings related to career, and determine the purpose of career-related work in their lives (Young et al., 1997). When parents and adolescents are given the opportunity to participate in career- and college-related conversations as part of a deliberate and planned component of the comprehensive school counseling program, then families can support adolescents in career and college problem solving, planning, and decision making. Through such conversations, adolescents and parents can be given a chance to explore the adolescent's feelings related to careers and college.

MIDDLE SCHOOL CAREER AND COLLEGE READINESS

As highlighted in Chapter 1, low college graduation rates have extensive personal and social costs. More importantly, the demand for college degrees is growing (Carnevale, Smith, & Strohl, 2010). Although not every student will go to college, it is important that stakeholders are aware of the skills that students need so that college can remain an option. According to the California College Board, these skills include participation in a rigorous high school curriculum and the development of skills in (a) higher order thinking, (b) studying and researching, (c) reasoning, (d) problem solving and analyzing, (e) writing, and (f) understanding career and college options, including college admissions and financing (Mijares, 2007). If these skills are important in high school, what career education and training are critical in middle school to prepare students for a rigorous high school curriculum?

Throughout this book, we propose a multisystemic approach to career and college readiness. It is important to underscore that parents, teachers, administrators, and community partners all play a vital role in the career and college development of middle school students. For example, Orthner (2012) identified benefits (including increased school engagement, higher performance on end of grade tests in math and reading, fewer unexcused absences and disciplinary referrals) among students whose teachers used *CareerStart*, an instructional strategy designed to help students connect academics to careers. CareerStart emphasizes a whole-school approach, including parent and community involvement, to improve school engagement and achievement. In the next section, we highlight how school counselors can address the career and college readiness needs of sixth and seventh graders through a comprehensive curriculum and a multisystems approach.

THE SCHOOL COUNSELING CURRICULUM

The school counseling career and college readiness curriculum in middle school should be centered on helping students explore their personal fit with careers and college by examining their interests, aptitudes, dispositions, and values related to career and postsecondary options. The curriculum also ideally should help build students' career decision-making self-efficacy (e.g., *The Career Horizons Program*; see O'Brien, Dukstein, Jackson, Tomlinson, & Kamatuka, 1999). We begin this section by including the ASCA Mindsets and Behaviors (2014) that may be particularly useful when developing the counseling curriculum for sixth- and seventh-grade students (Table 10.2). We also want to call readers' attention to the importance of including technology and assessment in the comprehensive career and college readiness curriculum to expose students to many possible options that are personally suited for them (i.e., focus on person–environment fit). Remember, middle school students love to talk about themselves and think about who they are, and that makes developing the career and college readiness curriculum particularly fun.

Assessment in Middle School Career and College Counseling

School counselors should use assessment to help middle school students discover the skills, aptitudes, interests, and values they hold that may impact their fit with potential careers and colleges. Although we covered various assessments in Chapter 5, we highlight a few in this section that are particularly useful in sixth- and seventh-grade classroom career and college readiness lessons. The activities we share may be helpful for promoting self-exploration and moving adolescents from diffusion and foreclosure to moratorium (Marcia, 1987), where they can actively begin to question who they are in relation to their future career and college choices.

   Values card sort. Knowdell's Career Values Card Sort (2005) can be used effectively with sixth- or seventh-grade students, as they are capable of understanding values they hold related to potential careers. The Knowdell Career

TABLE 10.2   ASCA Mindsets and Behaviors for Sixth- and Seventh-Grade Curriculum Planning Focus

CATEGORY 1: MINDSETS STANDARDS		
Self-confidence in ability to succeed Sense of belonging in the school environment Understanding that postsecondary education and lifelong learning are necessary for long-term career success		
CATEGORY 2: BEHAVIOR STANDARDS		
Learning Strategies	Self-Management Skills	Social Skills
Apply media and technology skills	Demonstrate ability to work independently	Create positive and supportive relationships with other students
Identify long- and short-term academic, career, and socioemotional goals	Demonstrate ability to overcome barriers to learning	Create relationships with adults that support success
Gather evidence and consider multiple perspectives to make informed decisions	Demonstrate personal safety skills	Use effective oral and written communication skills and listening skills

Values Card Sort is a deck of cards with each card listing a value related to careers (e.g., team work, creativity, and problem solving) and an explanation of the value.

The first author, when using the values card sort activity with students, would place students in small groups seated in a circle. Each group was given one deck of cards and one student was the dealer. The dealer gave each student six cards and students were asked to place the cards in order from the thing they valued most in a future career to the thing they valued least. Then the group discussed their values and why they chose their particular card order and how the card order they chose related to careers. The Knowdell Career Values Card Sort comes with activity sheets that the students fill out as they complete the activities. The sheets gave students a chance to think about the values they chose and to reflect on their own personal preferences of values related to careers. Students were then asked to remove the card they ranked as most valuable and give it to the student sitting on their right in the circle. Then they reordered their cards to integrate the new card they just received. As a follow-up activity, the English teacher had each student write a reflection on the things he or she valued in a future career. Students reported enjoying this activity, and the discussions in the small groups were generally lively. In addition, the cards gave students a chance to broaden their career values vocabulary.

Career genogram. According to Gibson (2005, 2012), the career genogram activity is one way to have students examine the influence of their family members and other significant adults on their career choice. It also can help them identify ways that their interests may be different from those of family members; remember, according to Erikson (1963) and Bowen (1976), adolescents are exploring their own individual beliefs and values and how they resemble or differ from those held by their family of origin. If a school counselor has not facilitated a genogram activity previously, he or she can access instructions from Gibson (2005, p. 358). In addition to filling out the genogram, Gibson (2012) recommends that students be provided with questions to ask family members that will deepen their knowledge, such as: (a) What influenced family members' career decisions? (b) Who influenced their career decisions? and (c) At what age did they decide on their career choice? To incorporate a focus on college, questions such as the following can be asked: (a) What type of education was needed for each family member's occupation? (b) What was the highest level of education each person attained? and (c) What factors affected the educational attainment of each family member? Figure 10.1 includes an example of Ainsley's career genogram (Ainsley is a student wishing to become a school counselor).

Based on this genogram, some questions that could be posed to Ainsley that may help her see the similarities and differences between her career choice and those of her family members include: Who in your family has a career that is similar to the career you have chosen? (In Ainsley's case, she may choose her mother, a substitute teacher.) How is his or her career similar to the career(s) you are considering? (Both involve working with children in an education setting.) Whose career is different? (Ainsley's father, a funeral director.) What similar characteristics or values exist between your career choice

FIGURE 10.1   Ainsley's Career Genogram

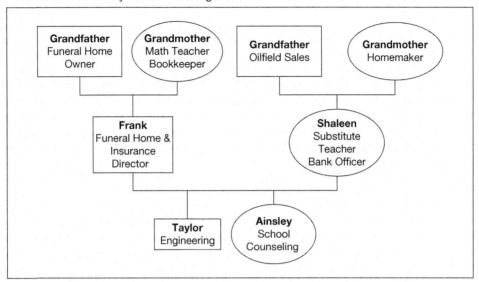

and the career choices of your family members? (Ainsley may identify similar characteristics of kindness or compassion.) How has your family influenced your career decisions? In what ways have you chosen your own career path?

PROMOTING STEM CAREERS IN MIDDLE SCHOOL

As previously noted (Chapter 1), there is a growing need to fill science, technology, engineering, and mathematics (STEM) careers, and STEM careers have a high college payoff (Chapter 2); yet females, African Americans, Hispanics, Native Americans, and students from low SES homes continue to be severely underrepresented in STEM fields. Based on a study by Aschbacher, Ing, and Tsai (2014), this underrepresentation might be partly due to low interest, but is more likely due to low self-perceptions students have of their abilities related to science. Therefore, they don't aspire to science careers. Early exposure and access may help.

Beyond exposing students to options for career and college opportunities in STEM through classroom presentations, school counselors should work collaboratively with others to consider ways to promote STEM beyond the classroom and academic curriculum. For example, Lawrence and Mancuso (2012) described ways to apply for and improve chances of getting funded for a small grant to develop a Girls Excited about Engineering, Mathematics, and Computer Science (GE2McS) program at your school. The program combines two 1 hour, hands-on workshops for students, a discussion of gender issues for counselors and teachers, and a student and career panel. Lawrence and Mancuso described the type of workshops that should be offered, how to design interesting panels, sample agendas, where to apply for funding, and ways to improve efficiency in delivering the program such as partnering with your local high school.

An out-of-school program, known as Lang Science, at the American Museum of Natural History promotes science identities for students from underrepresented groups in science fields (i.e., women, African Americans). This program is competitive, and students commit to being in the program from sixth grade through high school graduation. The program includes meetings every other Saturday during the school year and 3 weeks in the summer for a total of 165 contact hours per year (Adams, Gupta, & Cotumaccio, 2014). In a qualitative study, conducted by Adams et al., alumnae of the Lang Science program disclosed numerous benefits of the program that had impacted their science identities beyond the program in their postsecondary lives. Themes from the study included that the Lang Science program had (a) given the participants a collective identity by connecting them with a group of peers with similar interests and future goals where they didn't feel weird or different for their science interests; (b) created a sense of belonging in the physical place and ownership of the museum as participants had IDs with access to non-public spaces, were invited to social events at the museum, met with museum personnel, and were physically present at the museum frequently; (c) increased participants' understanding of the range of science careers beyond stereotypes (e.g., labs) through broad exposure; and (d) helped increase persistence in science, in spite of the participants not finding supportive environments in their postsecondary science pursuits.

Although school counselors cannot make every STEM opportunity available to students, making an effort to add cocurricular or extracurricular activities available is important. Please see Exhibit 10.1 for a science educator's explanation of how science identity may be fostered. Exhibit 10.2 highlights a school counselor who discusses how she supports students' STEM career interest through her role with the SeaPerch underwater robotics competition.

EXHIBIT 10.1
Voices From the Field: Fostering Science Identities in Middle School Students

Angela W. Webb, PhD

Science Educator, Louisiana State University, School of Education

STEM may seem inaccessible to students for a variety of reasons. After all, they receive implicit and explicit messages about what science is (and is not) and who can (and should) do it from myriad sources, ranging from family and friends to school and the media to religious leaders. Students take these messages to heart, which may have implications for their affiliation with science and their developing science identities. In fact, as early as elementary school, students start to wonder, "Is science me?" How can we reimagine school science so their answer is yes?

(continued)

EXHIBIT 10.1 (*continued*)

Robust in- and out-of-school programs focused on engaging students with STEM concepts and practices in authentic ways are needed to broaden the meanings of science and science persons with which students engage. SeaPerch (http://www.seaperch.org/index), which is sponsored by the Office of Naval Research, is one such context. Promoted as an "innovative underwater robotics program," SeaPerch "provides students with the opportunity to learn about robotics, engineering, science, and mathematics (STEM) while building an underwater remotely operated vehicle (ROV) as part of a science and engineering technology curriculum" (SeaPerch website). A wealth of STEM concepts are addressed through students' work on their SeaPerch ROV. As outlined on the SeaPerch website, these concepts include engineering design; buoyancy and displacement; propulsion; vectors; electricity, circuits, and switches; ergonomics; depth measurement; biological sampling; attenuation of light; and the physics of motion.

Although connections to relevant STEM careers are also drawn in the SeaPerch curriculum, it is students' engagement in the authentic practices of science that most affects their developing science identities. For students to see themselves as scientists, they must engage in the practices of scientists. Through SeaPerch, students are afforded opportunities to (a) ask scientific questions and define engineering problems related to their ROV and STEM concepts; (b) develop and use models pertaining to the construction and use of their ROV, and extend these ideas to ship and submarine construction; (c) plan and carry out investigations, and analyze and interpret data for variables such as buoyancy, control, speed, and friction of their ROV; (d) use mathematics and computational thinking to design, build, and fine-tune their ROV; (e) construct explanations of science concepts and design solutions for engineering problems, basing each in evidence; and (f) obtain, evaluate, and communicate information from trials and investigations of their ROV. (Please see the Next Generation Science Standards for more on the science and engineering practices.) These vast opportunities to engage with their SeaPerch ROV *as scientists* expose students to broad and accessible meanings of science and science person—opening up robust spaces for students to affiliate, and thus identify, with science. In this context, science becomes less about memorizing isolated facts (a narrow and often unappealing notion of science, and subsequently, science person) and more about using science concepts, laws, and theories to answer questions and solve problems (a more expansive, more accessible meaning of science, and subsequently, science person).

Liking science and affiliating (i.e., identifying) with science are not synonymous, and just liking science is an inadequate predictor of whether students will pursue postsecondary studies in STEM or STEM-related careers. To improve students' career and college readiness around STEM, we need to extend our notions of successful school science beyond students' acquisition of science-related knowledge and skills to include their science identities as well.

EXHIBIT 10.2
Voices From the Field: The School Counselor's Role in Promoting STEM
Careers and College Readiness

D'Jalon J. Jackson, PhD

Middle School Counselor, Kenilworth Science and Technology Charter School

Being employed as a school counselor at a STEM-focused, public charter school for middle school students provided a unique opportunity to actively address the vital need for STEM exploration. The student body I served was comprised of over 98% African American/Black or Hispanic students, the majority of whom qualified for free or reduced-price lunch. This demographic makeup further accentuated my responsibility as a school counselor to champion the integral infusion of STEM initiatives into a learning environment that catered to a population otherwise unlikely to pursue STEM careers due to lack of early access and exposure.

Fortunately, at this particular charter school, STEM exploration is built into the learning environment in myriad ways, including through curriculum. For example, each student is required to create a criteria-driven scientific demonstration that contains the appropriate level of difficulty respective to their grade level. These demonstrations range from simple chemistry experiments to complex physics and robotics projects and could potentially qualify students to participate in regional, national, and international science fairs. Along with engaging in curriculum that highlights STEM, the opportunity to participate in cocurricular school and after-school STEM activities is also provided to all students. It was during the preparation process surrounding these activities that I was able to support my students through my role as a school counselor. As students prepared for various competitions, such as our science fair and SeaPerch (see Exhibit 10.1), I provided them with feedback concerning visual aids (posters) and assisted them with their oral presentation skills to ensure clarity and conciseness. I also posed inquiries that could potentially surface from competition judges concerning their demonstrations and thought processes. Although I was not teaching them science content, I was promoting their critical thinking and problem-solving skills.

Ultimately, I contributed to their career and college readiness as it related to STEM awareness by aiding in the honing of their oral and written communication skills as well as evoking higher order thinking through the presentation of knowledge synthesized to adequately address scientific inquiry. Thus, from my personal experience, exposure to STEM fields, through my career and college presentations in classrooms, as well as my individual work preparing students for competition, like our science fairs and SeaPerch, has better equipped students for success in STEM careers and postsecondary education. More than that, I believe our students have had the experience of being in the role of scientists while still in middle school, and this enables them to envision, very realistically, their ability to be a scientist in the future.

ENGAGING STAKEHOLDERS

Johnson (2000) reported results of a study conducted with sixth- and ninth-grade students. Only about half of the students in the study could identify a skill needed for career success. More alarming, approximately 88% of the participants "reflected little or no awareness of how the skills, knowledge, or attitudes learned in the subject course work might relate to future employment" (Johnson, 2000, p. 269). However, Johnson (2000) also reported that sixth-grade students found schoolwork more useful to their careers than did ninth-grade students, an indication, according to Johnson, of students' feelings of increasing discontentment with their school experience between the sixth- and ninth-grade years. Therefore, sixth- and seventh-grade teachers have an important task in keeping students engaged in academics and connecting academics to career. Indeed, nearly every middle school teacher and counselor has heard students say about various content, "Why do I have to learn this? I'm never going to use it!" This feeling that the information being learned is not useful or applicable to students' lives may leave students feeling disengaged, frustrated, and unmotivated to learn. The *CareerStart* (Orthner, 2012) program is one evidence-based approach to help students feel more engaged in school. Lesson plans and suggested activities are provided, but teachers are encouraged to scaffold lessons to cater to their specific populations. Using a quasi-experimental design, Orthner, Jones-Sanpei, Akos, and Rose (2013) divided middle school students into experimental and control conditions. Using the *CareerStart* program, but controlling for prior school engagement, socioeconomic, and academic factors, the researchers found that the students in the experimental group who participated in the *CareerStart* program had significantly higher levels of school valuing and school engagement after being given career relevant instruction in their academic classes.

Teachers

Middle school teachers have the opportunity to engage middle school students in learning. Curry, Belser, and Binns (2013) highlighted numerous ways that middle school teachers can integrate career-related information in the education curriculum. For example, a middle school counselor, Mr. Braxton, met with all seventh-grade math teachers at Rock Creek Middle School. He explained that he would be introducing students to math careers every quarter in their math class and that he would like to coordinate this with the seventh-grade math teachers. Each quarter, the math teachers and Mr. Braxton met to discuss what types of math activities were being covered and how these might relate to careers. One example occurred after a unit on measurements (i.e., mass, volume, perimeter, and circumference). Mr. Braxton and the seventh-grade math teachers completed a lesson on careers where math measurements were used (e.g., chemist, engineer, construction worker, and architect). Students were then given an opportunity to discuss in small groups what they found challenging or interesting about the math skills learned in the unit and which, if any, of the related careers were of interest to them. Mr. Braxton did this with every math class each quarter and teachers reported that students seemed to take a greater interest in learning math skills as a result.

Moreover, there may be some evidence that career knowledge and maturity may result in positive student outcomes. For example, Legum and Hoare (2004) conducted a study with urban, at-risk middle school students. They divided the participants into control and experimental groups. Participants in the experimental group received a 9-week career intervention program that linked academics to careers; the control group received no intervention. At the end of the study there were no major statistical findings between the control and experimental groups in academic outcomes, but several qualitative changes were reported. Teachers were interviewed at the completion of the groups, and they identified positive changes in the students attending the experimental group at the end of the study including gains in self-esteem, academic achievement, academic motivation, participation in class, and more willingness to attempt class work. Teachers did not notice similar changes in the control group (Legum & Hoare, 2004). This study only lasted 9 weeks; therefore, what is not known is whether or not a longer and more systematic intervention would have a definitive and significant academic impact.

The major consideration based on Legum and Hoare's (2004) study is that career exploration may help students to feel more engaged in the educational agenda of middle school (motivation, willingness to attempt class work, and classroom participation), making career curriculum integration a worthwhile task for teachers. Further, there are many ways to include teachers, and it is most important to point out that much of the career and college readiness curriculum infusion does not require large amounts of time from teachers. Often, short quantities of time devoted to career and college (when done with frequency and consistency over time) may be effective. In Exhibit 10.3 we share an example of how a school counselor worked with teachers to provide a brief but consistent activity that promoted a college-going culture.

Other interventions that do not require significant use of class time may also be considered. Rinke, Arsenie, and Bell (2012) reported results of a study based on collaboration between college students and an urban middle school. The college students (undergraduate students in a teacher education program) hosted an after school program for 1 week where they helped urban middle school students develop personal and professional artifacts (artistic pieces and career projects) that showcased their future lives. They presented these to friends and families. Two weeks later, the middle school students and their faculty visited the partner college for a tour. Results of the study showed that college students who participated reported feeling more inclined to work with urban students and noted that working with the middle school students was the most meaningful aspect of the project. The middle school students in the study demonstrated increased confidence and perseverance for college (Rinke et al., 2012).

Another out-of-classroom experience is the summer program. Summer programs that promote the middle school to college pipeline, such as the Pathways Partnership, have been successful in terms of students' future aspirations without taking significant time from the classroom academic core (Ng, Wolf-Wendel, &

Lombardi, 2014). However, even without removing time from the classroom, programs like the Pathways Partnership often offer a teacher in-service component to assist teachers in bridging information on career and college in the classroom. This is an important model to follow as the school counselor must utilize all stakeholders to help, and even minor classroom integration of career and college curriculum sends a clear message that it is important.

Specific recommendations for teachers were made by Radcliffe and Bos (2013). They suggested that teachers could do some of the following to promote career and college readiness in conjunction with the school counselor: (a) have students create digital stories about their future careers and the preparation needed, (b) visit campuses and journal during the visits in a writing marathon approach, (c) create opportunities for academic tutoring, (d) have college students give presentations, and (e) have projects that include collaborations with college students if possible. School counselors and teachers will need to determine where in the curriculum these activities make the most sense.

Parents

Hall (2003) described the nuanced and complicated relationship between individuals' families and their career choices. One major factor creating this dynamic is that students who choose careers that are out of their family's perceived level of prestige (aiming too high or too low based on the perception of family members) are at emotional risk. In other words, students may suffer emotional consequences (e.g., stated disapproval or anger from parents) for making a decision that family members do not agree with (Hall, 2003). For example, one school counselor conducted a career and college planning session with a parent and student. The student was adamant about becoming a music major and the father, an accountant, told the student that if she wanted a career in music she would have to move out and pay for college herself. The father followed up by stating that if the student chose "a real major" he would support her and pay her way through school. In this way, the father was exerting an emotional and economic sanction for his disapproval of the student's career choice. The emotional, fiscal, cognitive, and social investments parents make in raising their children can lead them to have highly emotional reactions when discussing careers and college with their children.

As previously mentioned, Young et al. (1997) noted the importance of career communication and emotions between parents and their middle school children in developing positive career action. Usinger (2005) conducted a 5-year longitudinal, interpretive study of seventh-grade students in low-achieving schools and how they constructed their academic and career aspirations. Usinger focused on the parent/guardian role in this process. Based on her findings, Usinger asserted that parents need opportunities to reflect on their own career disappointments, regrets, triumphs, and insights. By including parents in career and college readiness activities and by creating opportunities for them to consider their own growth and development, the career and college counseling process can include the family system in a meaningful and relevant way. Usinger also highlighted

EXHIBIT 10.3
College Colors Day at Highland View Middle School

A middle school counselor, Mr. Burnett, delivered a classroom lesson on career exploration and postsecondary options. He found that many students did not understand the differences between universities, community colleges, and technical schools, and he wanted to do more to promote student awareness of postsecondary institutions and the types of degrees or training certificates they offer. More importantly, he thought students needed this information more consistently and that it should become a continuous part of the academic curriculum.

Mr. Burnett devised a plan with the help of his school counseling advisory committee, which they introduced at a faculty in-service on career and college readiness. The advisory committee collected information on universities, colleges, community colleges, and technical schools in their state and in all surrounding states in the region. At the beginning of each 6-week period, every teacher was given a postsecondary institution to present in each of their classes (each teacher taught six classes and had one planning period) on a day designated as *College Colors Day.*

On *College Colors Day,* teachers wore the colors of the postsecondary school they were assigned to present. In each of their six classes they gave a 5-minute presentation including: types of programs/degrees offered, number of students attending, strengths of the school (such as arts, specific degrees, and job placement), highlights about the town in which the school is located, and so on. Every 6 weeks the teachers were all given a different postsecondary institution with information to present on *College Colors Day.* Students were exposed to information about seven different postsecondary options each *College Colors Day.* By the end of the year they had heard about 42 different options, and discussions of postsecondary education became a more regular part of the academic discourse of the school.

the importance of parents discussing their own struggles and how they have overcome them in order to role model personal success for their children and also demonstrate that everyone has their own personal struggles. These kinds of conversations may become increasingly important, and deeper, as students in middle school contemplate their futures.

Moreover, based on a study by Turner and Lapan (2002), perceived parent support was a predictive factor in students' career self-efficacy as it accounted for 29% to 43% of total unique variance in career self-efficacy for a sample of middle school students, more evidence of the impetus to include parents. Similarly, Hill and Wang (2015) found that warmth, autonomy, and support had significant indirect effects on college enrollment (up to 3 years post-high school) through school engagement, aspirations, and grade point average. Both of these studies underscore how important it is to keep students and their parents talking, in positive ways, about careers and college in the middle school years. However, many families may need help doing this because it may not come as second nature. Other career skills that parents and students both need during the middle school years include how to effectively explore careers and colleges using technology, understanding education and labor market trends, and how to reduce the impact of socially constructed gender types for careers (Amundson & Penner, 1998; Turner & Lapan, 2002).

Literature provides some suggestions of career interventions for parents and students that school counselors can review before designing their own programs (e.g., Parent Involved Career Exploration [PICE]; see Amundson & Penner, 1998). However, before beginning to implement any parent-involved career curriculum, we suggest accurately identifying the career and college needs of the school population served through a needs assessment (ASCA, 2012). See Exhibit 10.4 and Table 10.3 for examples of school counseling program activities designed to include parents.

EXHIBIT 10.4
The Career Conversation Workshops

Mr. Drexler, a middle school counselor, decided to provide seventh-grade students and their parents with an opportunity to have career conversations as part of a large-scale career and college readiness program Mr. Drexler was implementing at Grove Middle School. Although students were receiving career education curriculum in their courses, Mr. Drexler also designed three parent–student workshops for family career exploration (one in September and two in October). He also partnered with a local counselor educator, Dr. Shelton, to collaborate and design the workshops. Dr. Shelton's school counseling graduate students were volunteers who helped with the parent night programs (nine volunteers in all). Three total workshops were provided lasting 2 hours each with homework assignments for the parents and students in between.

For the first program, parents and students were given an introduction to career and college readiness and the types of tasks they will need to complete from seventh grade to 12th grade. Then, parents and students were given a brief introduction to active listening (including videos with good and bad examples) and positive communication skills. Parents were then asked to discuss three questions with their children (taking turns with both adults and students answering each question): (a) If you could have any career in the world, what would it be? (b) What gifts or talents do you have to bring to the workplace? and (c) What skills do people need to be successful in the workplace? After parents and their children discussed these questions, they came together in groups (facilitated by the school counseling graduate students) to discuss their answers. Homework was assigned at the end of the workshop; the assignment was to fill out a worksheet exploring one career on the *Occupational Outlook Handbook* website and answer the questions on the worksheet.

For the second program, parents and students were reminded of active listening and positive communication skills, then all were introduced to family and individual values. Dr. Shelton provided a brief developmental overview of

(continued)

EXHIBIT 10.4 (continued)
The Career Conversation Workshops

how family values do influence youth, but also how students begin to develop their own unique value systems as they get older. Parents and students were given a list of 48 values (see Table 10.3) that may impact the fit between an individual and his or her career. Then, pictures of individuals working were posted on a screen and the parents and their child discussed the possible values that a person in that work might have that fit with that career. For example, when looking at a picture of a female firefighter, parents and students looked at the careers value list (Table 10.3) and came up with three to five values that a person with the career of firefighter might have (e.g., team work). Next, students and parents each chose three careers of interest to them (one of which they had explored in their homework assigned at the last session) and discussed what values they have that might be a fit for that career. They also talked about things they valued that may not be a fit. For example, one parent stated that a dream job of his was rock star but that he has strong family values and touring/being on the road would not be a fit. Finally, everyone was placed in groups (facilitated by the school counseling graduate students) and discussed values portrayed in social media and how those values may be confusing to people as they consider careers. In one group, a mother mentioned that women are often portrayed in clerical/secretarial roles or as housewives (she named several TV shows and commercials). She was bothered by this as these portrayals didn't reflect the values she was trying to teach her daughter about being a leader. She stated, "My daughter can be a CEO of a company. I don't want her to feel she can only be the CEO's assistant or wife." The homework assignment for the second workshop was to watch television together and count and list the number of careers seen in a specific show. The parent and student then filled out a worksheet about the values associated with each career and if the career was portrayed in a realistic, stereotypical, or nontraditional way (careers that are portrayed out of gender type, such as male nurses).

In the third parent and child career workshop, parents and students were given specific information about the types of career exploration assessments and activities that students would experience throughout the remainder of seventh grade (from October to May). Parents and students were reminded of communication and active listening skills, then they were asked to answer the following questions:

Parents: What do you wish you knew when you were making career and college decisions for yourself? What career might you have today if you had received the best possible information?

Students: What career concerns do you have today? As you think about the future, what three careers are of most interest to you?

In the final activity, students and parents co-created a collage about what they had learned about and what their wishes were for the student's future career (magazines were provided by a local distributor). Everyone was put in small groups and the school counseling graduate students facilitated the final discussions and presentations of the career collages.

TABLE 10.3   Career Values Chart

Intellectual status	Diversity	Independence	Make decisions
Friendships	Excitement	High earnings	Affiliation
Stability	Change and variety	Team work	Moral fulfillment
Competition	Power and authority	Honesty and integrity	Fast pace
Public contact	Influence people	Physical challenge	Adventure
Work under pressure	Location	Fun and humor	Family
Challenging problems	Precision work	Collaboration	Status
Time freedom	Security	Tradition	Recognition
Aesthetics	Job tranquility	Artistic creativity	Steep learning curve
Predictability	Spirituality	Feeling competent	Practicality
Help society	Work alone	Creative expression	Work–life balance
Supervision	Knowledge	Community	Fame

The parent workshop in Exhibit 10.4 illuminates some of the suggestions for student career development provided by Turner and Lapan (2002): having parents and students engage together in activities that reduce career gender typing (such as co-viewing media and improving media literacy skills to question stereotypes) and developing career exploration skills (e.g., considering values related to careers and using technology to explore and answer questions about a specific career). Moreover, the career conversations in the example provided a structured opportunity for parents and students to discuss careers in a meaningful way.

SUMMARY

In this chapter, we reviewed developmental concepts and career theory relevant to comprehensive career and college planning with sixth- and seventh-grade students. In particular, we highlighted Marcia's identity statuses and the importance of students learning about themselves in relation to their future careers and college plans. We highlighted how preadolescence and early adolescence are times of growth where students come to understand how their individual preferences may be similar to, or different from, their family of origin (Bowen) and how school counselors might help students explore these similarities and differences (career genogram, parent–student career, and college conversations). We also illuminated specific interventions for middle school students related to STEM. In summary, middle school is a time of vast changes and growth, and the perfect opportunity to promote student understanding of their future career and college options.

⋯❯ Test Your Knowledge

1. What tasks are involved in the development of positive identity formation (consider Erikson, Havighurst, and Marcia)?
2. In what ways is self-concept related to career and college development for sixth- and seventh-grade students?
3. What are the goals of career assessment measures for sixth and seventh graders? In other words, what types of knowledge or insights should they gain?

REFERENCES

Adams, J. D., Gupta, P., & Cotumaccio, A. (2014). Long-term participants: A museum program enhances girls' STEM interest, motivation and persistence. *Afterschool Matters, 20,* 13–20.

American School Counselor Association. (2012). *The ASCA national model: A framework for school counseling programs* (3rd ed.). Alexandria, VA: Author.

American School Counselor Association. (2014). *ASCA mindsets & behaviors for student success: K-12 college- and career-readiness standards for every student.* Alexandria, VA: Author.

Amundson, N. E., & Penner, K. (1998). Parent involved career exploration. *Career Development Quarterly, 47*(2), 135–144. http://dx.doi.org/10.1002/j.2161-0045.1998 .tb00547.x

Aschbacher, P. R., Ing, M., & Tsai, S. M. (2014). Is science me? Exploring middle school student's STEM career aspirations. *Journal of Science Education and Technology, 23,* 735–743. http://dx.doi.org/10.1007/s10956-014-9504-x

Ausubel, D. P. (1954). *Theory and problems of adolescent development.* New York, NY: Grune & Stratton.

Bowen, M. (1976). Theory in the practice of psychotherapy. In P. J. Guerin (Ed.), *Family therapy* (pp. 42–90). New York, NY: Gardner.

Bourdieu, P. (1977). *Outline of a theory of practice.* Cambridge, UK: Cambridge University Press.

Carnevale, A. P., Smith, N., & Strohl, J. (2010). Help wanted: Projections of jobs and education requirements through 2018. Retrieved from http://cew .georgetown.edu/jobs2018

Crow, L. D., & Crow, A. (1965). *Adolescent development and adjustment* (2nd ed.). New York, NY: McGraw-Hill.

Curry, J., Belser, C. T., & Binns, I. C. (2013). Integrating post-secondary college and career options in the middle school curriculum: Considerations for teachers. *Middle School Journal, 44*(3), 26–32.

Eisenberg, N., Miller, P. A., Shell, R., McNalley, S., & Shea, C. (1991). Prosocial development in adolescence: A longitudinal study. *Developmental Psychology, 27*(5), 849–858. http://dx.doi.org/10.1037/0012-1649.27.5.849

Erikson, E. H. (1963). *Childhood and society* (2nd ed.). New York, NY: W. W. Norton.

Gaertner, M. N., & McClarty, K. L. (2015). Performance, perseverance, and the full picture of college readiness. *Educational Measurement: Issues and Practice, 34*(2), 20–33.

Gibson, D. M. (2005). The use of genograms in career counseling with elementary, middle, and high school students. *Career Development Quarterly, 53*(4), 353–362. http:// dx.doi.org/10.1002/j.2161-0045.2005.tb00666.x

Gibson, D. M. (2012). Using career genograms in K-12 settings. Retrieved from http:// associationdatabase.com/aws/NCDA/pt/sd/news_article/5473/_PARENT/ layout_details/false

Gottfredson, L. S. (1981). Circumscription and compromise: A developmental theory of occupational aspirations. *Journal of Counseling Psychology, 28*(6), 545–579. http:// dx.doi.org/10.1037/0022-0167.28.6.545

Hall, A. S. (2003). Expanding academic and career self-efficacy: A family systems framework. *Journal of Counseling & Development, 81*(1), 33–39. http://dx.doi.org/10 .1002/j.1556-6678.2003.tb00222.x

Hall, G. S. (1904). *Adolescence.* New York, NY: Appleton.

Havighurst, R. J. (1972). *Developmental tasks and education* (3rd ed.). New York, NY: David McKay.

Hill, N. E., & Wang, M. T. (2015). From middle school to college: Developing aspirations, promoting engagement, and indirect pathways from parenting to post high school enrollment. *Developmental Psychology, 51*(2), 224–235. http://dx.doi.org/10.1037/ a0038367

Hindley, C. B. (1983). Psychological changes in adolescence related to physical changes. In W. Everaerd, C. B. Hindley, A. Bot, & J. J. van der Werff ten Bosch (Eds.), *Development in adolescence: Psychological, social and biological aspects* (pp. 28–48). Boston, MA: Martinus Nijhoff Publishers.

Holland, J. L. (1973). *Making vocational choices: A theory of careers.* Englewood Cliffs, NJ: Prentice Hall.

Holland, J. L. (1997). *Making vocational choices: A theory of vocational personalities and work environments* (3rd ed.). Odessa, FL: Psychological Assessment Resources.

Johnson, L. S. (2000). The relevance of school to career: A study in student awareness. *Journal of Career Development, 26*(4), 263–276. http://dx.doi.org/10.1177/089484530002600403

Jones, L. K. (2011). Holland's six personality types. Retrieved from http://www.careerkey.org/asp/your_personality/hollands_6_personalitys.asp

Knowdell, R. L. (2005). *Career values card sort.* San Jose, CA: Career Research & Testing.

Lawrence, D. A., & Mancuso, T. A. (2012). Promoting girls' awareness and interest in engineering. *Technology and Engineering Teacher, 72*(1), 11–16.

Legum, H. L., & Hoare, C. H. (2004). Impact of a career intervention on at-risk middle school students' career maturity levels, academic achievement, and self-esteem. *Professional School Counseling, 8*(2), 148–155.

Marcia, J. E. (1987). The identity status approach to the study of ego identity development. In T. Honess & K. Yardley (Eds.), *Self and identity: Perspectives across the lifespan* (pp. 161–171). New York, NY: Routledge.

Mijares, A. (2007). *Defining college readiness* (California Education Policy Convening). Retrieved from http://s3.amazonaws.com/zanran_storage/www.edsource.org/ContentPages/744695364.pdf

Ng, J., Wolf-Wendel, L., & Lombardi, K. (2014). Pathways from middle school to college: Examining the impact of an urban, precollege preparation program. *Education and Urban Society, 46,* 672–698. http://dx.doi.org/10.1177/0013124512470161

Niles, S. G., & Harris-Bowlsbey, J. (2009). *Career development interventions in the 21st century* (3rd ed.). Upper Saddle River, NJ: Merrill.

O'Brien, K. M., Dukstein, R. D., Jackson, S. L., Tomlinson, M. J., & Kamatuka, N. A. (1999). Broadening career horizons for students in at-risk environments. *Career Development Quarterly, 47*(3), 215–229. http://dx.doi.org/10.1002/j.2161-0045.1999.tb00732.x

Orthner, D. (2012). CareerStart: A proven approach to middle-school success. Retrieved from http://www.learnnc.org/lp/pages/7260

Orthner, D. K., Jones-Sanpei, H., Akos, P., & Rose, R. A. (2013). Improving middle school student engagement through career-relevant instruction in the core curriculum. *Journal of Educational Research, 106,* 27–38. http://dx.doi.org/10.1080/00220671.2012.658454

Piaget, J. (1969). *The intellectual development of the adolescent.* In G. Caplan & S. Lebovici (Eds.), *Adolescence: Psychosocial perspectives* (pp. 22–26). New York, NY: Basic Books.

Radcliffe, R. A., & Bos, B. (2013). Strategies to prepare middle school and high school students for college and career readiness. *Clearing House, 86,* 136–141. http://dx.doi.org/10.1080/00098655.20013.782850

Rinke, C. R., Arsenie, M. E., & Bell, S. (2012). "College is a good place to go to become what you want to become": A collaboration between liberal arts undergraduate and urban middle school students. *Teacher Education Quarterly, 39*(1), 99–120.

Sharf, R. S. (2006). *Applying career development theory to counseling* (4th ed.). Belmont, CA: Thomson.

Turner, S. L., Conkel, J., Starkey, M. T., & Landgraf, R. (2010). Relationships among middle-school adolescents' vocational skills, motivational approaches, and interests. *Career Development Quarterly, 59,* 154–168. http://dx.doi.org/10.1002/j.2161-0045.2010.tb00059.x

Turner, S., & Lapan, R. T. (2002). Career self-efficacy and perceptions of parent support in adolescent career development. *Career Development Quarterly, 51*(1), 44–55. http://dx.doi.org/10.1002/j.2161-0045.2002.tb00591.x

Usinger, J. (2005). Parent/guardian visualization of career and academic future of seventh graders enrolled in low-achieving schools. *Career Development Quarterly, 53*(3), 234–245. http://dx.doi.org/10.1002/j.2161-0045.2005.tb00993.x

Young, R. A. (1983). Career development of adolescents: An ecological perspective. *Journal of Youth and Adolescence, 12*(5), 401–417. http://dx.doi.org/10.1007/BF02088723

Young, R. A., Paseluikho, M. A., & Valach, L. (1997). The role of emotion in the construction of career in parent-adolescent conversations. *Journal of Counseling & Development, 76*(1), 36–44. http://dx.doi.org/10.1002/j.1556-6676.1997.tb02374.x

ELEVEN

Career and College Readiness for Grade 8: High School Transition Planning

The eighth grade is typically when students are expected to make important choices regarding their futures. In many states, students must decide by the end of their eighth-grade year what curriculum they want to follow in high school. Although they are referred to by various descriptors (e.g., courses of study, tracks, academic paths), the curricula from which students must choose typically reflect long-term career and college plans. For example, students might choose a career or technical curriculum that would prepare them to search for a job, enter the military right after high school, or attend a technical training program (e.g., culinary arts, welding). Conversely, students may choose a college preparatory curriculum that would enable them to pursue postsecondary training at a 2- or 4-year college, or they might choose a rigorous honors or Advanced Placement (AP) curriculum that would enable them to competitively pursue 4-year college degrees. Because of differing math, science, and foreign language requirements, among other things, students who choose a less rigorous curriculum may be limited in postsecondary school options should they decide later on that they do want to attend college; moreover, they might have to take remedial courses (such as algebra) or prerequisite courses (such as foreign languages) once in college in order to catch up with their collegiate peers. On the other hand, students who choose an honors college preparatory track may find that they took on more than they were ready for academically, and their grades may suffer accordingly.

Clearly, choosing a high school curriculum requires a lot of thought. Preparing for the transition to high school and the corresponding decisions that must be made also require a keen awareness both of self and of careers. Furthermore, knowledgeable school counselors and a collaborative approach involving families, teachers, and community members can help to ensure a smooth high school transition process. Middle or junior high school personnel must be familiar with high school requirements and expectations, and parents should be included in helping to make these important curricular decisions. In this chapter, we discuss student readiness for high school and focus on collaborative efforts to help students make the transition from eighth to ninth grade.

DEVELOPMENTAL OVERVIEW

The typical eighth grader, who has progressed through school in a traditional manner, is age 13 or 14. Although we acknowledge that students vary immensely in their development at any age, we highlight next some of the more common developmental characteristics of students in eighth grade. Later, we discuss appropriate interventions based on these developmental considerations.

Psychosocial Development

According to Erikson (1963), students in eighth grade would fall into the *identity versus role confusion* stage. Adolescents struggle to identify who they want to be now and in the future—both as people in general (e.g., beliefs, values) and in relation to their future career role. Students in this stage need opportunities to explore and try out new things so they can figure out what they like and don't like, as well as in what areas they possess strengths and weaknesses. Part of the challenge with developing a clear identity is that students at this age often struggle to reconcile their own desires and dreams with those of their friends or parents. Though the influence of family is still important (Young, 1983), these students are highly influenced by their peers and want to fit in. In fact, many of their decisions are based on what their peers are doing or what their peers value, including in the area of career development.

As we discussed in Chapter 10, Marcia (1989) elaborated on Erikson's stage of *identity versus role confusion* to look at how adolescents resolve the major life task of developing an identity. He proposed four statuses (moratorium, diffusion, foreclosure, and achievement) to describe the various ways in which adolescents form identity, and these statuses can be distinctly applied to career decision making. The four statuses are illustrated in Table 11.1.

Beyond career and identity development, social development is a major life task of adolescence. In particular, adolescents begin to develop a more keen awareness of social cues and, as a result, begin to monitor their own behavior to meet social expectations of their peer group. They may also become somewhat rebellious to adult figures in their lives and develop short-term, adolescence-limited turmoil as they are beginning to learn to negotiate conflict with others (Belsky, 2007). It is important that students at this age learn positive communication and conflict resolution strategies to set the stage for positive working relationships and future career success.

TABLE 11.1   Marcia's Identity Statuses as Related to Careers

	Active Career Exploration	No Career Exploration
No commitment to career choice	Moratorium	Diffusion
Committed to career choice	Achievement	Foreclosure

Cognitive Development

As we discussed in the previous chapter, according to Piaget (1977), students in middle school are becoming more sophisticated in their thinking and are likely entering the stage of *formal operations*. At minimum, most students in eighth grade possess concrete thinking abilities. They are able to understand cause and effect and can follow sequences. Although not everyone develops formal operational thought, many students in eighth grade will show some evidence, albeit inconsistent, of their abstract thinking abilities. These are the abilities that help students understand algebraic concepts and comprehensively explain how personal experiences might affect someone later in life (e.g., understanding and predicting consequences). Additionally, abstract thinking gives adolescents new skills to use, including thinking logically, engaging in inductive and deductive reasoning, generating hypotheses, and problem solving. These skills are essential to career and college planning, as doing so requires the ability to understand one's options, research possibilities, comprehend one's own talents and abilities, and project into the future (Belsky, 2007).

Despite their advanced thinking skills, many adolescents are still quite egocentric in their thinking (Elkind, 1978). They might be able to clearly explain the consequences of a specific choice, but at the same time they may believe that they are immune to any negative outcomes (i.e., their personal fable). It is this kind of thinking that leads some students to believe that things will work out for them no matter what they do.

Beyond promoting complex academic structures and capabilities, the emergence of formal operational thought supports the ability to take another person's perspective. Perspective taking creates a critical foundation for advanced interpersonal skills such as empathy, compassion, prosocial interest, and altruism (Eisenberg et al., 1999; Eisenberg, Miller, Shell, McNalley, & Shea, 1991), all of which are important for effective social interaction and positive collegial relationships in the workplace. Moreover, advanced abstract thought can promote moral development and affect career choices for adolescents who develop a strong sense of justice, an ethos of caring for others, and a propensity for activism (Belsky, 2007). Conversely, the ability to think abstractly may support critical thinking, which can manifest as students questioning authority and becoming argumentative. For students struggling academically, adolescence can become a time when they question why school is important or meaningful in their personal lives.

RELEVANT CAREER THEORIES: GOTTFREDSON (1981), HOLLAND (1973), AND YOUNG (1983)

Gottfredson's *Theory of Circumscription and Compromise* (1981, 2002) provides much insight into understanding the decision-making process in which many eighth-grade students engage as they make career- and college-related choices. Specifically, students in eighth grade would most likely fall into Gottfredson's third stage, *Orientation to Social Valuation*. In this stage, individuals narrow career choices based on their perceived social values of particular careers. Doing so requires students to assess their own social status as well as the social status of various careers they are considering. According to Gottfredson (2002), adolescents in this stage are noticing symbols of status including cars, home, and clothing, among other material possessions. Students may begin to consider careers that will afford them the status they desire.

Beyond social status, adolescents begin to consider perceived intellectual abilities in career choice. Adolescents will consider careers that are within a tolerable level boundary, meaning the status of the career must fit within the acceptable range of careers for the individual's perceived social status. For example, a student whose parents are surgeons will most likely find a career as a fast-food restaurant manager intolerable. Similarly, a student with a single mother who is a hotel housekeeper may find a career as a physicist intolerable. Individuals circumscribe and compromise out of careers based on the social value of the career and the individual's perception of his or her social value.

With students struggling to solidify their own identities at this age, however, messages from peers can greatly influence perceptions of which careers are valuable and/or how students view themselves, although peers' perceptions may or may not be accurate. Gottfredson's and Piaget's theories complement each other in helping to conceptualize the unique needs of eighth-grade students, particularly in regard to the development of self-concept and career decision making. We discuss ways to involve peers and address peer influence in the interventions we share later in this chapter.

Holland's *Theory of Vocational Choice* (1973) also serves as an important foundation for understanding and working with eighth-grade students. His emphasis on self- and career awareness as precursors to make satisfying career choices suggests that time spent helping students explore their identities and develop a realistic understanding of job requirements and characteristics might help set the stage for future career success and satisfaction. The use of assessments that target interests, abilities, and values is common with students in eighth grade, and the results of those assessments can serve as a starting point for identifying careers that are consistent with a student's personality type. More details about working with these types of assessments are presented later in this chapter.

Finally, Young's (1983) ecosystemic career concepts are particularly important both for understanding factors that can influence eighth-grade students and for conceptualizing interventions relevant to those students. Young discussed both explicit and implicit career influences that can come from the school. The intentional implementation of individual, group, classroom, and school-wide career activities would reflect explicit influence exerted by the school. The implicit influences, however, can come in the form of things such as what topics are or are not addressed; what messages counselors, teachers, and other school personnel send to students regarding their future; and what opportunities are afforded all students to engage in career and self-exploration.

Young (1983) also acknowledged the role of peer (social group) and parent (family) microsystems on students' career development. Specifically, direct or indirect messages from peers and parents can be integrated into students' decision-making process. Finally, the positioning of eighth-grade students in their transition to high school highlights the importance of examining mesosystemic influences. For example, the quality and extent of the relationships as well as the amount and type of communication that exists between the eighth-grade school personnel, parents, and high school personnel can affect how prepared students (and their families) are for the transition to ninth grade, the important choices that must be made regarding choosing a high school curriculum, and the resulting impact those choices have on students' future career and college outcomes.

EIGHTH-GRADE STUDENT CAREER AND COLLEGE READINESS OUTCOMES

As we discussed in Chapter 1, a multifaceted and systemic approach to career and college planning requires a focus on more than just career and college awareness. Things such as academic skills, interpersonal skills, and skills in self-regulation are all important to students' future career and college outcomes. We find each of these areas addressed throughout the American School Counselor Association's (ASCA) (2014) Mindsets and Behaviors. Furthermore, a clear emphasis on self-awareness, career awareness, and future planning is evident in the Mindsets and Behaviors and should be a core part of the classroom curriculum.

CAREER AND COLLEGE READINESS INTERVENTIONS

Career and college readiness interventions for eighth-grade students should be intentional, comprehensive, include a variety of activities and delivery methods, and involve a variety of stakeholders (ASCA, 2012; Brown, 2012). We will be sharing developmentally appropriate interventions that reflect the concepts and concerns we identified previously in the developmental and career theories and that allow school counselors to address many of the ASCA (2014) Mindsets and Behaviors (see Table 11.2). The primary goal of these activities is to focus on self-awareness, career awareness, and long-term career and college decision making—all critical to enable students to make decisions regarding their high school curriculum. The secondary goal is to address relevant career and college readiness skills. Of note, novice school counselors are often surprised by

TABLE 11.2 ASCA Mindsets and Behaviors for Eighth-Grade Curriculum Planning Focus

CATEGORY 1: MINDSETS STANDARDS		
Self-confidence in ability to succeed Belief in using abilities to their fullest to achieve high-quality results and outcomes		
CATEGORY 2: BEHAVIOR STANDARDS		
Learning Strategies	**Self-Management Skills**	**Social Skills**
Use time management, as well as organizational and study skills	Demonstrate self-discipline and self-control	Demonstrate ethical decision making and social responsibility
Identify long- and short-term academic, career, and socioemotional goals	Demonstrate ability to manage transitions and ability to adapt to changing situations and responsibilities	Demonstrate social maturity and behaviors appropriate to the situation and environment

how much middle school students enjoy exploring careers and colleges. Eighth grade is the pinnacle of that exploration, and students genuinely like having the opportunity to assess themselves and consider their options.

Career and College Readiness Curriculum

School counselors preparing classroom lessons for eighth-grade students may think about that delivery system as a means for efficiently and comprehensively working with students regarding their career and college readiness needs. Ideally, school counselors will be able to get into classrooms at least six times throughout the year (e.g., once a week over the course of one 6-week grading period) to administer weekly classroom lessons to eighth graders, and by partnering with teachers who can deliver supplemental lessons, they can ensure that career- and college-related concepts are addressed comprehensively. We present more information about teacher involvement later in this chapter. For school counselors, a three-unit approach that focuses on (a) self-assessment, (b) career awareness, and (c) decision making can be used to help them make the early career decisions requisite to their choosing a high school curriculum, which will ultimately lead to postsecondary choices. A manageable approach to presenting these lessons that is consistent with Holland's theory is presented in Table 11.3.

Unit 1: Self-assessment. As reflected in many of the theories presented in the beginning of this chapter (e.g., Erikson, Marcia), students in eighth grade are working to establish their identities, which involves being able to discuss their strengths, weaknesses, interests, values, and desires for the future. While self-exploration activities are an integral part of the core counseling curriculum in grades 6 and 7, as discussed in previous chapters, a formal assessment of interests, abilities, and values is critical in eighth grade so that students can begin to make high school academic choices that match their future career and college interests. One instrument that taps into those three areas is Holland's Self-Directed Search (SDS; see Chapter 5). The SDS is a reliable and valid self-report instrument that can be used to identify a student's career personality,

TABLE 11.3   Sample Career and College Readiness Curriculum

Week	Topic	Student Product
1	Unit 1. Self-assessment. Complete and discuss interest inventory	Interest ability results
2	Unit 1. Self-assessment. Complete and discuss abilities inventory	Ability assessment results
3	Unit 1. Self-assessment. Complete and discuss values inventory and calculate personality code	Values assessment results plus overall personality code
4	Unit 2. Career awareness. Understanding personality and occupation fit	List of potential occupations that match personality code
5	Unit 2. Career awareness. Exploring occupational training requirements	List of possible postsecondary options
6	Unit 3. Decision making. Making curriculum decisions	High school curriculum choice that matches potential postsecondary plans

as defined by Holland. After completing an interest inventory, self-rating their abilities, and identifying their values, students are able to calculate their three-letter personality code.

The SDS can be completed electronically, and numerous career guidance systems used in school districts throughout the United States (e.g., Kuder, EXPLORE, and DISCOVER) have been developed based on Holland's theory. The three lessons that comprise this self-assessment unit could be conducted in a computer lab or with classroom laptop sets where students would be able to complete assessments online. Moreover, having students complete online assessments reinforces the use of technology (ASCA, 2014) for career and college decision making. Having already discussed interests, abilities, and values in grades 6 and 7, school counselors should be able to facilitate the formal assessment process after a brief review of those constructs and the importance of self-awareness in finding a satisfying occupation.

Unit 2: Career awareness. After the self-assessment process is complete, students must be able to identify occupations that match their career personalities. By using Holland's Occupations Finder (a workbook that lists various occupations by Holland code) or other resources available in computerized career guidance systems such as *O*Net* and others (see Chapter 5), students can search for occupations that match their personality code. It is important to help students identify why different occupations have the codes they do so that they begin to understand the nuances that make one occupation slightly different from another similar one.

To facilitate students' understanding of what distinguishes one occupation from another, the *World-of-Work Map* (see Figure 11.1) may be a useful visual. Using this map also can help facilitate understanding for visual learners, as they can see and measure how close or far away from each other various occupations are on the map. The placement of occupations on the map in relation to people, data, things, or ideas also can become clearer when a visual representation is used.

One approach to facilitating career awareness is to determine what students know before sharing concrete information with them. For example, school counselors might ask students to name the occupation(s) they are most interested in, and then the class can try to guess the appropriate Holland code without looking it up. Interesting and insightful class discussion can occur as students try to explain to each other why they think one code is more appropriate than another. Evidence of formal operational thinking patterns also often emerge in these discussions and students can learn from each other.

Once students have an idea of which occupations might be good matches for them based on their current self-assessment of interests, abilities, and values, they need to thoroughly investigate those occupations. In addition to accessing information that often is connected to computerized career guidance systems, school counselors also might have students access information available online in *O*Net* and the *Occupational Outlook Handbook*. Having already introduced students to these resources in grade 7, school counselors simply may remind them of what information is available and how to locate it.

FIGURE 11.1   World-of-Work Map

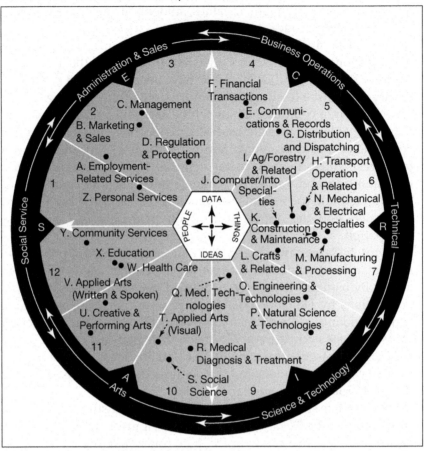

Reprinted with permission from ACT, Inc.

For students interested in a possible career in the military, it is critical that they also consider how their potential military career is related to civilian careers they might have when leaving or retiring from the military. One way to begin this exploration is by visiting Careers in the Military (careersinthemilitary.com), a useful tool for students who are curious about what occupations they might pursue in one of the five branches of the military or in the National Guard. Minimal expectations would be for students to identify requisite skills, existing pathways into those occupations, and educational opportunities (such as Reserve Officers Training Corps [ROTC]) and educational requirements.

Given the impending transition to high school and the requirement to choose a curriculum of study before finishing eighth grade, students can benefit from a thorough exploration of occupational training requirements. Although it is unlikely that every student will know exactly what he or she wants to do after high school, one way to approach this discussion is to ask students to identify the different educational and training requirements for all of the occupations in which they express an interest. This information will be important in their decision-making process. For example, perhaps one student knows that she wants to do something involving computers. She knows that she will need to pursue college, but she doesn't know if she wants to get a 2-year degree in programming, pursue a 4-year degree in computer science, or enter the military and become trained as a computer systems specialist. She doesn't need to decide right now—that will be one of her long-term goals. But what will be important is that she chooses a high school curriculum that will allow her to pursue as many postsecondary options as possible.

Unit 3: Decision making. Once students possess self-awareness and basic career awareness, they are in a position to make initial decisions about their long-term future and their upcoming high school curriculum choice. A psychoeducational approach is warranted, whereby school counselors review the high school curricular options to ensure that students understand the most logical postsecondary options associated with each career and college choice. To engage students collaboratively, a number of case scenarios could be developed for which the class would need to identify curriculum possibilities.

Another important consideration in the decision-making process relates to students who are undecided about whether or not they want to attend postsecondary school and/or what kind of postsecondary school they intend to pursue. Students might be tempted to choose a high school curriculum based on what their friends are doing or what might seem easiest to them academically. Given the importance of peers and the fact that many early adolescents believe things will work out for them no matter what they do, these scenarios are not uncommon. Students might not understand that earning a B in a weighted honors or AP English course would be more impressive to many colleges than earning an A in a general English course. School counselors should plan to integrate as many real-life examples as possible into classroom lessons to proactively address these issues, then they can supplement these lessons by providing students with firsthand opportunities to talk to individuals in the community and at postsecondary schools. Parents also will play a very important role in this high school curriculum decision process, and later in this chapter we discuss more ways in which school counselors might involve and educate parents about the various career and college options available to students.

One benefit of using classroom lessons to address career and college readiness is that most students can benefit from similar types of information, and they can learn from each other. Nevertheless, developmentally, students will vary in their readiness to make decisions or truly understand all of the information they have acquired. School counselors cannot dismiss the importance of working individually with students in an effort to address the unique questions and concerns of each student.

Individual Interventions

Given the developmental differences that exist among young adolescents, school counselors should do what they can to ensure that each student has an accurate understanding of self, career, and postsecondary options. Starting with self-assessment, school counselors want to check in to make sure that each student understands his or her results assessment. As such, a very important part of using an instrument like the SDS is taking time to process the results with students. Similarly, once students identify potential occupations and educational or training requirements, school counselors should make sure that their decisions are logical and well informed.

It is important to acknowledge that students' self-reported abilities may or may not be accurate indicators of their potential, and it is also important that students don't make decisions based solely on their own self-perceptions. Low self-efficacy related to skills and abilities needed for success in various occupations could lead students to rule out options unnecessarily. As such, school counselors should consider the ways in which they might supplement student self-ratings with less subjective data, and to assess and intervene regarding self-efficacy when relevant. For example, feedback from teachers, academic grades, and achievement test scores might be included in discussions with students in an effort to help them develop a comprehensive picture of their potential. Furthermore, while in the Kuder system students self-rate their abilities, the EXPLORE system generates scores in English, math, reading, and science based on student responses to items in those areas. The score report that students receive from EXPLORE explains their scores in relation to readiness for college-level course work, and this report could be a useful tool during individual planning sessions.

One of the challenges with trying to meet individually with every student relates to school counselor caseloads. With an average caseload exceeding a 300:1 ratio (American Counseling Association, 2011), school counselors have limited time to engage in individual planning meetings with students. Yet we know this type of approach can be critical for students as they prepare for a high school transition. For example, South Carolina requires that students and their parents or guardians participate in an individual graduation plan (IGP) meeting during the eighth-grade year. The purpose of these meetings is to review the students' self-assessment results and future plans and to decide on a high school program of study. In some middle schools, the school counselors are solely responsible for conducting these meetings; in other schools, teachers and career development facilitators take the lead, under the supervision of school counselors (later we discuss some ways that school counselors can engage teachers in this process). In any case, those IGP meetings typically run 15 to 20 minutes each, which hardly seems enough time to thoroughly invest in such an important discussion. Furthermore, the scheduling and rescheduling of those meetings can last for well over a month, leaving school counselors little time to engage in other tasks.

Classroom Curriculum Integration

Given the extensive time involved in adequately preparing students to make high school curricular decisions, school counselors should try to involve as many other stakeholders as possible. Classroom teachers may help in a number of ways. First, classroom teachers are the experts in their subject areas, and they possess knowledge of what types of subject-specific skills are needed for various occupations. They can use interactive strategies to expose students to the numerous occupations related to their subject areas (Exhibit 11.1). Also, classroom teachers may be encouraged to implement contextual learning strategies so that students are better able to understand the potential real-world application of class content, and to do so in reference to a variety of occupational choices. Examples ranging from basic arithmetic skills needed to successfully manage a cash register to advanced math skills necessary to calculate angles for a construction job or to generate complex formulas needed for accounting could be illustrated.

EXHIBIT 11.1
Helping Teachers Integrate Career and College Information

At one small, rural middle school in the Midwest, the eighth-grade school counselor collaborated with classroom teachers to expose students to a variety of careers. At the beginning of the academic year, she attended the eighth-grade teachers' team meeting and shared her career development goals for the upcoming year, explaining the activities she had planned to implement and identifying areas where she felt she needed help. One of those areas was career exposure. Students had access to lots of career information online, but they were missing personal discussions about specific careers. Also, she had attempted to host a career fair the previous year, but the school was in such a rural area that it was challenging to find enough and varied speakers. She did not feel comfortable on her own trying to discuss occupations across all subject areas in a way that really helped students understand how the skills they learned in those subject areas could be applied.

To introduce the teachers more specifically to what she had in mind, she pulled out a copy of the World-of-Work Map (see Figure 11.1). Most were not familiar with the map, so she briefly explained what it was and how the occupations were grouped. She proposed to the teachers that if they were willing to identify six occupations from the map related to their subject area and prepare brief classroom discussions about those occupations (highlighting skill application), then she would provide World-of-Work Maps for each of them and would provide them access to career information. She emphasized that she wanted them to choose at least one occupation that did not require postsecondary school, one that required vocational/technical training, and one that required a 4-year college degree. She also encouraged them to choose occupations that reflected varied career clusters as well as clusters from different Holland codes (i.e., RIASEC) and reflecting an emphasis on data, ideas, people, and things. The goal was to help students recognize that while some subjects tend to be more highly represented in certain career clusters, others cross over many career clusters.

The school counselor also wanted the teachers to help students identify requisite occupational skills. She shared with the teachers an activity whereby

(continued)

> **EXHIBIT 11.1** (continued)
> Helping Teachers Integrate Career and College Information
>
> they would introduce an occupation, have students locate it on the map, and then brainstorm the type and level of subject-specific skills that would be needed. By having to locate the occupation and then referencing other occupations located in proximity, students will be forced to think critically about the occupations.
>
> The teachers responded very positively to the idea, and each was able to spend at least 20 minutes discussing each of six occupations. They reported that students at first had difficulty locating the occupations on the map, but that over time as the students became more familiar and the teachers provided some facilitative questions (e.g., Do you think this occupation fits under data, people, ideas, or things? Would this occupation be classified as R, I, A, S, E, or C?), they more quickly located the occupations. The teachers also reported that they personally developed a clearer conceptualization of what students were learning in their counseling classroom lessons. They appreciated that the school counselor had checked in after the first couple of sessions, and the follow-up information she had provided regarding the RIASEC codes had been very helpful to them in helping the students.

Second, classroom teachers could invite guest speakers into their classes—people who use subject-specific skills in their jobs—to share their experiences. School counselors might help to organize these speakers, maintaining a database of individuals who are willing to volunteer their time on occasion. To find speakers, counselors and teachers can begin by utilizing the support of community partners, local universities, and family members of students. As teachers anticipate teaching specific skill sets, they could easily contact the volunteers who could help illustrate the concepts, helping to reinforce other contextual learning and experiential strategies they might be using.

Furthermore, classroom teachers also can help students explore their strengths and weaknesses as they relate to each subject area. School counselors only have limited information about students, and reviewing report cards and achievement test results may not give an accurate picture of a student's potential. This is one opportunity, however, where teachers can unintentionally influence students in positive and negative ways regarding their future potential. The teacher who discourages a student from enrolling in algebra mainly on the basis that the student has not demonstrated consistent, high achievement and not because the student is incapable can set that student up for limited career and college options. Indeed, encouraging students to take rigorous courses is a critical function of teachers in preparing students for career and college readiness. School counselors can help teachers understand the impact of their feedback and may encourage teachers to monitor their comments to provide students with helpful and constructive feedback regarding their academic futures. Helping teachers express perceptions about students' work ethics as separate from their perceptions of students' abilities may be helpful.

Finally, classroom teachers can be educated about the high school curriculum choices to the degree where they possess enough information to help students make choices. By providing them with a structured format, school counselors can rely on teachers to be collaborative partners in leading student–parent high school curriculum planning meetings. Realistically, school counselors cannot meet the individual needs of students on their own, but they can provide oversight to a school-wide effort.

Fouad (1995) found moderate success for an intervention that combined many of the activities just discussed. With a focus on increasing students' awareness of careers in math and science, partnerships were developed among the school counselor, teachers, a university, parents, and individuals in the community. The intervention involved eighth-grade students participating in a series of 6-week units built into core academic classes, which included general discussion of the career field (e.g., natural sciences, engineering), field trips to local businesses, guest speakers, and job shadowing opportunities. Fouad reported that a significantly higher proportion of students in the experimental group chose magnet high schools than did those in the control group. Further, there were significant differences in the type of math courses taken by minority students in the experimental versus control group, with students in the experimental group being more likely to enroll in algebra or geometry than applied math or pre-algebra.

PARTNERING WITH PARENTS AND THE COMMUNITY

We have mentioned parents a few times in this chapter, and most importantly we want to convey the importance of inviting parents/guardians to be partners in this high school curriculum decision-making process. Before they can become involved, however, parents must possess an understanding of the process and requirements. One way to avoid confusion is to give parents information more than once. For example, in a focus group of middle school parents regarding their perceptions of the school's efforts in preparing students for career and college readiness, the first author had multiple parents share the frustration of receiving eighth- to ninth-grade transition information in one presentation given at a meeting with over 300 parents in the school gymnasium. The parents reported feeling frustrated and overwhelmed by the amount of information and did not feel that they could help their children with the information they received. Just as it can be important to provide information to students in various ways, school counselors should consider that parents have different levels of knowledge as well as varying needs related to assisting their children in preparing for careers and college. School counselors should also consider the types of information that will be helpful to parents in assisting their children through the middle to high school transition, including information on the importance of extracurricular activities, time management, navigating increasing responsibilities, high school curriculum paths and programs, and high school registration and scheduling.

We reported in Chapter 4 that approximately one third of students are first-generation college students (Aud et al., 2012), meaning that neither of their parents attended college. Some percentage of parents in any school will likely possess little awareness of college, the requisite requirements for attending postsecondary school, or the different paths students can take to pursue various occupations. School counselors must be aware of the needs of the parents/guardians in their schools and provide relevant educational opportunities. Researchers have suggested that parental involvement is one of the most significant predictors and influencing factors of students' educational aspirations (Holcomb-McCoy, 2010) and schools need to provide support and information to assist families in making the most informed decision possible (Akos, Lambie, Milsom, & Gilbert, 2007).

During this critical transition period, school counselors need to ensure that parents are educated about high school curriculum choices and how those choices relate to career and college options. Just like students, parents who don't accurately understand the different types of courses available (e.g., AP, honors) or how weighted grades are viewed by postsecondary schools may be uncomfortable encouraging their child to enroll in the most rigorous curriculum. Also, parents who don't understand requirements to enter the military may not understand that a rigorous curriculum can still be important. As school counselors help parents and students understand the benefits of taking more rigorous courses, they will need to explain how the demands of more rigorous classes will translate into the need for greater time and stress management. School counselors also should anticipate the importance of sharing information with parents about specialized options available to students, including vocational/technical training options available through high school and unique local programs such as those available at magnet or charter schools.

Parent education may occur in a number of ways. Parent workshops are a common approach, but sometimes it is difficult for parents to attend meetings at the school. School counselors should consider alternative formats to make the information they want to share as accessible as possible, and they may have to be creative in order to reach the parents of the children in their school. For example, in one inner city school district with poor public transportation, school counselors visit community centers in housing projects. Further, publishing relevant information on the school website, sending information home in a newsletter, or partnering with local businesses to conduct breakfast or lunchtime information sessions for parents who cannot leave work are just a few ideas (see Exhibit 11.2).

A number of school counselors have been able to get local churches and other organizations to promote their workshops, and some school counselors have been able to partner with local libraries to conduct information workshops at night and on the weekends. Efforts to ensure that translating services are available are also important, as more and more students in the United States come from homes where English is not the first language. The more informed parents are and the more they believe the school wants to help them,

EXHIBIT 11.2
Community Partnership for Parent Involvement

In another rural middle school, the school counselor struggled to interact face to face with parents. Although the district included individuals from all socioeconomic levels, the overwhelming majority of parents either had not graduated from high school or had achieved a high school diploma as their highest level of education. Farming and factory work were common occupations, and neither of those occupations allowed parents flexibility to come to school during the day to attend meetings. Further, although many parents would happily drive to the school to attend sporting events, few made the effort to make the often 45-minute drive to attend a meeting. The school counselor decided she needed to be creative in reaching out to parents. She believed that many parents were interested in being involved but just were stuck. Those who worked in the local factory a half mile down the road were not able to take any time off during the day—they risked their pay being docked.

The school counselor decided to pursue a collaborative partnership with the factory in order to reach out to parents who worked there. After much discussion, the factory agreed to allow the school counselor to come over during the lunch break to meet with parents in small groups or individually as necessary. The school principal was completely on board and permitted her to leave the building during the day to do this. She was able to share information about high school choices, student academic progress, career development activities, and other related information. Through this approach, the school counselor was able to disseminate career and college information to more parents than she had in the past. She found that many of the students whose parents she had talked with followed up by coming in to talk with her about their future plans and to ask questions.

the more likely they will be to come in and ask questions. School counselors need to take the initiative to creatively reach out to parents and get them actively involved in students' career and college decision making.

FACILITATING THE EIGHTH- TO NINTH-GRADE TRANSITION

Although career exploration and academic advisement are essential for connecting school to the world of work for eighth-grade students, another important task for school counselors is facilitating the eighth- to ninth-grade transition. This transition is important for career and college readiness because ninth grade is a time when many students face critical decisions and challenges that can get them off track. Specifically, students need to be prepared for the greater autonomy, self-regulation demands, and responsibilities of ninth grade. With a clear understanding of what to expect in high school, students will be more successful in their transition, both academically and socially.

High school visits are a common transition intervention, and partnering with the high school is critical to developing a successful transition program. Middle school counselors can coordinate with high school counselors to provide several opportunities where parents and students can visit the high school, meet teachers, and receive instruction on how to make the transition. They also can invite ninth-grade students to answer questions and talk about their own transition experiences. In addition, eighth-grade teachers and school counselors might work together to cover topics that are of importance for transition success. Some possible topics might include stress management, time management, academic organization, extracurricular involvement, or goal setting. One eighth-grade counselor shared with these authors that during the eighth-grade year, she and the eighth-grade teaching team use *The 7 Habits of Highly Effective Teens* (Covey, 1998) to help the eighth graders develop prehigh school success skills. As part of the program, they provided parent workshops to assist parents in conceptualizing how to help their children develop those skills.

Another important transition activity is to review graduation and in-state scholarship requirements. The second author recalls having many conversations with high school students who had failed one or more courses in ninth grade. Although information had been provided to them upon their arrival at the high school (e.g., graduation requirements, the importance of passing classes and credits, the fact that colleges look at ninth-grade grade point average [GPA]), most students did not remember that information. Repetition is critical to ensuring that the message will eventually be heard, and if students can start out their high school experience with a clear understanding of how things work, perhaps more will demonstrate good academic and study skills from the start (Exhibit 11.3).

EXHIBIT 11.3
Voices From the Field: Eighth Grade and the Transition to
High School, College, and Career

Tristen Bergholtz, MEd

School Counselor, Woodlawn Middle School

As one of two school counselors at a large urban middle school in an urban setting, our time to implement activities related to each of the three domains of the ASCA National Model (2012) is limited, but through creativity, organization, and collaboration we do our best to adequately prepare our eighth graders for high school and beyond. As middle school counselors, we feel a great responsibility to our students and the preparation they need in order to set them up for success as they transition into high school. We provide tier two and three interventions (e.g., study skills and stress management groups, individual counseling, academic monitoring trackers) to students who have been identified as or who identify themselves as struggling students. At the tier one level, we provide a multitude of opportunities throughout the school

(continued)

EXHIBIT 11.3 (*continued*)

year to equip *all* students with the necessary attitudes, knowledge, and skills they will need to succeed in high school, college, and careers.

Fall Semester

One of the first major components of our school counseling program, which we complete at the beginning of each school year, is the school-wide needs assessment. Over the past 3 years, the top concerns and areas of need for our eighth-grade students have consistently been stress, fear of receiving one or more failing grades, dealing with change or new situations, and fear of making mistakes. While each of these areas is broad in scope, they can easily be linked to the many changes entailed in the process of transitioning out of middle school and into high school. From this data, we incorporate stress management and study skills techniques into all levels of our delivery system so that even after students transition out of middle school they have tools they can easily use in different situations.

Students involved in clubs attend a club meeting once a month for 30 minutes. However, students who do not sign up for a club are sent to classrooms with a supervising teacher. To maximize the use of the students' time and our school counseling program, the school counseling department provides supervising teachers with classroom lessons. Each of the lessons has a core focus on either the academic or socioemotional domain. At the end of each lesson, there is a concluding activity that encourages students to link the lesson to their postsecondary futures. Some of the lesson topics include malleable intelligence, persistence, and achieving their personal best. Club day was an unfilled use of time for students who are not involved in clubs, but now we use this time to help them build upon their strengths and in doing so reach about 200 students each month.

We administer a pretest prior to delivering the various transition-focused direct services we offer to our eighth-grade students. The pretest includes questions about the diploma tracks offered by our state, number of credits required to graduate from each diploma track, postsecondary education options and the differences between them, resources students can use during the career and college decision-making process, career clusters, and other high school, career, and college readiness topics we aim to cover by the end of the school year. At the end of the spring semester, we administer the posttest.

In the middle of October, we invite all of the high schools within the district that our eighth graders are eligible to attend. To start the event, we invite the ninth-grade counselor of our main feeder high school to introduce herself, review a few of the differences between middle school and high school, and introduce the various high school diploma tracks offered to students. We want to make sure our students are familiar with the high school jargon they'll be inundated with as soon as they start ninth grade (e.g., Carnegie units, credits, in-state scholarship language, FASFA). We encourage participation by offering a twofold extra credit opportunity for students; not only is their presence

(continued)

EXHIBIT 11.3 (continued)
**Voices From the Field: Eighth Grade and the Transition to
High School, College, and Career**

mandatory to earn extra credit, but they must also circulate to each school's table with a worksheet that includes questions they should ask about why that school would be a good fit for them. At the end of the night students whose worksheets are complete receive a signature from a counselor. These worksheets are then shown to each of their core teachers the following day for extra credit points.

In the middle of November, we host career week and career day. I have been able to grow this event from one that used to only serve a hand-selected group of eighth graders to one that now serves *all* students in *all* grades. At the beginning of the week, students are given a pretest and then each day they engage in a career lesson on various topics such as career role models, nontraditional careers, budgeting, conflict resolution, and the completion of an interest inventory that connects their interests to related careers. Many of these lessons have been adapted from Missouri's comprehensive career curriculum. On the final day, students complete the posttest and we also invite professionals from the community to speak with our students. Each student is exposed to four different guest speakers and completes a worksheet that provides him or her with questions the student can ask the guest speaker. These questions are specifically aligned with information found on the *Occupational Outlook Handbook*. According to posttest data we collect, students' career and college readiness increases an average of 75% as a result of the classroom guidance lessons we offer during this week.

At the end of the fall semester, eighth-grade students take a field trip to the high school. Students are divided up into groups and through a series of rotations are led through the school by high school student ambassadors. Our students learn about the school schedule and general rules and norms, meet the administration, watch performances by and learn about some of the extracurricular opportunities, and are able to ask questions to current high school students about what high school is like. One of the most beneficial aspects of this trip is that it provides eighth-grade students with an opportunity to visit the high school through the lens of a peer role model and helps them begin to think of themselves as high school students.

Spring Semester

At the beginning of the spring semester, the counseling department provides in-depth classroom lessons on the differences between middle school and high school (e.g., bell schedules, grading policies, promotion policies). We also discuss the differences between the college-bound and career-bound diploma tracks, postsecondary education options, and then help students complete their IGPs or 4-year high school plans. One of the most significant points that we highlight during the lesson is the Carnegie unit/credit system and how this positively or negatively affects their class selections for each of their remaining semesters in high school; we also underscore how these credits determine their graduation date and that the number of years spent in

(continued)

EXHIBIT 11.3 (*continued*)

high school does not equate to your class status (i.e., to become a sophomore students need six credits, not the same as starting your second year of high school). Students review the career clusters and identify which of the clusters their dream career fits into. From this selection, the school counselors help students plan which high school courses they should take to complete a career pathway that best prepares them for their chosen careers.

During the middle of the spring semester, the ninth-grade counselor speaks to our students during the school day. She again reviews the graduation requirements and diploma tracks and helps students complete their course request cards. The same day students are given their course request cards, we cohost a high school night event at the main feeder high school. Not only does this provide parents with an opportunity to tour the school and learn about the different programs and activities offered, but it also allows parents to ask questions about the course request cards and how their students' course selections affect their postsecondary options.

Toward the end of the semester, the school counseling department collects our final bulk of data from the students. Eighth-grade students complete the posttest related to the various transition and postsecondary planning topics covered throughout the school year. Upon review of this data, we see a 60% increase in the number of students whose knowledge, skills, and attitudes adequately demonstrate their awareness and preparedness for the transition to high school and postsecondary options because of our comprehensive school counseling program. We also offer students an end-of-year survey to learn about the school counseling programs they enjoyed and others they would like to see us offer. From this survey, we learned that students want us to host a college week in addition to career week. Through feedback from former students' parents, we have identified another area of improvement, which is to work more collaboratively with our former students and their parents to learn what they believe would best benefit our current students as they transition to high school and to ultimately help us better shape the services we offer through our school counseling program.

SUMMARY

In this chapter, we have highlighted career and college readiness interventions specifically for eighth-grade students. As we explained, students in eighth grade have a very important decision to make, one that could greatly impact their future. School counselors and educators must ensure that students and families are as prepared as possible to make this curricular decision. Opportunities for student self-, career-, and college-exploration, as well as for families and students to acquire information about career and college options, will enable them to make informed decisions. However, the process does not end with that decision; once students enter ninth grade they will continue to require more and more information as they narrow down their future plans. In the next chapter, we continue to look at the role of the school counselor in facilitating student career and college readiness as these students enter ninth grade.

···> Test Your Knowledge

1. What developmental stage would Erikson believe most eighth-grade students are in?
2. Explain the role of abstract thinking in future planning.
3. Name at least two career guidance systems you could use to assess student interests, abilities, and values.
4. Name at least two websites where students can gather occupational information.

REFERENCES

Akos, P., Lambie, G., Milsom, A., & Gilbert, K. (2007). Early adolescents' aspirations and academic tracking: An exploratory investigation. *Professional School Counseling, 11*(1), 57–64. http://dx.doi.org/10.5330/PSC.n.2010-11.57

American Counseling Association. (2011). United States student to counselor ratios for elementary and secondary schools. Retrieved from http://www.counseling.org/PublicPolicy/ACA_Ratio_Chart_2011_Overall.pdf

American School Counselor Association. (2012). *The ASCA national model: A framework for school counseling programs* (3rd ed.). Alexandria, VA: Author.

American School Counselor Association. (2014). *ASCA mindsets & behaviors for student success: K-12 college- and career-readiness standards for every student.* Alexandria, VA: Author.

Aud, S., Hussar, W., Johnson, F., Kena, G., Roth, E., Manning, E., . . . Zhang, J. (2012). *The condition of education 2012 (NCES 2012-045).* Washington, DC: U.S. Department of Education, National Center for Education Statistics. Retrieved from http://nces.ed.gov/pubs2012/2012045.pdf

Belsky, J. (2007). *Experiencing the lifespan.* New York, NY: Worth Publishers.

Brown, D. (2012). *Career information, career counseling, and career development* (10th ed.). Boston, MA: Pearson.

Covey, S. (1998). *The 7 habits of highly effective teens.* New York, NY: Fireside.

Eisenberg, N., Guthrie, I. K., Murphy, B. C., Shepard, S. A., Cumberland, A., & Carlo, G. (1999). Consistency and development of prosocial dispositions: A longitudinal study. *Child Development, 70*(6), 1360–1372. http://dx.doi.org/10.1111/1467-8624.00100

Eisenberg, N., Miller, P. A., Shell, R., McNalley, S., & Shea, C. (1991). Prosocial development in adolescence: A longitudinal study. *Developmental Psychology, 27*(5), 849–858. http://dx.doi.org/10.1037/0012-1649.27.5.849

Elkind, D. (1978). Understanding the young adolescent. *Adolescence, 13*(49), 127–134.

Erikson, E. H. (1963). *Childhood and society* (2nd ed.). New York, NY: W. W. Norton.

Fouad, N. A. (1995). Career linking: An intervention to promote math and science career awareness. *Journal of Counseling & Development, 73*, 527–534.

Gottfredson, L. S. (1981). Circumscription and compromise: A developmental theory of occupational aspirations. *Journal of Counseling Psychology, 28*(6), 545–579. http://dx.doi.org/10.1037/0022-0167.28.6.545

Gottfredson, L. S. (2002). Gottfredson's theory of circumscription, compromise, and self-creation. In D. Brown (Ed.), *Career choice and development* (4th ed., pp. 85–148). San Francisco, CA: Jossey-Bass.

Holcomb-McCoy, C. (2010). Involving low income parents and parents of color in college readiness activities: An exploratory study. *Professional School Counseling, 14*(1), 115–124.

Holland, J. L. (1973). *Making vocational choices: A theory of careers.* Englewood Cliffs, NJ: Prentice Hall.

Marcia, J. E. (1989). Identity and intervention. *Journal of Adolescence, 12*(4), 401–410. http://dx.doi.org/10.1016/0140-1971(89)90063-8

Piaget, J. (1977). *The development of thought: Equilibration of cognitive structure.* New York, NY: Viking Press.

Young, R. A. (1983). Career development of adolescents: An ecological perspective. *Journal of Youth and Adolescence, 12*(5), 401–417. http://dx.doi.org/10.1007/BF02088723

TWELVE

Career and College Readiness for Grade 9: Focus on Academic and Work Habits

Much has been written about the critical nature of the ninth-grade year on students' future outcomes. More and more school districts in the United States are acknowledging the need to target ninth graders via the formation of ninth-grade academies, or similar initiatives, where they can provide attention to the unique needs of this group of students and help them adjust to the increasing academic demands of high school (McCallumore & Sparapani, 2010). With an emphasis on facilitating the transition from eighth grade and promoting academic success, these kinds of initiatives often include specific instruction in development of self-regulatory mechanisms such as study skills, goal setting, academic progress monitoring, and time management. They also prioritize teachers' relationships with students and parents (Fields, 2008).

This kind of proactive approach has helped to improve student outcomes in many schools. For example, McIntosh and White (2006) reported a reduction in the number of classes failed, fewer expulsions, and increased attendance. Further, Cook, Fowler, and Harris (2008) examined outcomes associated with students attending ninth-grade academies in North Carolina. Compared to state averages, the students in ninth-grade academies had lower grade-level retention rates (15% vs. 22%) and lower dropout rates (6.6% vs. 12.5%). As we discussed earlier in this book, keeping kids in school and helping them achieve academic success can be critical to them envisioning increased career and postsecondary educational possibilities. As students experience success, they develop self-efficacy beliefs that lead them to persist even in the midst of challenges.

In ninth grade, some students realize for the first time that their academic grades affect the possibilities they have for the future. Students begin to learn the importance of setting goals, and they also acquire necessary study and time management skills that will carry them through their high school careers, college, and future work life. Ninth-grade academies facilitate the development of core academic and self-regulatory skills that are the cornerstone of career and college readiness. In the absence of these kinds of specialized programs, counselors and educators who work with ninth-grade students can integrate numerous activities into their curricula to promote skill and knowledge development in these areas.

DEVELOPMENTAL OVERVIEW

Unless they have been retained in school, most ninth graders are around age 14 or 15. They are in a phase of life where they are trying to figure out who they are and who they want to become, and their peers play very important roles in their lives and their overall development. Next, we highlight some of the more common developmental characteristics of students in ninth grade, and we later discuss relevant career and college readiness interventions based on these developmental considerations.

Psychosocial Development

Picking up with our discussion in the previous chapter, Erikson's (1963) *identity versus role confusion* stage is where most ninth-grade students can be categorized. Developmentally, students who are in this stage strive to be viewed as unique and special, but at the same time want to be accepted by their peers. They want to stand out in the crowd but also to fit in. In their attempt to navigate this challenge, students often experiment with different groups of friends, clothing styles, and interests and hobbies to try to determine where they want to fit.

Further, while many ninth-grade students choose classes and activities based on their own interests, others make decisions based on what their friends are doing. Similarly, students may even choose career paths and postsecondary options based on peer influence rather than personal choice. Ideally, we hope that students develop the confidence to make choices based on what *they* really like and value, but in many ways the exploration that occurs as they try to fit in with their peers may be of benefit in the long run.

During this stage, students also begin to differentiate from their families of origin, determining their own values and identifying ways that they are similar to, and different from, members of their family. Some stress and tension can result in the family system that might even manifest in academic and career advisement in school settings. For example, parents may expect their children to take courses that are aligned with the values they hold for their children's future. However, students may wish to take courses that align with a different set of values, ones that conflict with their parents' expectations. School counselors need to be prepared to explore and understand students' and parents' expectations and help them to navigate these difficult decisions.

Recall Marcia's (1989) theory (introduced in Chapter 10). It could be argued that ninth-grade students ideally should be in a moratorium status, when they are actively exploring careers or colleges without committing to anything specific. During this stage, parents and teachers may be frustrated with students' lack of commitment, so school counselors should assure these stakeholders that this is a normal transition. It is also helpful to remind students and parents that in ninth grade, there is still plenty of time for them to finalize their future decisions.

Although middle school career and college readiness interventions focus primarily on helping students explore abilities, interests, and values, it is not realistic to think that those activities alone will be sufficient in helping students finalize their career and college plans. Formal career and college readiness activities implemented throughout high school are designed to further assist students in developing self- and career awareness as well as in narrowing down their choices. Additionally, as students interact with their peers and try out new identities and activities, they are, in fact, informally engaging in the process of exploring aspects of themselves that are very relevant to career development—they just may not realize it.

Although we all can think of success stories associated with students who foreclosed on a career choice very early (e.g., a ninth-grade student, Martin, who has known forever he wanted to be a taxidermist because he has been actively involved in his family's business), there is value in encouraging exploration throughout high school. If Martin, who was an exceptional writer and avid reader in addition to doing well in his art classes, had been encouraged to explore careers in the liberal arts, would he still have decided to pursue taxidermy? Despite his talents, after exploring possible liberal arts careers Martin indeed might have decided that taxidermy was for him, or perhaps he would have identified a new potential career path and corresponding college choice.

We encourage exploration not to force students down different career paths than they initially chose, but rather to help them solidify and feel confident in their choices. By doing so, we also hope to reduce some of the confusion they might feel in college surrounding choice of major. Further, we want to help students explore options within fields. For example, a female student, Tori, wanted to work in nursing but was unsure of what type of nursing (psychiatric, neonatal, surgical). By exploring careers more thoroughly, students may be able to learn about the salient differences between related occupations. It is also hoped that when adolescents have opportunities to fully explore career options, they may feel greater career commitment and satisfaction in their future work lives rather than a sense of regret. Fortunately, the natural tendency for adolescents to try new things with peers as they are working to solidify their identity can provide an avenue to help them explore various career and college options more easily.

Cognitive Development

Anyone who has worked with students in the ninth grade knows that they have a tendency to be egocentric. Although many ninth graders are beginning to develop formal abstract thought (Piaget, 1977), they often oscillate between concrete thinking and abstraction. So, for example, while they may be able to use complex math skills and scientific theory in academic course work, they are not always capable of thinking about their futures in a more abstract manner, particularly in regard to problem solving, generating solutions, and considering consequences of the choices they make.

Specifically, Elkind's (1978) discussion of the *personal fable* holds much relevance to career and college readiness for these students. For instance, despite possessing some abstract thinking skills and the ability to understand cause and effect, many ninth-grade students believe that nothing bad will happen to them. It is this kind of thinking that leads students not to worry about their grades or about engaging in risky behavior—they refuse to believe that negative consequences could result. They also tend to be confident that things will work out for them, which can lead to apathy and procrastination regarding career and college planning as well as schoolwork.

Indeed, it is not uncommon for a student with a very low grade point average (GPA) to come in for academic advisement and proclaim the aspiration of attending Harvard and being a doctor in the future. Because students often don't make the connection between the consequences of present behavior on future options, they may unrealistically believe that their current academic standing won't matter for career and college success. Categorized according to Marcia (1989) as in a state of *identity diffusion*, these students can show little to no interest in exploring career or college options or planning for their future; they are the ones who will be resistant to, or ambivalent about, participating in career or college readiness interventions and often not worried about receiving low grades.

RELEVANT CAREER THEORIES: GOTTFREDSON (1981), HOLLAND (1973), AND SUPER (1980)

Many career counseling theories inform the types of interventions that would be useful to address the needs of ninth-grade students. For these students, *self-concept* and *personality* are particularly important career constructs. In the career counseling theories presented in the following, we illustrate the connection between these constructs and career development outcomes for ninth graders.

Gottfredson's Theory of Circumscription and Compromise

Consistent with their internal struggle to develop an identity, students in ninth grade typically fall into Gottfredson's (1981, 2002) fourth stage, *Orientation to Internal, Unique Self*. During this stage, self-concepts are evolving, and students are able to articulate their beliefs regarding idealistic and realistic future careers. These beliefs reflect the careers that they have circumscribed not only based on power, sex roles, and social valuation but also based on their own *self-concept*. This includes students' beliefs about what they are capable of and their evaluation of what skills, talents, and intelligence they have that may apply to a specific career.

For example, when he was younger, Martin (the aspiring taxidermist) may have admired his father as a taxidermist and may have thought that career took a lot of skill and strength. Later, despite his love for writing, he may have ruled out careers in the liberal arts (and writing in particular) because he believed they are not acceptable for men (orientation to gender role). At the same time, he retained the possibility of being a taxidermist, because in the rural location where he lives, both his peers and family would consider that to be a very prestigious career path (orientation to social value). Now that he is older, Martin also is considering how taxidermy fits for him personally (orientation to internal, unique self).

During the fourth stage of Gottfredson's theory (1981, 2002), students take a more introspective look at their futures, determining what is and is not realistic based on how they view themselves and how accessible they perceive specific careers to be. It is not uncommon for students to abandon their most preferred or ideal occupations for less compatible, but what they perceive to be accessible, alternatives. Gottfredson (2005) refers to this situation as *compromise*, and indicates that people frequently compromise on careers due to limited or inaccurate information regarding educational requirements or pathways to pursue various careers. That is, students' inaccurate beliefs lead them to make somewhat uninformed decisions.

Continuing with Martin, because his family has been heavily involved in taxidermy, he has a very clear idea of how to enter that profession and he has a guaranteed position in the family business. Therefore, he perceives it as very accessible. Martin can easily apprentice with his family and obtain the requisite on-the-job training, and he knows that the certification requirements can be completed quickly. Martin's main interest in taxidermy relates to his love of art. He thinks he can put up with the initial hands-on work removing the animal hide—but it is creating the mold and sculpting the final product that really interests him. Martin has a talent for sculpting; he often creates carvings out of wood and sells them in his father's shop. He is unfamiliar, however, with what other careers in art might look like; he has not been exposed to other art-related occupations.

Further, although Martin could pursue other career opportunities in art, he does not believe them to be accessible to him. No one in Martin's family has completed any formal education beyond high school, and the idea of art school is foreign to him. Martin would not know where to start when it comes to researching, applying, enrolling, and registering for art school, and doesn't know how he would pay for school or what financial options he has. Further, Martin's family tells him that an expensive technical degree is not necessary since he can work at the family business. They encourage and expect him to work in the family business full time when he graduates from high school. Without intervention focused on helping Martin and his family acquire more information about postsecondary school and additional career possibilities in art, Martin will likely compromise on these options because they do not appear accessible to him. He will stick with what is familiar and immediately in reach. Perhaps, he will be very successful and happy being a taxidermist, but by compromising, Martin may have missed out on other opportunities that could have been equally or more satisfying to him.

Holland's Theory of Vocational Choice

Holland's theory (1973) works well in conjunction with Gottfredson's. That is, in order for students to avoid compromising on careers, they must have an accurate understanding of themselves and of careers. Holland's focus on thoroughly assessing and examining person–environment match is consistent with efforts to help students avoid compromise. As they determine their own *personality code* and examine the personality types associated with various occupations, students should develop a more accurate understanding of the connection among their interests, skills, and various occupations (see Chapters 10 and 11 for more information about Holland's theory). For this reason, self- and career exploration activities continue to be important for ninth graders.

Super's Life-Span, Life-Space Theory

According to Super (1980), students in ninth grade would probably be transitioning from the *growth stage* (typically up to age 15) into the *exploration stage.* They should have a general understanding of the world of work as well as of their interests and abilities, and should be starting to engage in activities (e.g., hobbies, job shadowing) to get more specific information about occupations in order to try to narrow down their choices. At this age, Super indicates that students should be engaged in the developmental task of *crystallization—* the process of developing a tentative career goal. Interventions spanning the types of activities associated with the growth and exploration stages would be appropriate in ninth grade to help students progress toward crystallizing their career goals.

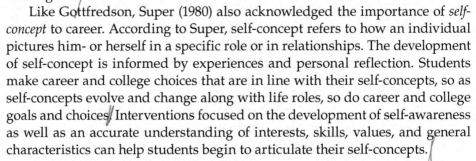
Like Gottfredson, Super (1980) also acknowledged the importance of *self-concept* to career. According to Super, self-concept refers to how an individual pictures him- or herself in a specific role or in relationships. The development of self-concept is informed by experiences and personal reflection. Students make career and college choices that are in line with their self-concepts, so as self-concepts evolve and change along with life roles, so do career and college goals and choices. Interventions focused on the development of self-awareness as well as an accurate understanding of interests, skills, values, and general characteristics can help students begin to articulate their self-concepts.

FACILITATING THE EIGHTH- TO NINTH-GRADE TRANSITION: FOLLOW-UP ACTIVITIES

In the previous chapter, we talked a lot about what middle schools can do to prepare students for the transition to high school. We must remember that transition is a process, however, and that follow-up activities on the back end of the transition can be equally as important as those on the front end. Ninth-grade counselors and teachers play an important role in ensuring a successful transition. Many students will adjust very quickly to ninth-grade expectations, but others will struggle to find their place and feel motivated to work.

One of the biggest struggles students have when transitioning into ninth grade relates to academics. The percentage of students who fail ninth grade continues to be fairly high in many schools (McCallumore & Sparapani, 2010), and the *ninth-grade bulge* is a term used to refer to the disproportionate number of students enrolled in grade 9 compared to those enrolled in grades 10 to 12.

Wheelock and Miao (2005) reported ninth- to 10th-grade promotion rates as being much lower than promotion rates to 11th or 12th grade. Furthermore, research suggests that these ninth-grade repeaters are more likely to drop out of high school than their peers who move on to 10th grade on time (Kennelly & Monrad, 2007). For this reason, an emphasis on the academic transition in ninth grade is warranted. Students who graduate from high school have increased career and college opportunities than do their peers who drop out of school.

As mentioned at the beginning of this chapter, the idea of ninth-grade academies came about in response to concerns surrounding the transition to ninth grade. Even without having a formal academy, schools might be able to put into place some of the critical components of those initiatives. For example, instruction and monitoring of academic and study skills can be implemented by counselors or teachers (see the next section) or through specialized workshops. Recognizing that students might need help adjusting to different academic expectations, counselors may search for ways to build in study hall time or provide opportunities for peer tutoring, as well as providing information on homework help resources (e.g., homework help lines and helpful websites).

Due to the increased demands in ninth grade on students to monitor their own work habits by managing multiple assignments, projects, and homework at any given time, and increased metacognition applied to academics (i.e., problem solving, critical thinking), many students find ninth grade very stressful, and their grades suffer. Without support, students falling behind may find that as they struggle over time, their difficulties become compounded. For example, if a student is struggling with the demands of reading comprehension, then reading material in six classes every night and not absorbing the information adequately can quickly lead to the student falling behind. The further behind a student gets in high school, the more likely she or he is to suffer long-term consequences in college.

THE HIGH SCHOOL ACADEMIC PATHWAY

Many school districts now require students to choose a specific academic path while they are in high school. This path often requires a prescribed program of study. As part of this plan, each student identifies a particular career goal and a school counselor helps identify the courses that the student will take during high school that will align the student's secondary and postsecondary training. This is meant to offer the best preparation possible for students for their career and to reduce the amount of remedial courses required in college as well as to maximize the amount of credit earned in high school.

For example, imagine a student, Celeste, would like to be a biological engineer. Her school counselor is going to want to ensure that while in high school she takes any courses required to enter most 4-year engineering programs including Calculus and 2 years of foreign language. In addition, given that she is interested in biological sciences, she will need 4 years of science. Her school counselor will want to monitor her grades, extracurricular activities, and college entrance exam scores as well to challenge her to take honors and Advanced Placement (AP) courses where possible throughout

TABLE 12.1 Comparable Ninth-Grade Schedules for Celeste and Jackson

Celeste's Schedule	Jackson's Schedule
Honors Algebra I	Algebra I
Honors English I	English I
Honors Biology I	Environmental Science
Spanish I	Civics
Honors U.S. History	Introduction to Business Computer Applications
P.E./Health	Career Education
Elective I—Public Speaking	Physical Education I

her high school career. All of these considerations should be part of her plan for leaving eighth grade and entering ninth grade. Her ninth-grade school counselor will want to ensure that after engaging in more career exploratory activities in ninth grade, Celeste is still interested in this path of course work.

Now imagine that another student, Jackson, would like to be a mechanical drafter. His high school has drafting courses that will count toward an Associate's Degree through his local community college. There is also a technical school in town where he can earn certification in about 1 year. His school counselor knows that he will need strong math skills and plans a path where he can take basic core courses in English, math, science, and social studies. His electives will be in drafting and will count through an articulation agreement with either the technical college or the community college. Please see Table 12.1 for a comparison of Celeste and Jackson's schedules in their first year of high school.

During the first year, these schedules are not largely dissimilar. Many of the courses taken would satisfy the same requirements, and they will both earn a total of seven high school credits. However, Celeste is taking nearly all honors courses in preparation for more rigor, likely AP or Dual Enrollment classes later in high school. She is also taking a foreign language, a requirement for most 4-year colleges. What if they want to change career trajectories later? What if, during his junior year, Jackson decides he wants to become an architect rather than a drafter? The good news is that Jackson will still be able to go to a 4-year college. However, he will likely have to do a lot of work to prepare for the rigor of a 4-year college and he may not have all of the requisite courses. He and his school counselor will need to fully analyze his transcript to determine what course work he is missing from his program of study to meet college and program entry requirements.

NINTH-GRADE STUDENT CAREER AND COLLEGE READINESS OUTCOMES

Throughout this chapter we have identified some of the main focus areas for ninth-grade students with regard to career and college readiness—academic and self-regulatory skills, and self- and career knowledge. How to address and evaluate outcomes in those areas in school can once again be informed by referring to the ASCA Mindsets and Behaviors (2014). Table 12.2 lists the Mindset and Behavior standards that might be most developmentally relevant to ninth graders, but school counselors will always have to choose what works best for their populations.

Looking closely at the Mindsets and Behaviors (ASCA, 2014), we can see parallels with many of the constructs we have discussed in this chapter. Basic self- and career awareness activities can be designed around career development. Additionally, academic and self-regulatory skill sets we have identified as important for career and college readiness are of key importance in ninth grade. They also connect to goal setting and future planning activities. In the following sections, we share some ideas for how to address these different areas with ninth-grade students. We begin with Exhibit 12.1, Voices From the Field, from a school counselor who focuses on assessments that help students examine who they are in relation to personal values, personality type, and interests related to career, academic success, and postsecondary planning.

TABLE 12.2 ASCA Mindsets and Behaviors for Ninth-Grade Curriculum Planning Focus

CATEGORY 1: MINDSETS STANDARDS		
Sense of belonging in the school environment Understanding that postsecondary education and lifelong learning are necessary for long-term career success Belief in using abilities to their fullest to achieve high-quality results and outcomes Positive attitude toward work and learning		
CATEGORY 2: BEHAVIOR STANDARDS		
Learning Strategies	**Self-Management Skills**	**Social Skills**
Use time-management, organizational, and study skills	Demonstrate ability to assume responsibility	Create positive and supportive relationships with other students
Apply self-motivation and self-direction to learning	Demonstrate self-discipline and self-control	Use effective collaboration and cooperation skills
Identify long- and short-term academic, career, and socioemotional goals	Demonstrate ability to manage transitions and ability to adapt to changing situations and responsibilities	Create relationships with adults that support success

EXHIBIT 12.1
Voices From the Field: Helping Ninth-Grade
Students Figure Out *Who Am I?*

Frank Phinney, MS, NCC, LPC

School Counselor, Walker Freshman High School

My work at a ninth-grade academy as the sole counselor with 480 students is very hectic. My school is in a rural community where 93% are White, 4% are African American, 2% are Hispanic, and 1% are Native American/Pacific Islander. We have over 60% of our students receiving free or reduced-price lunch. Many of our students will be first-generation college students, so my role in assisting them in career and college exploration is critical.

(continued)

EXHIBIT 12.1 (continued)
Voices From the Field: Helping Ninth-Grade
Students Figure Out *Who Am I?*

According to Erik Erikson's stages of psychosocial development, adolescents are on a journey to answer these fundamental questions and to achieve identity formation. Having this understanding of adolescent development provides context for my role as a school counselor—to facilitate students' quest to fully understand who they are and how that relates to career options. This is the motivation for why we do career counseling and why we, as school counselors, must form a strong repertoire of career and college readiness counseling and assessment techniques. Having worked over a decade with adolescents has proven to me that a consistent message only enhances their ability to be engaged in career and college exploration and increases their capacity to learn.

I have found Holland's *Theory of Vocational Types* to be best suited for my work with adolescents; understanding one's personality and its congruency to career choice aligns perfectly with the developmental stage of adolescents. Employing Holland's framework provides me with a substantial amount of tools and resources that work well with ninth-grade students.

Personality has a critical role in Holland's theory and is the first thing I address with my students. There are multiple instruments that exist to assist you in navigating a student's personality profile: ACT Career Interest Inventory, Kuder Career Interest Inventory (ACT and Kuder both use Holland's Realistic, Investigative, Artistic, Social, Enterprising, and Conventional [RIASEC] hexagon), True Colors© Personality profile, Myers-Briggs, and so forth. I have found more success in using a combination of assessments rather than one specific instrument because one rarely supplies the complete picture.

The foundation of my career and college program, and one that I find to be the most fun and relatable with adolescents, is True Colors. There is cost involved with becoming a certified facilitator for True Colors, but I have found it to be well worth the expense. True Colors simplifies the Myers-Briggs Type Indicator by using four colors (Orange, Blue, Green, and Gold) and allows the user to rank personality descriptors in order of preference. This tool provides a relevant and concentrated experience for the students as they begin to identify with themselves. Once the student identifies his or her personality type, I am able to demonstrate careers that are congruent with the student's personality and provide relevant information as it relates to the course of study while in high school. As an added benefit, this discovery process has proven invaluable in all three domains of my counseling program. Although I primarily use True Colors in my career lessons, I have seen remarkable returns in the academic and personal/social domains.

In regards to the academic domain, this program has allowed students to identify their personality's role in their learning style. This realization

(continued)

EXHIBIT 12.1 (*continued*)

has resulted in better performance in core classes and an almost 100% reduction in retentions. Additionally, having students be more aware of their personality type and how they relate to others (increased personal awareness) has resulted in a significant reduction in referrals resulting from interpersonal conflict—this included teacher-to-student/student-to-teacher conflict.

In addition to True Colors I also use resources such as the ACT Interest inventory, which utilizes Holland's Vocational Types: RIASEC. The interactive tools available on the ACT website, which includes an interactive World-of-Work Map, assists students in their efforts to deepen their knowledge of potential careers and solidifies their understanding of their identified personality type as it relates to those careers. This process empowers students by synthesizing information gathered from True Colors and the ACT interest inventory and gives them a concentrated direction regarding potential careers. Experience has shown that once students become fully engaged in the career selection process there is a positive correlation in having a positive career self-efficacy.

Regardless of resources and assessments you have at your disposal, you ultimately want to make the career decision process as engaging as possible. Millennials are often seen as distracted or having short attention spans, but I believe the opposite is true. At the core of their being exists the same questions we have all had to answer—"Who am I?" "What role will I play?" To be an effective school counselor, we must learn their language and be willing to adapt our lessons to fully embrace what sets them apart as learners. Henry Kissinger once said, "The task of a leader is to get his people from where they are to where they have not been." Take your students to the precipice of their future and make a lasting impact on their lives.

CAREER AND COLLEGE READINESS INTERVENTIONS: COLLABORATING WITH TEACHERS

Interventions for ninth-grade students must be developed with consideration of the importance of peers, the developmental task of establishing an identity, the relevance of self-concept, and the career development goal of crystallization. At the same time, they must address the transition-related needs of these students, specifically in relation to academic and self-regulatory skills. A proactive, collaborative approach to addressing these needs can be very manageable in a high school.

Career and College Counseling Curriculum

The career and college readiness curriculum should not be administered only by school counselors. In fact, a collaborative approach can help ninth-grade students recognize that teachers and other school staff are all on the same page when it comes to the skills and knowledge that are important for their future success. Counselors often find it challenging to implement the counseling curriculum in a high school, but once it is developed and objectives identified, there are a few different ways that it can be implemented without detracting from students' time in other classes.

A traditional school counselor-implemented approach is one option for addressing career and college readiness in ninth grade. As a junior/senior high school counselor, I (second author) provided classroom lessons weekly to all ninth-grade students. Even though students in my school were in the same building for grades 7 to 12, they still had areas of transition. The students rotated through my class opposite their physical education and health classes; in this manner, they were still on a more typical middle school or junior high schedule, and it was familiar to them.

Further, I had the ability to design and implement whatever curriculum I chose, allowing for flexibility to accommodate students' needs throughout the year. My curriculum, based on school counseling standards and needs assessment data, addressed the importance of ninth grade and how academic skills and habits would be critical to students' future success, career and college planning activities (e.g., interest inventories), and goal setting. As report cards came out and teachers reported concerns, I revisited various topics or added new ones. This approach was proactive and reactive as well as collaborative and flexible.

Another approach to implementing the counseling curriculum is to involve teachers more directly. Working together to develop the curriculum, school counselors and teachers can prepare units to be implemented throughout the year. Given that the content might be more familiar to school counselors, it is advised that they take the lead to ensure that everyone who will be implementing the intervention understands the content and how to present it. For example, in some ninth-grade academies in Louisiana, students actually take semester-long education-for-careers courses. Although these courses are taught by classroom teachers, the counselor often oversees the curriculum. In this way, the school counselor is able to find additional time throughout the year to offer supplemental lessons.

Another way to have teachers implement the curriculum is to use teacher advisory periods. These advisory periods might be scheduled weekly, or they might be built in only during certain times of the year (e.g., every morning for 1 week each marking period). With a specific group of students to work with throughout the year, teachers can monitor student needs and seek assistance from the school counselor in modifying the curriculum if necessary. This type of approach is collaborative and efficient but does require someone monitoring for consistency to ensure all content is covered adequately.

Readiness for career decision making involves possessing self- and career knowledge. Because ninth-grade students often have difficulty realistically projecting what their lives might be like in the future (e.g., they imagine being a teacher who drives a fancy car and lives in a huge house), school counselors should be sure to include in their curriculum activities that help students develop a concrete understanding of occupational choices. That is, they should provide opportunities to help students understand the kind of salary they might make in various occupations as well as how far that money would stretch depending on the lifestyle they envision; this can be very beneficial to their future satisfaction. Numerous activities and resources exist to help students examine how various budgets would impact their lives and how to make informed career decisions that include the lifestyle they would like.

For example, school counselors might find the *California Career Zone* (www.cacareerzone.org) to be a useful resource in this effort. Some states have similar online programs. This free web resource enables students to choose occupations and/or a specific salary, as well as to indicate the type of location where they envision living (e.g., small town, large city). Then they walk through choosing options related to things like housing, utilities, food, transportation, health care, social activities, and savings. An estimated budget is produced, which enables students to have a concrete understanding of how much money they would need in order to live a certain lifestyle, as well as how much money they might make in a certain occupation. Using this kind of activity may be coupled with discussions of values in order to help students make informed career decisions. Other types of information that students need to know include projected growth for the career, necessary education and training, related careers, and any requisite specialized skills.

Large Group Information Sessions

High school students need a lot of information throughout the year in order to make informed career and college decisions, and large group information sessions may be used to disseminate this type of information. Whether it is providing an overview of the graduation requirements and 4-year planning, or sharing information about job shadowing opportunities, school counselors should think about what topics might be important to discuss in person with students. Topics about which students need basic information (e.g., completing their graduation plan, how to identify educational requirements for jobs) rather than extended practice or explanation are ideal for this delivery format.

Although much of the information school counselors deliver via large groups might be available in writing in a student handbook or on a web page, for many students hearing someone talk about things and walk them through the process helps them comprehend better and allows them the opportunity to ask questions. In an ideal scenario, counselors expect students to review information and come to them with questions, but only a small minority of students do this. Some do not feel comfortable approaching counselors with questions, many lack initiative, and others don't even know what to ask. By meeting them where they are developmentally, counselors might proactively facilitate their acquisition of important information. Further, providing information in numerous formats (e.g., written, oral) also can help to accommodate different learning styles.

Scheduling large-group information sessions can be challenging at times, as having too large of a group will deter questions, but having too small of a group means holding more sessions. In a small high school where

I (second author) worked, I noted that with a few exceptions (i.e., students in self-contained classrooms), all ninth-grade students had the same English teacher and the same civics teacher. I approached those teachers to inquire about the possibility of targeting students during their class time, while appreciating that those teachers likely could not afford to give up much time. Planning in advance, the English teacher and I were able to identify one day each marking period where the teacher could spend time grading papers while I shared information with students. With this approach, I only had a few students to reach individually (including those who had been absent) and the teacher was appreciative of the work time; the teacher stayed in the room and heard what was being shared with the students.

On that note, working closely with teachers to ensure they understand academic requirements also can be helpful, but not all teachers will be able to sit in on the discussions counselors have with students. At a large, urban school, the school counselors provided a faculty in-service training each year on student academic planning in order to promote teachers' understanding of academic paths, postsecondary preparation, in-state scholarships, and graduation plans. Details of their approach are outlined in Exhibit 12.2. Because school counselors are responsible for large numbers of students, providing teachers with information about graduation requirements and academic planning allows students to have greater access to information through all of the adults in the building.

EXHIBIT 12.2
Instructing Teachers on Academic Requirements

At West Orange High School, Mrs. Olivares, the ninth-grade school counselor, along with the counseling team, presented a faculty in-service on student academic planning at the beginning of each school year. The training lasted approximately 30 minutes and was meant to serve as a refresher for faculty on academic path options and related course work, changes to graduation requirements and certificates (either legislatively or in the district), and the purpose and logistics of graduation plans (e.g., 5-year plans). By doing this, all faculty members were prepared to answer day-to-day questions from students regarding graduation requirements and academic paths. Each quarter (9 weeks), the school counselors prepared the faculty to give short, 10- to 15-minute presentations in homeroom on a topic chosen by the school counselors. Presentations included topics such as updating graduation plans, registering for courses, and reviewing transcripts to ensure academic courses taken match requirements for career paths.

Beyond the faculty in-service at the beginning of the year, Mrs. Olivares and the school counselors also designated trainings once per quarter for new faculty. In those trainings, the school counselors gave more specific, detailed information to new faculty including an overview of the developmental needs (personal/social, academic, and career) of high school students. New teachers were given information on how to best utilize the school counseling

(continued)

EXHIBIT 12.2 (*continued*)

program and were given the opportunity to ask questions about their concerns of working with parents, motivating students, identifying students having personal problems, and how to deal with classroom management and conduct problems. Additionally, they were given information on how to integrate study strategies, self-regulatory time management, and other academic skills training in the daily educational curriculum.

Individual Planning

Although finding time to provide individual advising to all students in their caseloads can be challenging, school counselors need to provide opportunities for students to get some individual attention to discuss their long-term goals (ASCA, 2012). They cannot adequately meet the unique needs of each student without finding some time to talk with him or her personally. The default approach seems to be to block off 3 weeks and hold back-to-back meetings with students. Although not ideal in terms of being able to provide a comprehensive counseling program and curriculum during that time frame, that approach does allow school counselors to meet with all students within a designed period of time. Many schools have the luxury of a career or college counselor who has fewer general counseling responsibilities and therefore more time to focus on career and college planning discussions. Other school counselors need to be more creative in finding these opportunities.

During part of her counseling class time, one school counselor built in time in December where the class could work on career projects while she called them up one at a time for approximately 15 minutes each. The purpose of those individual discussions was to check in prior to the start of course registration in the spring in the hopes that registration would go more smoothly if students had thought in advance about their future plans and relevant courses. Although 15 minutes isn't much, that brief amount of time helped her provide some personalized attention to each student. For a large percentage of students, the combination of classroom activities, large group information sessions, and these brief informational meetings was sufficient to help them move forward in their career and college planning. During the meetings, the school counselor was able to identify students who needed follow-up intervention, but those were fewer in number and therefore much more manageable to target outside of class.

Prior to meeting with each student, the school counselor asked all the students to be ready to answer the following general questions: What do you want to do after high school? How do you know? How certain are you? What do you know about how to reach that goal? What is your plan? What do you need from me? After hearing their initial answers, she used various probes to clarify or specify their responses. Some students came up with very well-thought-out responses and others were very vague or hadn't thought about things. Their overall responses informed how she proceeded in terms of identifying relevant interventions for them, as well as when and how to involve their parents/guardians. Table 12.3 includes some of the things she was listening for during these discussions.

One noteworthy way to positively utilize the adolescent inclination toward peer influence is to encourage opportunities for them to have peer interaction and dialogue that is meaningful about career and college. McPhillip, Rawls, and Barry (2012) suggested that early exposure to college counseling should start in ninth grade rather than in upper grades, and that having students meet for peer advisement and share their college questions and the information they collected could be very helpful. We suggest lending structure to peer advisement by asking students to think in advance about the same kinds of questions we mention in the earlier paragraph.

Another approach to individual planning involves partnering with teachers. In most schools, students in ninth grade are asked to develop a high school or graduation plan where they map out their high school courses. These plans are developed to be in line with career and college goals. With a little preparation, teachers can be asked to help with this process. In fact, in one southeastern high school, teachers are responsible for holding planning conferences with all of the students in their homeroom and with their parents. Two evenings are set aside during which these sessions are scheduled. The school counselors prep the teachers, and then walk around that evening from room to room answering questions as needed. The school counselors are able to handle "make-up" sessions for anyone who could not attend during the evening. All in all, the process is efficient, and the collaboration seems to work well.

TABLE 12.3   Individual Advisement Discussions

Initial Question	Listening for
What do you want to do after high school?	Has student thought about the future? Is student in *diffusion*? Does student have a specific future goal? Does student plan to graduate from high school? Does student have a specific occupational goal in mind? Is student interested in attending college?
How do you know?	What led student to the choice? Is student's choice based on peer choices? Is student's choice based on family preference? Has student *foreclosed* career choice? Has student *circumscribed or compromised* career choice? Has student explored self? Can student articulate self-concept? Has student explored career? Does student make connection between self and career? Does student have accurate career information?
How certain are you?	Use rating scale. If not completely certain, what else is student considering? What questions does student still have about choice? What would help student feel more certain with choice? (Often real and perceived barriers came up here, such as lack of information, parental pressure, etc.)
What do you know about how to reach that goal?	Does student have accurate information?
What is your plan?	Has student thought much about this? Is student ready to actively pursue the goal? Is the plan realistic? Comprehensive? Relevant?
What do you need from me?	Is student actively interested in working on goal? Are others helping the student? What interventions might I need to plan?

Partnering With Parents

Parents/guardians play an important role in students' career and college outcomes. At one extreme, they can hold incredibly high aspirations for their children and limit their career or college options to a few acceptable, rigorous alternatives. These kinds of parents are likely to want their child enrolled in every AP class, encourage them to take the Scholastic Aptitude Test (SAT) every year starting in middle school, and push their kids to become involved in lots of activities. At the other extreme are parents/guardians who express very limited aspirations for their children and/or discourage careers that require much education, focusing rather on those students finding immediate employment. Often these parents just want their child to graduate, but some don't even care about high school completion and see little value in future planning. It is important that school counselors do not judge parents but, rather, try to appreciate their perspective. For example, parents may believe, based on their own experience and life knowledge, that a college education is not necessary for making a living. Counselors should be respectful while introducing other possibilities and explaining information in a sensitive manner.

The majority of parents, however, even those at the extremes, mainly want their children to be happy. They want them to find satisfaction in their future occupations and to make choices that fit for them. Many parents are well informed about career and college planning, while others have little to no information to help their children navigate this process or navigate high school. Parents can benefit just as much as students can from learning about the career and college planning process, and school counselors would be wise to involve them as much as possible. Just like students, parents are often reluctant to reach out to the school and ask for help or information. A proactive approach to disseminating information to parents and involving them in career and college planning activities can help to encourage their involvement over time.

As mentioned, involving parents in the high school planning process can be helpful in many ways. By chatting with parents and students together, counselors can examine the dynamics and listen for what messages parents send their children regarding careers and college. Further, involving parents directly ensures, in general, that they receive information, and that they have accurate information. We all know how easy it is for students unintentionally to leave out an important detail or to provide partially accurate information. For parents to be able to effectively help and reinforce school initiatives, they need to be informed.

As with students, providing information in a handbook and on a web page is always a good idea, but counselors should reach out in more ways to parents. Not all parents have access to the Internet, so technology cannot be the sole form of disseminating information to them. Some parents also do better when they have a chance to interact with someone and ask questions, as opposed to just reading information. School counselors must think of the best ways to provide these kinds of interactive opportunities. They also should remember that one-shot approaches are not likely to be effective. Just as students can benefit from receiving information in multiple formats repeated over time, parents also are more likely to understand and retain information if they are afforded different kinds of opportunities throughout their child's schooling to acquire information and ask questions.

Thinking about specific populations, school counselors might consider planning informational activities to target specific needs. For example, it is likely that some parents have helped older siblings through the career and college planning process, so their needs would differ from those of parents dealing with their first child entering high school. While some parents value hearing information each year because they want to be reassured nothing has changed, for others it can be frustrating to not learn anything new. Information sessions could be advertised as beginner or advanced, for example, so that parents could make more intentional choices about what or what not to attend.

Finally, more and more families in the United States speak English as a second language. As we try to help students achieve success, we need to find ways to involve a diverse group of parents. School counselors must be conscious of the language barriers that exist and find ways to communicate effectively with parents. Providing materials in other languages and involving translators are two common ways to do this. Anticipating the unique needs of these parents is also important. Because educational systems in other countries can vary greatly from that in the United States, it is not uncommon for parents to be confused about what options are available and what expectations schools have. Providing an *Orientation to High School* or some type of similar workshop where the structure, format, and expectations are discussed can help parents understand what they can do at home to reinforce school expectations as well as to facilitate their child's learning. Similar workshops could be held regarding career and college planning in the United States.

SUMMARY

In this chapter, we have highlighted career and college readiness interventions specifically for ninth-grade students. A crucial year in terms of setting the stage for future opportunities, ninth grade is a time when students must really start focusing on who they want to be and what they want to do. Self-awareness, skill development, and future planning all are important. As they develop interventions and programming for these students, counselors and educators must keep in mind the developmental milestones that ninth-grade students are moving through as well as the transition-related issues associated with entering ninth grade.

••> Test Your Knowledge

1. Provide an example of a ninth-grade student's career choice that illustrates your understanding of circumscription and compromise.
2. Provide an example of a statement that a ninth-grade student might make reflecting his or her personal fable, and explain how that belief could affect career and college outcomes.
3. Define in your own words Super's notion of crystallization.

REFERENCES

American School Counselor Association. (2012). *The ASCA national model: A framework for school counseling programs* (3rd ed.). Alexandria, VA: Author.

American School Counselor Association (ASCA). (2014). *ASCA mindsets & behaviors for student success: K-12 college- and career-readiness standards for every student.* Alexandria, VA: Author.

Cook, C., Fowler, H., & Harris, T. (2008). *Ninth grade academies: Easing the transition to high school.* Raleigh, NC: North Carolina Department of Public Instruction.

Elkind, D. (1978). Understanding the young adolescent. *Adolescence, 13*(49), 127–134.

Erikson, E. H. (1963). *Childhood and society* (2nd ed.). New York: W. W. Norton.

Fields, G. M. (2008). *Reinventing 9th grade: Academics through personalization.* International Rexford, NY: Center for Leadership in Education.

Gottfredson, L. S. (1981). Circumscription and compromise: A developmental theory of occupational aspirations. *Journal of Counseling Psychology, 28*(6), 545–579. http://dx.doi.org/10.1037/0022-0167.28.6.545

Gottfredson, L. S. (2002). *Gottfredson's theory of circumscription, compromise, and self-creation.* In D. Brown (Ed.), *Career choice and development* (4th ed., pp. 85–148). San Francisco, CA: Jossey-Bass.

Gottfredson, L. S. (2005). Applying Gottfredson's theory of circumscription and compromise in career guidance and counseling. In S. D. Brown & R. W. Lent (Eds.), *Career development and counseling: Putting theory and research to work* (pp. 71–100). Hoboken, NJ: John Wiley & Sons.

Holland, J. L. (1973). *Making vocational choices: A theory of careers.* Englewood Cliffs, NJ: Prentice Hall.

Kennelly, L., & Monrad, M. (2007). *Easing the transition to high school: Research and best practices designed to support high school learning.* Washington, DC: National High School Center.

Marcia, J. E. (1989). Identity and intervention. *Journal of Adolescence, 12*(4), 401–410. http://dx.doi.org/10.1016/0140-1971(89)90063-8

McCallumore, K. M., & Sparapani, E. F. (2010). The importance of the ninth grade on high school graduation rates and student success in high school. *Education, 130*(3), 447–456.

McIntosh, J., & White, S. (2006). Building for freshman success: High schools working as professional learning communities. *American Secondary Education, 34*(2), 40–49.

McPhillip, M. E. M., Rawls, A., & Barry, C. (2012). Improving college access: A review of research on the role of high school counselors. *Professional School Counseling, 16*(1), 49–58. Retrieved from ERIC database (EJ987532).

Piaget, J. (1977). *The development of thought: Equilibration of cognitive structure.* New York, NY: Viking Press.

Super, D. E. (1980). A life-span, life-space approach to career development. *Journal of Vocational Behavior, 16*(3), 282–298. http://dx.doi.org/10.1016/0001-8791(80)90056-1

Wheelock, A., & Miao, J. (2005). The ninth-grade bottleneck: An enrollment bulge in a transition year that demands careful attention and action. *School Administrator, 62*(3), 36–40.

THIRTEEN

Career and College Readiness for Grade 10: Career and College Planning

In the previous chapter, we encouraged counselors to spend a lot of time helping ninth-grade students develop the academic and self-regulatory skills (e.g., time management, academic progress monitoring, and study skills) that would carry them through high school and beyond. We also encouraged counselors to help these students explore self and careers so that they could continue working to narrow down their choices. By no means are 10th graders done working on those skills or have finalized their career and college decisions; they still can benefit from interventions targeting those specific areas.

Nevertheless, 10th grade also is a year when counselors and educators can help students to examine the internal and external factors that affect their choices, and to start thinking more concretely about career and college planning activities. By 10th grade, students should start actively preparing for their future careers and postsecondary educational choices, which means narrowing their choices and engaging in activities that will help them move forward. In this chapter, we share a number of ideas for helping students engage in early career and college preparation activities. As in previous chapters, we start with a review of salient developmental characteristics and career theories, and then provide recommendations for intervention.

DEVELOPMENTAL OVERVIEW

Students in 10th grade fall into the category known as mid-adolescence (ages 15–18). These students are very similar to ninth graders in many ways; they still struggle to develop an identity and their peers are very important. Additionally, many mid-adolescents are transitioning into a more advanced stage of formal operational thinking. In the following, we highlight some of the more common developmental characteristics of students in 10th grade and discuss their relevance to career and college readiness.

Physical Development

By the time students reach 10th grade, many of the physical changes associated with puberty are slowing down. For the most part, these students have moved beyond what many refer to as the *awkward stage* (i.e., due to disproportionate features) and are beginning to look more like adults. Because the majority of drastic physical changes are slowing down, mid-adolescents tend to be less volatile; that is, the concerns about emotional regulation that we discussed in Chapter 10 seem to lessen. However, physical development still plays an important role in career and college development for these students.

Although 10th-grade boys typically will experience more physical changes over the next 5 years (e.g., they might grow another few inches, develop more lean muscle, and have more noticeable facial hair growth), by 10th grade most boys are now as tall as, if not taller than, girls their age. Most also have completed one of the more embarrassing changes associated with puberty, such as the change that was so well illustrated in *The Brady Bunch* when Peter Brady had to sing—the changing voice. Increased testosterone associated with puberty causes the larynx and facial bones to grow, which results in the development of a lower voice. The process is gradual, however, and the inconsistent, cracking voice that many boys experience during that process may cause them great anxiety and embarrassment. Anyone who is able to observe boys as they develop will often notice increased confidence once they are taller than girls (or of similar height to their male peers) and once their voice has finally changed. With these types of changes, boys might start to envision the types of careers that may or may not be possible based on physical requirements.

Most girls in 10th grade have reached their adult height, and they have begun to settle in to their new body shapes. However, body image concerns are still present for many mid-adolescent girls, and some struggle with the realization that they might not be able to do some of the physical things they were good at prior to puberty. For example, Maria had been attending an arts school for ballet, and was hoping that once she adjusted to her changed body shape (i.e., wider hips, larger breasts, different weight distribution) she would be able to continue progressing toward her goal of becoming a professional ballet dancer. She was quite talented and her career path had always been clear; she had never considered other options. Although most girls are quite capable of pursuing various athletic pursuits after puberty, Maria's new body was not designed for ballet. She needed to develop a new plan and cope with the loss of her long-term dream.

Cognitive Development

According to Piaget (1969), mid-adolescents are capable of abstract and hypothetical thinking, which enables them to look into the future, predict outcomes, and consider the perspectives of others. Nevertheless, the personal fable (as noted in Chapter 12) is still very influential, and it is not uncommon for 10th graders to seemingly bounce back and forth between making healthy and unhealthy decisions. Despite cognitively being able to predict the consequences of their actions, peer influence often leads these students to engage in behaviors that they know are not in their best interests. The personal fable allows them to develop the faulty assumption that negative consequences won't happen to them. In terms of career and college readiness, students functioning under the personal fable might make poor choices such as procrastinating on major projects, not preparing for the ACT, choosing not to work in the summer, or not accepting an internship opportunity because they don't think it will affect their long-term goals. Counselors and educators should be prepared to continue challenging these students to examine the positive and negative consequences related to their choices and the potential for new opportunities to arise as a result of their choices (as we discussed in Chapter 1 in relation to Krumboltz's (2009) *Happenstance Learning Theory*).

As many mid-adolescents develop formal operational thinking skills, their awareness of and interest in the perspectives and experiences of others often leads, in general, to increased concern for others and a sense of personal responsibility. This is because formal abstract thought lends to an increased ability to take others' perspectives (Piaget, 1969), a necessary cognitive skill in the development of empathy and prosocial behavior (Curry, Smith, & Robinson, 2009). Students with these cognitive abilities may show an interest in engaging in volunteer work, helping underserved populations, or demonstrating an appreciation for discussions about social and global issues. For many of these students, this awareness may lead them to shift their thinking about their futures.

For example, a high school counselor was working with Tonja, who had always wanted to be an accountant like her mother. Tonja came in to see the counselor one day and asked him about starting a student organization that would focus on community service. She had talked with her older cousin over Thanksgiving about her previous spring break volunteer efforts in another state, and Tonja was intrigued and felt quite compelled to try to reach out locally. She also mentioned that maybe she wanted to think about career opportunities where she would be able to make an impact on others.

Psychosocial Development

Students in 10th grade continue to move through the *identity versus role confusion* stage (Erikson, 1963). Peers remain an important influence in their lives and in the decisions they make. For example, even though a student knows that she needs to study for her geometry test so that she can pass the class (cognitively she understands the potential consequences of going into the test unprepared and/or tired), she is easily convinced by her friends to sneak out to attend a late night party. Her decision-making process is challenged, as she attempts to balance her role as a friend wanting to fit in with her peers and her desire to be a good student and obtain a high grade point average (GPA).

Students in 10th grade also frequently *experiment* with their identities, or *try on* different identities in an attempt to figure out what fits. Their self-concept is still forming (see the following discussion of Super's theory), and these experimental activities are very important to their overall development. Although parents often get concerned when their children engage in behaviors like changing the way they dress, hanging out with different peer groups, or wanting to go to a different church or no church, these behaviors are not necessarily indicative of larger concerns. They can be sometimes, but in most instances those types of behaviors simply reflect the adolescent progression through typical developmental milestones and the process of individuation.

In their search to solidify their identity, 10th-grade students often explore their values by challenging others, especially their parents. It is not uncommon for these students to openly resist or reject their parents' views during this time, and parents often view their children as argumentative or disrespectful as they do this. Many students do not possess the skills to maturely engage in discussions involving differences of opinion, and this time period offers a unique opportunity to help students be able to articulate their beliefs as well as to develop the interpersonal and conflict resolution skills that will be so critical to their future success in the workplace.

RELEVANT CAREER THEORY: SUPER (1980) AND LENT, BROWN, AND HACKETT (1994)

Interventions related to Holland and Gottfredson (see Chapter 12) continue to be very relevant for 10th-grade students. In this chapter, however, we are highlighting two theories with constructs that speak specifically to the developmental challenges we already discussed. *Life roles, self-efficacy beliefs,* and *outcome expectations* are important considerations when helping 10th-grade students engage in career and college preparation activities.

Super's Life-Span, Life-Space Theory

When we presented Super's (1980) theory in Chapter 12, we discussed the role of self-concept and the importance of helping students develop increased self-awareness. Super's discussion of life roles is very important to understanding career development and self-concept, particularly for students in 10th grade. First, according to Super, people assume various roles throughout their lives and hold many roles simultaneously. Super charted an individual's life roles through a chart known as a *Life Career Rainbow* (see Figure 13.1). The relative importance of each role (known as *role salience*) will vary, so that some roles are more important than others. In Figure 13.1, darker shading reflects increased role salience. Super identified the nine most common roles people hold as: (a) child, (b) student, (c) leisurite (i.e., time spent in leisure activities), (d) citizen, (e) worker, (f) spouse, (g) homemaker, (h) parent, and (i) pensioner (retired citizen). Furthermore, he acknowledged that people might identify other salient roles, such as friend or sibling, and that the length of time someone fills any given role can vary. He stated that people not only assume certain roles throughout much of their lives (e.g., a person is a child until his or her parents die), but also that not all people experience all roles during their lifetime.

Second, to understand life roles, Super (1980) addressed the relevance of role expectations (of the individual and of others) and the manner in which roles change over time and by situation. For example, there might be different

FIGURE 13.1   Example of a Life Career Rainbow

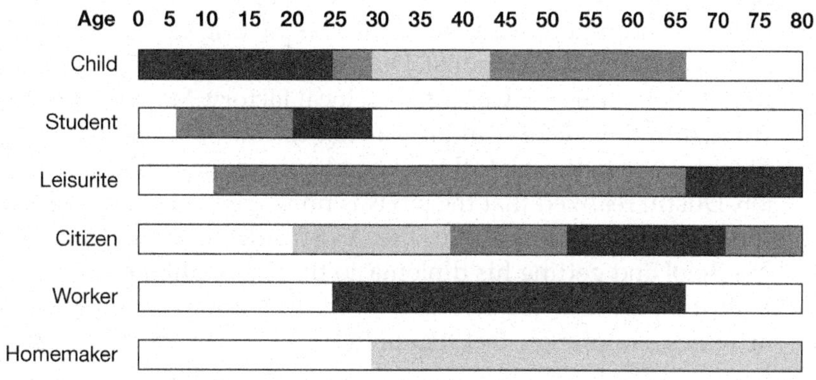

Note: Darker shading reflects increased role salience. *Adapted from Super's (1980) life career rainbow.*

expectations of the *child* life role depending on a person's age and/or based on cultural factors. People typically would expect a child at age 5 not to question his or her parents, but might not have the same expectations of a child who is 16 (think about the previous discussion of children exploring their own values by challenging or rejecting their parents' values). Nevertheless, some people and some cultural groups expect children to honor and respect their parents' wishes, no matter how old they are, while others allow for more independence of thought as children age. A student's perception of his or her expectations as a child may or may not differ from the expectations of others.

Major life roles for students in 10th grade tend to include child, student, friend, leisurite, citizen, and, in some cases, worker. Students' personal expectations and the expectations of others inform how they approach various roles. For example, Richard prioritizes his life role as child above all others and feels an expectation to honor his parents. They also have an expectation that he honor their wishes. His parents are experiencing financial difficulties and have asked him to find a job to help bring in more income to support their family. In one possible scenario, Richard prioritizes the child and worker roles more than others, so he chooses to drop out of high school to find full-time employment. In this way, he meets both his and his parents' expectations. And he also finds a way to fulfill his preferred life roles. In a second potential scenario, Richard prioritizes the child and student roles above others, so he chooses to stay in school in the hopes of going to college, and seeks part-time employment to try to help his family. Again, doing this allows Richard to fill expectations as well as his life role preferences.

According to Super (1980), as people try to fulfill expectations for multiple roles, their experiences in those roles naturally influence other roles they occupy. Some 10th-grade students acquire new roles, such as parent, that may result in unexpected changes to other roles. For example, a student, Carla, who becomes a *parent* may have significantly less time to devote to the concurrently held and highly important life roles of *student* and *friend* than she had before having a baby. Carla might benefit from discussing ways to manage all of the expectations that she places upon herself related to those roles, and may need help reprioritizing her roles and developing a long-term plan.

In a different illustration of roles impacting each other, the second author recalls one particular student, Dustin, who followed the lead of his friends and found a part-time job working in a local factory. Many of the students' parents worked in this factory, and it was not uncommon for students to drop out of school at age 16 to seek full-time employment there. Shortly after obtaining the job, Dustin realized that the job was not something he wanted to do on a full-time basis or for the rest of his life. As a result, he became much more interested in school and getting his diploma so that he might have more options. Dustin kept the part-time job because he wanted to have money to fund his social activities. Despite the fact that holding a job decreased the amount of time he had available for studying, Dustin's grades started to improve, reflecting that his life role as *worker* positively impacted his role as *student* (see Figure 13.2).

Finally, the way in which people see themselves in one or more roles (i.e., their self-concept) is reflected in their life role beliefs. Examples of life role beliefs include statements such as "I enjoy learning," "I am a thoughtful friend," and "I am a dependable worker." Students develop life role beliefs by observing others, as well as through their own firsthand experience. The important role that peers play during adolescence, and the struggle students

FIGURE 13.2 Dustin's Partial Life Career Rainbows

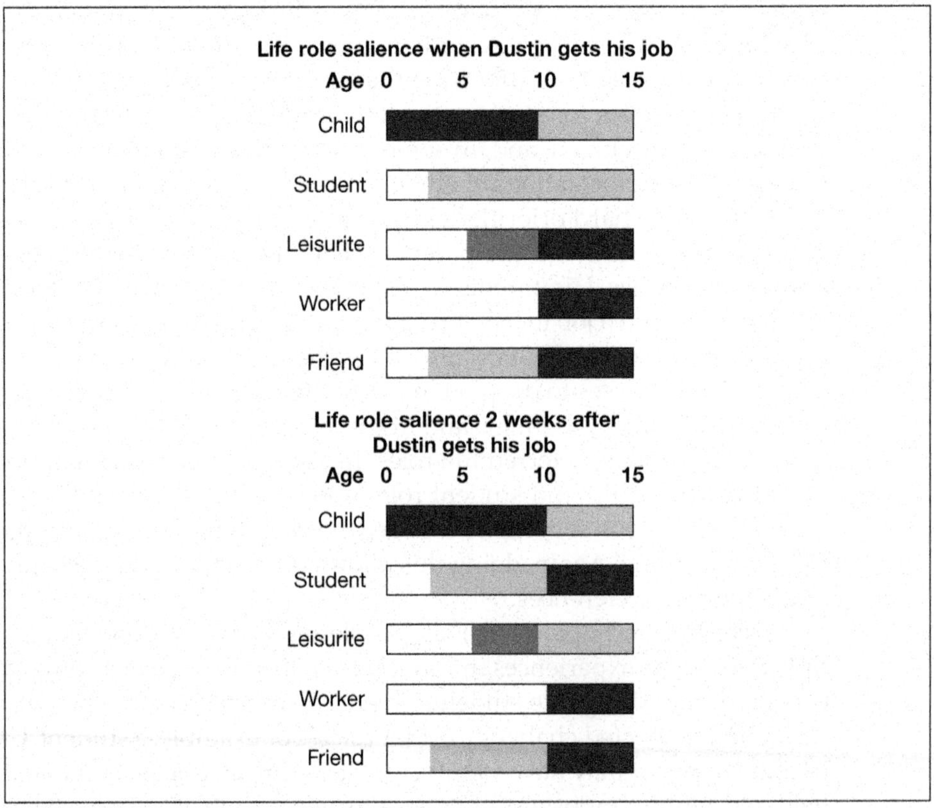

Note: Darker shading reflects increased role salience. *Adapted from Super's (1980) life career rainbow.*

have to solidify their identities, can create much confusion with regard to their life roles and, as a result, their self-concepts. For example, because many students see positive outcomes associated with belonging to a certain group, they often prioritize the life role of friend and may make positive or negative choices (e.g., taking Advanced Placement classes, skipping school) based more on their friends' role expectations of them rather than basing their choices on their parents' role expectations. Students in this mid-adolescent stage can benefit from opportunities to explore their life roles, and later in this chapter we provide an example of how to help them do that.

Lent, Brown, and Hackett's Social Cognitive Career Theory

In their *Social Cognitive Career Theory* (SCCT), Lent, Brown, and Hackett (1994) explain how people develop vocational interests and make occupational choices. We focus on the former (vocational interests) in this chapter. In SCCT, Lent et al. (1994) identify the relationships among self-efficacy, outcome expectations, and personal goals. Importantly, and consistent with our focus on a student's environment and the systems in which he or she lives, they also discuss the role of personal and environmental/contextual factors in career development.

Grounded in social cognitive theory, SCCT adheres to Bandura's (1997) assertion that *self-efficacy* can be strengthened or weakened through the influence of a number of factors, with mastery experiences being one of the most influential factors. Recall our discussion in Chapter 9 about self-efficacy. Bandura believed that individuals who successfully complete tasks would, upon completion, feel more confident in their ability to perform similar tasks in the future. Further, particularly for 10th-grade students, who are still a bit egocentric and for whom their social world is very influential, vicarious learning and verbal persuasion (e.g., encouragement or positive feedback) also can greatly influence self-efficacy beliefs.

Why is self-efficacy relevant for mid-adolescents? Lent et al. (1994) suggested that self-efficacy influences an individual's intentions or goals, and students limit career and college possibilities based on what they think they can or cannot do. We introduced the concept of self-efficacy in Chapter 9, and focused on the importance of helping young children develop confidence in their abilities and learn to develop self-regulatory behaviors in order to achieve goals. Ongoing efforts to address those focus areas are important.

So why revisit this topic in high school? Importantly, mid-adolescence provides a wealth of opportunities for counselors to help students examine self-efficacy beliefs. As students engage in a variety of activities in their efforts to explore and solidify their identities, they encounter new experiences and receive positive and negative feedback from others that will inform their self-efficacy beliefs. They also hopefully have some of their own *mastery experiences* that will impact their self-efficacy. Furthermore, as their bodies change, students become increasingly aware of the strengths and limitations they might have related to their ability to fulfill the physical requirements of various careers (e.g., Maria's realization that she cannot pursue a career as a professional ballerina).

FIGURE 13.3 Carla's Goal Influences

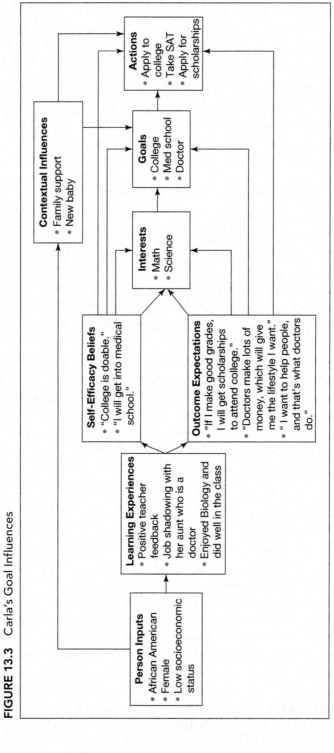

Source: Adapted from Lent et al. (1994).

As discussed in Chapter 8, many males aspire to become professional athletes. By high school, these students begin to understand how limited their opportunities are to enter professional sports based on individual talent and genetics.

Two other important constructs comprise a model that explains the development of career interests. First, Lent et al. (1994) described *outcome expectations* as the beliefs a person holds about the outcomes of engaging in certain behaviors. For example, Carla (the new teen parent) is confident she would be successful in college (high self-efficacy) and she believes that getting good grades in high school will enable her to secure a scholarship to attend college (outcome expectations). Since her family cannot afford to send her to college, a scholarship would be very important in helping her pursue her goal of attending college. Second, *personal goals* refer to an individual's plans to pursue a certain career or engage in a specific behavior (Lent et al., 1994). These goals are informed by self-efficacy beliefs and outcome expectations (see Figure 13.3 for an illustration of the factors that influenced Carla's interests and goals of becoming a doctor), but also by contextual factors. In Carla's case, her new family responsibilities will influence her goals and the actions she takes toward pursuing them.

Notice that in Figure 13.3, one of the contextual influences in Carla's life includes her new baby. Even if Carla has high self-efficacy and outcome expectations, it is possible that factors related to being a mom and caring for her baby will deter her from successfully pursuing her goals. In this sense, SCCT acknowledges an environmental component that might warrant attention. Examining life role balance concerns could be critical to helping Carla navigate the new demands that she faces related to being a mom.

MINDSETS AND BEHAVIORS FOR 10TH GRADE

As we suggested for other grade levels, interventions for 10th-grade students ideally should be grounded in theory and connected to the American School Counselor Association (ASCA) Mindsets and Behaviors (2014). In Table 13.1, we highlight some of the Mindsets and Behaviors that are particularly relevant for 10th-grade career and college planning. Note that most of them closely correspond to the constructs we have reviewed in this chapter, things such

TABLE 13.1 ASCA Mindsets and Behaviors for 10th-Grade Curriculum Planning Focus

CATEGORY 1: MINDSETS STANDARDS		
Self-confidence in ability to succeed Understanding that postsecondary education and lifelong learning are necessary for long-term career success Belief in using abilities to their fullest to achieve high-quality results and outcomes		
CATEGORY 2: BEHAVIOR STANDARDS		
Actively engage in challenging course work	Demonstrate ability to delay immediate gratification for long-term rewards	Use leadership and teamwork skills to work effectively in diverse teams
Identify long- and short-term academic, career, and socioemotional goals	Demonstrate perseverance to achieve long- and short-term goals	Demonstrate advocacy skills and ability to assert self, when necessary

as future planning, career goals, strengths, and balancing life roles. In the sections that follow, we share examples of interventions that can be used to address many of these key areas.

Collaborating With Teachers and the Community to Target Future Goals

In most schools, 10th-grade students have some sort of tentative program of study, grounded in a career and postsecondary plan and outlining the high school course work and experiences that would facilitate them reaching their career and college goals. An example of this was introduced in Chapter 11 with the individual graduation plan (IGP) used in South Carolina schools. Using these IGPs or similar plans as a foundation, school personnel can help students develop long-term goals and thoroughly examine the choices they make related to those goals, as well as the factors that influence those goals. The interventions described in the following focus on identifying and/or addressing influences to self-efficacy.

Developing and evaluating career plans. Because 10th-grade students are still developing their identities and experimenting with new interests and activities, ongoing examination of their career plans is warranted. School personnel cannot assume that career plans developed at the beginning of ninth grade will remain relevant throughout high school. Opportunities to identify their talents and strengths can serve as entry points to revisit and more closely examine students' long-term career plans.

Although school and career counselors traditionally assume responsibility for working with students to develop their programs of study, teachers easily can become more involved in that process. Recall in Chapter 12 when we mentioned a high school where teachers facilitated IGP meetings. In gathering accountability data, the school counselor, Carney, discovered that the teachers did not always feel confident facilitating those meetings and that they sometimes weren't sure how helpful they had been.

After talking with many teachers, Carney realized that they were looking for something more concrete to help them walk students and parents through their decision-making process. She decided to provide them with a template that would allow them to help students identify and connect their strengths and goals (and that fits very well with our SCCT focus), and she provided a worksheet for them to follow as well (see Exhibit 13.1). The example in Exhibit 13.2 illustrates an abbreviated version of a teacher-led conversation using this approach.

Optimizing feedback to students (verbal persuasion). We have talked about the factors that affect self-efficacy beliefs, and adults with whom students interact can play very important roles in the formation of students' self-efficacy beliefs and future aspirations. To maximize opportunities for encouragement (verbal persuasion), school counselors can facilitate adult involvement in a number of ways.

First, school counselors can lead a faculty in-service session during that time to discuss the ways in which the teacher's feedback can influence student goals (review the factors that influence self-efficacy). School counselors

EXHIBIT 13.1
Teacher-Led Student Future Planning Conference Worksheet

Pull up the student's **IGP**. Review his or her career goal and ask if it is still accurate. If Yes, go to **(A)**; if No, go to **(X)**.

(A) Ask how confident the student feels he or she is that he or she can achieve the goal: (not confident) 1 2 3 4 5 6 (very confident) 	**(X)** Ask what the new goal is, what led to the change, and how much the student knows about the job requirements. Make notes here, then jump over to **(A)**:

(B) Ask the student what kinds of related activities (e.g., course work, job shadowing, hobbies) he or she has engaged in this past year and list them here:

(C) Comment on the relevance of those activities in relation to the goal:

(D) Ask the student what reinforcement he or she has received related to that goal and list responses here:
*   Evidence of potential (mastery experiences):
*   Encouragement from parents, teachers, peers, others (verbal persuasion):

(E) Finally, develop a list of activities for this year to help the student make further progress toward his or her goal and/or to allow for some opportunities for reinforcement:

EXHIBIT 13.2
Sample IGP Meeting

Marcus, a 10th-grade student, and his mother have come to meet with his teacher for their annual career and college planning session. Marcus has been taking general level academic classes, thinking he will attend a 2-year college or technical school, and he has a 3.4 GPA. After engaging in introductions, Mr. Thompson walks them through the session using the template (see Exhibit 13.1) provided by the school counselor:

Mr. Thompson: So, Marcus, it looks like last year you had indicated a desire to work on computers . . . like a tech support person? Is that still something you want to do?

(continued)

EXHIBIT 13.2 (continued)
Sample IGP Meeting

Marcus: Yeah, that's what I did want to do. I understand computers pretty good, so I thought that could be fun.

Mr. Thompson: Sounds like something you feel pretty confident about—like you would be good at it?

Marcus: That's right, but I have a different plan now.

Marcus's mother: He keeps changing his mind. I tell him he needs to pick something and stick with it.

Mr. Thompson: I'm sure it's difficult to see your son still trying to come up with a long-term plan. I can reassure you, however, that most kids at his age are still trying out new things. The important thing is that we help him move forward in a way that will keep as many options open as possible, and we can do that today. What's your new idea, Marcus?

Marcus: I want to join the Air Force. My friend's cousin was telling me about how he is like a weather forecaster for the Air Force. He got all of his training there and now he gets to work with these cool computer programs to predict the weather.

Mr. Thompson: So I hear you saying that finding out about this new job through your friend's cousin got you thinking about it. (Mr. Thompson takes some time to explore what Marcus knows about the job expectations and training . . . he seems to have thought a lot about it, so Mr. Thompson proceeds to Step A on the worksheet.)

Mr. Thompson: You have done your homework and seem to have a clear idea of what is required. I'm wondering how confident you are that you could complete the requirements? If 1 = not confident and 6 = very confident . . . give me a number where you would be.

Marcus: I think a 5. I mean, I really want to do it, so I'll work hard.

Mr. Thompson: Okay, so you're pretty confident. Aside from talking with your friend's cousin, what else have you done that is related to being a weather forecaster? Any classes you've taken that are relevant?

Marcus: Well, the earth science I have is. I got an A in that class. I'm good with computers, too, like I said before. Nothing else I can think of.

Marcus's mother: He really hasn't done anything. He hasn't even talked to the Air Force—I know we need to do that.

Mr. Thompson: Definitely. Before we leave today we'll try to come up with a plan. I know that, Marcus, you have done well in science and computer classes, so it makes sense that you feel pretty confident. You mentioned that your teachers have been very encouraging of your abilities as well, and that

(continued)

EXHIBIT 13.2 (*continued*)

your friend's cousin was pretty confident you could do it because he and you are a lot alike, is that right?

Marcus: Yep—I can't think of any reason not to try.

Mr. Thompson (to Marcus's mother): How do you feel?

Marcus's mother: To be honest, I'm a little hesitant. I don't know much about the military, but he does seem really excited. I just want to make sure he does what needs to be done.

Mr. Thompson: Alright then . . . sounds like we need to develop a new action plan to help you move forward with this new goal. (Mr. Thompson leads them in a discussion to explore activities he should complete including things like taking the Armed Services Vocational Aptitude Battery (ASVAB), meeting with the Air Force recruiter, job shadowing with a meteorologist, signing up for advanced science classes, and so on. He also refers them back to the school counselor, just so they can make sure that the plan makes sense and nothing critical is missing.)

may also provide concrete examples of how to phrase or rephrase feedback in an effort to not sound discouraging. For example, rather than a frustrated teacher saying to a student who does poorly on tests, "You'll never pass this class if you don't study for the tests," that teacher can be encouraged to provide more positive and encouraging feedback such as, "You always pay attention in class but seem to do poorly on the tests—I'm wondering if we can talk about how we might help you do better on the next one." Sharing a chart like that in Table 13.2 could help teachers understand how their words can be internalized. Sometimes asking teachers to come up with statements they have made or heard, and then asking them to generate ideas for what messages students might hear, can help them to get into the mindset of their students a little better.

In addition to demonstrating to teachers how students might internalize their feedback, school counselors also can help all school personnel become more intentional about sharing feedback. We talked earlier in this book about the need to encourage all students to consider nontraditional careers; to help more minority students, those from low socioeconomic status (SES) families, and students with disabilities consider college as a possibility; and to help females and minority students aspire to enter science, technology, engineering, and mathematics (STEM) careers. Although we aren't suggesting that school personnel target some students over others, knowing how their words effect students could make a difference; thus, we are encouraging them to make an intentional effort to reach out when they find opportunities.

For example, Dimitrius is an African American male from a low SES background. Neither of his parents graduated from high school, and his older sister found employment right after high school. Dimitrius is very bright and

TABLE 13.2 Examples of How Students Internalize Feedback

Feedback Statement	Message Heard	Student Action
You'll never pass the class if you don't study for the tests.	He doesn't think I can pass.	Student stops studying.
You always pay attention in class but seem to do poorly on the tests—I'm wondering if we can talk about how we might help you do better on the next one?	He thinks I can do better and is willing to work with me.	Student is willing to get tutoring and keep working.
You need to spend more time on school and less with your girlfriend.	She doesn't understand how hard I'm really trying to balance everything.	Student shuts down when teacher talks to him.
You seem to be juggling a lot of things lately and your schoolwork has dropped; would it help to talk about ways to balance everything?	She understands me and is willing to help me figure out how to bring my grades up.	Student and teacher talk, or student approaches school counselor for help.

has excelled in all of his classes. He has strong academic potential to pursue college in a math or science major. Recognizing that Dimitrius might receive little information about college at home, and that he probably would need financial aid, his teachers and counselor could be very intentional and proactive in pointing out his strengths and conveying their belief in his potential (e.g., "Your work ethic would serve you well in college—are you thinking about that?" or "I would like to see you enroll in AP Chemistry—it would be great if you could get college credit now, and I think you have a good shot"). Planting the idea of college early enough so that he would have plenty of time to enroll in requisite courses and explore financial aid options would be critical to facilitating the transition for a potential first-generation college student.

Role models and mentors (vicarious learning). Students are most influenced by individuals with whom they feel a connection based on some salient characteristic (Bandura, 1997). Those connections often are initially based on factors like race/ethnicity or gender, but sometimes students connect with certain people for other reasons. For example, lots of high school students look up to athletes who may or may not look like them, but whom they want to emulate because of their status. In any event, school counselors can work to identify individuals who can serve as mentors or role models for students and to create opportunities for them to interact. These kinds of experiences can allow for vicarious learning and verbal persuasion influences to occur.

Similar to the mentoring scenario in Exhibit 13.3, by partnering with various organizations or groups in their local community, school counselors can recruit adult mentors to pair with specific students. These kinds of arrangements may be established with local businesses, by contacting civic groups, or by soliciting parent volunteers. School counselors should be prepared to provide some information to the mentors about the purpose of the partnerships as well as how they might spend their time with the students. They also should make efforts to recruit individuals who reflect the diversity of the school population as well as nontraditional careers (e.g., male nurse). If time permits, school counselors should host a mentor training workshop that outlines what

EXHIBIT 13.3
Partnering With a College to Identify Mentors

To help promote a college-going culture, one southeastern school partnered with a local university to establish ongoing mentoring relationships. Providing monthly opportunities for lunch meetings at the school, the school counselors solicited college student volunteers whom they matched with students they thought could benefit from having a mentor (i.e., most of these students were potential first-generation college students). Mentors were paired in order to match salient characteristics as much as possible (e.g., a Latina college student majoring in engineering with a Mexican American student who excels in math and science). As the mentors talked about their backgrounds and their experiences in college, the students were able to better envision the same kinds of possibilities for themselves. The mentors were encouraged to emphasize the importance of academics, to provide information and encouragement relevant to the student's career goals, and to share the things that they believed helped them be successful.

the role of a mentor is, the goals of mentoring, activities to engage in during a mentoring session, and how to avoid and address problems in the mentoring relationship.

Another way to connect students with role models is through a career fair. Thoughtfully planned to include individuals who represent nontraditional careers, a career fair can help students recognize that people like them can succeed in any number of careers. Kolodinsky et al. (2006) discussed the positive outcomes of a career fair involving mainly females who worked in a variety of nontraditional careers. The women who served as the career role models discussed and demonstrated various aspects of their work to participants during small-group breakout sessions. Through pre-/postsurveys, the researchers found increased occupational self-efficacy among adolescent girls who attended the career fair, specifically in relation to their confidence to engage in tasks needed for various occupations.

A final way to expose students to role models is through job shadowing. Many students need to see or experience someone being successful in order for vicarious learning to crystallize. That is, seeing someone perform an activity may be more influential to a student's self-efficacy beliefs than simply talking with someone about his or her ability to perform an activity. Logistical concerns sometimes make organizing job-shadowing activities challenging, but school counselors can be creative in making these opportunities work.

Perhaps in an ideal world, every student is provided an opportunity to participate in a meaningful job-shadowing opportunity, and with any luck he or she might have a couple of opportunities during high school to do this. The main challenge is that someone needs to coordinate these kinds of activities (e.g., identify relevant employees, match the mentor with students, coordinate schedules, address liability issues, and complete any relevant paperwork), ensure transportation is available (don't assume that all students would be able to transport themselves to and from these opportunities), and address issues related to students missing school. In schools that employ a career counselor, this type of arrangement might be very realistic. Most schools, however, are limited in staff available to organize such a comprehensive career-related initiative.

One solution to help eliminate logistical concerns related to job shadowing is to provide opportunities for students to engage in virtual job shadowing. Numerous websites (e.g., www.virtualjobshadow.com/) are available for students to learn about jobs, to hear from individuals who work in those jobs, and to capture a glimpse of what the job environment might look like. In addition to providing an option that is accessible to all students, virtual job shadowing also affords students an opportunity to explore jobs that might not be readily accessible to them. These experiences also can be completed any time of day, which means that students would not need to miss school in order to participate. Finally, when relevant, parents or counselors could participate along with students.

Mastery experiences. We will talk more about mastery experiences in the next chapter, as school personnel can facilitate opportunities for students in numerous ways. In 10th grade, however, school personnel can address self-efficacy related to academic potential by focusing on college preparatory experiences. One way to do this is to challenge students to take the most rigorous course work that they are capable of rather than allowing students to choose their own courses based on their comfort level or what their peers are choosing. As noted in Chapter 2, as part of their admissions process, colleges consider the type of course work that students have undertaken in high school. Students who are able to experience success in rigorous high school classes should feel more confident in their ability to complete college-level course work. Exhibit 13.4 highlights a school counselor who identified a population of students at her school that were not equitably represented in Advanced Placement (AP) course work and how she focused on changing that pattern. By encouraging more African American students to take AP courses at her school, this school counselor fostered opportunity for appropriate and equitable mastery experiences.

Another type of mastery experience school counselors should keep in mind for 10th-grade students relates to college entrance examinations. Specifically, the Preliminary Scholastic Aptitude Test (PSAT) can serve as an important factor influencing self-efficacy related to reading, writing, and math. The PSAT serves as a practice test for the Scholastic Aptitude Test (SAT) as well as an opportunity to qualify for certain scholarships and use some career planning tools (The College Board, 2012). Some students start taking the actual SAT in middle school, in order to get as much exposure and practice with the real exam as possible, but for many students, that is not a financially viable option. Most students wait to take the less-expensive PSAT in their sophomore year. In this way, they can get a sense of how they might do the following year on the PSAT (when they first become eligible for certain scholarship opportunities based on their scores) and later when they take the SAT.

EXHIBIT 13.4
Voices From the Field: Pushing 10th-Grade Academic
Rigor for College Preparation

Wendy Rock, PhD, LPC-S, NCC, NCSC

School Counselor, Hahnville High School

My school district has been encouraging school counselors to intentionally use data to support their work for the past 10 years and has provided school counselors with a number of professional development opportunities to support this endeavor. In 2011, my state implemented an evaluation system that required all teachers, administrators, librarians, and school counselors to establish student learning targets (SLTs) as part of their annual performance review. SLTs require the use of baseline data and goal setting to improve student achievement. As a result, school counselors in my state have had no choice but to become results-oriented and use data to support our school counseling interventions and programs.

My school is somewhat diverse. We have nearly 1,500 high school students: 1% Asian/Pacific Islander, 32% African American, 3% Hispanic, and 63% White, non-Hispanic, with 48.5% on free or reduced-price lunch. I think a lot about who receives the best preparation for college, and I feel personally responsible to ensure all students have the opportunity to achieve to their highest capability. In planning my SLT for the 2012–2013 school year, I considered the enrollment in our growing AP program. In my high school only 19% of minority students were enrolled in an AP course for the 2012–2013 school year, while the minority population made up 37% of the total enrollment.

I was working with 10th-grade students and wanted to start slow. My objective was to increase minority enrollment in AP U.S. History, an 11th-grade course my students might consider scheduling. My baseline data indicated that 15% (26 out of 171) of students enrolled in the feeder class, Honors Civics, were minority students. My goal was to have at least 18% of the enrollment in AP U.S. History be minority students.

My interventions included identifying and encouraging 10th-grade students to enroll in AP U.S. History for the 2013–2014 school year. Minority students in particular were targeted with the aim to increase minority student enrollment and thus close the achievement gap that existed. Course grades and assessment results (including EXPLORE, PSAT, and PLAN) were used to identify talented minority students not taking honors courses that could potentially be successfully challenged in AP U.S. History. I consulted with non-Honors Civics teachers at the beginning of the school year, communicating my plan and asking their help in identifying students with potential to succeed in AP. I met with students individually and in small groups to discuss the benefits and challenges of taking an AP course. We held two AP nights, one in the fall and one in the spring, to provide information to students and parents about the AP program.

(continued)

EXHIBIT 13.4 (continued)
Voices From the Field: Pushing 10th-Grade Academic Rigor for College Preparation

My results were even greater than I hoped. At the conclusion of scheduling for the 2013–2014 academic year, 25% of the students who requested AP U.S. History were minority students. An achievement gap still existed considering the total school enrollment was composed of 37% minority students; however, to increase the enrollment from Honors Civics to AP U.S. History from 15% to 25% was significant.

Utilizing data, I was able to identify an achievement gap that existed in my school and develop an action plan to help close the gap. Students benefited from the targeted interventions and, looking at the ASCA Mindsets and Behaviors, developed specific mindsets: "self-confidence in the ability to succeed" and "sense of belonging in the school environment" and behaviors: "set high standards of quality," "actively engage in challenging course work," and "create relationships with adults that support success." AP courses matter because they prepare students for the rigor of college. Professionally I grew through this process as well and I know that when I grow as a professional, my students benefit. The school counselor competencies included: ". . . demonstrate an understanding of impediments to student learning and use of advocacy and data-driven school counseling practices to act effectively in closing the achievement/opportunity gap" (I-A-3), "advocates for student success" (I-B-3), ". . . demonstrate an understanding of data-driven decision making (IV-A-5), and "uses student data to demonstrate a need for systemic change in areas such as course enrollment patterns; equity and access; and the achievement, opportunity and information gap" (IV-B-3c).

What is most concerning about this experience is that I know that everyday across America, students don't take the highest rigor courses simply because they aren't challenged to do so. My take away from this experience is that when we present our students with opportunities to be their best, they often will. This was a valuable learning experience for me and one that definitely affected how I think about data and challenging my students.

The ACT is a similar, but slightly different, college entrance exam that students typically take in grades 11 or 12. Where the SAT assesses reading, writing, and math, the ACT assesses English, reading, math, and science skills and offers an optional writing test (ACT, Inc., 2012). Similar to the SAT, a practice test of sorts, PLAN, is available to help students estimate their future ACT scores. The test format of PLAN is identical to the ACT, but questions are a little less difficult. PLAN is meant to be taken in 10th grade.

Their experiences taking the PSAT and/or PLAN can inform students' future goals in positive and negative ways. For example, a student who does well on the PSAT might experience increased self-efficacy related to taking the SAT in the future. Anticipating that he or she might be able to get into competitive colleges, a student who does well on the PSAT may feel more motivated to put effort into academic work and/or may be inspired to investigate colleges not previously considered (due to increased self-efficacy and outcome expectations). Assuming he or she will do well, this student also might be more motivated to register for challenging high school classes. Upon receiving a good score, another student who had not really considered college but who was encouraged to take the PSAT might actively start looking at careers requiring a 4-year college degree. Some students who do not fare as well on the PSAT might be motivated to work harder in school so that they can improve their scores. Conversely, some who don't score very high may get discouraged (i.e., lower self-efficacy) and start exploring other career paths not requiring college degrees.

We encourage school counselors to use the PSAT and PLAN tests as opportunities to engage students in discussion to find out how they make sense of their scores. For instance, school counselors should clarify that students must be careful about making strong inferences based on a single test. They could explore with students things like how they felt going into the test, how much they prepared for it, and how they felt during the exam. School counselors also can emphasize that there are many things students can do to improve their scores for future tests. Building these conversations into the annual career and college planning meetings will ensure that parents receive the same information.

Defining the career and college needs of each unique school's population. Each school will be different. Conducting a thorough needs assessment of the career and college goals of 10th graders at the beginning of the year will help school counselors tailor intervention for 10th graders at individual schools. Because 10th grade is such a pivotal year in career and college decision making, it is necessary to consider what knowledge and skills the specific students at a particular school have and what they need. Asking the faculty as well as students and parents about what is needed also is important.

The types of skills that are noted throughout the literature are broad. For students preparing for 4-year and 2-year college, these skills include technology, financial literacy, research skills and information literacy, time management, social and communication skills (including social media and self-representation), to name a few (Strom, Strom, Whitten, & Kraska, 2014). For students focusing on technical and career paths, such as students obtaining industry recognized credentials (IRCs), the development of employability skills is crucial such as writing resumes, focusing on team work, developing leadership, learning about industry credentials, and improving technical skills, personal budgeting and finance, problem solving, and workplace communication. School counselors will need to adapt their curriculum for their distinct school environments and plan accordingly.

Targeted Interventions to Address Life Role Challenges

Given the number of students in 10th grade who may start to increase and/ or reprioritize the number of life roles they need to balance (e.g., adding the worker role through part-time jobs, adding the parent role by having a baby), we wanted to provide an example of how school counselors might address their concerns. To focus on students currently experiencing difficulties related to life role balance, school counselors can implement small-group interventions. Nevertheless, over the course of their lives, all students will experience life role balance challenges. As such, all students potentially could benefit from engaging in similar discussions so they can develop skills to navigate similar changes in the future; large-group or classroom-based interventions could be implemented.

Earlier in this chapter we introduced Carla, the teen mom who aspired to become a doctor. She and a few other girls in her school are all struggling with the newly acquired role of parent. Even though the students have different future goals, they can benefit from exploring their life role challenges together in a small group where they can experience peer support and a sense of universality.

One way to help students thoroughly examine the life role changes that have occurred is to have them create their own life career rainbow. These rainbows don't need to be complicated—students can simply label different bars with the life roles they assume (as in Figure 13.1) and then shade in the bars accordingly. To better illustrate the changes, students may be asked to create one rainbow to represent their life before the baby (and the acquisition of the parent role) and another to represent their life with the baby (more along the lines of Figure 13.2). To expand the rainbow, they can be asked to list the daily activities that go along with each role and/or to estimate the percent of time each day that they engage in that role.

Many students who become teenage parents may understandably feel some resentment or frustration about losing some of their youth. They may have less time with their friends or less time to focus on school, and they might start to rethink their future plans. For example, while trying to care for her baby, Carla is struggling to maintain her high academic standing in the hopes that she can still get a scholarship to attend college, but she also feels torn between prioritizing school and prioritizing her daughter. For students like Carla, creating a "reality" life role rainbow as well as a "desired" life role rainbow can encourage the identification and acknowledgment of these kinds of feelings. These rainbows also can serve as the foundation for discussing how to move forward toward pursuing future goals including examining potential barriers and brainstorming ways to navigate them.

SUMMARY

In this chapter, we focused on life roles and self-efficacy as important target areas for career- and college-related interventions. Tenth-grade students should be encouraged to engage in a variety of activities, so they can hone in on their talents and skills; those mastery experiences will shape their interests and goals. Further, opportunities for vicarious learning and encouragement can be provided through school-wide initiatives and connecting with the community. Counselors and educators should be intentional in their efforts to influence students' self-efficacy.

> **⋯❯** Test Your Knowledge
>
> 1. Explain the relationship between outcome expectations, self-efficacy, and personal goals.
> 2. Identify at least four life roles that most 10th graders hold.

REFERENCES

ACT, Inc. (2012). Description of the ACT. Retrieved from http://www.actstudent.org/testprep/descriptions/index.html

American School Counselor Association. (2014). *ASCA mindsets & behaviors for student success: K-12 college- and career-readiness standards for every student.* Alexandria, VA: Author.

Bandura, A. (1977). *Social learning theory.* Englewood Cliffs, NJ: Prentice Hall.

Curry, J., Smith, H., & Robinson, E. H. (2009). The development and manifestation of altruistic caring: A qualitative inquiry. *Counseling and Values, 54*, 2–16.

Erikson, E. H. (1963). *Childhood and society* (2nd ed.). New York, NY: W. W. Norton.

Kolodinsky, P., Schroder, V., Montopoli, G., McLean, S., Mangan, P. A., & Pederson, W. (2006). The career fair as a vehicle for enhancing occupational self-efficacy. *Professional School Counseling, 10*, 161–167.

Krumboltz, J. D. (2009). The happenstance learning theory. *Journal of Career Assessment, 17*(2), 135–154. http://dx.doi.org/10.1177/1069072708328861

Lent, R. W., Brown, S. D., & Hackett, G. (1994). Toward a unifying social cognitive theory of career and academic interest, choice, and performance. *Journal of Vocational Behavior, 45*, 79–122.

Piaget, J. (1969). *The intellectual development of the adolescent.* In G. Caplan & S. Lebovici (Eds.), *Adolescence: Psychosocial perspectives* (pp. 22–26). New York, NY: Basic Books.

Strom, P. S., Strom, R. D., Whitten, L. S., & Kraska, M. F. (2014). Adolescent identity and career exploration. *NASSP Bulletin, 98*(2), 163–179. http://dx.doi.org/10.1177/0192636514528749

Super, D. E. (1980). A life-span, life-space approach to career development. *Journal of Vocational Behavior, 16*(3), 282–298. http://dx.doi.org/10.1016/0001-8791(80)90056-1

The College Board. (2012). About the PSAT/NMSQT. Retrieved from http://www.collegeboard.com/student/testing/psat/about.html

FOURTEEN

Career and College Readiness for Grade 11: Beginning the Career and College Transition

Although many students and their parents start anticipating and planning for the end of high school as far back as middle school, grade 11 is a time when most students really start to acknowledge that high school graduation is not that far away. Evidence of this shift in thinking includes students beginning to take school more seriously, worrying about being involved in enough activities to boost their college applications, and seeming eager, ready, and willing to actively engage in activities to prepare them for their future careers. Students who are still uncertain about their future plans may start to feel pressure from peers and parents to make a choice. As such, activities implemented for 11th-grade students should be designed to help them narrow down or confirm their future plans and then to help them take concrete steps toward pursuing those plans. In this chapter, we briefly review relevant developmental and career theories, and then focus on interventions to help them attain their career and college goals.

DEVELOPMENTAL OVERVIEW

Students in 11th grade have passed most major physical, cognitive, and psychosocial milestones, and their development starts to flatten out, so to speak. Therefore, developmental changes in the junior year may be more subtle than in previous grades. Most 11th-grade students fall into the mid-adolescence (ages 15 to 18) category and still possess many of the characteristics discussed in the previous chapter. In particular, peer influence and abstract thinking skills (e.g., problem-solving skills) are very important to their career and college decision-making process.

Recall our discussion of identity statuses (Marcia, 1987) in Chapter 10. As students in 11th grade are finalizing their future plans, it is not uncommon to hear them talk about pursuing options that their peers are pursuing. Relying too much on their peers' preferences can result in identity foreclosure and possible future dissatisfaction with their choices. Similarly, some students may choose the same careers as their parents or careers that fit with a family business, rather than exploring their own personal interests, aptitudes, and values before making a career decision. Further, when students engage in career and college exploration activities and find that they have numerous options that might make sense, it sometimes can be easier to just do what everyone else is doing. Students in a moratorium status (i.e., exploring but unable to commit; Marcia, 1987) may be more easily influenced by their peers than would students who have committed to an identity (i.e., identity achievement) and chosen a unique career path. That is, when students feel strongly about something, they can be less susceptible to influence from others.

Decisions about college (including whether or not to attend, the type of school to attend, and which particular school to attend) also are often influenced by others' opinions and choices. Both authors have worked with students who were set on attending a specific college (often based on peer or parent influence, family tradition, or because they had a good football team) without thinking about whether or not they could major in something they liked at a particular school. In essence, they foreclosed on a college choice because they didn't feel any need to explore other options.

As these students were eventually able to narrow down possible majors, they often realized that their preferred colleges did not offer those majors. These students then had to choose between attending the school they had become excited about and finding a major at that college that they might find satisfactory, or taking a risk to branch out away from their peers and explore colleges that would allow them to pursue their career goals.

Whether it is choosing a career or a college, the influence of peers or other important individuals can supersede logical thinking. For example, students might be able to explain very clearly why one college might be a more logical choice than another based on their career goals or characteristics they value (e.g., religious affiliation). Yet, the idea of leaving peers behind or disappointing someone they care about can be too overwhelming for some students, and they end up making a choice that will not help them get what they want in the long run. To an outsider, their decision-making process may seem illogical.

How can students make choices and life decisions that don't match their personal goals? Even when adolescents can accurately discuss the potential consequences of their actions, they still sometimes believe that things will work out for them. In other instances, the desire to fit in and do what their peers do is just too great. For these reasons, it is important to foster autonomy and help students learn to make decisions that *they* believe to be in their best interest (even if those decisions are based on the preferences of others). We believe that decisions made in the absence of exploration (i.e., students who are in identity diffusion or foreclosure) are ones that students might question later.

We hope that very few students in 11th grade are apathetic about their future (i.e., identity diffusion), but realistically a good number of students fall into this category. Some are not ready to leave the comforts of high school, so they avoid planning. Others have a difficult time picturing themselves living a successful life, leaving them unmotivated to plan. Yet another subset of students don't envision themselves working or attending school, so they believe there is nothing to plan for. Later in this chapter, we discuss ideas for helping these students become more engaged in thinking about and preparing for their futures.

RELEVANT CAREER THEORY: LENT, BROWN, AND HACKETT (1994) AND SAVICKAS (2005)

In Chapter 13, we introduced *Social Cognitive Career Theory* (SCCT; Lent, Brown, & Hackett, 1994), and we elaborate on that theory in this chapter by focusing on factors that affect student *performance* on academic and career tasks. In addition, we present another theory that can be used to help students finalize their career decisions: Savickas's (2005) *Career Construction Theory*. These two theories provide the framework for interventions we review later in this chapter.

Lent, Brown, and Hackett's Social Cognitive Career Theory

In the previous chapter, we introduced the Lent et al. (1994) model to help explain the personal and environmental factors that influence the development of career and college interests. Continuing with the example from the previous chapter of Carla, the teen mom who wants to become a doctor, in this chapter we review SCCT's *performance model* (see Figure 14.1). This model explains success at, and persistence toward, academic- and career-related tasks. Notice that self-efficacy and outcome expectations continue to play important roles.

According to Lent et al. (1994), the ability/past performance box in Figure 14.1 refers to task-specific knowledge and skills that Carla has acquired. For example, by doing well in a trigonometry class, Carla develops math-related skills and strategies that will help her to achieve success in more advanced math classes. In this way, her acquired skills directly affect her performance attainment (i.e., level of performance). As illustrated through the arrows in Figure 14.1, past performance also indirectly affects performance attainment by influencing self-efficacy and outcome expectations.

FIGURE 14.1 Carla's Task Performance Model

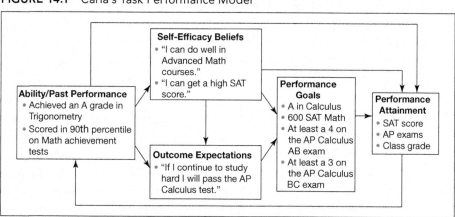

Source: Adapted from Lent et al. (1994).

Recall from previous chapters our discussions of how *mastery performances* can greatly influence self-efficacy beliefs; as Carla achieves success, she feels more and more confident that she has the ability to achieve success in similar tasks in the future. Further, in seeing that her study habits seem to be working, Carla's outcome expectation is that approaching future math classes as she did her trigonometry class should result in academic success. Based on her self-efficacy beliefs and outcome expectations, Carla develops performance goals. The more confidence she has in her ability to achieve success and attain desired outcomes, the more challenging goals she will set.

Persistence is an important construct in relation to the performance model. Lent et al. (1994) indicated that students who persist are more likely to achieve success in academic or career tasks (e.g., graduate from high school) than are their peers who do not persist. They believe that persistent students are probably more competent at specific tasks than are students who are not persistent. That is, students who had successful mastery experiences would naturally feel more confident in their future capabilities, and therefore they would put forth continual effort (i.e., persist) toward a goal. This sentiment holds true especially for students who encounter obstacles or barriers; to persist in the face of obstacles suggests positive and high self-efficacy beliefs and outcome expectations. Interestingly, in examining the career beliefs of inner city youth, Turner and Conkel Ziebell (2011) found that only 24% of participants believed that effort was linked to success; these students had low outcome expectations. Without knowing how their beliefs developed, SCCT would suggest that past performance would play a role.

Finally, Lent et al. (1994) discussed the importance of examining self-efficacy beliefs in relation to a person's past performance/abilities. More specifically, they articulate that both overconfidence and underconfidence in one's actual abilities can be detrimental to performance attainment. Thinking they are very capable, overconfident individuals may mistakenly believe that they do not have to put forth much effort. Further, these individuals may set unrealistic or unattainable goals, often resulting in failure because they did not possess the requisite skills or knowledge to be successful. For example, students with average or below average grades may set the goal of attending medical school, not realizing that their academic record may prohibit them from meeting admissions requirements or underestimating the amount of effort it will take to be successful in such an endeavor. As a result, high schools often try to set students up for success by requiring teacher recommendations before students can enroll in higher level or Advanced Placement (AP) courses.

Underconfident individuals possess similar challenges. Feeling less hopeful, these students tend to exert less effort, give up more quickly, and set less challenging goals (Lent et al., 1994). Because they have little confidence in their abilities, the anxiety that many of these students experience before engaging in tasks can prevent them from achieving success. By missing out on opportunities that would allow them to advance their skills, underconfident students often fail to reach their potential.

Savickas's Theory of Career Construction

Although a thorough discussion of Career Construction Theory is beyond the scope of this book (refer to Savickas, 2002, 2005 for more information), we want to highlight a few key aspects of this theory that are particularly relevant to working with 11th-grade students. Savickas (2005) wrote, "Individuals construct their careers by imposing meaning on their vocational behavior and occupational experiences" (p. 43). Career Construction (Savickas, 2002) is a postmodern theory that is grounded in the belief that the best way to understand individuals is in the context of their environment and how they experience it, as well as by examining how they make meaning of their experiences. Further, according to Savickas, Career Construction

> views careers from a contextualist perspective, one that sees development as driven by adaptation to an environment rather than by maturation of inner structures. Viewing careers from constructionist and contextual perspectives focuses attention on interpretive processes, social interaction, and the negotiation of meaning. Careers . . . are constructed as individuals make choices that express their self-concepts and substantiate their goals in the social reality of work roles. (p. 43)

Understandably, Career Construction relies on subjective measures and qualitative assessments as opposed to objective and quantitative measures, and counselors using this approach focus on individual perceptions and stories or personal narratives (Savickas, 2005). Nevertheless, Savickas's theory complements theories such as those of Holland (1973) and Super (1980) that rely on objective, or concrete, assessments of person and/or environment. Savickas does not discount the value of examining objective assessment data (e.g., Holland Codes); rather, he believes that subjective data are necessary to truly understand career behaviors. That is, while Savickas values Holland's RIASEC types, he cautions that those types are socially constructed categories that may or may not make sense to a client. When they use objective assessments like interest inventories, counselors who adhere to a career construction approach use the results as a starting point for discussion about things such as how their clients view their interests and experiences in relation to various occupations and how those interests evolved.

Similar to Holland (1973), Savickas (2005) defined *vocational personality* as comprised of factors like abilities, values, and interests. He also indicated that those factors are evident long before people engage in work through things like hobbies, school activities, and other leisure activities. Unlike focusing on an objective assessment of traits to identify an individual's vocational personality, using Career Construction Theory, a counselor would focus on acquiring a more subjective understanding of an individual's vocational self-concept and *life themes*. This counselor would be interested in examining how clients understand and make sense of themselves and their world, and how they find meaning in life. Savickas (2005) believes that no matter what occupation they are in or what job they hold, everyone can find ways to express themselves (i.e., their self-concept) and find meaning through their work. With this idea in mind, counselors can help high school students begin to examine self-concept and life themes through their hobbies, activities, and formal or informal work experience.

Savickas (2005) indicated that beliefs about self and life are reflections of one's purpose, and that one's purpose truly explains career behaviors. That is, people make choices that fit with who they are and who they want to be. It is through subjective assessment, where life patterns and themes emerge, that Savickas (2005) says an individual's purpose becomes elucidated. Later in this chapter, we illustrate how the *Career Style Interview* introduced in Chapter 5 can be used to facilitate the process of examining purpose through self-concept and life themes.

11TH-GRADE CURRICULUM DEVELOPMENT

Career and college readiness curricula for 11th-grade students, like all other grades, should follow a logical, developmental, and sequential order. Although we are advocating the American School Counselor Association (ASCA; 2014) Mindsets and Behaviors listed in Table 14.1 as a focus for 11th-grade curriculum, we encourage school counselors to consider the populations at their schools when designing and developing all program components. School counselors may wish to emphasize interventions for 11th-grade students that allow for concrete and experiential opportunities to engage in career-related tasks (examples include internships, job shadowing, career interviews, and resume writing). We illustrate some such present interventions in the next section.

TABLE 14.1   ASCA Mindsets and Behaviors for 11th-Grade Curriculum Planning Focus

CATEGORY 1: MINDSETS STANDARDS		
Self-confidence in ability to succeed Understanding that postsecondary education and lifelong learning are necessary for long-term career success Belief in using abilities to their fullest to achieve high-quality results and outcomes		
CATEGORY 2: BEHAVIOR STANDARDS		
Learning Strategies	**Self-Management Skills**	**Social Skills**
Identify long- and short-term academic, career, and socioemotional goals	Demonstrate ability to delay immediate gratification for long-term rewards	Use effective oral and written communication skills and listening skills
Gather evidence and consider multiple perspectives to make informed decisions	Demonstrate perseverance to achieve long- and short-term goals	Use leadership and teamwork skills to work effectively in diverse teams
Participate in enrichment and extracurricular activities	Demonstrate ability to manage transitions and ability to adapt to changing situations and responsibilities	Demonstrate advocacy skills and ability to assert self, when necessary

INTERVENTIONS: COLLABORATING WITH TEACHERS

As we discussed in previous chapters, teachers can continue to play very important roles in helping 11th-grade students prepare for their futures. By partnering with teachers, school counselors can expand opportunities for students to identify mastery experiences, articulate their strengths, and develop challenging performance goals. In the following we provide specific suggestions for collaborating with teachers in this regard.

Using Clubs and Activities to Facilitate Mastery Experiences

Consistent with Savickas's (2005) belief that the factors comprising vocational personality are evident in the activities in which people engage, it makes sense to find instances to help students identify strengths through their activities and hobbies. Because teachers often tend to be engaged with students as club advisors and coaches, they have frequent opportunities to monitor students and recognize students' strengths. These advisors and coaches (who are often parents or community members) may or may not, however, do anything when they notice innate abilities or talents in their students. School counselors can encourage these individuals to be proactive and intentional in identifying strengths and offering encouragement (verbal persuasion). In Exhibit 14.1, we offer an example of a teacher initiating a conversation with a student and being intentional in her use of verbal persuasion.

In Exhibit 14.1, Mrs. Talley could have very easily made a comparison between Maria's behavior in class and what she was seeing on the project. Her comment might have been something along the lines of, "You were so quiet in class last year, I never expected to see you taking charge the way you are now." We all have heard many people share that kind of feedback, meant with the best of intentions but sometimes heard by the student as condescending. Rather than mention weaknesses or negative characteristics, teachers and school personnel can simply choose to highlight the positive things they are seeing, in the hopes that students internalize their feedback.

Before advisors and coaches can offer encouragement in activities, students need to get involved in activities. Classroom teachers often are in the best position to identify students' interests and strengths, as well as encourage their involvement in meaningful activities where they can develop or hone their talents. Teachers can quickly pick up on which students possess innate talents and which students express strong interest and persistence. With intentional effort, teachers can facilitate opportunities for mastery experiences by recommending that students join various clubs or activities. For example, math teachers might identify students whom they believe would do well on the math team or who might benefit from participating in a robotics competition. Similarly, English teachers might identify students who could do well on the debate team or in drama club.

EXHIBIT 14.1
Teacher Highlights Student Strengths

The purpose of the Key Club is to foster school and community relationships. Students work all year to implement a spring activity that will serve to connect the school and community and to raise money for a designated charity. About halfway through the year the advisor, Mrs. Talley, begins to notice the leadership role that Maria is playing. She taught Maria in a History class last year, and recalls her having been very shy and reserved, but quite bright. The energy, initiative, and confidence she sees Maria displaying in this task are quite different from what she saw in class.

Mrs. Talley decides to approach Maria. She mentions how impressed she is with Maria's leadership, initiative, and assertiveness in relation to the project. Maria responds by explaining her interest in the project, talking about how she feels passionate about it because of her own personal experiences related to the charity cause as well as from her general interest in sociology. Mrs. Talley then takes the opportunity to provide encouragement and to comment on how happy she is to experience Maria's passion and how it seems this type of work might make her very happy. She expresses curiosity about Maria's future career plans.

Many students are not aware of the different clubs or activities available at school or in the community. Others might be aware, but also might be reluctant to join for any number of reasons—because none of their friends are members, because they lack self-efficacy, or because they have assumptions about what the experience might be like. A little encouragement (i.e., verbal persuasion) from teachers who can share why the activity might be beneficial or why they think the student would be a good fit can sometimes be enough to pique students' interest. As we discussed in the previous chapter, students engage in activities when they believe they can succeed and when they believe positive outcomes will result from their involvement (Lent et al., 1994). Tapping into the power of peer influence, teachers also might invite current members of different clubs and activities to talk about their experiences and the benefits of joining various organizations. This kind of information can help students more clearly envision potential outcomes of becoming involved. Simply seeing other students with whom they sense a connection or similarity to themselves can provide the impetus for them to take a risk on something new.

In addition to extracurricular activities, teachers can include mastery experiences in the classroom. For example, through a federal grant program, one school district was able to redesign all of their science classrooms and to provide learning materials that were very hands-on. In biology lab, students had the equipment and space to dissect animals, in the physics lab students worked on designing and developing models of bridges, and in chemistry class students had the equipment to run and evaluate experiments. These types of hands-on, mastery activities are helpful for the learning process, but also enable students to envision themselves doing the work of a biologist, chemist, or physicist. Teachers should be encouraged to seek the professional development and resources necessary to provide these kinds of activities.

In considering accessibility of activities, teachers and school personnel should be aware of the associated costs. It is very likely that some students do not join activities because they cannot afford to do so. Schools might consider engaging in discussions about if and how to support students who possess strong talents but who lack opportunities because of financial concerns. As we discussed in the beginning of this book, students from low socioeconomic status (SES) families often have lower aspirations because they have not had the same kinds of opportunities or exposure to career and educational options that tend to be more readily accessible to students from higher SES families. For that reason alone, it becomes all the more important to provide experiential opportunities in school when possible. Ideally, schools should have support systems (such as a student activity fund) in place to ensure accessibility of activities and clubs for all students.

Creating Resumes to Highlight Mastery Experiences

English classes are logical places for students to work on a variety of writing projects, such as resumes. In fact, because many students who are enrolled in general or lower-level English classes enter the workforce right after graduating, it is common for teachers of those English classes to include resume and cover letter writing in their curriculum. Unfortunately, for many 11th-grade students who are enrolled in AP or honors classes, a resume may not be a regular part of their curriculum. We believe that all students can benefit from preparing resumes, and school counselors can partner with English teachers in this regard. Later in this chapter (see Exhibit 14.4), you can read about a school counselor who used this and many other collaborative interventions with her high school students.

In keeping with the idea that mastery experiences and outcome expectations inform future performance goals and attainment, resume writing can be approached with an emphasis on helping students identify experiences and successes relevant to their future goals. For example, using the resume preparation form in Exhibit 14.2, a teacher could assign students to gather the background information needed to write their resume in a way that requires them to identify accomplishments and strengths. Hopefully through the process of completing this form, students will become more aware of their ability/past performance and mastery experiences.

After students compile their resume background information, school counselors could partner with the English teachers to conduct lessons during which they help students make the connections between their experiences, skills, and future goals. While the teachers could focus on helping students format and write their resumes, the school counselor can engage in targeted career discussions. Through this activity, students who might benefit from additional career and college development assistance could easily be identified. See Figure 14.2 for an example of how the student example in Exhibit 14.2 would translate into a resume.

EXHIBIT 14.2
Sample Resume Preparation Form

Pull out your graduation plan/program of study, and use that information as a starting point for completing this form.

1. List your career goal—the occupation you would like to pursue:
- *I want to be a preschool teacher.*

2a. List any paid or volunteer jobs you have held in which you did things related to that occupation:	2b. List examples of things you accomplished in those jobs:
• *Babysit* • *Volunteer at the children's summer program at my church*	• *Kept kids entertained* • *Monitored child's behavior* • *Used fun activities* • *Was team leader last summer*

3. List any hobbies or activities you have participated in that relate to that occupation:
- *I like doing crafty things and scrapbooking.*
- *I like to play games.*

4. List the school subjects/classes you completed, and the grades you received, that relate to that occupation:
- *Parenting class—B, Art—A, Chorus—A*
- *Overall grade point average (GPA)—3.64*

5. List any other experiences you have had that you think are relevant to your occupational goal:
- *Not sure*

6. Go back through what you listed previously and * any items that you think would be important to include on your resume—as evidence of your potential for success in your desired occupation.

To make this type of assignment appealing to English teachers, especially those teaching advanced classes, an extra component could be added that would connect back to the basic career and college readiness skills that we reviewed earlier in this book. To foster and assess critical thinking skills, the resume and an accompanying cover letter could be used as part of an assignment focusing on how well students are able to make a convincing argument. Specifically, English teachers could grade the resume and cover letter not only based on the required format, but also on how well the student convinced the reader of his or her potential for success; that is, how well the content supported his or her career and college goals.

TARGETED COUNSELING INTERVENTIONS

A large number of 11th-grade students usually are not quite certain about their career paths, and they might benefit from creative ways to explore possible options outside of the more traditional trait-and-factor approaches used in many schools. Other students in 11th grade have difficulty narrowing

FIGURE 14.2 Resume Generated From Content in Exhibit 14.2

Ashley B. Peters

1234 MayBerry Lane
Abby Creek, WA 97825
(878) 555-4321
apeters@gmail.com

Objective
To become a preschool teacher.

Education
Abby Creek High School
Expected Graduation – May 2014
Honors Student
GPA – 3.64/4.00

Work Experience

Volunteer, Children's Summer Program   Summer 2009 and 2010

Abby Creek Church

- Served as Team Leader (2010) for a staff of four student volunteers
- Planned and set up activities for children based on predetermined themes
- Led craft activities for kids in grades 1 and 2

Babysitter   2009-present

Three families in Abby Creek (references available upon request)
- Worked with children ages 1-10
- Fed and cared for infants
- Helped one child learn to tie his shoes
- Provided educational activities for children in grades 1-5

Activities
- Abby Creek High School Chorus
- Abby Creek High School Yearbook Club
- Abby Creek High School Girl's Track

Skills
- Singing
- Art (painting)

---

down college choices, or have made tentative choices of schools that don't seem to closely match their desired majors. The interventions discussed in the following could be implemented with individuals or with small groups of students who are struggling with similar career and college development concerns.

Narrowing Down Possible Career Paths via the *Career Style Interview*

As we discussed in Chapter 5, the *Career Style Interview* (Savickas, 2005) can be a useful tool for helping students examine personal interests and themes that might inform possible career options. This type of assessment can be particularly beneficial for students who have Holland Code profiles that lack differentiation (i.e., their RIASEC scores are very similar across categories). When students have an aptitude for a lot of things and are interested in a lot of things, they often need extra assistance in trying to figure out how to narrow down career options. They often cannot simply answer questions like, "What are you most interested in?" or "In which classes do you do the best?"

The constructionist approach of the *Career Style Interview* can help noteworthy interests and skills emerge. Students who are used to answering concrete questions about their interests and abilities through assessments, like those offered through the Kuder® (2006) system, sometimes are thrown off by this type of subjective interview. Nevertheless, school counselors who use the *Career Style Interview* should make sure to explain up front why they are asking certain questions and how they will use the information to help students narrow down career and college possibilities.

School counselors also can be creative in how they approach the *Career Style Interview*. As suggested in Chapter 5, although the interview can be conducted in person, school counselors realistically do not have time to engage in long interviews with many students. As such, they might first use an introductory session to briefly review the assessment, then they can ask the student to complete the assessment as homework to be turned in to them sometime before the two of them meet again. Students can be asked to provide responses in writing, or they might be encouraged to create a collage of images or words in response to each interview item. Sometimes students cannot generate the exact words they want to express their ideas, but they might find pictures or lyrics that very clearly capture their experiences. Allowing for flexibility in the format of the interview helps to accommodate different learning styles.

By turning in their responses in advance, students give school counselors time to review the responses and look for themes, which allows them to make the most of their next session together. The follow-up session with the student could then be devoted to reviewing the counselor's and student's interpretation, soliciting feedback from the student, and generating next steps. The example in Exhibit 14.3 illustrates a sample *Career Style Interview* interpretation session between a counselor and student.

EXHIBIT 14.3
Career Style Interview Interpretation Session

A student submitted the following written responses:

- **Role models:** when I was little, it was all superheroes—I always liked the idea of catching the bad guys and saving people; I also admire my grandfather—he died helping put out a fire
- **Books:** ones by Sherlock Holmes and by James Patterson
- **Magazines:** I don't read magazines
- **Leisure activities:** baseball, video games, sudoku
- **School subjects:** History, English, Physical Education
- **Mottos:** everyone gets what they deserve
- **Ambitions:** make my grandfather proud, play baseball
- **Decisions (how made):** I talk to people (friends or parents) to get their opinions

(continued)

EXHIBIT 14.3 (continued)

The counselor generated the following:

- **Career style**—he values communication and collaborative problem solving; he expects people to take responsibility for their actions and to be held accountable
- **Career path**—his future career likely will involve using analytical and communication skills
- **Interests**—he appreciates the humanities, communication, and being physically active
- **Occupational prospects**—many areas in the Law and Public Safety cluster
- **Guiding fiction**—I will make a difference if I can help to protect others from harm

Counselor–Client Meeting (Abbreviated)

Counselor: So, I've reviewed the answers (see previous text) you provided last week to the *Career Style Interview.* I have identified some patterns, but I'm wondering if anything stood out to you as you reflected on what you wrote?

Student: Not really. I didn't know what to put for some of the questions.

Counselor: That's okay. Even when students give short responses, sometimes patterns come out. I definitely noticed some patterns for you. Would you like me to tell you what I picked up on?

Student: Sure, I'm kinda curious.

Counselor: Well, for one thing, it seemed like you connect with law enforcement and protectors—superheroes, detectives, police, firefighters. I noticed that in your role models and books, and kind of in your motto. Did you notice that at all?

Student: I hadn't, but I see what you're saying. I guess I always have liked the idea of helping make sure people are safe.

Counselor: I wonder if there are any other places in your life where that idea of protecting comes up—maybe in some of the video games you play or things you like about history?

(Counselor explores this further since student had not expanded on those items in his previous responses.)

Counselor: So we've determined, then, that you have a pretty long history of being interested in these kinds of protecting and detective roles, and it crosses over many activities you engage in. Even though this wasn't really an area that you initially could narrow down as worth exploring, I'm wondering if you might want to now? We're really talking about the Law and Public Safety career cluster.

Student: Yeah—that actually sounds a lot like something that I might like.

(continued)

EXHIBIT 14.3 (continued)
Career Style Interview Interpretation Session

Counselor: Well, there are a lot of different possibilities within that cluster, some that require college and others that don't. I know you also weren't sure about how much education you wanted to get, so maybe we can keep exploring your responses to see if we can make some decisions about that, too?

Student: Sure.

Counselor: Well, a few things stand out to me from your responses that I thought were worth pointing out. First is I see that you like history and English. I also know that you have a very good GPA and scored high on the PSAT. If you were to pursue something like law, which would require a 4-year college degree and a law school degree, based only on your responses, it seems like that might be interesting to you and that you would be good at that. I also notice that you like PE and baseball—being active and athletic. Your grandfather was a firefighter. Maybe the idea of doing something that is pretty active physically would be more appealing—like being a firefighter or police officer. Those types of positions don't require formal college, but they do require specialized training. Finally, I see that you like detective books and you also like sudoku puzzles. I'm thinking maybe you like figuring things out—solving problems. Becoming a police detective or something similar might appeal to you, and you could achieve that goal with or without college. I do notice that you want to play baseball, though, and I know you are pretty good. Is playing in college something you're hoping to do—have you talked with your coaches about that?

Student: I really do want to play college ball, and it sounds like I have a good chance . . . so I think I do want to try to go to college.

Counselor: So with college in mind, what do you think of my interpretations? What do you think about some of those possibilities?

(Counselor and client continue to explore career options as well as educational requirements.)

Exploring Postsecondary Options With Students Who Envision College in Their Futures

Many students in 11th grade will express their intentions to pursue postsecondary education, yet a large number will approach that decision as they do their career decisions; they will choose colleges that are familiar to them or ones that their friends plan to attend. With this awareness, school counselors should be very intentional about providing opportunities to increase students' (and their parents') awareness of the variety of postsecondary institutions that exist. They also should help students find a good match; students need to know if the institutions they are considering offer majors that match their career goals.

Students also need to consider what type of environment they might prefer or that would best support their academic and social needs. General factors such as cost, financial aid, location, class size, and religious affiliation (to name but a few) are important to explore. Students with disabilities ideally would want to explore the types of disability support services available to them on a particular campus, first-generation college students might specifically examine the general college transition programs available, and students seeking to connect with others like themselves might explore the availability of student organizations such as the Latino Student Association or the Gay/Straight Alliance.

School counselors might already have college comparison forms that students can use to record information about postsecondary institutions, but numerous worksheets also are available online. The authors conducted an online search using the phrase "college comparison worksheet" that generated a long list of resources. These types of forms could be introduced during large group sessions with students and parents/guardians and then discussed more thoroughly during individual or smaller group sessions.

Given the continued importance of peers during high school, the use of peers can be important in the college exploration process. For many students, seeing someone like them being successful (vicarious learning) can provide the impetus to persist. As such, school counselors should be conscientious about trying to secure the involvement of a group of individuals who are representative of the current student body—hopefully students will identify someone with whom they feel a connection.

For example, every high school has graduates who go on to attend a variety of postsecondary institutions, and numerous ways exist to involve them in helping future graduates explore colleges. In a more general approach, recent graduates who are doing well in college could be invited back to participate in a panel discussion. Their focus would be to (a) identify steps the current students should be taking now to prepare for college, (b) discuss their experiences in exploring and choosing colleges, and (c) talk about characteristics that have been important to their success.

For a more targeted approach, recent graduates also could be invited back to talk about their specific institutions or majors. For example, knowing that everyone experiences a setting differently, a number of graduates who are all attending the same institution could be invited back to compare and contrast their experiences at that institution. Similarly, a number of students who are majoring in the same degree areas but across different institutions could be invited to discuss their experiences across those different schools. Additionally, a group of graduates who are now first-generation college students could participate in an informational workshop for students and their parents. The possibilities are endless for how targeted opportunities could be set up involving the use of peers and the needs of numerous populations could be addressed in this manner. To ensure accessibility and to enable new topics to be presented each year, school counselors might consider preserving these kinds of workshops and discussions electronically, either as webinars that can be posted on the school website or as DVDs that can be checked out for viewing at home. They also should consider ways in which they can accommodate the needs of parents who do not speak English.

Helping All Students and Their Families "Visit" Colleges

Students and their families can probably best learn about colleges by visiting them; there is nothing like walking around a campus and interacting with people to truly get a sense of what it might be like to be a student there. During the spring of the junior year and the summer following that year, many students participate in college tours and visits. Postsecondary schools all have various options (ranging from weekend events to afternoon tours) for orienting prospective students and their families to campus and their programs. By discussing these visits proactively with students and their families, school counselors can provide suggestions for how to maximize the visit and gather important information that may or may not be included in the planned activities. Visiting schools can be expensive, however, and not realistic for many families.

In order to increase accessibility to postsecondary schools that may not be geographically close, school counselors can encourage the use of virtual tours. Websites like www.campustours.com or www.ecampustours.com provide access to information about schools across the United States. An online search using the phrase "college virtual tour" will pull up links to other similar sites that can assist students in identifying and exploring schools based on a variety of factors (e.g., location, religious affiliation). Many postsecondary institutions have virtual tour links on their own websites as well, so school counselors could help students access those links directly. In preparing students and families for viewing the virtual tours, school counselors can suggest they have the college comparison worksheets handy so they can make notes and list questions that may not have been answered.

Assigning Summer Homework

The summer before the senior year of high school might be considered one of the most important in terms of career development, especially for students who plan to attend college. School counselors can encourage students and their families to take full advantage of the summer months to complete tasks and participate in activities that will help them be prepared to submit college applications in the fall. We already discussed the importance of college visits, and the summer months are a good time for students and their families to visit any schools they are still considering. As they are gathering final comparison information about prospective schools, students also can be encouraged to create a list of application deadlines and required materials for the application process.

Regarding the application process, many postsecondary institutions require some sort of application essay, and its importance varies from school to school. In addition to hosting a workshop on application essays during the school year in conjunction with the English teachers, school counselors can encourage students to prepare draft essays over the summer. If they come back to school at the start of their senior year with drafts, they can seek feedback early, leaving time for revisions before applications are due.

EXHIBIT 14.4
Voices From the Field: Preparing Students in Career and Technical
Education Programs for Postsecondary Transitions

Bianca W. Brown, EdD

Former School Counselor, Port Hudson Academy
Assistant Principal of Assessment and Student Services

As a counselor for one of our state's premier public high schools, my goal was to academically advise students to take the most rigorous course work that will adequately prepare them for postsecondary education. Over 75% of those students planned to enter a 4-year college or university upon graduating from high school. The remaining 25% of students hoped to attend either a 2-year college, enlist in the military, or enter the workforce. In 2013, our district opened a satellite campus for students to experience a blended learning (online/traditional) atmosphere as well as course work in the career and technical field. During the process, my superintendent asked that I serve as the school counselor for that campus. Traditionally, students who attended this campus shared a passion for hands-on workplace experiences and course work such as auto technology and carpentry. Additionally, these students were eager to graduate from high school while earning training and a credential that would lead to a viable career. Our programs allowed students to gain all of those aspects to education. For me, both counseling experiences allowed me to approach academic and career counseling in a different manner based on the child's goal after high school. Overall, I discovered a common theme among parents; they shared the same desire: to witness their child's success in both school and life.

While working at Port Hudson, I hosted various activities to prepare our students for their future careers. Being a member of a professional team who shared the same vision allowed me to create remarkable opportunities for students. For example, in an effort to adequately prepare students for postsecondary education and the workforce, I hosted an annual college and career week for students to take field trips to college campuses as well as job sites to witness firsthand what a job and/or career would entail. Additionally, I invited an etiquette trainer to demonstrate professional appearance and demeanor for success. After the training, students received preparation time in order to practice interview skills. I also partnered with our English department so that students received resume writing assistance. Following the resume writing, students were invited to participate in on-campus interviews with local industries and other organizations, including business partners, to employ future auto technicians and carpenters. This practice was essential to our program as it secured future employment and prepared students for the workforce.

Working with students who plan to enter the workforce forced me to take risks and create practical opportunities for students. I felt it was important for students to understand all educational training beyond high school is considered postsecondary education. I educated students

(continued)

EXHIBIT 14.4 (continued)
Voices From the Field: Preparing Students in Career and Technical
Education Programs for Postsecondary Transitions

on the requirements needed to graduate from high school. I also provided them with information that led to postsecondary education and/or a viable career upon completing high school. I believe it is essential to equip students with knowledge and tools necessary to make sound decisions about their future. With that in mind, I encouraged all students to learn beyond high school to create opportunities for advancement in their future profession.

Working with a career and technical education program is essential to our community. It is very important to build partnerships with local business and community members in order to create pipelines to careers for students. Additionally, our profession builds partnerships with the community to provide resources to students in need. As a counselor, I noticed many students attending the campus were from low income and at-risk backgrounds. With this in mind, I knew it was even more important for stakeholders to work together to meet the needs of students through donations, school involvement, job placement/ job shadowing, and more. Partnering with the community was essential to the success of our school.

I consider our Career and Technical Center as a success and asset to our school district. The school provided an alternative to the traditional high school setting, which enabled students to graduate from high school or earn a GED diploma. Our school district experienced higher percentages in graduation rates and school performance scores due to academic growth within the low income and at-risk population. Much of the success may be attributed to the campus. The school provided students with viable careers and certifications in auto technology and carpentry. Most importantly, students were able to pursue postsecondary education through partnerships formed with ABC Welding School, which provides additional training in career fields.

Finally, all students can benefit from focusing on building their resumes over the summer through work and/or volunteer experiences. Students who are preparing to attend college might get a part-time job to help save some money for college. They also could use paid or volunteer work to gain valuable experience related to their future career plans. Similarly, individuals who plan to enter the workforce after college could start looking for employment that would boost their potential for finding a good job upon graduation.

SUMMARY

In this chapter, we focused on mastery experiences as a critical focus of career- and college-related interventions. Eleventh-grade students should be encouraged to engage in a variety of activities so they can hone in on their talents and skills; their mastery experiences will shape their interests and goals. Further, opportunities for vicarious learning and encouragement can be provided through school-wide initiatives and connections with peers and the community. Counselors and educators should be intentional in their efforts to influence students' self-efficacy by helping them identify and develop their strengths and make connections to future goals.

···> Test Your Knowledge

1. Discuss which students might benefit from something like the *Career Style Interview* and explain why.
2. Compare and contrast Lent, Brown, and Hackett's (1994) performance model with the interest model discussed in the previous chapter. Explain how these models jointly explain career and college choice and behavior for students in mid-adolescence.

REFERENCES

American School Counselor Association. (2014). *ASCA mindsets & behaviors for student success: K-12 college- and career-readiness standards for every student.* Alexandria, VA: Author.

Holland, J. L. (1973). *Making vocational choices: A theory of careers.* Englewood Cliffs, NJ: Prentice Hall.

Kuder, F. (2006). *Kuder career planning system.* Adel, IA: Kuder, Inc.

Lent, R. W., Brown, S. D., & Hackett, G. (1994). Toward a unifying social cognitive theory of career and academic interest, choice, and performance. *Journal of Vocational Behavior, 45,* 79–122.

Marcia, J. E. (1987). The identity status approach to the study of ego identity development. In T. Honess & K. Yardley (Eds.), *Self and identity: Perspectives across the lifespan* (pp. 161–171). New York, NY: Routledge.

Savickas, M. L. (2002). Career construction: A developmental theory of vocational behavior. In D. Brown & Associates (Eds.), *Career choice and development* (4th ed., pp. 149–205). San Francisco, CA: Jossey-Bass.

Savickas, M. L. (2005). The theory and practice of career construction. In S. D. Brown & R. W. Lent (Eds.), *Career development and counseling: Putting theory and research to work* (pp. 42–70). Hoboken, NJ: John Wiley & Sons.

Super, D. E. (1980). A life-span, life-space approach to career development. *Journal of Vocational Behavior, 16*(3), 282–298. http://dx.doi.org/10.1016/0001-8791(80)90056-1

Turner S. L., & Conkel Ziebell, J. L. (2011). The career beliefs of inner city adolescents. *Professional School Counseling, 15,* 1–14.

FIFTEEN

Career and College Readiness for Grade 12: Postsecondary Transitions

A student's senior year of high school can bring about many conflicting emotions, including excitement, fear, sadness, hope, and even apathy. Some students would prefer to remain in high school forever rather than face the unknowns and responsibilities of the real world, while others can't escape fast enough. No matter how students feel, in order to be successful after high school, they all need to spend some time during their senior year focusing on their future careers. In this chapter, we discuss factors important to their postsecondary transition as well as interventions that could be implemented to help them move forward.

DEVELOPMENTAL OVERVIEW

Students in 12th grade still fall cleanly into Erikson's (1963) *identity versus role confusion* stage. Although many of them can pretty clearly articulate their interests and abilities and identify future career and postsecondary educational goals, a large majority of students are uncertain about who they are and who they want to become. The importance of peers and the experimentation with various roles that we discussed in previous chapters continues into and beyond the senior year of high school.

Further, as students move closer to finishing high school, a sense of urgency to make decisions can set in. This urgency can come not only from parents putting pressure on them to make decisions, but also from their own competitiveness to keep up with peers who solidify their decisions more quickly than they do, as well as from the reality that decisions about college are, to some degree, time limited. Unfortunately, this kind of pressure can lead some students to make decisions in haste and based on the interests and values of others rather than their own desires.

Peer relationships continue to play important roles, and romantic relationships also take on more prominence as students often consider future plans with their partners in mind. Many students limit their future options based on friends or romantic partners, prioritizing their relationships over their own dreams or desires. These are the students who choose to live at home and either work or attend a local college because their friends/partner plans to stay in town, or the students who choose to attend a college only because their friends/partner is doing so. The idea of leaving behind a support system or significant other can be overwhelming to students who may naturally be a little scared about moving forward into something unknown. By making decisions that will allow them to have a familiar face or support system, students' choices may not feel as scary.

In addition to the typical pressures associated with graduating, students who are in their senior year of high school experience one specific milestone that can affect their decision making; they reach the age of consent. Many adolescents start to exert their independence during high school, especially as they secure driver's licenses and part-time employment. By the senior year and as they get closer to age 18, many students start to feel more comfortable expressing their own opinions and making decisions that their parents may or may not support. It is not uncommon to hear students and parents talk about changes in their relationships that involve more arguments. As students struggle to break away, parents do what they can to regain control.

The confusion that many high school seniors experience related to their identities, their independence, their relationships, and their future suggests that interventions targeting 12th-grade students should be designed to help them and their parents navigate this transition to life after high school. Activities to further allow students to gain self-awareness, identify their values, and make decisions with future goals in mind are discussed later in this chapter. Additionally, suggestions for working with parents to help them appreciate and cope with the uncertainty of their children's futures are shared.

RELEVANT CAREER THEORY: SAVICKAS (2005) AND BROWN (2002)

In this chapter, we expand on Savickas's *Theory of Career Construction* (2005), which we introduced in Chapter 14, to discuss how it explains career development behaviors. We also introduce another career theory, Brown's *Values-Based Theory* (1996). Brown discussed the ways in which values, which have cognitive and emotional components, influence career goals and behaviors. These two theories provide the framework for interventions we review later in this chapter.

Savickas's Theory of Career Construction

In the previous chapter, we discussed how Savickas's theory could be useful for working with students who have difficulty narrowing down career options based only on trait and factor approaches. Through the identification of a construct called *career adaptability*, the Theory of Career Construction also helps to explain the career-related behaviors that students engage in over time.

Similar to Super's *Life-Span, Life-Space Theory* (1980), in the Theory of Career Construction, Savickas (2005) discussed five developmental stages: growth, exploration, establishment, management, and disengagement. The growth and exploration stages are relevant for P–12 students, and most

12th-grade students would be in the exploration stage. Successful completion of each stage leads to greater likelihood of success for task completion in future stages. Savickas indicated that to successfully transition from task to task, individuals must possess *career adaptability*.

According to Savickas (2005), career adaptability is "a psychosocial construct that denotes an individual's readiness and resources for coping with current and imminent vocational development tasks, occupational transitions, and personal traumas" (p. 51). It allows people to implement their self-concept and regulate their behavior. Savickas identified four dimensions of career adaptability as: (a) concern, (b) control, (c) curiosity, and (d) confidence.

Career concern refers to an individual's interest in his or her future (Savickas, 2005). In addition to recognizing that planning for future activities is important, understanding the connection between past and current experiences and behaviors and future goals is critical to successfully navigate career development tasks. Savickas believes that optimism is also important in fostering a concern for the future. Individuals who are pessimistic about future outcomes are more likely to exhibit what Savickas refers to as *career indifference*.

According to Savickas (2005), *career control* refers to individuals believing that it is their responsibility to construct their careers. Savickas emphasizes that in both individualistic and collectivistic cultures, individuals still can control their careers; it is not as much about making decisions independently as it is about feeling that you have some level of control over your choice. Choosing to take into consideration the opinions of others, such as family, still reflects control. For some people, career or college options may be limited (e.g., everyone in your family expects you to be a doctor, or your father and I will only pay for you to attend a state school), but personal control exists in an individual's ability to make that limited choice meaningful and personal (e.g., meeting your parents' wishes of you becoming a doctor, but choosing to become a pediatrician because you want to help kids as opposed to being a dermatologist like your dad, or applying for scholarships to help you afford an out-of-state school). *Career indecision* is the opposite of career control. People have a difficult time putting energy into making career decisions if deep down they do not believe that the outcome will be within their control.

Career curiosity refers to being inquisitive about people and work (Savickas, 2005). Curiosity leads people to seek out self and occupational knowledge and also to be willing to try new things. Savickas did not identify a specific term to refer to a lack of career curiosity, but he indicated that people who are not curious tend to lack accurate information about themselves and the world of work. As such, these individuals might develop unrealistic plans or expectations.

Finally, *career confidence* refers to one's sense of self-efficacy about planning and carrying out a course of action to implement his or her career choices (Savickas, 2005). Concepts like mastery experiences, from *Social Cognitive Career Theory* (Lent, Brown, & Hackett, 1994), are particularly useful in understanding career confidence. Savickas explained that a lack of career confidence results in *career inhibition*; people who are inhibited often lack the courage to try new things or fail to persist when challenged.

In a nutshell, school counselors should want students to be concerned about their future and feel a sense of control over it. They also should hope that students demonstrate curiosity about it and a willingness to explore themselves and careers (and colleges), as well as feel confident in their ability to achieve their goals. By identifying where students fall on these four dimensions, school counselors can identify relevant interventions to target any of the dimensions that are low.

Brown's Values-Based Theory

Brown's (2002) theory focuses on the importance of a person's values in his or her career decision making. Brown explained that values are what we use to evaluate our and others' actions; they are those things that are important to us and that influence our behavior and goals. As such, values that we prioritize inform our occupational choices. When our occupations do not match our values, over time, we become dissatisfied. School counselors proactively can help students identify and consider values as they are making important life decisions.

When discussing values, Brown (2002) not only includes what he considers to be work values—things such as helping others or being able to use one's creativity—but he also includes cultural values like collectivism versus individualism. Brown indicated that values can be examined through standardized assessment instruments like the *Life Values Inventory* (Brown & Crace, 2002), or through more informal assessments such as card sorts or checklists. Many of the computerized career guidance programs widely used by schools also have a values exploration component. Once values are identified, counseling sessions can be used to help students explore career and college choices that would match prioritized values and also to integrate interests, abilities, and values into their future decisions. Interventions we present later in this chapter demonstrate a focus on values.

12TH-GRADE CURRICULUM DEVELOPMENT

By 12th grade, school counselors should use the ASCA (2014) Mindsets and Behaviors to design curricula that allow students to reflect upon and apply the skills and knowledge they have developed throughout their schooling. Interventions for 12th-grade students should allow them opportunities to review the information they have gathered about themselves and careers; to set concrete goals that match their interests, abilities, and values; and to complete initial steps toward achieving those goals. The curriculum should assist students in beginning the postsecondary transition (Table 15.1).

COUNSELING AND EDUCATIONAL INTERVENTIONS

Skills and knowledge needed for successful postsecondary transitions are highlighted in the interventions we present in the following. In this section, we share interventions targeting both students and parents. We also focus on interventions that are grounded in the two theories we presented earlier in this chapter.

TABLE 15.1 ASCA Mindsets and Behaviors for 12th-Grade Curriculum Planning Focus

CATEGORY 1: MINDSETS STANDARDS		
Self-confidence in ability to succeed Understanding that postsecondary education and lifelong learning are necessary for long-term career success Belief in using abilities to their fullest to achieve high-quality results and outcomes		
CATEGORY 2: BEHAVIOR STANDARDS		
Identify long- and short-term academic, career, and socioemotional goals	Demonstrate ability to assume responsibility	Demonstrate ethical decision making and social responsibility
Demonstrate critical-thinking skills to make informed decisions	Demonstrate perseverance to achieve long- and short-term goals	Use leadership and teamwork skills to work effectively in diverse teams
Gather evidence and consider multiple perspectives to make informed decisions	Demonstrate ability to manage transitions and ability to adapt to changing situations and responsibilities	Demonstrate social maturity and behaviors appropriate to the situation and environment

Summer Interventions

As noted in Chapter 14, having homework (e.g., write draft college application essays) between the junior and senior year is one way to ensure that students are staying on track toward their career and college readiness goals. Another option is to hold formal events, such as workshops for parents and students. During these events, students can receive information about writing college application essays, interviewing for jobs, and other topics. One school counselor, Mrs. Hinote, ran a summer program called "Seize the Day" (Exhibit 15.1).

Teachers Helping Students Become "Concerned" About Their Futures

As students get closer and closer to graduation, many find it easier and often preferable to avoid making decisions rather than face the difficult choices they have ahead of them. Further, by not thinking about their life after high school, they can put off dealing with the conflicting feelings they have about their futures. Teachers can help students consider their futures through class assignments, which can be less intimidating and sometimes easier to do than if they were just asked to talk about their plans.

Although 12th-grade students might be enrolled in a variety of English classes, a common assignment could be put into place to help them practice their writing skills and think about their futures. By having students write an autobiography that would reflect their life at age 25 or 30, teachers can encourage students to dream big. By collaborating with teachers in this endeavor, school counselors can help to design the assignment in a way that will require students to articulate important things like what they will be doing, how they got there, what their strengths are, and other accomplishments that came

EXHIBIT 15.1
Seize the Day Summer Program for High School Seniors

Seize the Day was a 2-day career and college readiness summer program developed by Mrs. Hinote to help students between their junior and senior years develop skills and make informed decisions about their postsecondary options. Partnering with the community, she was able to run the program for little to no expense. Volunteer community members who had expertise in many of the content areas served as guest speakers for the seminar sessions. Further, local restaurants donated breakfast and lunch. She was able to offer a variety of seminars, and students could choose the seminars most relevant to their postsecondary plans. For example, some of the seminar topics included essay writing, financial literacy, using technology to search college admissions information, participating in volunteer service, preparing a resume, and developing college study skills.

Financial presentations were provided for a range of monetary issues including opening bank accounts, saving money, using credit wisely, understanding the difference between a credit card and debit card, and navigating college financial aid. These presentations were provided through a local bank and credit union.

In a college planning seminar, students were given the opportunity to create timelines for their senior year that document deadlines for relevant activities including but not limited to things such as attending college fairs, taking the Scholastic Aptitude Test (SAT), submitting college applications, and submitting financial aid forms. In the career readiness seminars, students were given information about the types of communication skills that employers are looking for, and they participated in games and activities that demonstrated these skills. In the job interviewing seminar, students learned about and role-played interviewing skills. They also could sign up to participate in mock interviews with community members. Although parents were not included in this activity, the format could be changed to an evening program and parents could be invited to participate.

along the way. Curricular objectives might include students being able to "articulate a concrete future plan" and "accurately identifying steps needed to reach their goal."

After reviewing the students' papers, school counselors could use the information in a couple of ways. For example, they could identify any students who appear to be lacking concern about their future; that is, those who did not meet the objective of having a concrete future plan. Additionally, they can look for consistency between the futures articulated in the students' papers and the behaviors the students are engaging in currently: Are they doing the things they would need to do now in order to achieve that future? Finally, school counselors can pay attention to the process students describe, looking for signs of potential barriers the students anticipate. Interventions could be designed accordingly to address identified needs.

Focusing on Values to Address Career Indecision

Examining values can be helpful for students struggling with career and college indecision. Whether their indecision relates to choosing a career path or making a final college choice, students need to have some sense of control over their future (Savickas, 2002). As we discussed previously, pressure from peers, partners, or family may lead some students to feel like they have no say about their futures. These students can benefit from understanding the ways in which they *do* have control. When working with a student who is struggling with indecision, or is lacking a sense of control over his or her future, a school counselor can administer the *Life Values Inventory* (Brown & Crace, 2002). The following case (Exhibit 15.2) illustrates how this kind of assessment can be useful in these situations.

Notice how Carole (in Exhibit 15.2) was able to help Dimitrius prioritize his values. In discussing what was important to him, he was able to realize that the control he had in this situation was more in relation to how he made his decisions than what those decisions actually were. After realizing that he did have some control and was able to accept his responsibility to make a choice, Dimitrius was able to move forward exploring solutions to his dilemma.

EXHIBIT 15.2
Using the Life Values Inventory With a Student

A school counselor, Carole, has been working with Dimitrius, a 12th-grade student, for the past 3 years as he has explored his future plans. He has completed honors course work and has a 3.48 GPA. Dimitrius is an African American male and the youngest of four children; his older sisters have all completed 2-year degrees. He is the son of an auto mechanic and secretary, and lives in a lower-middle class suburban neighborhood. Dimitrius has been dating his girlfriend for the past 2 years and hopes to marry her.

In their recent sessions, Carole has noticed that Dimitrius seems less excited about his initial plans to attend a 4-year college to study mechanical engineering. Having worked alongside his dad for many years, Dimitrius became excited when he learned about the possibility of contributing to the design of cars. He had been encouraged throughout high school by his math and science teachers, and has identified a number of scholarships geared to help students like him enter science, technology, engineering, and math (STEM) fields.

When discussing his plans recently, Carole learned that Dimitrius was feeling pressure from his family to attend school close to home, and from his girlfriend to not move away. He indicated that his girlfriend threatened to break up with him if he chose to move away. His family doesn't understand why he needs to pursue a 4-year degree when everyone else has been successful attending the local technical college. Dimitrius was struggling because he really wants to pursue engineering but also does not want to disappoint

(continued)

EXHIBIT 15.2 (continued)
Using the Life Values Inventory With a Student

the people who are important to him. As they talked, it became apparent that Dimitrius was feeling resentful that others were limiting his future options. He didn't think that he had much of a choice, especially given his girlfriend's ultimatum to break up with him if he moves away. Carole thought that a values inventory might be something that could help him to explore this challenge a little more concretely.

After he completed the *Life Values Inventory*, they discovered that his highest rated values were belonging (being accepted by others and feeling included), interdependence (following family expectations), and achievement (challenging oneself). Carole discussed and normalized the internal conflict that is resulting from his conflicting values. They also talked about how he felt about the results, if he agreed with the priority order, and if he wanted to maintain that priority order for the future. Carole helped Dimitrius to realize that he had a choice of whether or not to place value on his family and girlfriend's opinions—that he had some control over how much he allowed others to influence his future. Once he realized the degree to which he could exert control over his future, they were able to brainstorm ways to help him fulfill both his achievement and belonging values while trying to pursue mechanical engineering.

Counselors also can use a focus on values to help students narrow down college choices. If a student is trying to decide between two schools and is feeling stuck, sometimes bringing things back to core values can make a difference. For example, if the schools are fairly comparable in terms of the quality of a particular program, exploring things like size, organizations, or the religious affiliation may help a student make a final decision. Further, perhaps a student is trying to choose between two schools that are different mainly in terms of distance from their home. If the student values independence and wants to gain further autonomy, perhaps choosing the school that is farther away might afford him or her more opportunities to be independent. Rather than focus so much on the details, sometimes a broader focus on values can make decisions easier.

Encouraging College Curiosity: It Is Not Too Late

Although possessing accurate information about the world of work and one's self is critical to informed decision making, for high school seniors that might not be enough. It is equally important that students acquire accurate knowledge of a transitional experience—attending college. Many students enter their senior year still uncertain if they want to attend college or not quite clear about the differences between 2- and 4-year colleges. Although ideally students would have explored schools and visited colleges prior to their senior year, many avoid doing so until the last minute. School counselors can help those in need of a crash course and can provide them with information in time to make decisions before they miss application deadlines.

The first thing school counselors can do is to remind students of opportunities to visit colleges, virtually or in person. We talked about this in Chapter 14, as ideally students would start visiting schools *no later than* grade 11 or the summer in between 11th and 12th grades. Reminders can be made over school announcements and placed on the school counseling website. Individual students may need to meet with their school counselor for in-person reminders and career advisement.

School counselors can involve peers in the process of sharing information about colleges (see Exhibit 15.3). Additionally, school counselors can take advantage of opportunities to heavily promote existing activities and events that might be in place. For example, fall is a time when college recruiters and admissions counselors are making rounds to high schools to meet with prospective students. School counselors should ensure that notices about these upcoming meetings are widely disseminated (e.g., morning announcements, website, school newsletter) to students and parents. Ideally, they should also identify students who express curiosity but who need more information before finalizing their plans. Personal invitations sent to students encouraging them to attend can sometimes increase the probability they will attend. For these students, one-on-one conversations with individuals who can provide first-hand information about the schools can be very valuable.

Finally, college fairs are commonly held during the early fall semester, organized either by individual schools, school districts, or local communities. These fairs provide opportunities for students and their families to gather information from a variety of schools, learn what majors and special programs they offer, and talk to recruiters and admissions counselors. As they would with the other opportunities already discussed, school counselors can target specific 12th-grade students who need more information about colleges in order to narrow down their plans, encouraging them and their families to participate. For these students in particular, follow-up conversations with school counselors can be useful to help them process what they learned and weigh pros and cons of their options in relation to their career goals.

EXHIBIT 15.3
Sharing College Information Through Peer Interventions

One high school counselor organized a week-long lunchtime sharing session. She set aside separate lunch tables with information and brochures about various colleges, posted a college banner at the table, and asked students who had attended in-person visits during the past year to talk about what they saw and experienced. These students also were able to field specific questions from other students. Some of the students shared pictures that they took when they were on campus as well as pictures of the surrounding community (before they visited, the school counselor had encouraged them to take pictures to bring back for sharing). Students who had not been able to visit those colleges or who wanted other perspectives about the college were able to sit at a different table each day during lunch to learn about multiple schools throughout the week.

Addressing Career Inhibition Through Peer Support

Earlier in this book, we discussed the different rates at which students apply to and attend college, with certain populations (e.g., Latinos) being underrepresented. We have talked a lot in this chapter about the role that beliefs and self-efficacy can play in career- and college-related behaviors. Many students will complete high school with all of the requirements that will enable them to pursue college, and they will also engage in many relevant preparatory activities (e.g., visiting colleges). When it comes to submitting a college application, however, some students do not follow through because they lack the confidence in their ability to be successful. This lack of confidence can be particularly true for students who would be the first in their family to attend college. These potential first-generation college students can use a lot of support and encouragement as they engage in the process of applying to college, and opportunities for peer support and encouragement can help to increase their self-efficacy about this process. The state of South Carolina has provided a unique opportunity to address this lack of confidence and attempt to increase the number of students who apply to college (see Exhibit 15.4).

EXHIBIT 15.4
College Application Day Event

A large number of high schools in South Carolina organize College Application Day events during the month of October (The Riley Institute at Furman University, 2012). The main purpose of these days is to assist first-generation students or others who might not typically apply to college to successfully complete their online college applications. High schools are, however, encouraged to provide opportunities for all seniors. School counselors, in collaboration with volunteers and staff from the South Carolina Commission on Higher Education, assist students with the online application process. In the first five years, the number of high schools participating increased from 12 in 2009 to 215 in 2015, resulting in just under 300,000 complete college applications submitting across that time frame (South Carolina Commission on Higher Education, n.d.).

At one high school, school counseling staff and volunteers made themselves available all day in the computer lab to assist students. Teachers agreed to come in to help during their planning periods, as the school believed that students would appreciate seeing familiar faces there to provide encouragement. Agreements were made with classroom teachers to permit students to leave specific classes in order to participate, and students were permitted to come in before and after school or during lunch or other free times. Comments heard from students throughout the day supported the idea that many students felt less intimidated knowing that help was available, that many students would not have completed applications at home on their own because they didn't know how to start and were afraid to ask for help, and that students were glad to know that lots of other students were confused about the process.

Creating a vicarious learning opportunity, school counselors also might consider involving former graduates in a college application day process. By inviting diverse students who were able to successfully navigate the college application process and who are attending college to assist with college application days, school counselors can provide role models for a variety of students. These student volunteers can help to normalize the fears or uncertainty that many of the seniors might be experiencing, as well as provide encouragement through sharing their own successes.

Assisting Students Not Pursuing Postsecondary School

Students who do not have postsecondary education plans need assistance in developing career-related skills. School counselors can use classroom time to provide instruction and support for things like resume writing, crafting cover letters, developing interview skills, and approaching the job search process. One creative way to provide this assistance for students is to recruit local community partners and form a mock interview committee. Students can develop their resumes and cover letters and the mock interview committee can set up interviews with students. Appropriate interview attire also should be discussed with students and resources provided (if possible) to help them look their best. For example, one inner city school in an economically disadvantaged area provides a clothing donation closet where students are loaned shirts, ties, dresses, and other interview appropriate clothing when they go on job interviews.

Interventions to Foster Parent–Student Relationships

As we mentioned earlier in this chapter, parents and students often experience tension as students try to separate themselves and parents try to keep them close. For many parents, especially those who have had very strong and comfortable relationships with their children, this tension can be heartbreaking and confusing. They may begin to catastrophize, fearing that their teenager will move out after graduation and never want to come home. The tendency of some parents in these situations will be to exert greater control by setting and enforcing stricter rules. Other parents will give up, afraid that if they push too hard, they will lose the relationship they have with their teenager.

Although everyone was an adolescent at some point, it can be challenging to take oneself back to that age. Arguably, adolescents today have different challenges to face than their parents did at that same age. Furthermore, some adolescents are preparing for very different kinds of postsecondary plans than their parents did (e.g., first-generation college students), so it can be difficult for their parents to really know what they are experiencing. Understandably, parents can benefit from information to help them understand what their adolescents are going through.

One thing school counselors might do is offer parent workshops or information via a newsletter regarding adolescent development. Important topics to address would include information about identity development and peer relationships. By providing examples of the range of ways that adolescents interact with peers and family and experiment with and explore new identities (see Exhibit 15.5), school counselors can help to normalize what parents might be experiencing. Specific examples related to preparing for graduation and leaving home can be provided, along with concrete suggestions for what parents can do to support their adolescents throughout that process.

Parents also can benefit from information about issues specific to career and college development. The second author vividly recalls working with many parents who experienced extreme stress because their adolescent was planning to start college with an undeclared major. A lot of parents, even those who did attend college, have unrealistic expectations that their adolescents must know *exactly* what they want well before they graduate from high school. Providing them with data that are available can sometimes help alleviate their concerns. For example, school counselors could share that approximately 80% of students enter college without a declared major, and that 50% of college students who do enter with a specific major will change their major at least once (Ronan, 2005). They also could talk about the types of programs that are available at most colleges to help students explore and choose a major—things

EXHIBIT 15.5
Engaging Parents and Students in a Values Comparison

One of the things that many parents struggle most with is acknowledging that their children may not adopt the same values that they did. At the core of many parent–adolescent arguments is a difference in values. One high school counselor found himself addressing these kinds of issues a lot with parents, and he developed a way to help parents and students get to the core issues. He developed a list of values that he found commonly came up when working with adolescents—things like making money, being respected, having a sense of control, fitting in. He gave this list to students and their parents, asking them to fill it out by rating the values that were important to them personally, then asking them to rate as if they were each other.

Engaging them in discussion, the school counselor was quickly able to identify similarities and differences. Helping people identify commonalities can go a long way toward building relationships, so in discussing the results with them, the school counselor would focus on pointing out those things they had in common. He then would move on to discuss the differences as well as the assumptions they had about each other, specifically examining the accuracy of their assumptions as well as how their assumptions played out in their relationship. Although school counselors are not family counselors and do not have the time or expertise to engage in family counseling sessions, this school counselor found that he could be quite effective in helping to make inroads during a 30-minute meeting following this basic approach. He would encourage them to continue focusing on the things that they did agree on, and offered them suggestions for how to address differences.

such as first-year seminar courses, career exploration courses, and academic advisors. The fact that these types of services exist suggests a great need among college students for career exploration.

Just like students value their peers, sometimes parents are more receptive to hearing from their peers. School counselors can organize panel discussions involving parents of recent graduates. During these sessions, the parents can discuss their experiences—including challenges and successes—as well as their adolescents' experiences. Parents often just want to know that their children fit into a norm, so to speak, and the more schools can help them understand what is typical and common, the less pressure they might put on their adolescents to make decisions before they are developmentally ready to do so.

A final way that school counselors can help parents of 12th graders is to provide them with suggestions about how they might talk with their adolescents. Many adolescents will say that adults don't listen to them, that they always try to tell them what to do. By understanding that what their adolescents probably want most is to be heard and supported, parents can approach conversations with them differently than they might have in the past. School counselors can offer case studies, engage in role-play demonstrations, and provide verbiage that parents might use to convey empathy and support before they challenge or question.

Teaching Parents and Students About Financial Literacy

Whether students are college bound or not, teaching them and their parents about finances is a critical step in their transition from high school student to young adult. Abundant evidence exists that Americans are in chronic debt and that the economy has caused difficulties for many families. Specifically, in 2011, there were over 800,000 home foreclosures in the United States (Veiga, 2012) and in 2010 over 1.5 million Americans filed for bankruptcy (Dugas, 2010). Furthermore, the average credit card holder has approximately $6,500 in credit card debt and 1 in 10 consumers have 10 or more credit cards (Economy Watch, 2011).

It is important that regardless of the type of school in which they work (i.e., inner city, private, public), school counselors need to understand that students and parents may not comprehend the core principles of financial independence. Also, depending on their own financial status and experiences, parents may have a limited understanding of common financial challenges people experience. Conducting a joint parent–student workshop on financial literacy is one way to educate families and promote conversation about money. Three major pieces of information that should be covered are (a) how to create a budget, (b) problems with credit card debt, and (c) creating an emergency fund.

Creating a budget may be a new life skill for both parents and students. Moreover, according to a survey of 16- to 18-year olds by Charles Schwab (2011), only 35% of teens knew how to balance a checkbook or check the accuracy of a bank statement. Given how important these skills are, it is critical to help parents and teens talk about money, including how to create a budget, how to balance a checkbook, and how to avoid spending pitfalls. One interesting approach for teaching budgeting involves using a simulation program, such as the Budget

Challenge program that can be done on computer (www.budgetchallenge.com). In the Budget Challenge simulation, students are assigned a job, salary, and options such as the types of services they wish to purchase (e.g., having cable, owning a car, having a cell phone), where to bank and a choice of bank accounts (checking, savings, etc.), and retirement savings options. Students and parents can learn the value of savings and how to create financial growth over time.

According to Charles Schwab (2011), only 31% of teens understand credit card interest and fees. One resource for teaching how credit cards work is the *House of Cards: Credit Card Project* (Espana, Fegette, Islip, Sampson, & Walker, 2004). This comprehensive lesson packet is free, downloadable, and covers credit card interest, how to calculate compound interest, credit card amortization, and how to calculate an average daily balance.

The third financial literacy component that should be covered is the importance of an emergency fund. Students and parents should consider the types of emergencies and occasional expenses that young adults commonly encounter (e.g., extra college expenses, car repairs, deposits on housing and utilities). Next, students and parents should consider how large the emergency fund needs to be and should devise a plan to set money aside weekly until that amount is achieved. In general, an emergency fund should cover necessary expenses (food, shelter) for several months in the event that income is lost.

CELEBRATING THE HIGH SCHOOL TRANSITION

As has been evident throughout this book, the milestone of leaving high school and transitioning to career or college is one of life's major moments. As we have cautioned, this postsecondary transition period is an important time to identify students who may need extra support (e.g., first-generation college students, students with disabilities, English-language learners, homeless students) and connect them to resources. However, it also is a time to celebrate (in ways that are befitting to each unique school community) students' accomplishments.

For example, at a private school in Florida, the senior counselor hangs a pennant in the school cafeteria for every college that a student in the senior class has committed to attend. By the end of each school year, the cafeteria is full of the different colleges' pennants. At a high school for pregnant and parenting teens, the graduation ceremony includes the teen mother walking across the stage with her child, honoring the work and commitment of getting through high school and being a parent. During graduation at a high school near a military post, the ROTC color guard does a presentation and all students who have chosen to go into the military are honored during the ceremony. Many schools around the country have formal celebrations for students making this critical transition. School counselors should determine what types of celebrations are appropriate for their populations and consider ways to positively send students forward into their postsecondary futures. Exhibit 15.6 gives an example of how one school counselor helped seniors navigate finances, focus on finishing high school, utilize community relationships, and celebrate the high school to postsecondary transition.

EXHIBIT 15.6
Voices From the Field: The College Transition Process

Nmah, Juterh MEd

Regional Coordinator, Louisiana Office of Student Financial Assistance

As a senior counselor, one of the biggest challenges I faced when preparing students for college was getting them to see the importance of planning early. Students struggle with activities that require long-term planning and multiple steps such as applying to college, filling out the FAFSA, and applying for scholarships. Additionally, I had to often remind them to complete their course work thoroughly including any credit recovery for courses they had not passed and taking ownership of their current schoolwork. As a senior counselor, I realized that parents, students, teachers, and administrators saw me as the go-to person to answer all things related to career and college readiness. Although some students had parents that did attend college and could provide limited support, others did not have parents or families with a college background to assist. Further, although I have worked with some wonderfully high achieving students, and had students receive numerous scholarships and be accepted to top-tier colleges and universities, I noticed that most of the students needed some assistance when it came to acquiring financial aid and scholarships to fund their postsecondary education. However, the bulk of my time was spent encouraging and planning with students who were unsure of their postsecondary decisions. Thankfully, I was fortunate to work with a great group of school counselors who provided support to me and had several senior teachers who were eager to learn about the college planning process to assist with answering students' questions about the college/application process.

Although I loved being a school counselor, when offered a job as a regional coordinator for the state financial aid office, I accepted the position because of my passion for career and college readiness and student success. In my current role, I have been fortunate to learn a lot about current federal initiatives and was lucky enough to attend the White House Convening for Reach Higher in 2014 and 2015. Through attending these national events, I learned the importance of the stakeholders at the school level (school counselors, educators, parents, and students) in creating a college-going culture. I also learned about national policies and initiatives that help prevent major barriers to student success in education. For example, I learned about *summer melt*, a term used to describe the phenomenon where college-eligible and enrolled students graduate from high school but don't go to college in the fall. This mainly happens to low-income students. I learned how to assist these students through the summer and to bridge the high school to college experience, connect financial resources, and help to ensure that the institution match is not an over or under match, but rather an appropriate fit. Senior counselors need very specific professional development and I would encourage them to seek professional training on all of these topics.

(continued)

EXHIBIT 15.6 (continued)
Voices From the Field: The College Transition Process

There are lots of things senior counselors can do to be effective in helping students get financial support and resources for college. The first and most important thing is to identify local and regional agencies and organizations that have a vested interest in career and college readiness. These organizations have resources and personnel who are willing and eager to assist students through the college application process. They often will come out to schools across the state and work with underperforming schools to provide students with adequate access to career and college activities. This is extremely beneficial for school counselors, as it allows them to expand the school counseling program offerings for seniors such as campus field trips, financial literacy workshops for parents and students, and cross-curricular activities. Although the school counselor is not always the person providing each of these programs, he or she is coordinating with the local agencies and organization that can provide them. For example, as a senior counselor, I coordinated with a state agency to assist me in helping my students and their families get accurate information regarding applying for state and federal aid, and one organization raffled off a $1,000 scholarship.

Working in my current position, I really see the power of collaboration and using creative and alternative methods to assist and give important information to students. Rather than explain debt and financial aid to students using PowerPoints or lectures, we developed skits, involving current songs that were written by my colleagues, to inform students of the different types of financial aid, and how to use it wisely. This was very important because the students (high school seniors) were very receptive to the entertaining, yet informative way to get the information. Local high school students attend our presentations and enjoy themselves. They are able to tell me what they learned from the presentations. School counselors should also consider having mentorship programs for seniors to help them set college and career goals. Mentors can help students set goals for applications, goals for developing budgets, and goals for choosing postsecondary options.

Finally, senior counselors should be prepared to celebrate with students. Working with school-level stakeholders to celebrate being accepted to college was a high point for me as a senior counselor. We had a "National College Signing Day" event where the seniors wore the shirts of the colleges and universities where they had been accepted and decided to attend. They proudly wore their shirts and enjoyed being asked by their teachers and younger students about their college choices. We invited the local paper to come and feature some of the students who wore their shirts. We even had a College Signing Parade through the main hall of the school between homeroom and first period, which served as an unveiling of their choices. The underclassmen lined the halls and the seniors went through the halls in their shirts. It was a source of great pride. If students chose the military, they wore those shirts as well or technical schools, careers, and community college. The most important piece was acknowledging that all students were choosing a postsecondary opportunity, and that is the goal.

SUMMARY

In this chapter, we focused on helping high school seniors prepare for their transitions to college or the workforce. These students should be provided with concrete opportunities to explore self, make connections between self and career, and develop confidence in their ability to direct their futures. Their parents are important partners as they navigate the postsecondary transition, and school counselors and educators should consider the various ways in which they can educate and involve parents.

··**>** Test Your Knowledge

1. Name and define the four dimensions of career adaptability.
2. Explain the connection between Lent et al.'s (1994) Social Cognitive Career Theory and Savickas's Theory of Career Construction.
3. List three components of financial literacy training.

REFERENCES

American School Counselor Association (ASCA). (2014). *ASCA mindsets & behaviors for student success: K-12 college- and career-readiness standards for every student*. Alexandria, VA: Author.

Brown, D. (1996). Brown's values-based, holistic model of career and life-role choices and satisfaction. In D. Brown, L. Brooks, & Associates (Eds.), *Career choice and development* (pp. 337–372). San Francisco, CA: Jossey-Bass.

Brown, D. (2002). The role of work values and cultural values in occupational choice, satisfaction, and success: A theoretical statement. In D. Brown & Associates (Eds.), *Career choice and development* (4th ed., pp. 465–509). San Francisco, CA: Jossey-Bass.

Brown, D., & Crace, R. K. (2002). *Life values inventory*. Williamsburg, VA: Applied Psychology Resources.

Charles Schwab, Inc. (2011). Charles Schwab 2011 teens & money survey findings: Insights into money attitudes, behaviors and expectations of 16–18 year olds. Retrieved from http://www.schwabmoneywise.com/public/file/P-4192268/110526-SCHWAB-TEENSMONEY.pdf

Dugas, C. (2010, March 3). More consumers file for bankruptcy protection. *USA Today*. Retrieved from http://usatoday30.usatoday.com/money/economy/2010-03-03-bankruptcy03_ST_N.htm

Economy Watch. (2011, May 23). 9 Alarming U.S. consumer debt statistics. Retrieved from http://articles.businessinsider.com/2011-05-23/markets/30101275_1_consumer-debt-credit-cards-student-loans#ixzz2E1Prmcqz

Erikson, E. H. (1963). *Childhood and society* (2nd ed.). New York, NY: W. W. Norton.

Espana, S., Fegette, K., Islip, B., Sampson, J., & Walker, M. (2004). House of cards: Credit card project. Retrieved from http://commproj101.weebly.com/uploads/2/3/8/7/23873444/economics-house-of-cr-cards.pdf

Lent, R. W., Brown, S. D., & Hackett, G. (1994). Toward a unifying social cognitive theory of career and academic interest, choice, and performance. *Journal of Vocational Behavior, 45*, 79–122.

Ronan, G. B. (2005, November 29). College freshmen face major dilemma. *MSNBC News*. Retrieved from http://www.msnbc.msn.com/id/10154383/ns/business-personal_finance/t/college-freshmen-face-major-dilemma/#.UJgoNoU88a0

Savickas, M. L. (2002). Career construction: A developmental theory of vocational behavior. In D. Brown & Associated (Eds.), *Career choice and development* (4th ed., pp. 149–205). San Francisco, CA: Jossey-Bass.

Savickas, M. L. (2005). The theory and practice of career construction. In S. D. Brown & R. W. Lent (Eds.), *Career development and counseling: Putting theory and research to work* (pp. 42–70). Hoboken, NJ: John Wiley & Sons.

South Carolina Commission on Higher Education. (n.d.). College application month results. Retrieved from http://sccango.org/cam-results

Super, D. E. (1980). A life-span, life-space approach to career development. *Journal of Vocational Behavior, 16*(3), 282–298. http://dx.doi.org/10.1016/0001-8791(80)90056-1

The Riley Institute at Furman University. (2012). College application month. Retrieved from http://riley.furman.edu/sites/default/files/docs/CEPLClearinghouseCollege ApplicationMonth5.25.12.pdf

Veiga, A. (2012, August 9). Number of homes facing foreclosure rose in July: Lenders placed more homes on foreclosure path in July, but repossessions decline. Retrieved from http://finance.yahoo.com/news/number-homes-facing-foreclosure-rose -040831645.html

Appendices

National Career Development Association Minimum Competencies for Multicultural Career Counseling and Development

(This document replaces the 1997 Career Counseling Competencies)
Approved by the NCDA Board—August 2009

INTRODUCTION

The purpose of the multicultural career counseling and development competencies is to ensure that all individuals practicing in, or training for practice in, the career counseling and development field are aware of the expectation that we, as professionals, will practice in ways that promote the career development and functioning of individuals of all backgrounds. Promotion and advocacy of career development for individuals are ensured regardless of age, culture, mental/physical ability, ethnicity, race, nationality, religion/ spirituality, gender, gender identity, sexual orientation, marital/partnership status, military or civilian status, language preference, socioeconomic status, or any other characteristics not specifically relevant to job performance, in accordance with NCDA and ACA policy. Further, they will provide guidance to those in the career counseling and development field regarding appropriate practice with regard to clients of a different background than their own. Finally, implementation of these competencies for the field should provide the public with the assurance that they can expect career counseling and development professionals to function in a manner that facilitates their career development, regardless of the client's/student's background.

If you believe that you need assistance with performing at these minimum levels, or would like to further develop your skills in these areas, please visit the NCDA website www.ncda.org for contact information regarding sources for increasing your competence in dealing with individuals with different cultural backgrounds than yourself.

For those seeking a designation of competency, NCDA offers the Master Career Counselor and Master Career Development Professional Special Memberships. Visit www.ncda.org for more information.

THE MULTICULTURAL CAREER PROFESSIONAL

Career Development Theory

- Understands the strengths and limitations of career theory and utilizes theories that are appropriate for the population being served.

Individual and Group Counseling Skills

- Is aware of his or her own cultural beliefs and assumptions and incorporates that awareness into his or her decision making about interactions with clients/students and other career professionals.
- Continues to develop his or her individual and group counseling skills in order to enhance his or her ability to respond appropriately to individuals from diverse populations.
- Is cognizant when working with groups of the group demographics and monitors these to ensure appropriate respect and confidentiality is maintained.

Individual/Group Assessment

- Understands the psychometric properties of the assessments he or she is using in order to effectively select and administer assessments and interpret and use results with the appropriate limitations and cautions.

Information, Resources, and Technology

- Regularly evaluates the information, resources, and use of technology to determine that these tools are sensitive to the needs of diverse populations, amending and/or individualizing for each client as required.
- Provides resources in multiple formats to ensure that clients/students are able to benefit from needed information.
- Provides targeted and sensitive support for clients/students in using the information, resources, and technology.

Program Promotion, Management, and Implementation

- Incorporates appropriate guidelines, research, and experience in developing, implementing, and managing programs and services for diverse populations.
- Utilizes the principles of program evaluation to design and obtain feedback from relevant stakeholders in the continuous improvement of programs and services, paying special attention to feedback regarding specific needs of the population being served.
- Applies his or her knowledge of multicultural issues in dealings with other professionals and trainees to ensure the creation of a culturally sensitive environment for all clients.

Coaching, Consultation, and Performance Improvement

- Engages in coaching, consultation, and performance improvement activities with appropriate training and incorporates knowledge of multicultural attitudes, beliefs, skills, and values.
- Seeks awareness and understanding about how to best match diverse clients/students with suitably culturally sensitive employers.

Supervision

- Gains knowledge of and engages in evidence-based supervision, and pursues educational and training activities on a regular and ongoing basis inclusive of both counseling and supervision topics. Further, is aware of his or her limitations, cultural biases and personal values and seeks professional consultative assistance as necessary.
- Infuses multicultural/diversity contexts into his or her training and supervision practices, makes supervisees aware of the ethical standards and responsibilities of the profession, and trains supervisees to develop relevant multicultural knowledge and skills.

Ethical/Legal Issues

- Continuously updates his or her knowledge of multicultural and diversity issues and research and applies new knowledge as required.
- Employs his or her knowledge and experience of multicultural ethical and legal issues within a professional framework to enhance the functioning of his or her organization and the image of the profession.
- Uses supervision and professional consultations effectively when faced with an ethical or legal issue related to diversity, to ensure he or she provides high-quality services for every client/student.

Research/Evaluation

- Designs and implements culturally appropriate research studies with regards to research design, instrument selection, and other pertinent population-specific issues.

NCDA Headquarters
305 N. Beech Circle
Broken Arrow, OK 74012
918/663-7060 Toll-free 866-FOR-NCDA
Fax: 918/663-7058
www.ncda.org

B

Career Counselor Assessment and Evaluation Competencies

Adopted by the National Career Development Association on January 10, 2010 Association for Assessment in Counseling and Education on March 20, 2010

The purpose of these competencies is to provide a description of the knowledge and skills that career counselors must demonstrate in the areas of assessment and evaluation. Because effectiveness in assessment and evaluation is critical to effective career counseling, these competencies are critical for career counselor practice and service to students, clients, and other customers.

The competencies can be used by counselors as a guide in the development and evaluation of workshops, in-service, and other continuing education opportunities, as well as to evaluate their own professional development, and by counselor educators as a guide in the development and evaluation of career counselor preparation programs.

Competent career counselors strive to meet each of the eight numbered competencies and exhibit the specific knowledge, understandings, and skills listed under each competency.

Career counselors are skilled in:

Competency 1. Choosing assessment strategies. Career counselors . . .
a. Can describe the nature and use of different types of formal and informal assessments, including questionnaires, checklists, interviews, inventories, tests, observations, surveys, and performance assessments, and they work with individuals skilled in clinical assessment.
b. Can specify the types of information most readily obtained from different assessment approaches.
c. Can identify the type of information needed to assist the client and select the assessment strategy accordingly.
d. Are familiar with resources for critically evaluating each type of assessment and can use the resources to choose appropriate assessment strategies.
e. Are able to advise and assist organizations, such as educational institutions and governmental agencies, in choosing appropriate assessment strategies.
f. Use only those assessments for which they are properly and professionally trained.

343

Competency 2. Identifying, accessing, and evaluating the most commonly used assessment instruments. Career counselors . . .

a. Know which assessment areas are most commonly assessed in career counseling, such as ability, skills, personality, preference of work style, career thoughts and barriers, work values, and interests, including alternate formats.

b. Know the factors by which assessment instruments should be evaluated, including developmental procedures, target audience, purpose, validity, utility, norms, reliability and measurement error, score reporting method, cost, and consequences of use.

c. Obtain and evaluate information about the quality of career assessment instruments used.

d. Use the highest quality instruments available with their students, clients, or customers.

Competency 3. Using the techniques of administration and methods of scoring assessment instruments. Career counselors . . .

a. Implement appropriate administration procedures, including administration using computers.

b. Follow strict standardized administration procedures as dictated by the directions and resulting interpretation.

c. Modify administration of assessments to accommodate individual differences consistent with publisher recommendations and current statements of professional practice.

d. Provide consultation, information, and training to others who assist with administration and scoring, and follow the guidance of others who are more extensively trained.

Competency 4. Interpreting and reporting assessment results. Career counselors . . .

a. Can explain scores that are commonly reported, interpret a confidence interval for an individual score based on a standard error of measurement, and always consider the impreciseness of assessment results.

b. Evaluate the appropriateness of a norm group when interpreting the scores of an individual or a group.

c. Are skilled in communicating assessment information to the client and others, including peers, supervisors, and the public.

d. Evaluate their own strengths and limitations in the use of assessment instruments and in assessing clients with disabilities or linguistic or cultural differences.

e. Know how to identify professionals with appropriate training and experience for consultation.

f. Follow the legal and ethical principles regarding confidentiality and disclosure of assessment information, and recognize the need to abide by professional credentialing and ethical standards on the protection and use of assessments.

Competency 5. Using assessment results in decision making. Career counselors . . .

a. Recognize the limitations of using a single score in making an educational or career decision and know how to access multiple sources of information to improve decisions.

b. Evaluate their own expertise for making decisions based on assessment results, and also the limitations of conclusions provided by others, including the reliability and validity of computer-assisted assessment interpretations.

c. Determine whether the available technical evidence is adequate to support the intended use of an assessment result for decision making, particularly when that use has not been recommended by the developer of the assessment instrument.

d. Can evaluate the consequences of assessment-related decisions and avoid actions that would have unintended negative consequences.

Competency 6. Producing, interpreting, and presenting statistical information about assessment results. Career counselors . . .

a. Can describe data (e.g., test scores, grades, demographic information) by forming frequency distributions, preparing tables, drawing graphs, and calculating descriptive indices of central tendency, variability, and relationship.

b. Can compare a score from an assessment instrument with an existing distribution, describe the placement of a score within a normal distribution, and draw appropriate inferences.

c. Interpret statistics used to describe characteristics of assessment instruments, especially reliability coefficients, validity studies, and standard errors of measurement.

d. Can use computers for data management, statistical analysis, and production of tables and graphs for reporting and interpreting results.

Competency 7. Engaging in professionally responsible assessment and evaluation practices. Career counselors . . .

a. Act in accordance with ACA's *Code of Ethics and Standards of Practice* and NCDA's *Ethical Guidelines.*

b. Adhere to professional codes and standards, including the *Code of Fair Testing Practices in Education,* to evaluate counseling practices involving assessments.

c. Understand test fairness and avoid the selection of biased assessment instruments and biased uses of assessment results.

d. Do not violate the legal and ethical principles and practices regarding test security, reproducing copyrighted materials, and unsupervised use of assessment instruments that are not intended for self-administration.

e. Obtain and maintain available credentialing that demonstrates their skills in assessment and evaluation and update their skills on a regular basis.

Competency 8. Using assessment results and other data to evaluate career programs and interventions. Career counselors . . .

a. Collect data to determine the impact of the career development activities on clients.
b. Use appropriate statistics when comparing groups, making predictions, and drawing conclusions about career programs and strategies.
c. Use evaluation results to improve current practices or implement more successful techniques to assist the client.
d. Can explain evaluation results to relevant persons, colleagues, agencies, and other stakeholders.

DEFINITION OF TERMS

Competencies describe knowledge, understanding, and skills that a career counselor must possess to perform assessment and evaluation activities effectively.

Assessment is the systematic gathering of information for decision-making about individuals, groups, programs, or processes. Assessment targets include abilities, achievements, personality variables, aptitudes, attitudes, preferences, interests, values, demographics, beliefs, and other characteristics. Assessment procedures include, but are not limited to, standardized and nonstandardized tests, questionnaires, inventories, checklists, observations, portfolios, performance assessments, rating scales, surveys, interviews, card sorts, and other measurement techniques.

Evaluation is the collection and interpretation of information to make judgments about individuals, programs, or processes that lead to decisions and future actions.

Committee:

Cheri Butler (NCDA, Chair), Belinda McCharen (NCDA, Chair), Janet Wall (AACE/NCDA, Chair), Rick Balkin (AACE), Lori Ellison (AACE), Chester Robinson (AACE), Brian Taber (NCDA), and Pat Nellor Wickwire (AACE).

C

ASCA Mindsets & Behaviors for Student Success:

K-12 College- and Career-Readiness Standards for Every Student

The ASCA Mindsets & Behaviors for Student Success: K-12 College- and Career Readiness for Every Student describe the knowledge, skills and attitudes students need to achieve academic success, college and career readiness and social/emotional development. The standards are based on a survey of research and best practices in student achievement from a wide array of educational standards and efforts. These standards are the next generation of the ASCA National Standards for Students, which were first published in 1997.

The 35 mindset and behavior standards identify and prioritize the specific attitudes, knowledge and skills students should be able to demonstrate as a result of a school counseling program. School counselors use the standards to assess student growth and development, guide the development of strategies and activities and create a program that helps students achieve their highest potential. The ASCA Mindsets & Behaviors can be aligned with initiatives at the district, state and national to reflect the district's local priorities.

To operationalize the standards, school counselors select competencies that align with the specific standards and become the foundation for classroom lessons, small groups and activities addressing student developmental needs. The competencies directly reflect the vision, mission and goals of the comprehensive school counseling program and align with the school's academic mission.

RESEARCH-BASED STANDARDS

The ASCA Mindsets & Behaviors are based on a review of research and college- and career-readiness documents created by a variety of organizations that have identified strategies making an impact on student achievement and academic performance. The ASCA Mindsets & Behaviors are organized based on the framework of noncognitive factors presented in the critical literature review "Teaching Adolescents to Become Learners" conducted by the University of Chicago Consortium on Chicago School Research (2012).

This literature review recognizes that content knowledge and academic skills are only part of the equation for student success. "School performance is a complex phenomenon, shaped by a wide variety of factors intrinsic to students and the external environment" (University of Chicago, 2012, p. 2). The ASCA Mindsets & Behaviors are based on the evidence of the importance of these factors.

Organization of the ASCA Mindsets & Behaviors

The ASCA Mindsets & Behaviors are organized by domains, standards arranged within categories and subcategories and grade-level competencies. Each is described in the following text.

Domains

The ASCA Mindsets & Behaviors are organized in three broad domains: academic, career and social/emotional development. These domains promote mindsets and behaviors that enhance the learning process and create a culture of college and career readiness for all students. The definitions of each domain are as follows:

Academic Development – Standards guiding school counseling programs to implement strategies and activities to support and maximize each student's ability to learn.

Career Development – Standards guiding school counseling programs to help students 1) understand the connection between school and the world of work and 2) plan for and make a successful transition from school to postsecondary education and/or the world of work and from job to job across the life span.

Social/Emotional Development – Standards guiding school counseling programs to help students manage emotions and learn and apply interpersonal skills.

Standards

All 35 standards can be applied to any of the three domains, and the school counselor selects a domain and standard based on the needs of the school, classroom, small group or individual. The standards are arranged within categories and subcategories based on five general categories of noncognitive factors related to academic performance as identified in the 2012 literature review published by the University of Chicago Consortium on Chicago School Research. These categories synthesize the "vast array of research literature" (p. 8) on noncognitive factors including persistence, resilience, grit, goal-setting, help-seeking, cooperation, conscientiousness, self-efficacy, self-regulation, self-control, self-discipline, motivation, mindsets, effort, work habits, organization, homework completion, learning strategies and study skills, among others.

Category 1: Mindset Standards – Includes standards related to the psychosocial attitudes or beliefs students have about themselves in relation to academic work. These make up the students' belief system as exhibited in behaviors.

Category 2: Behavior Standards – These standards include behaviors commonly associated with being a successful student. These behaviors are visible, outward signs that a student is engaged and putting forth effort to learn. The behaviors are grouped into three subcategories.

a. **Learning Strategies:** Processes and tactics students employ to aid in the cognitive work of thinking, remembering or learning.

b. **Self-management Skills:** Continued focus on a goal despite obstacles (grit or persistence) and avoidance of distractions or temptations to prioritize higher pursuits over lower pleasures (delayed gratification, self-discipline, self-control).

c. **Social Skills:** Acceptable behaviors that improve social interactions, such as those between peers or between students and adults.

The ASCA Mindsets & Behaviors for Student Success: K-12 College- and Career-Readiness Standards for Every Student

Each of the following standards can be applied to the academic, career and social/emotional domains.

CATEGORY 1: MINDSET STANDARDS		
School counselors encourage the following mindsets for all students.		
1. Belief in development of whole self, including a healthy balance of mental, social/emotional and physical well-being 2. Self-confidence in ability to succeed 3. Sense of belonging in the school environment 4. Understanding that postsecondary education and life-long learning are necessary for long-term career success 5. Belief in using abilities to their fullest to achieve high-quality results and outcomes 6. Positive attitude toward work and learning		

CATEGORY 2: BEHAVIOR STANDARDS		
Students will demonstrate the following standards through classroom lessons, activities and/or individual/small-group counseling.		
Learning Strategies	**Self-Management Skills**	**Social Skills**
1. Demonstrate critical-thinking skills to make informed decisions	1. Demonstrate ability to assume responsibility	1. Use effective oral and written communication skills and listening skills
2. Demonstrate creativity	2. Demonstrate self-discipline and self-control	2. Create positive and supportive relationships with other students
3. Use time-management, organizational and study skills	3. Demonstrate ability to work independently	3. Create relationships with adults that support success
4. Apply self-motivation and self-direction to learning	4. Demonstrate ability to delay immediate gratification for long-term rewards	4. Demonstrate empathy
5. Apply media and technology skills	5. Demonstrate perseverance to achieve long- and short-term goals	5. Demonstrate ethical decision making and social responsibility
6. Set high standards of quality	6. Demonstrate ability to overcome barriers to learning	6. Use effective collaboration and cooperation skills
7. Identify long- and short-term academic, career and social/emotional goals	7. Demonstrate effective coping skills when faced with a problem	7. Use leadership and teamwork skills to work effectively in diverse teams
8. Actively engage in challenging course work	8. Demonstrate the ability to balance school, home, and community activities	8. Demonstrate advocacy skills and ability to assert self, when necessary

(continued)

CATEGORY 2: BEHAVIOR STANDARDS Students will demonstrate the following standards through classroom lessons, activities and/or individual/small-group counseling. (*Continued*)		
Learning Strategies	**Self-Management Skills**	**Social Skills**
9. Gather evidence and consider multiple perspectives to make informed decisions	9. Demonstrate personal safety skills	9. Demonstrate social maturity and behaviors appropriate to the situation and environment
10. Participate in enrichment and extracurricular activities	10. Demonstrate ability to manage transitions and ability to adapt to changing situations and responsibilities	

Grade-Level Competencies

Grade-level competencies are specific, measurable expectations that students attain as they make progress toward the standards. As the school counseling program's vision, mission and program goals are aligned with the school's academic mission, school counseling standards and competencies are also aligned with academic content standards at the state and district level.

ASCA Mindsets & Behaviors align with specific standards from the Common Core State Standards through connections at the competency level. This alignment allows school counselors the opportunity to help students meet these college- and career-readiness standards in collaboration with academic content taught in core areas in the classroom. It also helps school counselors directly align with academic instruction when providing individual and small-group counseling by focusing on standards and competencies addressing a student's developmental needs. School counselors working in states that have not adopted the Common Core State Standards are encouraged to align competencies with their state's academic standards and can use the competencies from the ASCA Mindsets & Behaviors as examples of alignment.

ASCA Mindsets & Behaviors Database

The grade-level competencies are housed in the ASCA Mindsets & Behaviors database at *www.schoolcounselor.org/studentcompetencies*. School counselors can search the database by keyword to quickly and easily identify competencies that will meet student developmental needs and align with academic content as appropriate. The database also allows school counselors to contribute to the competencies by sharing other ways to meet or align with a specific standard.

Citation Guide

When citing this ASCA publication, use the following reference:

American School Counselor Association (2014). *Mindsets and Behaviors for Student Success: K-12 College- and Career-Readiness Standards for Every Student.* Alexandria, VA: Author.

AMERICAN
SCHOOL
COUNSELOR
ASSOCIATION

Resources Used in Development of ASCA Mindsets & Behaviors
The following documents were the primary resources that informed ASCA Mindsets & Behaviors.

Document	Organization	Description
ACT National Career Readiness Certificate	ACT	Offers a portable credential that demonstrates achievement and a certain level of workplace employability skills in applied mathematics, locating information and reading for information.
ASCA National Standards for Students	American School Counselor Association	Describes the knowledge, attitudes and skills students should be able to demonstrate as a result of the school counseling program.
AVID Essentials at a Glance	AVID	Promotes a college readiness system for elementary through higher education that is designed to increase schoolwide learning and performance.
Building Blocks For Change: What it Means to be Career Ready	Career Readiness Partner Council	Defines what it means to be career-ready, and highlights the outcome of collaborative efforts of the Career Readiness Partner Council to help inform policy and practice in states and communities.
Career and Technical Education Standards	National Board of Professional Teaching Standards	Defines the standards that lay the foundation for the Career and Technical Education Certificate.
Collaborative Counselor Training Initiative	SREB	Offers online training modules for middle grades and high school counselors that can improve their effectiveness in preparing all students for college, especially those from low-income families who would be first-generation college students.
Cross Disciplinary Proficiencies in the American Diploma Project	Achieve	Describes four cross disciplinary proficiencies that will enable high school graduates to meet new and unfamiliar tasks and challenges in college, the workplace and life.
Eight Components of College and Career Readiness Counseling	College Board	Presents a comprehensive, systemic approach for school counselors to use to inspire and prepare all students for college success and opportunity, especially students from underrepresented populations.
English Language Arts Standards	National Board of Professional Teaching Standards	Defines the standards that lay the foundation for the English Language Arts Certificate.
Framework for 21st Century Learning	Partnership for 21st Century Skills	Describes the skills, knowledge and expertise students must master to succeed in work and life; it is a blend of content knowledge, specific skills, expertise, and literacies.
NETS for Students 2007	International Society for Technology in Education	Describes the standards for evaluating the skills and knowledge students need to learn effectively and live productively in an increasingly global and digital world.
Ramp-Up to Readiness	University of Minnesota	Provides a schoolwide guidance program designed to increase the number and diversity of students who graduate from high school with the knowledge, skills and habits necessary for success in a high-quality college program.

(continued)

(*continued*)

Document	Organization	Description
Social and Emotional Learning Core Competencies	CASEL	Identifies five interrelated sets of cognitive, affective and behavioral competencies through which children and adults acquire and effectively apply the knowledge, attitudes and skills necessary to understand and manage emotions, set and achieve positive goals, feel and show empathy for others, establish and maintain positive relationships and make responsible decisions.
Teaching Adolescents to Become Learners: The Role of Non-Cognitive Factors in Shaping School Performance	The University of Chicago Consortium on Chicago School Research	Presents a critical literature review of the role of noncognitive factors in shaping school performance.
What is "Career Ready"?	ACTE	Defines what it means to be career-ready, involving three major skill areas: core academic skills, employability skills, and technical and job-specific skills.

D

ASCA Ethical Standards for School Counselors

(Adopted 1984; revised 1992, 1998, 2004 and 2010, 2016)

PREAMBLE

The American School Counselor Association (ASCA) is a professional organization supporting school counselors, school counseling students/interns, school counseling program directors/supervisors and school counselor educators. School counselors have unique qualifications and skills to address preK–12 students' academic, career and social/emotional development needs. These standards are the ethical responsibility of all school counseling professionals.

School counselors are advocates, leaders, collaborators and consultants who create systemic change by providing equitable educational access and success by connecting their school counseling programs to the district's mission and improvement plans. School counselors demonstrate their belief that all students have the ability to learn by advocating for an education system that provides optimal learning environments for all students.

All students have the right to:

- Be respected, be treated with dignity and have access to a comprehensive school counseling program that advocates for and affirms all students from diverse populations including but not limited to: ethnic/racial identity, nationality, age, social class, economic status, abilities/disabilities, language, immigration status, sexual orientation, gender, gender identity/expression, family type, religious/spiritual identity, emancipated minors, wards of the state, homeless youth and incarcerated youth. School counselors as social-justice advocates support students from all backgrounds and circumstances and consult when their competence level requires additional support.
- Receive the information and support needed to move toward self-determination, self-development and affirmation within one's group identities. Special care is given to improve overall educational outcomes for students who have been historically underserved in educational services.
- Receive critical, timely information on college, career and postsecondary options and understand the full magnitude and meaning of how college and career readiness can have an impact on their educational choices and future opportunities.

- Privacy that should be honored to the greatest extent possible, while balancing other competing interests (e.g., best interests of students, safety of others, parental rights) and adhering to laws, policies and ethical standards pertaining to confidentiality and disclosure in the school setting.
- A safe school environment promoting autonomy and justice and free from abuse, bullying, harassment and other forms of violence.

PURPOSE

In this document, ASCA specifies the obligation to the principles of ethical behavior necessary to maintain the high standards of integrity, leadership and professionalism. The ASCA Ethical Standards for School Counselors were developed in consultation with state school counseling associations, school counselor educators, school counseling state and district leaders and school counselors across the nation to clarify the norms, values and beliefs of the profession.

The purpose of this document is to:

- Serve as a guide for the ethical practices of all school counselors, supervisors/directors of school counseling programs and school counselor educators regardless of level, area, population served or membership in this professional association.
- Provide support and direction for self-assessment, peer consultation and evaluations regarding school counselors' responsibilities to students, parents/guardians, colleagues and professional associates, schools district employees, communities and the school counseling profession.
- Inform all stakeholders, including students, parents/guardians, teachers, administrators, community members and courts of justice of best ethical practices, values and expected behaviors of the school counseling professional.

A. RESPONSIBILITY TO STUDENTS

A.1. Supporting Student Development

School counselors:

a. Have a primary obligation to the students, who are to be treated with dignity and respect as unique individuals.
b. Aim to provide counseling to students in a brief context and support students and families/guardians in obtaining outside services if the student needs long-term clinical counseling.
c. Do not diagnose but remain acutely aware of how a student's diagnosis can potentially affect the student's academic success.
d. Acknowledge the vital role of parents/guardians and families.
e. Are concerned with students' academic, career and social/emotional needs and encourage each student's maximum development.

f. Respect students' and families' values, beliefs, sexual orientation, gender identification/expression and cultural background and exercise great care to avoid imposing personal beliefs or values rooted in one's religion, culture or ethnicity.

g. Are knowledgeable of laws, regulations and policies affecting students and families and strive to protect and inform students and families regarding their rights.

h. Provide effective, responsive interventions to address student needs.

i. Consider the involvement of support networks, wraparound services and educational teams needed to best serve students.

j. Maintain appropriate boundaries and are aware that any sexual or romantic relationship with students whether legal or illegal in the state of practice is considered a grievous breach of ethics and is prohibited regardless of a student's age. This prohibition applies to both in-person and electronic interactions and relationships.

A.2. Confidentiality

School counselors:

a. Promote awareness of school counselors' ethical standards and legal mandates regarding confidentiality and the appropriate rationale and procedures for disclosure of student data and information to school staff.

b. Inform students of the purposes, goals, techniques and rules of procedure under which they may receive counseling. Disclosure includes informed consent and clarification of the limits of confidentiality. Informed consent requires competence, voluntariness and knowledge on the part of students to understand the limits of confidentiality and, therefore, can be difficult to obtain from students of certain developmental levels, English-language learners and special-needs populations. If the student is able to give assent/consent before school counselors share confidential information, school counselors attempt to gain the student's assent/consent.

c. Are aware that even though attempts are made to obtain informed consent, it is not always possible. When needed, school counselors make counseling decisions on students' behalf that promote students' welfare.

d. Explain the limits of confidentiality in developmentally appropriate terms through multiple methods such as student handbooks, school counselor department websites, school counseling brochures, classroom curriculum and/or verbal notification to individual students.

e. Keep information confidential unless legal requirements demand that confidential information be revealed or a breach is required to prevent serious and foreseeable harm to the student. Serious and foreseeable harm is different for each minor in schools and is determined by students' developmental and chronological age, the setting, parental rights and the nature of the harm. School counselors consult with appropriate professionals when in doubt as to the validity of an exception.

    f. Recognize their primary ethical obligation for confidentiality is to the students but balance that obligation with an understanding of parents'/guardians' legal and inherent rights to be the guiding voice in their children's lives. School counselors understand the need to balance students' ethical rights to make choices, their capacity to give consent or assent, and parental or familial legal rights and responsibilities to make decisions on their child's behalf.

    g. Promote the autonomy of students to the extent possible and use the most appropriate and least intrusive method to breach confidentiality, if such action is warranted. The child's developmental age and the circumstances requiring the breach are considered, and as appropriate, students are engaged in a discussion about the method and timing of the breach. Consultation with peers and/or supervision is recommended.

    h. In absence of state legislation expressly forbidding disclosure, consider the ethical responsibility to provide information to an identified third party who, by his/her relationship with the student, is at a high risk of contracting a disease that is commonly known to be communicable and fatal. Disclosure requires satisfaction of all of the following conditions:

        1. Student identifies partner, or the partner is highly identifiable

        2. School counselor recommends the student notify partner and refrain from further high-risk behavior

        3. Student refuses

        4. School counselor informs the student of the intent to notify the partner

        5. School counselor seeks legal consultation from the school district's legal representative in writing as to the legalities of informing the partner

    i. Request of the court that disclosure not be required when the school counselor's testimony or case notes are subpoenaed if the release of confidential information may potentially harm a student or the counseling relationship.

    j. Protect the confidentiality of students' records and release personal data in accordance with prescribed federal and state laws and school board policies.

    k. Recognize the vulnerability of confidentiality in electronic communications and only transmit student information electronically in a way that follows currently accepted security standards and meets federal, state and local laws and board policy.

    l. Convey a student's highly sensitive information (e.g., a student's suicidal ideation) through personal contact such as a phone call or visit and not less-secure means such as a notation in the educational record or an e-mail. Adhere to state, federal and school board policy when conveying sensitive information.

    m. Advocate for appropriate safeguards and protocols so highly sensitive student information is not disclosed accidentally to individuals who do not have a need to know such information. Best practice suggests a very limited number of educators would have access to highly sensitive information on a need-to-know basis.

n. Advocate with appropriate school officials for acceptable encryption standards to be utilized for stored data and currently acceptable algorithms to be utilized for data in transit.

o. Avoid using software programs without the technological capabilities to protect student information based upon currently acceptable security standards and the law.

A.3. Comprehensive Data-Informed Program

School counselors:

a. Collaborate with administration, teachers, staff and decision makers around school-improvement goals.

b. Provide students with a comprehensive school counseling program that ensures equitable academic, career and social/emotional development opportunities for all students.

c. Review school and student data to assess needs including, but not limited to, data on disparities that may exist related to gender, race, ethnicity, socio-economic status and/or other relevant classifications.

d. Use data to determine needed interventions, which are then delivered to help close the information, attainment, achievement and opportunity gaps.

e. Collect process, perception and outcome data and analyze the data to determine the progress and effectiveness of the school counseling program. School counselors ensure the school counseling program's goals and action plans are aligned with district's school improvement goals.

f. Use data-collection tools adhering to confidentiality standards as expressed in A.2.

g. Share data outcomes with stakeholders.

A.4. Academic, Career and Social/Emotional Plans

School counselors:

a. Collaborate with administration, teachers, staff and decision makers to create a culture of postsecondary readiness.

b. Provide and advocate for individual students' preK–postsecondary college and career awareness, exploration and postsecondary planning and decision making, which supports the students' right to choose from the wide array of options when students complete secondary education.

c. Identify gaps in college and career access and the implications of such data for addressing both intentional and unintentional biases related to college and career counseling.

d. Provide opportunities for all students to develop the mindsets and behaviors necessary to learn work-related skills, resilience, perseverance, an understanding of lifelong learning as a part of long-term career success, a positive attitude toward learning and a strong work ethic.

A.5. Dual Relationships and Managing Boundaries

School counselors:

a. Avoid dual relationships that might impair their objectivity and increase the risk of harm to students (e.g., counseling one's family members or the children of close friends or associates). If a dual relationship is unavoidable, the school counselor is responsible for taking action to eliminate or reduce the potential for harm to the student through use of safeguards, which might include informed consent, consultation, supervision and documentation.

b. Establish and maintain appropriate professional relationships with students at all times. School counselors consider the risks and benefits of extending current school counseling relationships beyond conventional parameters, such as attending a student's distant athletic competition. In extending these boundaries, school counselors take appropriate professional precautions such as informed consent, consultation and supervision. School counselors document the nature of interactions that extend beyond conventional parameters, including the rationale for the interaction, the potential benefit and the possible positive and negative consequences for the student and school counselor.

c. Avoid dual relationships beyond the professional level with school personnel, parents/guardians and students' other family members when these relationships might infringe on the integrity of the school counselor/student relationship. Inappropriate dual relationships include, but are not limited to, providing direct discipline, teaching courses that involve grading students and/ or accepting administrative duties in the absence of an administrator.

d. Do not use personal social media, personal e-mail accounts or personal texts to interact with students unless specifically encouraged and sanctioned by the school district. School counselors adhere to professional boundaries and legal, ethical and school district guidelines when using technology with students, parents/guardians or school staff. The technology utilized, including, but not limited to, social networking sites or apps, should be endorsed by the school district and used for professional communication and the distribution of vital information.

A.6. Appropriate Referrals and Advocacy

School counselors:

a. Collaborate with all relevant stakeholders, including students, educators and parents/guardians when student assistance is needed, including the identification of early warning signs of student distress.

b. Provide a list of resources for outside agencies and resources in their community to student(s) and parents/guardians when students need or request additional support. School counselors provide multiple referral options or the district's vetted list and are careful not to indicate an endorsement or preference for one counselor or practice. School counselors encourage parents to interview outside professionals to make a personal decision regarding the best source of assistance for their student.

c. Connect students with services provided through the local school district and community agencies and remain aware of state laws and local district policies related to students with special needs, including limits to confidentiality and notification to authorities as appropriate.

d. Develop a plan for the transitioning of primary counseling services with minimal interruption of services. Students retain the right for the referred services to be done in coordination with the school counselor or to discontinue counseling services with the school counselor while maintaining an appropriate relationship that may include providing other school support services.

e. Refrain from referring students based solely on the school counselor's personal beliefs or values rooted in one's religion, culture, ethnicity or personal worldview. School counselors maintain the highest respect for student diversity. School counselors should pursue additional training and supervision in areas where they are at risk of imposing their values on students, especially when the school counselor's values are discriminatory in nature. School counselors do not impose their values on students and/or families when making referrals to outside resources for student and/or family support.

f. Attempt to establish a collaborative relationship with outside service providers to best serve students. Request a release of information signed by the student and/or parents/guardians before attempting to collaborate with the student's external provider.

g. Provide internal and external service providers with accurate, objective, meaningful data necessary to adequately evaluate, counsel and assist the student.

h. Ensure there is not a conflict of interest in providing referral resources. School counselors do not refer or accept a referral to counsel a student from their school if they also work in a private counseling practice.

A.7. Group Work

School counselors:

a. Facilitate short-term groups to address students' academic, career and/or social/emotional issues.

b. Inform parent/guardian(s) of student participation in a small group.

c. Screen students for group membership.

d. Use data to measure member needs to establish well-defined expectations of group members.

e. Communicate the aspiration of confidentiality as a group norm, while recognizing and working from the protective posture that confidentiality for minors in schools cannot be guaranteed.

f. Select topics for groups with the clear understanding that some topics are not suitable for groups in schools and accordingly take precautions to protect members from harm as a result of interactions with the group.

g. Facilitate groups from the framework of evidence-based or research-based practices.

h. Practice within their competence level and develop professional competence through training and supervision.

i. Measure the outcomes of group participation (process, perception and outcome data).

j. Provide necessary follow up with group members.

A.8. Student Peer-Support Program

School counselors:

a. Safeguard the welfare of students participating in peer-to-peer programs under their direction.

b. Supervise students engaged in peer helping, mediation and other similar peer-support groups. School counselors are responsible for appropriate skill development for students serving as peer support in school counseling programs. School counselors continuously monitor students who are giving peer support and reinforce the confidential nature of their work. School counselors inform peer-support students about the parameters of when students need to report information to responsible adults.

A.9. Serious and Foreseeable Harm to Self and Others

School counselors:

a. Inform parents/guardians and/or appropriate authorities when a student poses a serious and foreseeable risk of harm to self or others. When feasible, this is to be done after careful deliberation and consultation with other appropriate professionals. School counselors inform students of the school counselor's legal and ethical obligations to report the concern to the appropriate authorities unless it is appropriate to withhold this information to protect the student (e.g., student might run away if he/she knows parents are being called). The consequence of the risk of not giving parents/guardians a chance to intervene on behalf of their child is too great. Even if the danger appears relatively remote, parents should be notified.

b. Use risk assessments with caution. If risk assessments are used by the school counselor, an intervention plan should be developed and in place prior to this practice. When reporting risk-assessment results to parents, school counselors do not negate the risk of harm even if the assessment reveals a low risk as students may minimize risk to avoid further scrutiny and/or parental notification. School counselors report risk assessment results to parents to underscore the need to act on behalf of a child at risk; this is not intended to assure parents their child isn't at risk, which is something a school counselor cannot know with certainty.

c. Do not release a student who is a danger to self or others until the student has proper and necessary support. If parents will not provide proper support, the school counselor takes necessary steps to underscore to parents/guardians the necessity to seek help and at times may include a report to child protective services.

d. Report to parents/guardians and/or appropriate authorities when students disclose a perpetrated or a perceived threat to their physical or mental well-being. This threat may include, but is not limited to, physical abuse, sexual abuse, neglect, dating violence, bullying or sexual harassment. The school counselor follows applicable federal, state and local laws and school district policy.

A.10. Underserved and At-Risk Populations

School counselors:

a. Strive to contribute to a safe, respectful, nondiscriminatory school environment in which all members of the school community demonstrate respect and civility.

b. Advocate for and collaborate with students to ensure students remain safe at home and at school. A high standard of care includes determining what information is shared with parents/ guardians and when information creates an unsafe environment for students.

c. Identify resources needed to optimize education.

d. Collaborate with parents/guardians, when appropriate, to establish communication and to ensure students' needs are met.

e. Understand students have the right to be treated in a manner consistent with their gender identity and to be free from any form of discipline, harassment or discrimination based on their gender identity or gender expression.

f. Advocate for the equal right and access to free, appropriate public education for all youth, in which students are not stigmatized or isolated based on their housing status, disability, foster care, special education status, mental health or any other exceptionality or special need.

g. Recognize the strengths of students with disabilities as well as their challenges and provide best practices and current research in supporting their academic, career and social/emotional needs.

A.11. Bullying, Harassment and Child Abuse

School counselors:

a. Report to the administration all incidents of bullying, dating violence and sexual harassment as most fall under Title IX of the Education Amendments of 1972 or other federal and state laws as being illegal and require administrator interventions. School counselors provide services to victims and perpetrator as appropriate, which may include a safety plan and reasonable accommodations such as schedule change, but school counselors defer to administration for all discipline issues for this or any other federal, state or school board violation.

b. Report suspected cases of child abuse and neglect to the proper authorities and take reasonable precautions to protect the privacy of the student for whom abuse or neglect is suspected when alerting the proper authorities.

c. Are knowledgeable about current state laws and their school system's procedures for reporting child abuse and neglect and methods to advocate for students' physical and emotional safety following abuse/neglect reports.

d. Develop and maintain the expertise to recognize the signs and indicators of abuse and neglect. Encourage training to enable students and staff to have the knowledge and skills needed to recognize the signs of abuse and neglect and to whom they should report suspected abuse or neglect.

e. Guide and assist students who have experienced abuse and neglect by providing appropriate services.

A.12. Student Records

School counselors:

a. Abide by the Family Educational Rights and Privacy Act (FERPA), which defines who has access to students' educational records and allows parents the right to review and challenge perceived inaccuracies in their child's records.

b. Advocate for the ethical use of student data and records and inform administration of inappropriate or harmful practices.

c. Recognize the difficulty in meeting the criteria of sole-possession records.

d. Recognize that sole-possession records and case notes can be subpoenaed unless there is a specific state statute for privileged communication expressly protecting student/school counselor communication.

e. Recognize that electronic communications with school officials regarding individual students, even without using student names, are likely to create student records that must be addressed in accordance with FERPA and state laws.

f. Establish a reasonable timeline for purging sole-possession records or case notes. Suggested guidelines include shredding paper sole-possession records or deleting electronic sole-possession records when a student transitions to the next level, transfers to another school or graduates. School counselors do not destroy sole-possession records that may be needed by a court of law, such as notes on child abuse, suicide, sexual harassment or violence, without prior review and approval by school district legal counsel. School counselors follow district policies and procedures when contacting legal counsel.

A.13. Evaluation, Assessment and Interpretation

School counselors:

a. Use only valid and reliable tests and assessments with concern for bias and cultural sensitivity.
b. Adhere to all professional standards when selecting, administering and interpreting assessment measures and only utilize assessment measures that are within the scope of practice for school counselors and for which they are licensed, certified and competent.
c. Are mindful of confidentiality guidelines when utilizing paper or electronic evaluative or assessment instruments and programs.
d. Consider the student's developmental age, language skills and level of competence when determining the appropriateness of an assessment.
e. Use multiple data points when possible to provide students and families with accurate, objective and concise information to promote students' well-being.
f. Provide interpretation of the nature, purposes, results and potential impact of assessment/evaluation measures in language the students and parents/guardians can understand.
g. Monitor the use of assessment results and interpretations and take reasonable steps to prevent others from misusing the information.
h. Use caution when utilizing assessment techniques, making evaluations and interpreting the performance of populations not represented in the norm group on which an instrument is standardized.
i. Conduct school counseling program evaluations to determine the effectiveness of activities supporting students' academic, career and social/emotional development through accountability measures, especially examining efforts to close information, opportunity and attainment gaps.

A.14. Technical and Digital Citizenship

School counselors:

a. Demonstrate appropriate selection and use of technology and software applications to enhance students' academic, career and social/emotional development. Attention is given to the ethical and legal considerations of technological applications, including confidentiality concerns, security issues, potential limitations and benefits and communication practices in electronic media.
b. Take appropriate and reasonable measures for maintaining confidentiality of student information and educational records stored or transmitted through the use of computers, social media, facsimile machines, telephones, voicemail, answering machines and other electronic technology.
c. Promote the safe and responsible use of technology in collaboration with educators and families.
d. Promote the benefits and clarify the limitations of various appropriate technological applications.

e. Use established and approved means of communication with students, maintaining appropriate boundaries. School counselors help educate students about appropriate communication and boundaries.

f. Advocate for equal access to technology for all students.

A.15. Virtual/Distance School Counseling

School counselors:

a. Adhere to the same ethical guidelines in a virtual/distance setting as school counselors in face-to-face settings.

b. Recognize and acknowledge the challenges and limitations of virtual/distance school counseling.

c. Implement procedures for students to follow in both emergency and nonemergency situations when the school counselor is not available.

d. Recognize and mitigate the limitation of virtual/distance school counseling confidentiality, which may include unintended viewers or recipients.

e. Inform both the student and parent/guardian of the benefits and limitations of virtual/distance counseling.

f. Educate students on how to participate in the electronic school counseling relationship to minimize and prevent potential misunderstandings that could occur due to lack of verbal cues and inability to read body language or other visual cues that provide contextual meaning to the school counseling process and school counseling relationship.

B. RESPONSIBILITIES TO PARENTS/ GUARDIANS, SCHOOL AND SELF

B.1. Responsibilities to Parents/Guardians

School counselors:

a. Recognize that providing services to minors in a school setting requires school counselors to collaborate with students' parents/guardians as appropriate.

b. Respect the rights and responsibilities of custodial and noncustodial parents/guardians and, as appropriate, establish a collaborative relationship with parents/guardians to facilitate students' maximum development.

c. Adhere to laws, local guidelines and ethical practice when assisting parents/guardians experiencing family difficulties interfering with the student's welfare.

d. Are culturally competent and sensitive to diversity among families. Recognize that all parents/guardians, custodial and noncustodial, are vested with certain rights and responsibilities for their children's welfare by virtue of their role and according to law.

e. Inform parents of the mission of the school counseling program and program standards in academic, career and social/emotional domains that promote and enhance the learning process for all students.

f. Inform parents/guardians of the confidential nature of the school counseling relationship between the school counselor and student.

g. Respect the confidentiality of parents/guardians as appropriate and in accordance with the student's best interests.

h. Provide parents/guardians with accurate, comprehensive, and relevant information in an objective and caring manner, as is appropriate and consistent with ethical and legal responsibilities to the student and parent.

i. In cases of divorce or separation, follow the directions and stipulations of the legal documentation, maintaining focus on the student. School counselors avoid supporting one parent over another.

B.2. Responsibilities to the School

School counselors:

a. Develop and maintain professional relationships and systems of communication with faculty, staff and administrators to support students.

b. Design and deliver comprehensive school counseling programs that are integral to the school's academic mission; driven by student data; based on standards for academic, career and social/emotional development; and promote and enhance the learning process for all students.

c. Advocate for a school counseling program free of non-school-counseling assignments identified by "The ASCA National Model: A Framework for School Counseling Programs" as inappropriate to the school counselor's role.

d. Provide leadership to create systemic change to enhance the school.

e. Collaborate with appropriate officials to remove barriers that may impede the effectiveness of the school or the school counseling program.

f. Provide support, consultation and mentoring to professionals in need of assistance when in the scope of the school counselor's role.

g. Inform appropriate officials, in accordance with school board policy, of conditions that may be potentially disruptive or damaging to the school's mission, personnel and property while honoring the confidentiality between the student and the school counselor to the extent feasible, consistent with applicable law and policy.

h. Advocate for administrators to place in school counseling positions certified school counselors who are competent, qualified and hold a master's degree or higher in school counseling from an accredited program.

i. Advocate for equitable school counseling program policies and practices for all students and stakeholders.

j. Strive to use translators who have been vetted or reviewed and bilingual/multilingual school counseling program materials representing languages used by families in the school community.

k. Affirm the abilities of and advocate for the learning needs of all students. School counselors support the provision of appropriate accommodations and accessibility.

l. Provide workshops and written/digital information to families to increase understanding, improve communication and promote student achievement.

m. Promote cultural competence to help create a safer more inclusive school environment.

n. Adhere to educational/psychological research practices, confidentiality safeguards, security practices and school district policies when conducting research.

o. Promote equity and access for all students through the use of community resources.

p. Use culturally inclusive language in all forms of communication.

q. Collaborate as needed to provide optimum services with other professionals such as special educators, school nurses, school social workers, school psychologists, college counselors/admissions officers, physical therapists, occupational therapists, speech pathologists, administrators.

r. Work responsibly to remedy work environments that do not reflect the profession's ethics.

s. Work responsibly through the correct channels to try and remedy work conditions that do not reflect the ethics of the profession.

B.3. Responsibilities to Self

School counselors:

a. Have completed a counselor education program at an accredited institution and earned a master's degree in school counseling.

b. Maintain membership in school counselor professional organizations to stay up to date on current research and to maintain professional competence in current school counseling issues and topics. School counselors maintain competence in their skills by utilizing current interventions and best practices.

c. Accept employment only for those positions for which they are qualified by education, training, supervised experience and state/national professional credentials.

d. Adhere to ethical standards of the profession and other official policy statements such as ASCA Position Statements and Role Statements, school board policies and relevant laws. When laws and ethical codes are in conflict school counselors work to adhere to both as much as possible.

e. Engage in professional development and personal growth throughout their careers. Professional development includes attendance at state and national conferences and reading journal articles. School counselors regularly attend training on school counselors' current legal and ethical responsibilities.

f. Monitor their emotional and physical health and practice wellness to ensure optimal professional effectiveness. School counselors seek physical or mental health support when needed to ensure professional competence.

g. Monitor personal behaviors and recognize the high standard of care a professional in this critical position of trust must maintain on and off the job.

School counselors are cognizant of and refrain from activity that may diminish their effectiveness within the school community.

h. Seek consultation and supervision from school counselors and other professionals who are knowledgeable of school counselors' ethical practices when ethical and professional questions arise.

i. Monitor and expand personal multicultural and social-justice advocacy awareness, knowledge and skills to be an effective culturally competent school counselor. Understand how prejudice, privilege and various forms of oppression based on ethnicity, racial identity, age, economic status, abilities/disabilities, language, immigration status, sexual orientation, gender, gender identity expression, family type, religious/spiritual identity, appearance and living situations (e.g., foster care, homelessness, incarceration) affect students and stakeholders.

j. Refrain from refusing services to students based solely on the school counselor's personally held beliefs or values rooted in one's religion, culture or ethnicity. School counselors respect the diversity of students and seek training and supervision when prejudice or biases interfere with providing comprehensive services to all students.

k. Work toward a school climate that embraces diversity and promotes academic, career and social/emotional development for all students.

l. Make clear distinctions between actions and statements (both verbal and written) made as a private individual and those made as a representative of the school counseling profession and of the school district.

m. Respect the intellectual property of others and adhere to copyright laws and correctly cite others' work when using it.

C. SCHOOL COUNSELOR ADMINISTRATORS/SUPERVISORS

School counselor administrators/supervisors support school counselors in their charge by:

a. Advocating both within and outside of their schools or districts for adequate resources to implement a comprehensive school counseling program and meet their students' needs.

b. Advocating for fair and open distribution of resources among programs supervised. An allocation procedure should be developed that is nondiscriminatory, informed by data and consistently applied.

c. Taking reasonable steps to ensure school and other resources are available to provide appropriate staff supervision and training.

d. Providing opportunities for professional development in current research related to school counseling practice and ethics.

e. Taking steps to eliminate conditions or practices in their schools or organizations that may violate, discourage or interfere with compliance with the ethics and laws related to the profession.

f. Monitoring school and organizational policies, regulations and procedures to ensure practices are consistent with the ASCA Ethical Standards for School Counselors.

D. SCHOOL COUNSELING INTERN SITE SUPERVISORS

Field/intern site supervisors:

a. Are licensed or certified school counselors and/or have an understanding of comprehensive school counseling programs and the ethical practices of school counselors.

b. Have the education and training to provide clinical supervision. Supervisors regularly pursue continuing education activities on both counseling and supervision topics and skills.

c. Use a collaborative model of supervision that is ongoing and includes, but is not limited to, the following activities: promoting professional growth, supporting best practices and ethical practice, assessing supervisee performance and developing plans for improvement, consulting on specific cases and assisting in the development of a course of action.

d. Are culturally competent and consider cultural factors that may have an impact on the supervisory relationship.

e. Do not engage in supervisory relationships with individuals with whom they have the inability to remain objective. Such individuals include, but are not limited to, family members and close friends.

f. Are competent with technology used to perform supervisory responsibilities and online supervision, if applicable. Supervisors protect all electronically transmitted confidential information.

g. Understand there are differences in face-to face and virtual communication (e.g., absence of verbal and nonverbal cues) that may have an impact on virtual supervision. Supervisors educate supervisees on how to communicate electronically to prevent and avoid potential problems.

h. Provide information about how and when virtual supervisory services will be utilized. Reasonable access to pertinent applications should be provided to school counselors.

i. Ensure supervisees are aware of policies and procedures related to supervision and evaluation and provide due-process procedures if supervisees request or appeal their evaluations.

j. Ensure performance evaluations are completed in a timely, fair and considerate manner, using data when available and based on clearly stated criteria.

k. Use evaluation tools measuring the competence of school counseling interns. These tools should be grounded in state and national school counseling standards. In the event no such tool is available in the school district, the supervisor seeks out relevant evaluation tools and advocates for their use.

l. Are aware of supervisee limitations and communicate concerns to the university/college supervisor in a timely manner.

m. Assist supervisees in obtaining remediation and professional development as necessary.

n. Contact university/college supervisors to recommend dismissal when supervisees are unable to demonstrate competence as a school counselor as defined by the ASCA School Counselor Competencies and state and national standards. Supervisors consult with school administrators and document recommendations to dismiss or refer a supervisee for assistance. Supervisors ensure supervisees are aware of such decisions and the resources available to them. Supervisors document all steps taken.

E. MAINTENANCE OF STANDARDS

When serious doubt exists as to the ethical behavior of a colleague(s) the following procedures may serve as a guide:

a. School counselors consult with professional colleagues to discuss the potentially unethical behavior and to see if the professional colleague views the situation as an ethical violation. School counselors understand mandatory reporting in their respective district and states.

b. School counselors discuss and seek resolution directly with the colleague whose behavior is in question unless the behavior is unlawful, abusive, egregious or dangerous, in which case proper school or community authorities are contacted.

c. If the matter remains unresolved at the school, school district or state professional practice/standards commission, referral for review and appropriate action should be made in the following sequence:
   • State school counselor association
   • American School Counselor Association (Complaints should be submitted in hard copy to the ASCA Ethics Committee, c/o the Executive Director, American School Counselor Association, 1101 King St., Suite 310, Alexandria, VA 22314.)

F. ETHICAL DECISION MAKING

When faced with an ethical dilemma, school counselors and school counseling program directors/supervisors use an ethical decision-making model such as Solutions to Ethical Problems in Schools (STEPS) (Stone, 2001):

a. Define the problem emotionally and intellectually
b. Apply the ASCA Ethical Standards for School Counselors and the law
c. Consider the students' chronological and developmental levels
d. Consider the setting, parental rights and minors' rights
e. Apply the ethical principles of beneficence, autonomy, nonmaleficence, loyalty and justice
f. Determine potential courses of action and their consequences
g. Evaluate the selected action
h. Consult
i. Implement the course of action

GLOSSARY OF TERMS

Advocate

a person who speaks, writes or acts to promote the well-being of students, parents/guardians and the school counseling profession. School counselors advocate to close the information, opportunity, intervention and attainment gaps for all students.

Assent

to demonstrate agreement when a student is not competent to give informed consent to counseling or other services the school counselor is providing.

Assessment

collecting in-depth information about a person to develop a comprehensive plan that will guide the collaborative counseling and service provision process.

Boundaries

something that indicates or affixes an extent or limits.

Breach

disclosure of information given in private or confidential communication such as information given during counseling.

Competence

the quality of being competent; adequacy; possession of required skill, knowledge, qualification or capacity.

Confidentiality

the ethical duty of school counselors to responsibly protect a student's private communications shared in counseling.

Conflict of Interest

a situation in which a school counselor stands to personally profit from a decision involving a student.

Consent

permission, approval or agreement; compliance.

Consultation

a professional relationship in which individuals meet to seek advice, information and/or deliberation to address a student's need.

Conventional Parameters

general agreement or accepted standards regarding limits, boundaries or guidelines.

Cultural Sensitivity

a set of skills enabling you to know, understand and value the similarities and differences in people and modify your behavior to be most effective and respectful of students and families and to deliver programs that fit the needs of diverse learners.

Data Dialogues

inquiry with others around student information to uncover inequities, promote informed investigations and assist in understanding the meaning of data and the next steps to have an impact on data.

Data Informed

accessing data, applying meaning to it and using data to have an impact on student success.

Developmental Level/Age

the age of an individual determined by degree of emotional, mental and physiological maturity as compared with typical behaviors and characteristics of that chronological age.

Disclosure

the act or an instance of exposure or revelation.

Diversity

the inclusion of individuals representing more than one national origin, gender/gender identity, color, religion, socio-economic stratum, sexual orientation, and the intersection of cultural and social identities.

Dual Relationship

a relationship in which a school counselor is concurrently participating in two or more roles with a student.

Empathy

the action of understanding, being aware of, being sensitive to and vicariously experiencing the feelings, thoughts and experience of another without having the feelings, thoughts and experience fully communicated in an objectively explicit manner.

Emancipated Minor

a minor who is legally freed from control by his or her parents or guardians, and the parents or guardians are freed from any and all responsibility toward the child.

Encryption

process of putting information into a coded form to control and limit access to authorized users.

Ethical Behavior

actions defined by standards of conduct for the profession.

Ethical Obligation

a standard or set of standards defining the course of action for the profession.

Ethics

the norms and principles of conduct and philosophy governing the profession.

Ethical Rights

the fundamental normative rules about what is allowed of people or owed to people, according to some legal system, social convention or ethical theory.

Feasible

capable of being done, effected or accomplished.

Gender Expression

the ways in which students manifest masculinity or femininity in terms of clothing, communication patterns and interests, which may or may not reflect the student's gender identity.

Gender Identity

One's personal experience of one's own gender. When one's gender identity and biological sex are not congruent, the student may identify as transsexual or transgender.

Harassment

the act of systematic and/or continued unwanted disturbing or troubling persecution.

Informed Consent

assisting students in acquiring an understanding of the limits of confidentiality, the benefits, facts and risks of entering into a counseling relationship.

Intervention

to provide modifications, materials, advice, aids, services or other forms of support to have a positive impact on the outcome or course of a condition.

Legal Mandates

a judicial command or precept issued by a court or magistrate, directing proper behavior to enforce a judgment, sentence or decree.

Legal Rights

those rights bestowed onto a person by a given legal system.

Mandatory Reporting

the legal requirement to report to authorities.

Minors

persons under the age of 18 years unless otherwise designated by statute or regulation.

Peer Helper

peer-to-peer interaction in which individuals who are of approximately the same age take on a helping role assisting students who may share related values, experiences and lifestyles.

Peer Support

programs that enhance the effectiveness of the school counseling program while increasing outreach and raising student awareness of services.

Perception

a mental image or awareness of environment through a physical sensation. a capacity for understanding or a result of an observation.

Privacy

the right of an individual to keep oneself and one's personal information free from unauthorized disclosure.

Privileged Communication

conversation that takes places within the context of a protected relationship, such as that between an attorney and client, a husband and wife, a priest and penitent, a doctor and patient and, in some states, a school counselor and a student.

Professional Development

the process of improving and increasing capabilities through access to education and training opportunities.

Relationship

a connection, association or involvement.

Risk Assessment

a systematic process of evaluating potential risks.

School Counseling Supervisor

a qualified professional who provides guidance, teaching and support for the professional development of school counselors and school counseling candidates.

Serious and Foreseeable

when a reasonable person can anticipate significant and harmful possible consequences.

Sole-Possession Records

exempted from the definition of educational records and the protection of FERPA, are records used only as a personal memory aid that are kept in the sole possession of the maker of the record and are not accessible or revealed to any other person except a temporary substitute for the maker of the record and provide only professional opinion or personal observations.

Stakeholder

a person or group that shares an investment or interest in an endeavor.

Supervision

a collaborative relationship in which one person promotes and/or evaluates the development of another.

Title IX of the Education Amendments of 1972

a law that demands that no person in the United States shall, on the basis of sex, be excluded from participation in, be denied the benefits of or be subjected to discrimination under any education program or activity receiving federal financial assistance.

Virtual/Distance Counseling

counseling by electronic means.

AMERICAN
SCHOOL
COUNSELOR
ASSOCIATION

1101 King Street, Suite 310, Alexandria VA 22314
www.schoolcounselor.org

Author Index

ACT, Inc., 6, 43, 75, 77
Akos, P., 1
Alexander, N. P., 127
Allensworth, E., 43
Almonte, J. L. J., 38
American Association of University Women, 9, 36
American Counseling Association, 62, 244
American Psychological Association, 188
American School Counselor Association (ASCA), 23, 24, 25, 28, 33, 59, 61, 62, 63, 92, 121, 139, 215, 239, 285, 304
American Welding Society (AWS), 48
Amundson, N. E., 180, 181, 182, 229
ASCA. *See* American School Counselor Association
Association for Career and Technical Education (ACTE), 3
Auger, R. W, 144, 170
Aune, E, 84
Austenfeld, J. L., 191
Ausubel, D. P., 212, 215

Baer, R. M., 83
Bailey, D. F., 92
Baker, B., 87
Baker, J. C., 77
Bandura, A., 24, 126, 165, 189, 190, 191, 192, 193, 200, 201, 283, 290
Barbaranelli, C., 191, 193
Barker, J., 174
Bayer Corporation, 82
Baylor, E., 36
Belfield, C., 76
Belser, C. T., 26, 155, 225
Belsky, J., 141, 142, 143, 164, 165, 166, 167, 186, 187, 236, 237
Bickmore, D., 1
Binns, I. C., 26, 155, 225
Black, M. D. 59, 64, 65, 66
Blackhurst, A. E., 144, 170

Bloom, B. S., 123
Blumenstyk, G., 2, 5, 36
Boden, K., 75
Bodley, G., 76, 92, 94
Borders, L. D., 91, 110
Bourdieu, P., 16, 126, 167, 168, 193, 213
Bowen, M., 213, 220
Brandon, E., 24
Briggs, K. C., 111
Briggs Myers, I., 111
Brissett, A. E. A., 79
Brock, T., 23
Bronfenbrenner, U., 12, 13, 14, 15, 167
Brooks, M., 77, 335
Brown, C., 80
Brown, D., 122, 128, 320, 322, 325, 339
Brown, E. R., 81
Brown, S. D., 283, 301, 317, 321
Bureau of Labor Statistics, 4, 6, 9, 35, 84

California Career Zone, 129, 269
California College Board, 218
Cameto, R., 83
Campbell, D., 109
Caprara, G. V., 191, 193
Carnevale, A. P., 4, 5, 6, 9, 35, 36, 218
Carter, M., 14, 129
Carty, K., 77
Caster, T. R., 146
Center for the Study of Education Policy, 93
Center on Education Policy (CEP), 75
Charles Schwab, Inc., 331, 332
Cheah, B., 9, 35
Chen-Hayes, S. F., 23, 92
Choate, L. H., 16, 81, 187
Clark, E. K., 81
Clarke, C. P., 196
Clinedinst, M. E., 40, 41, 42
Coca, V., 40
Cocco, K., 84

College Board, 73, 218, 292
Conkel Ziebell, J. L., 302
Conkel, J., 216
Conley, D., 2, 3
Connolly, P., 167, 168
Conwill, W., 79
Cook, C., 257
Correa, M., 43
Council for Accreditation of Counseling
    and Related Educational Programs
    (CACREP), 60, 63, 64, 66, 67
Covey, S., 250
Crace, R. K., 322, 325
Cramer, S. H., 163
Creed, P., 27
Crow, A., 212, 214
Crow, L. D., 212, 214
Curry, J. R., 1, 16, 26, 38, 39, 79, 81, 187,
    188, 189, 203, 225, 279
Curtis, D., 129

Daiger, D. C., 110
Dalke, C., 84
Dasgupta, N., 82
Deil-Amen, R., 56
Department of Defense, 109
Diamond, K. E., 13
Diantoniis, J. M., 145
Dickinson, D. L., 83
Diekman, A. B., 81, 82
Diez-Nicolas, J., 191
Di Giacomo, F. T., 44
Dolan, T. G., 75
Dugas, C., 331
Dukstein, R. D., 219
Durodoye, B. A., 76, 92, 94

Ecklund, T. R., 80
Economy Watch, 331
Education Week, 82, 83
Eisenberg, N., 141, 213, 237
Elkind, D., 237
Ellis, B., 73
Engelhart, M. D., 123
Engberg, M. E., 56
Erford, B. T., 1
Erikson, E. H., 140, 167, 213, 214, 220,
    236, 279
Espana, S., 332
Ewing, M., 45

Fahs, M., 77
Fegette, K., 332
Ferguson, L. R., 186
Fernandez-Ballesteros, R., 191, 193
Fields, G. M., 257
Fjordbak, B. S., 146
Flexer, R. W., 83

Fouad, N. A., 247
Fowler, H., 257
Frank, L. K., 145
Franke, U., 146
Freeman, E., 175
Furst, E. J., 123

Gardner, H., 127, 201
Garrett, M. T., 79
Gasman, M., 40
Getch, Y. Q., 92
Gibbons, M. M., 91, 110
Gibson, D. M., 113, 220
Gibson, R. L., 27, 92
Gay, Lesbian and Straight Education
    Network (GLSEN), 85
Goodman, R. D., 77
Gottfredson, L. S., 17, 20, 76,
    105, 126, 144, 146, 238, 261
Graves, M., 121
Grbevski, S., 78
Greene, M. J., 174
Griffith, A. L., 82
Gushue, G. V., 196
Guyker, W., 80

Hackett, G., 105, 283, 301, 321
Hagner, D., 85
Hall, A. S., 196, 227
Hall, G. S., 211
Hanrahan, P., 13
Harris, T., 257
Harris-Bowlesby, J., 25, 121, 164,
    196, 217
Harrison, J. D., 50
Hart Research Associates, 6
Harter, S., 167
Hartley, M. T., 84
Hartung, P. J., 185
Havighurst, R. J., 185, 213, 215
Hawkins, D. A., 40
Heinrich, R., 124
Helwig, A., 176, 179
Henderson, C., 83
Herlihy, B., 92
Herr, E. L., 163, 167, 172
Holcomb-McCoy, C., 23, 92, 248
Holland, J. L., 18
Holland, M. M., 49, 50
Holland, N. E. 38
Hossler, D., 27
Howell, J., 41, 45
Hunsinger, M., 82
Hurley, S. F., 40
Hurwitz, M., 41

Isenberg, J. P., 121, 1?
Islip, B., 332, ?

Ivers, N. N., 76, 98
Ivey, A., 143, 160
Ivey, M., 143, 160

Jackson, A. P., 80
Jackson, D. J., 224
Jackson, S. L., 219
Jalongo, M. R., 121, 126, 129
Jenkins, D., 75
Johnson, L. S., 1, 225
Johnson, T., 78
Johnston, A. M., 81
Johnston, J., 113
Jones, G. B., 105
Jones, L. K., 111, 217
Jones-Sanpei, H., 225

Kamatuka, N. A., 219
Kemp, C., 14
Kennelly, L., 263
Kim, J. K., 40
Kimmel, M. S., 189
Knowdell, R. L., 113, 219, 220
Koebler, J., 81
Kohlberg, L., 142, 143
Kolodinsky, P., 291
Krathwohl, D. R., 123
Krieshok, T., 113
Krieshok, T. S., 59, 64, 65, 66
Krumboltz, J. D., 17, 21, 91, 105, 110, 279
Kuder, F., 112, 310

Lambie, G., 248
Lambie, G. W., 203
Landgraf, R., 216
Landreth, G. L., 145
Lapan, R. T., 228, 229, 231
Latham, S. J., 38, 54,
Lavish, L. A., 80
Lee, J., 87, 89
Lee, K. A., 38
Leff, E. H., 83
Legum, H. L., 226
Lent, R. W., 105, 280, 283, 284, 285, 301, 302, 306, 321
Lenz, J. G., 110
Levin, H., 76, 77
Lewin, T., 81
Lilis, M. P., 38
Long, J., 80
Lucas, M. S., 78
Luft, P., 83

Macias, E. E., 75
Maddux, J. E., 193
Madriaga, M., 83
Man- N., 45
      95

Marcia, J. E., 214, 219, 231, 236, 240, 260, 299, 300
Martin, P. J., 10
Marvasti, J. A., 147
Masten, A. S., 193
McCallumore, K. M., 257, 262
McIntosh, J., 257
McMahon, L., 145, 146
McMahon, M., 1, 185
McManus, M. A., 82
McNalley, S., 213, 237
McNutt, M. I., 37
Miao, J., 263
Mihesuah, J. K., 80
Mijares, A., 218
Miller, E. M., 1
Miller, M., 25
Miller, P. A., 213, 237
Milsom, A., 13, 84, 248
Missouri Center for Career Education, 128, 149
Mitchell, A. M., 105
Mitchell, M. H., 27, 92
Moeller, E., 40
Molenda, M., 124
Monrad, M., 263
Mortenson, T. G., 36
Muennig, P., 76
Muennig, P. A., 77
Murrell, P., 78
Myers, J., 143
Myers, J. E., 1
Myers, R. A., 110

Nagoka, J., 40
National Association for College Admissions Counseling (NACAC), 33, 34
National Career Development Association (NCDA), 59, 60, 62, 63, 64, 66, 67, 103, 120, 232
National Center for Educational Statistics (NCES), 5
National Financial Educators Council, 23
National Guard, 242
National Math and Science Initiative, 139, 161
National Poverty Center, 144, 161
National Research Center for Career and Technical Education, 48
Nelson, R. C., 146, 161
Newman, L., 83, 94, 99
Newsome, D. W., 76, 98
Niles, S. G., 1, 25, 121, 137, 163, 164, 183, 196, 209, 217, 233

O'Brien, K. M., 219, 233
Occupational Outlook Handbook, 129, 155, 173, 197, 229, 241

Orthner, D., 218, 225
Owens, D., 78

Pantzer, K. M., 196
Parris, G. P., 78
Parsa, A., 191
Parsons, F., 17, 18, 104
Paseluikho, M. A., 217
Pastorelli, C., 193
Patterson, B. F., 44
Patton, W., 27
Pearson, F., 78
Pellegrini, A. D., 148, 149
Penner, K., 180, 181, 229
Peterson, G. W., 105, 110
Phillips, P., 84
Piaget, J., 141, 166, 167, 212, 237, 259, 278, 279
Ponec, D. L., 79
Ponisciak, S., 43
Porfeli, E. J., 185
Power, P. G., 110

Raphael, D. L., 77
Reardon, R., 105, 110
Reed, M. J., 193
Remley, T. P., 92
Reynolds, A. L., 80
Rivera, E. T., 79, 95
Roach, R., 81
Robinson, E. H., 279
Robinson, S. G., 10
Rock, E., 83
Roderick, M., 40, 41, 49
Roessler, R. T., 84
Ronan, G. B., 330
Rose, R. A., 225
Rose, S. J., 9, 35
Rouse, C., 76
Rumrill, P. D., 84
Russell, J. D., 124

Sampson, J., 332
Sampson, J. P. Jr., 105, 110
Sands-Dudelczyk, K., 141
Satcher, J., 174
Saunders, D. E., 110
Savickas, M. L., 115, 116, 301, 303, 304, 309, 320, 321, 325
Scanlan, K. R. L., 196
Schmit, J., 27, 85, 86
Schultheiss, D. E. P., 185, 195
Shaffer, D. R., 180, 186
Sharf, R. S., 23, 125, 140, 144, 169, 193, 216
Shea, C., 213, 237
Shell, R., 213, 237
Simmons, C. H., 141
Simmons, T. J., 83

Smaldino, S. E., 124
Smith, J., 41
Smith, H., 279
Smith, N., 4, 218
Smith, S. A., 80
Sodano, S. M., 80
Solis, C., 75
Sparapani, E. F., 257, 262
Sparks, D., 45
Spiegel-McGill, P., 13
Stanton, A. L., 191
Starkey, M. T., 216
Stout, J. G., 82
Strohl, J., 4, 218
Super, D. E., 17, 19, 20, 105, 110, 125, 126, 154, 262, 280, 281, 303
Sweeny, T. J., 1
Sylvest, K., 38

Taningco, M. T., 75, 76, 100
Task Force on the Sexualization of Girls, 188
Taylor, K. M., 110, 120
Tevis, T. L., 56
The Center for Public Education, 82, 100
The College Board, 42, 44, 73, 100, 292, 297
The Economist, 37
The Institute for College Access & Success, 37
The Pell Institute, 47
The Riley Institute at Furman University, 328, 336
Thompson, M., 84, 98
Tian, R. G., 38
Tomlinson, M. J., 219, 233
Tracey, T. J. G., 78, 101
Trinder, M., 175, 183
Turner, S. 228, 229, 231
Turner, S. L., 79, 80, 81, 95, 100, 302, 317

U. S. Bureau of Labor Statistics, 84, 96
U. S. Census Bureau, 73, 74, 76, 79, 80, 96, 100
U. S. Department of Education, 10, 46, 47, 53, 89, 95, 99, 101, 254
U. S. News and World Report, 37

Valach, L., 217, 234
Veiga, A., 331, 336
Verbeek, R. L., 83, 96
Vesper, N., 27
Vondracek, F. W., 185, 209
Vygotsky, L. S., 142, 161

Wadsworth, J., 84
Wagner, M., 83, 99
Wahl, K. H., 144, 160, 170, 183
Walker, A., 98
Walker, M., 335
Walker, T., 101

Walker, T. L., 101
Watson, M., 185
Wertheim, E., 175
West-Olatunji, C. A., 77, 78, 79, 82
Wettig, H. H. G., 146, 161
Wheelock, A., 263
White House, 80, 98, 100
White, S., 275
Wilcox, D., 48
Witmer, J. M., 1
Wolniak, G. C., 56

Wong, S. C., 113
Woodard, L. E., 85
Wood, J. L., 50
Wood, C. 105, 120
Wright, L. L., 77, 101
Wyatt, J. N., 44

Yawkey, T. D., 145
Youn, M. J., 38
Young, R. A., 12, 15, 16, 140, 143, 144, 145, 161, 185, 194, 195, 202, 209, 217, 218, 227, 234, 236, 237, 238, 255

Subject Index

A Counselor's Guide to Career
    Assessment Instruments, 105
ABCD method, 124, 150
abilities inventory, 240
ability assessment results, 240
abstract thinking, 237, 254, 260, 299
academic
    abilities, 20
    achievement, 10, 40, 41, 50, 81, 93, 188,
        205, 206, 226
    advisement, 43, 60, 249, 260
    choices, 240
    content, 37, 128, 156, 178
    curriculum, 121, 155, 221, 228
    deficiency, 77
    demands, 75, 83, 257
    development, 168
    domain, ASCA, 122, 266
    enrichment, 182, 206
    expectations, 263
    growth, 178, 316
    motivation, 226
    opportunities, 156
    outcomes, 226
    planning, 270
    potential, 78, 82, 290, 292
    progress, 108, 249, 257, 277
    requirements, 75, 270,
    skills, 2, 3, 75, 79, 178, 185, 239, 268, 271
    standing, 260, 296
    success, 139, 142, 155, 167, 189, 207, 257,
        265, 302
    support, 46, 78
    transition, 203, 263
accelerated reader programs, 165
accessibility, 20, 78, 307, 313
    college, 4, 314
accommodate, 65, 107, 130, 268, 269, 310
accountability, 10, 48, 52, 104, 155, 286
accreditation, 53, 60, 104
acculturation, 80, 109

achievement, 3, 6, 24, 74, 75, 76, 81, 92, 93,
    103, 196, 218, 236, 244, 246, 293, 294,
    301, 326
    academic, 10, 40, 41, 50, 81, 93, 188, 205,
        206, 226
    gap, 10, 29, 63, 76, 83, 91, 118, 293, 294
    identity, 214, 236, 300
    test, 107, 109, 244, 246, 301
acquired skills, 128, 301
ACT, 6, 42, 43, 53, 69, 75, 77, 103, 118, 279, 294
ACT Aspire, 109
ACT WorkKeys, 109
active learning, 121
active listening, 23, 175, 229, 230
administrative support, 4, 33, 122
administrators, 15, 25, 26, 33, 47, 54, 177,
    179, 218, 293, 333
admissions, 27, 40, 43, 47, 53, 67, 70, 77, 81,
    89, 91, 131, 292, 324
    counselors, 71, 131, 327
    requirements, 40, 302, 324
    terminology, 41–42
adolescence, 211
    cognitive development in, 212, 237
    early, 185, 186, 211, 213, 214, 215, 236
    late, 139
    mid-, 277, 299, 317
    physical development in, 186, 211, 277
    psychosocial development in, 186, 213,
        236, 258, 280
adolescent
    career development, 15, 17, 20, 180, 215,
        260, 280, 301
    career growth
    development, 211, 258, 277, 299
adult, 121, 142, 143, 144, 146, 153, 154, 155, 164,
    165, 186, 213, 220, 236, 270, 278, 286, 331
    career development, 185, 214
    role models, 79, 86, 94, 219, 265, 290, 294
    roles, 20, 215
    workplace expectations, 15

adulthood, 180, 211
advanced degrees, 4
advanced placement (AP), 33, 40, 44, 45, 54, 78, 88, 91, 92, 93, 108, 235, 243, 248, 263, 264, 273, 283, 290, 292, 293, 294, 301, 302, 307
advising the college-bound student, 40
advisors, 78, 305, 331
advisory council, 118, 122, 130
advocacy, 92, 285, 294, 304
advocate, 34, 50, 70, 92, 104, 139, 294
African American, 9, 44, 76, 78, 88, 265, 292
    access to careers and colleges, 79
    college attendance, 4
    communities, 79
    degree attainment, 5
    earnings, 9, 74–75
    females, 36, 82, 284
    graduation rates, 4, 76, 77
    males, 50, 77, 289
    parent education levels, 5
    STEM majors, 12, 221
Afrocentric values, 79
afterschool enrichment program, 199
age of consent, 320
Ainsley, 220, 221
altruism, 237
American Community Survey, 73
American Indians. See Native Americans
American School Counselor Association (ASCA), 11, 33, 70, 121, 175
    Ethical Standards, 59
    Mindsets and Behaviors, 28, 33, 59, 150, 169, 170, 178, 196, 199, 204, 205, 219, 239, 264, 265, 285, 304, 322, 323
    National Model, 33, 68, 92, 121, 139, 145, 150
ancillary classes, 164, 176
anger management counseling, 212
anxiety, 40, 110, 141, 163, 188, 191, 193, 214, 278, 302
application
    college, 34, 40, 41, 42, 46, 69, 299, 314, 324, 328, 328, 333, 334
    deadlines, 69, 314
    essay, 323
    job, 84
aptitudes, 22, 26, 82, 103, 109, 195, 214, 215, 216, 218, 219, 299
Armed Services Vocational Aptitude Battery (ASVAB), 103–104, 109, 289
arts, 10, 112, 173, 176, 200, 201, 217, 228, 242, 278
ASCA. See American School Counselor Association
Asian, 40, 44, 78, 136, 293
    college attendance, 4
    degree attainment, 5
    earnings, 9, 74
    graduation rates, 4

parent education levels, 5
STEM majors, 12, 78
aspirations, 78, 216, 226, 228, 273, 286, 307
    career, 20, 38, 76, 78, 82, 144, 188, 215, 227
    educational, 40, 49, 91, 167, 179, 248
    occupational, 61, 176
assessment
    data, 64, 65, 103, 104, 105, 116, 117, 118, 268, 303
    instruments, 69, 105, 108, 118, 322
    procedures, 103
    resources, 26, 110
    results, 65, 66, 105, 116, 117, 122, 130, 240, 244, 293
    self-, 104, 110, 240, 241, 243, 244
Associate of Science in Nursing (ASN) degree, 34
associate's degrees (ADs), 8, 33, 40, 47, 49, 50, 51, 264
Association for Career and Technical Education, 3, 71
ASVAB. See Armed Services Vocational Aptitude Battery
athletics, 176, 177, 178, 186, 207, 216
at-risk students, 93
attendance, 41, 53, 78, 89, 90, 92, 256
    college, 4, 47, 50, 87, 110
    reports, 63
attitudes
    for success, 14
    positive, 149, 199
    work, 155, 199
auditory learners, 127
autism, 82
autonomy, 15, 61, 62, 142, 146, 228, 249, 300, 326
awareness
    career, 22, 147, 158, 238, 239, 240, 241, 243, 259, 265
    self-, 17, 22, 23, 34, 84, 108, 141, 167, 211, 217, 239, 241, 243, 262, 320

baby boomer generation, 73
Bachelor of Science in Nursing (BSN), 35
bachelor's degree, 5, 7, 8, 12, 24, 27, 35, 46, 49, 69, 188
Bandura's Social Learning Theory, 24, 185, 189, 202, 207
Barack Obama, 10, 11
barriers, 41, 64, 73, 75, 76, 80, 82, 86, 87, 88, 89, 91, 92, 105, 110, 115, 167, 170, 219, 272, 274, 296, 302, 324
behavior, 12, 14, 19
    prosocial, 141, 186, 279
    risk-taking, 189
    self-regulatory, 24, 178, 187, 199, 207, 214, 283
beliefs, 13, 22, 23, 59, 61, 62, 80, 81, 94, 103, 105, 108, 110, 119, 134, 143, 150, 168, 213, 220, 236, 260, 261, 280, 282, 285, 302, 304, 328

self-efficacy, 82, 193, 207, 257, 280, 283, 284, 286, 291, 301, 302
best practices, 26, 93, 175
biases, 23, 63, 76, 79, 92, 95, 118
biological traits, 216
biology, 12, 45, 69, 264, 284, 306
birth order, 15
Bloom's Taxonomy, 28, 123, 124
blue-collar employment, 6
bodily kinesthetic intelligence, 127
body image, 186, 212, 278
bridge programs, 46, 56
Bronfenbrenner's Bioecological Theory, 12–14, 167
Brown's Values-Based Theory, 320, 322
budget, 16, 23, 36, 37, 39, 84, 129, 158, 182, 202, 252, 269, 295, 331, 332, 334
business, 61, 67, 70, 77, 78, 111, 112, 173, 182, 188, 200, 201, 202, 217, 242, 247, 248, 259, 261, 264, 290, 299, 315, 316

California Career Zone, 129, 269
Campbell Interest and Skill Survey (CISS), 109
card sorts, 103, 113, 322
career activities, 169, 203, 238
career adaptability, 320, 321, 335
career and college
　choice, 219, 243, 262, 317, 322
　decisions, 76, 86, 105, 150, 230, 269, 277
　options, 26, 35, 154, 216, 218, 231, 243, 246, 248, 253, 259
　outcomes, 5, 140, 239, 273, 274
　planning, 34, 54, 62, 64, 66, 67, 69, 227, 231, 237, 239, 260, 268, 271, 273, 274, 277, 285, 287, 295
　preparation, 10, 34, 180, 204, 277, 280
career and college readiness, 2, 10, 12, 13, 15, 16, 21, 25, 33, 34, 44, 54, 56, 59, 60, 61, 63, 64, 66, 67, 71, 73, 76, 79, 83, 92, 94, 103, 104, 105, 107, 108, 116, 118, 122, 123, 129, 139, 140, 141, 143, 145, 150, 153, 157, 163, 167, 168, 175, 179, 180, 182, 185, 194, 198, 199, 202, 207, 212, 215, 218, 223, 224, 227, 228, 229, 240, 243, 246, 247, 249, 251, 252, 253, 257, 259, 260, 264, 265, 267, 279
　capital, 56
　counseling, 59, 60, 61, 63, 71, 104, 182, 207, 266
　curriculum, 28, 37, 122, 124, 126, 128, 129, 130, 136, 145, 150, 153, 170, 175, 198, 218, 219, 226, 267
　definition, 2, 3, 29
　development, 13, 277
　framework, 15
　interventions, 17, 26, 28, 60, 63, 67, 70, 74, 95, 105, 121, 145, 167, 196, 211, 258, 259, 274

programming, 27, 28, 63, 67, 68
programs, 16, 129, 151, 229
roles of stakeholders, 24, 25, 26, 27, 178, 179, 202
skills, 22, 43, 84, 239
trends, 3
career assessment, 70, 78, 104, 105, 231
Career Beliefs Inventory (CBI), 110,
career choice, 1, 19, 38, 69, 82, 84, 86, 125, 130, 144, 154, 176, 194, 215, 220, 221, 227, 236, 237, 238, 259, 266, 272, 274, 321
career cluster, 63, 112, 118, 122, 125, 127, 130, 152, 153, 154, 166, 171, 172, 173, 174, 178, 179, 180, 196, 201, 204, 245, 251, 253, 311
career competency, 174
career concern, 80, 230, 321
Career Construction Theory, 115, 301, 303
career conversation, 218, 229, 230, 231
career counseling, 18, 21, 59, 60, 62, 63, 69, 70, 71, 104, 105, 139, 217, 260, 266, 315
career counselor, 59, 70, 286, 292
career curiosity, 321
career curriculum, 26, 172, 189, 217, 229, 252
　development, 150
　integration, 226
　objectives, 130
career decision making, 22, 85, 104, 105, 110, 143, 147, 149, 195, 236, 238, 268, 322
　self-efficacy, 82, 196, 219
　skills, 78
Career Decision-Making Self-Efficacy Scale (CDSE), 110
Career Development Inventory (CDI), 110
career expectancy, 188
career exploration, 47, 78, 81, 110, 112, 122, 146, 147, 171, 178, 195, 196, 197, 198, 216, 217, 226, 229, 230, 236, 249
　activities, 22, 52, 54, 127, 170, 195, 196, 262
　courses, 331
　opportunities, 228
　skills, 22, 231
　software programs, 129
career exposure, 151, 245
career fair, 131, 245, 291
career gender typing, 231
career goals, 22, 34, 37, 63, 76, 204, 217, 262, 286, 291, 300, 312, 320, 327, 334
career growth, 60, 126, 140, 167, 168, 178, 180, 215
career guidance, 78, 108, 180, 322
career guidance systems, 108, 241, 322
　DISCOVER, 112, 241
　EXPLORE, 112, 241, 244, 293
　Kuder, 112, 241, 244, 266, 310
　O*Net, 52, 66, 129, 155, 173, 197, 241

career indecision, 85, 86, 321, 325
career indifference, 321
career influences, 238
career information, 127, 173, 174, 178, 182, 195, 196, 245, 272
career inhibition, 321, 328
career interests, 62, 81, 105, 195, 285
Career Key, 111
career knowledge, 15, 28, 142, 171, 226, 264, 268
career language, 148, 149
career maturity, 82, 85, 110, 125, 149, 195
career opportunities, 154, 217, 261, 279
career options, 35, 143, 144, 151, 152, 172, 217, 259, 266, 309, 312, 320
career outcomes, 37, 84, 188
career planning, 66, 110, 112, 174, 180, 196, 292
career play, 142, 163–182
career preparation, 75, 84, 204
career role, 149, 236
career role models, 192, 195, 252, 291
career self-efficacy, 79, 207, 228, 267
career shadowing, 15
Career Style Interview (CSI), 115, 304, 309, 310, 311, 312
career success, 1, 23, 54, 73, 75, 83, 85, 174, 189, 191, 207, 219, 225, 236, 238, 265, 285, 304, 323
Career Thoughts Inventory (CTI), 110
career values, 125, 130, 220, 231
Career Values Card Sort, 113, 219, 220
career-bound student, 33, 47
CareerOneStop website, 52
careers in the military, 242
census data, 74
Center for Credentialing in Education (CCE), 71
central tendency, 66
certification requirements, 261
certified nurse assistant (CNA), 34
certified welder (CW) program, 48
characteristics
  cultural, 76, 128
  developmental, 236, 258, 277
  familial, 15
  individual, 80, 168
  inherent, 18
  personal, 21, 75, 104, 197
  secondary sexual, 186, 211
checklists, 103, 322
child labor laws, 16
child life role, 280, 282
childhood, 20
  early, 149, 163, 185
  late, 186, 187
  middle, 163, 165, 166, 167, 168, 169, 171, 175, 179, 182, 185, 187

circumscription, 20, 76, 86, 143, 144, 146, 169, 193, 215, 216, 237, 260, 274
citizen, 4, 5, 87, 145, 280, 281
classification system, 18, 19
classroom teachers, 169, 176, 178, 198, 204, 244, 245, 246, 247, 268, 305, 328
clubs, 15, 78, 165, 200, 251, 305, 306, 307
coaches, 154, 177, 305, 312
cognitive abilities, 279
cognitive deficits, 113
cognitive development, 28, 141, 142, 143, 145, 166, 171, 187, 212, 213, 214, 237, 259, 278
cognitive skills, 23, 109, 166, 213
collaboration, 3, 13, 26, 28, 47, 54, 61, 67, 122, 129, 145, 153, 165, 171, 175, 176, 178, 226, 227, 231, 250, 265, 272, 328, 334
collectivism vs. individualism, 322
collectivistic cultures, 321
college admissions, 42, 43, 44, 47, 67, 70, 71, 91, 131, 218, 324
college admissions terminology, 41
college affordability, 73
college application assistance, 40, 46
college applications, 34, 40, 41, 42, 299, 314, 324, 328
college aspirations, 40, 49, 91, 167, 179
college choice, 11, 38, 89, 216, 219, 243, 259, 262, 300, 309, 317, 322, 325, 326, 334
college credit, 37, 44, 47, 50, 88, 290
college decision-making factors, 26, 38
college degree, 2, 4, 5, 23, 27, 33, 49, 77, 90, 115, 218, 235, 245, 295, 312
college enrollment, 4, 40, 228
college entrance exams, 33, 43, 91
college entrance requirements, 46, 67, 75
college exploration process, 313
college fairs, 27, 52, 68, 129, 197, 198, 324, 327
college graduation rates, 4, 218
college life, 75, 83
college majors, 112, 113, 155
College Navigator, 11, 53
college pay off, 34
college persistence rates, 75
college preparatory curriculum, 24, 235
college recruiters, 327
College Signing Day, 11, 53, 54, 334
college tours, 52, 314
college transition programs, 313
college virtual tour, 314
college visits, 34, 314
college-bound, 40, 56, 62, 252
college-bound culture, 40, 150
college-going culture, 40, 52, 155, 156, 179, 226, 291, 333
college-ready student, 2, 39

communication skills, 23, 174, 178, 219, 224, 229, 295, 304, 311, 324
community activities, 79, 197
community and social responsibility, 155
community college stigma, 49
community colleges, 4, 33, 46, 49, 50, 75, 228
community helpers, 148, 149
community members, 130, 235, 305, 316, 324
community partnerships, 156
community service, 242, 279
compromise, 20, 30, 76, 86, 132, 143, 169, 193, 215, 237, 238, 260, 261, 262, 272, 274
concrete operations, 166, 167, 187
concrete thinking, 166, 237, 259
confidence, 55, 164, 165, 170, 171, 192, 226, 258, 278, 283, 291, 302, 306, 321
  career, 55, 321, 321, 328, 335
  over-, 189, 302
  self-, 140, 145, 170, 197, 199, 219, 239, 285, 294, 304, 323
  under-, 302
confidentiality, 61, 65
conflict, 23, 85, 110, 141, 149, 165, 175, 258, 267, 326
conflict resolution, 146, 165, 166, 175, 178, 199, 236, 252, 280
conservation, 166, 187
Consortium on Chicago School Research (CCSR), 40, 41, 49
consultation, 61, 67, 153, 155
content knowledge, 2
contextual learning strategies, 142, 245
Council for Accreditation of Counseling and Related Educational Programs (CACREP), 60, 66
Council for Exceptional Children's Division on Career Development and Transition, 71
course offerings, 15, 26, 75, 93
course registration, 78, 271
courses of study, 235
cover letter, 84, 197, 198, 307, 308, 329
creativity, 18, 79, 145, 146, 170, 212, 220, 231, 250, 322
critical data elements, 92
critical thinking, 3, 23, 37, 43, 44, 49, 132, 133, 139, 199, 224, 237, 263, 308, 323
cross-age program, 199, 200
crystallization, 125, 262, 267, 274
Cubans, 5
cultural
  beliefs and values, 13, 16, 20
  bias, 107
  considerations, 20, 23, 73, 95
  expectations, 16
  group, 78, 93, 281
  heritage, 23
  insensitivity, 79

sensitivity, 23, 28, 92, 174, 175
  stereotypes, 82, 171
  values, 76, 78, 322
culturally responsive curriculum, 28, 30, 126
culturally sensitive practices, 28, 95
culture, 2, 14, 16, 33, 38, 40, 54, 63, 74, 80, 83, 94, 126, 128, 134, 153, 157, 167, 168, 182, 187, 215, 321
curricular choices, 24, 240, 243, 247, 248
curriculum, 15, 24, 26, 28, 30, 37, 40, 52, 54, 61, 92, 121, 122, 123, 124, 125, 126, 128, 129, 130, 136, 139, 145, 147, 149, 150, 151, 153, 154, 155, 157, 159, 169, 170, 172, 175, 176, 179, 189, 191, 196, 197, 198, 199, 200, 203, 204, 205, 211, 217, 218, 219, 221, 225, 226, 227, 229, 235, 239, 240, 242, 243, 244, 247, 248, 265, 267, 268, 286, 295, 304, 307, 322
curriculum design, 61, 169
curriculum development, 28, 121, 122, 136, 150, 151, 196, 304, 322

Deferred Action for Childhood Arrivals (DACA), 87, 88
deafness, 82
dean's list, 81
debt, 23, 24, 35, 37, 39, 331, 334
decision-making self-efficacy, 82, 110, 147, 196, 219
decision-making model, 62
decision-making process, 56, 104, 144, 195, 237, 238, 242, 243, 247, 251, 279, 286, 299, 300
decision-making skills, 78
decisions, 1, 11, 19, 21, 22, 26, 30, 38, 40, 42, 52, 53, 62, 64, 66, 68, 76, 78, 80, 85, 86, 103, 104, 105, 110, 115, 116, 117, 122, 130, 133, 147, 150, 192, 213, 219, 220, 221, 230, 231, 235, 236, 239, 240, 243, 244, 249, 253, 258, 261, 269, 277, 278, 279, 300, 301, 304, 310, 311, 312, 316, 319, 320, 321, 322, 323, 324, 325, 326, 331, 333
deficit, 36, 46, 78, 113, 189
depression, 188, 193
developmental
  delay, 82
  differences, 243
  level, 13, 62, 65
  milestones, 27, 163, 182, 207, 274, 279
  needs, 116, 129, 204, 270
  overview, 140, 163, 185, 211, 229, 236, 258, 277, 299, 319
Differential Aptitude Test (DAT), 109
differentiation, 213, 309
diffusion, 214, 219, 236, 260, 272, 300
disabilities, 2, 10, 21, 31, 47, 64, 67, 71, 82, 83, 84, 85, 106, 107, 111, 118, 145, 163, 289, 312, 332

disability status, 63
disability support services, 313
disaggregate data, 118
discrimination, 76, 85, 86, 168
discriminatory practice, 77
disengagement, 19, 50, 320
disparity in educational achievement, 76
disparity of earnings, 8
dispositions, 2, 22, 214, 216, 218
diverse learners, 126
diverse populations, 4, 61, 63, 71, 93, 107
diversity, 2, 23, 30, 60, 126, 131, 132, 133,
    136, 182, 215, 231, 290
doctoral degree, 4, 35, 36, 38, 56, 81
dreams, 87, 154, 236, 319
dropout rates, 92, 257
dual enrollment (DE), 33, 44, 48, 49, 93, 364

early action, 42
early decision, 42
earnings, 36, 52, 231
    by education level, 7, 9
    by race or ethnicity, 9,
    female/women's, 9,
    male/men's, 9
ecological and systems theories, 12
ecological frameworks, 168
economic concern, 16
economic recession, 8, 12, 36
ecosystemic, 1, 15, 140, 144, 238
Education and Economic Development
    Act, 26
education policy, 75
educational
    achievement, 76, 83, 92
    aspirations, 248
    attainment, 5, 9, 27, 31, 32, 180, 220
    disparities, 92
    opportunities, 61, 91, 242
    planning, 34, 70, 75, 182
    requirements, 20, 242, 261, 269, 312
educators, 2, 22, 23, 24, 27, 60, 64, 65, 66,
    67, 68, 70, 71, 74, 82, 105, 106, 107, 108,
    114, 115, 117, 118, 123, 124, 253, 257, 274,
    277, 279, 296, 317, 333, 335
efficacy, 24, 47, 145, 165, 189, 191, 192, 196,
    197, 198, 199, 200, 201, 202, 207
efficacy beliefs, 24, 193
egocentric, 141, 237, 259, 283
Elementary and Secondary Education Act, 10
elementary school, 50, 139, 143, 144, 146,
    151, 155, 156, 158, 163, 172, 174, 176, 179,
    181, 182, 185, 186, 194, 197, 200, 203
elementary school counselor, 136, 146, 154,
    170, 172, 175, 176, 180, 185, 192, 194, 199,
    203, 222
elementary students, 113, 115, 121, 143,
    144, 145, 150, 172, 179, 195

emotional
    arousal, 192
    development, 140, 141, 186
    independence, 213
    risk, 227
    self-regulation, 141, 155, 186, 191, 212
    support, 165
emotions, 141, 189, 190, 191, 192, 193, 205,
    206, 212, 214, 217, 218, 227, 319
empathy, 132, 141, 146, 170, 186, 189, 197,
    237, 279, 331
employability, 24, 35, 48
    issues, 8
    skills, 3, 22, 24, 47, 71, 73, 295
employed, 8, 76, 77, 224
employment, 1, 3, 8, 12, 14, 24, 36, 47, 52,
    73, 84, 89, 90, 115, 154, 168, 225, 242, 273,
    281, 282, 289, 315, 316, 320
    blue-collar, 6
    outcomes, 6
    of parents, 16
    rates, 2, 8
encouragement, 26, 82, 164, 165, 176, 192,
    283, 286, 287, 291, 296, 305, 306, 317,
    328, 329
English, 43, 87, 107, 109, 112, 206, 220, 240,
    243, 244, 248, 264, 270, 274, 294, 305, 307,
    308, 310, 312, 313, 314, 315, 323, 332
    benchmarks, 3, 6
English-language learners (ELL), 2, 74, 192
English proficiency, 47, 75
English teachers, 305, 307, 308, 314
English speaking skills, 111
enrichment programs, 182
enrollment, 2, 4, 29, 34, 36, 40, 45, 46, 53,
    56, 83, 92, 228, 293, 294
environmental factors, 5, 86, 189, 211,
    215, 301
equilibrium, 212
equity, 2, 33, 92, 133, 294
    -based programming, 2
ethical
    issues, 61, 62, 63
    system, 213
ethnicity, 9, 31, 36, 38, 40, 74, 118, 216, 290
evaluation, 59, 66, 67, 68, 103, 104, 105, 116,
    118, 128, 129, 130, 135, 212, 216, 260, 293
Every Student Succeeds Act, 10, 33, 139
evidence of academic rigor and college
    preparation, 42
experiential learning, 142
experiential opportunities, 304, 307
explicit influence, 15, 238
exploration, 19, 22, 35, 47, 52, 54, 55, 56,
    73, 78, 81, 86, 91, 110, 112, 118, 122, 127,
    129, 136, 139, 142, 146, 147, 157, 163, 164,
    169, 170, 171, 172, 174, 178, 193, 195, 196,
    197, 198, 202, 211, 214, 216, 217, 219, 224,

226, 228, 229, 230, 231, 236, 240, 242, 249, 253, 258, 259, 262, 265, 266, 300, 313, 320, 322, 331
exploration stage, 320, 321
extracurricular activities, 15, 24, 40, 202, 216, 222, 247, 263, 304, 306

faculty, 39, 78, 93, 94, 108, 131, 176, 179, 182, 226, 270, 295
faculty in-service, 25, 28, 54, 94, 131, 153, 155, 228, 270, 286
family
  income, 75, 180
  involvement, 115, 202
  members, 13, 16, 54, 76, 80, 115, 143, 153, 194, 213, 220, 221, 227, 246
  of origin, 213, 220, 231
  socioeconomic status (SES), 16, 26
  system, 213, 227, 258
  values, 27, 230
federal initiatives, 10, 12, 16, 29, 33, 139, 181, 333
feedback, 21, 68, 92, 129, 166, 192, 224, 224, 246, 253, 283, 284, 286, 289, 290, 305, 310, 314
females, 12, 16, 20, 76, 82, 88, 106, 168, 187, 216, 217, 221, 290, 291
field trips, 15, 132, 179, 201, 204, 247, 315, 334
fifth- to sixth-grade transition, 203, 204
financial aid, 24, 27, 34, 41, 50, 53, 88, 90, 91, 290, 312, 324, 333, 334
Financial Aid Shopping Sheet, 11, 53
financial literacy skills, 23
financial resources, 11, 78, 333
financial support, 37, 333
fine motor skills, 164
first-generation college students, 2, 5, 41, 63, 90, 118, 248, 265, 291, 313, 328, 329, 332
first year seminar courses, 331
focus group, 204, 248
follow-up activities, 115, 128, 262
foreclosure, 214, 219, 236, 299, 300, 331
foreign language, 10, 46, 176, 235, 263, 264
formal abstract thought, 212, 215, 259, 279
formal assessment, 108, 109, 110, 116, 240, 241
foster student, 88, 89
Frank Parsons, 17
Free Applications for Federal Student Aid (FAFSA), 11, 24, 41, 331
full-time employment, 73, 281, 282
future careers, 55, 214, 227, 231, 260, 277, 299, 315, 319
future goal, 213, 214, 222, 272, 286, 294, 296, 307, 317, 320, 321
future planning, 239, 254, 267, 273, 274, 284, 297

Gaining Early Awareness and Readiness for Undergraduate Programs (GEAR UP), 47, 91
Gay/Straight Alliance, 313
gender development, 185
gender ideals, 187
gender pay gap, 36
gender roles, 146, 147, 169, 187
gender socialization, 143, 189
gender stereotypes, 76
gender type, 143, 229, 230
General Education Development Test (GED), 87, 316
genogram, 113, 114, 115, 127, 220, 221, 231
gifted, 40, 78
gifted education, 77, 78, 92
Global Career Development Facilitator (GCDF), 71
global economies, 16
goal setting, 34, 66, 81, 178, 182, 205, 250, 257, 265, 268, 293
Gottfredson's Theory of Circumscription and Compromise, 20, 76, 143, 169, 193, 215, 237
grade level expectations (GLEs), 122
grade point average (GPA), 38, 40, 42, 43, 45, 47, 53, 69, 75, 81, 85, 92, 228, 250, 260, 279, 287, 308, 309, 312, 325
graduate school, 4, 81
graduates, 37, 43, 44, 71, 96, 261, 313, 329, 331
graduation plans, 270
graduation rate, 4, 53, 68, 77, 80, 316
  college, 2, 5, 8, 11, 12, 218
  high school, 4, 6, 79
graduation requirements, 67, 250, 253, 269, 270
gross motor skills, 163
growth rate, 4, 49, 52
growth spurts, 211
growth stage, 262

habitus, 167, 168
hands-on learning, 142, 156
health impairments, 82, 83
height, 144, 212, 278
helping students research career and technical programs, 51
heredity, 216
heritage, 23, 74
high school counselors, 250
high school
  courses, 78, 253, 272
  curriculum, 40, 218, 235, 239, 240, 243, 247, 248
  diploma, 5, 6, 8, 9, 71, 87, 249, 251
  dropouts, 76
  education, 27
  graduation rates, 4, 79

program of study, 244
transition, 235, 244, 247, 332
high-stakes testing, 155
higher education, 33, 36, 42, 46, 47, 52, 53, 75, 91, 131, 139, 178, 328
higher order thinking skills, 15, 22, 23, 28
Hispanic males, 76
Hispanics, 5, 74, 75, 76, 221
historically Black colleges and universities (HBCUs), 79
hobbies, 116, 216, 258, 262, 287, 303, 305, 308
Holland Code, 18, 19, 52, 78, 110, 241, 245, 303, 309
Holland type, 112, 216, 217
Holland's Occupations Finder, 19, 241
Holland's Self Directed Search (SDS), 240
Holland's Theory of Vocational Choice, 18, 216, 238, 261
homeless student, 67, 88, 89, 90, 332
homemaker, 221, 280, 281
honors, 81, 93, 40, 45, 54, 63, 81, 93, 131, 235, 248, 263, 264, 293, 294, 307, 309, 325
hormones, 186, 212
hospitality, 112, 171
hypothetical thinking, 278

identification with parents, 15, 217
identities, 81, 133, 134, 222, 223, 238, 240, 259, 279, 283, 286, 320, 330
identity achievement, 214, 300
identity development, 236, 330
identity diffusion, 214, 260, 300
identity foreclosure, 214, 299
identity formation, 213, 231, 266
identity statuses, 214, 23, 236, 299
identity vs. role confusion, 213, 214, 236, 258, 279, 319
implementation, 66, 67, 68, 83, 87, 176, 178, 238
income, 2, 4, 6, 8, 9, 23, 35, 46, 47, 53, 74, 75, 76, 77, 80, 90, 92, 158, 180, 201, 215, 281, 316, 332, 333
independence, 90, 185, 205, 213, 231, 281, 320, 326, 331
Individual Education Plan (IEP), 65, 83
Individual Graduation Plan (IGP), 244, 252, 286, 287, 288
individual planning, 28, 61, 244, 271, 272
individualism, 322
Individuals with Disabilities Education Act (IDEA), 82
industry, 1, 12, 15, 33, 37, 47, 67, 127, 140, 154, 164, 165, 167, 186, 213, 295
industry recognized credentials (IRCs) or industry-based credentials (IBCs), 33, 47–49, 51, 56, 295,
advantages of, 48–49

industry vs. inferiority, 140, 164, 167, 186, 213
informal assessments, 108, 112, 113, 116, 118, 119, 322
information sessions, 118, 248, 269, 271, 274
initiative vs. guilt, 140
integration, 15, 26, 81, 129, 159, 182, 199, 226, 227, 244
intellect, 18
intellectual abilities, 238
intelligence, 27, 50, 127, 201, 212, 215, 251, 260
interaction, 13, 15, 17, 18, 21, 22, 23, 55, 61, 62, 77, 121, 153, 155, 159, 178, 189, 205, 212, 213, 216, 217, 237, 272, 303
interest inventory, 111, 112, 117, 250, 241, 252, 262, 267
internal motivation, 165
internalization, 167, 168
Internet, 77, 134, 156, 157, 173, 174, 273
interpersonal relationships, 213
interpersonal skills, 18, 55, 174, 185, 206, 237, 239
interpretation, 65, 103, 109, 116, 117, 118, 217, 310, 312,
intersectionality, 74
interview protocols, 22
interviewing skills, 34, 84, 94, 324

Jean Piaget, 141, 187, 212, 237, 238, 278
job application, 3, 84
job environment, 292
job growth, 12, 73
job market, 73
job satisfaction, 18
job shadowing, 22, 27, 67, 247, 262, 269, 284, 287, 289, 291, 292, 304, 316
job success, 18
John Holland, 17, 18

kindergarten, 123, 139, 140, 147, 148, 149, 151, 152, 155–157, 171
kinesthetic learners, 127
Kuder Career Planning System, 112

labor market information, 66, 182
language barriers, 274
Latin America, 74
Latino Student Association, 313
Latinos, 9, 74, 75, 95, 328
learned helplessness, 165
learning disability, 82, 111
learning objectives, 28, 122, 123, 130
learning strategies, 142, 145, 170, 197, 219, 239, 245, 265, 304
learning styles, 65, 107, 118, 126, 127, 128, 130, 269, 310
legacy applicants, 42
leisure, 12, 205, 280, 303. 310

leisurite, 280–282
LGBT, 85–86
life decisions, 300, 322
life plan, 217, 286, 306, 316
life roles, 19, 205, 262, 280, 281, 283, 286, 295–297
life skills training, 84
Life-Span, Life-Space Theory, 19, 262, 280, 320
Life Values Inventory, 322, 325, 326
Life Career Rainbow, 280–282, 296
life-long learning, 1, 219, 265, 285, 304, 323
lifestyle, 23, 186, 269, 284
linguistic Intelligence, 127
loan, 23–24, 36–37, 39
logical-mathematical intelligence, 127
low performing schools, 334
low SES, 10, 41, 49, 180, 221, 289
lower-level thinking, 28

macrosystems, 13, 187
magnet or charter schools, 284
maintenance, 14, 19, 36, 76, 242
male bravado, 189
manners, 144, 174
marginalized groups, 167
marketing, 15, 111–112, 131, 177, 201–202, 242
master's degree, 4, 35–36
mastery experiences, 283, 287, 292, 296, 302, 305–307, 316, 321
math activities, 181, 225
math careers, 225
math skills, 181, 225–226, 245, 259, 264
matriculate, 5, 82
McKinney–Vento, 89
measurement techniques, 103
mechanical abilities, 212
media literacy, 231
mental health, 62, 90, 163, 188, 191
mental retardation, 82, 111
mentoring, 16, 39, 47, 199, 205, 290–291
mentors, 17, 27, 37, 76, 78–79, 86, 88, 91, 94, 188, 200, 290–291, 334
mesosystem, 13–15
Mexicans, 5
Michael and Susan Dell Foundation, 11
Michelle Obama, 11, 53
microaggressions, 77, 134–135
microinsults, 79
microinvalidations, 79
microsystems, 13–15, 238
middle childhood, 163, 165–169, 171, 175, 179, 182, 185, 187
middle school counselor, 121, 136, 203–204, 207, 212, 214, 224, 225, 228, 229, 250

middle school students, 34, 110, 202–203, 206, 215–217, 218–219, 222, 224–226, 228, 231, 240
middle school transition, 185, 196, 204
migratory children, 10
milestones, 27, 67, 163, 182, 207, 274, 280, 299
military, 67, 87, 104, 109, 235, 242–243, 248, 289, 315, 332, 334
military career, 242
Missouri Grade Level Expectations (GLEs), 122
moral development, 79, 142, 237
moratorium, 214, 219, 236, 258, 300
motivation, 145, 165, 168, 170, 197, 199, 211, 215, 218, 226, 265–266
motor skills, 163–164, 212
multiple intelligences, 127, 201
musical Intelligence, 127
My Vocational Situation, 110
Myers-Briggs Type Indicator, 111, 266

National Association for College Admission Counseling (NACAC), 33–34, 40, 71
National Career Development Association (NCDA), 59–60, 62–64, 66–67, 70, 103
  Code of Ethics, 62
  Minimum Competencies for Multicultural Career Counseling and Development, 59
National Science Foundation (NSF), 75
Native Americans, 79–80, 221
naturalistic intelligence, 127
naviance, 112
NCDA. *See* National Career Development Association
need-blind admission, 42
needs assessment, 123, 150, 229, 251, 268, 295
negative feedback, 21, 192, 283
neighborhood, 13–14, 54, 325
Net Price Calculator Center, 53
newsletter, 156, 157, 248, 327, 329
No Child Left Behind Act (NCLB), 10
nonstandardized tests, 103
nontraditional careers, 107, 169, 252, 289–291
nonverbal assessment, 111
norms, 2, 107, 112, 165, 252

O*Net, 52, 66, 129, 155, 173, 197, 241
Obama administration, 87
objectives, 25, 28, 121–126, 128–131, 136, 153, 268, 324
observations, 15, 103
occupation clusters, 6
occupation fit, 240, 246
occupational choices, 17, 245, 268, 283, 322

occupational information, 108, 110, 112, 125, 254

Occupational Outlook Handbook, 35, 38, 49, 66, 129, 155, 173, 197, 229, 241, 252

occupational skills, 245

occupational status, 180

online application, 328

on-the-job training, 173, 261

open admission, 42, 46

oppression, 76–77, 95, 168

optimism, 144, 321

Orientation to Internal, Unique Self, 20, 260–261

Orientation to Sex Roles, 20, 144, 169, 182, 187

Orientation to Size and Power, 20, 144

Orientation to Social Valuation, 20, 193, 215–216, 237

orthopedic impairment, 82

outcome expectations, 280, 283–285, 295, 301–302, 307

parent education, 92, 180, 248

parent engagement, 156, 179, 182, 202

parent volunteers, 201, 290

parent workshops, 25, 28, 54, 131, 153, 158, 204, 248, 250, 329

parent–child interaction, 15, 217

parent–teacher conference, 13, 157

partnering, 64, 203, 221, 240, 247–248, 250, 272–273, 290–291, 316, 324

partnership, 12, 14, 47, 156, 179, 200, 226, 247, 249, 290, 316

part-time college students, 5

part-time employment, 281, 320

part-time jobs, 295

part-time work, 15

past performance, 301–302, 307

pedagogy, 28, 126

peer group, 186, 194, 236, 279

peer influence, 38, 238, 258, 272, 278, 299, 306

peer relationships, 319, 330

peer tutoring, 199, 263

pensioner, 280

perceptions, 20, 75, 86, 117, 127, 144, 188, 219–217, 221, 238, 244, 247, 303

perceptual abilities, 212

performance accomplishment, 192, 194, 196, 198–201

performance assessments, 103

performance attainment, 301–302

performance goals, 301–302, 305, 307

performance model 301–302

persistence, 45, 56, 75, 82, 110, 191, 222, 251, 301–302, 305

personal characteristics, 21, 75, 104, 197

personal fable, 237, 260, 274, 278, 279

personal goals, 283, 285, 297, 300

personal narratives, 303

personal responsibility, 91, 178, 187, 196, 279

personality, 18, 19, 103–105, 212, 216, 238, 240, 241, 260, 262, 265–267, 303, 305

personality styles, 104

personality traits, 111, 216

personality types, 18–19, 262
    artistic, 18
    conventional, 18
    enterprising, 18
    investigative, 18
    realistic, 18
    social, 18

physical change, 186, 211, 212, 277, 278

physical development, 163, 164, 186, 211, 277, 278

physical education and health classes, 268

physical requirements, 278, 283

physiological, 186, 190

Pictorial Inventory of Careers, 111

PLAN, 293–295

play techniques, 140, 142, 145–147, 159

play therapy, 146, 147

Plyler v. Doe, 87

popular culture, 187

populations, 2, 4, 8, 10, 11, 28, 29, 36, 61, 63, 64, 66, 67, 71, 73, 74, 76, 79, 83, 90, 93, 95, 106, 107, 118, 145, 170, 225, 264, 274, 279, 304, 313, 328, 332

portfolio, 103, 112, 113, 203

positive reinforcement, 199

postsecondary education, 2–4, 6, 11, 23, 24, 27, 33, 34, 38, 40, 46, 47, 49, 53, 61, 64, 66, 70, 71, 75, 79, 83, 87, 88, 91, 129, 143, 154, 156, 170, 179, 194, 197, 206, 219, 224, 228, 251, 252, 257, 265, 277, 285, 304, 312, 315, 316, 319, 323, 329, 333

postsecondary enrollment, 29

postsecondary institutions, 46, 83, 167, 228, 312–314

postsecondary life, 1, 23, 175

postsecondary options, 34, 35, 37, 56, 75, 76, 94, 139, 144, 170, 174, 188, 219, 228, 240, 243, 253, 258, 312, 324, 334

postsecondary plans, 240, 324, 329

postsecondary preparation, 73, 84, 93, 163, 270

postsecondary success, 16, 76, 77, 79, 159, 158, 167

postsecondary training, 82, 112, 140, 235, 263

postsecondary transitions, 315, 316, 319, 321, 322

potential, 11, 16, 25, 35, 38, 41, 44, 49, 51, 53, 60, 61, 63, 68, 74, 78, 82, 88–90, 92, 108, 118, 174, 190, 204, 212, 219, 224, 240, 242,

244–246, 259, 267, 279, 281, 287, 290–293, 296, 300, 302, 306, 308, 316, 324, 328
poverty, 2, 6, 8, 75, 77, 80, 144, 157
Preliminary Scholastic Aptitude Test (PSAT), 292–295, 312
preoperational stage, 142
preoperational thought, 141, 142
prestige, 20, 78, 168, 180, 193, 194, 212, 215, 227
private schools, 39, 332
problem solving, 3, 37, 43, 44, 49, 79, 139, 166, 174, 175, 193, 218, 220, 224, 237, 259, 263, 295, 299, 311
professional development, 26, 34, 69–72, 175, 293, 307, 333
professional learning communities, 93, 95
program of study, 244, 263, 264, 286, 308
program planning, 67, 68, 117, 118
prosocial behavior, 141, 186, 279
psychosocial development, 164, 167, 213, 236, 258, 266, 279
puberty, 186, 277, 278
Puerto Ricans, 5
puppets, 128, 147, 151, 152

quality of life, 11

Race to the Top Fund, 12
Reach Higher, 10, 11, 33, 53, 54, 333
reading, 6, 10, 11, 43, 44, 65, 83, 107, 109, 111, 112, 127, 130, 150, 152, 156, 165, 180, 182, 218, 244, 263, 273, 292, 294
Reading-Free Vocational Interest Inventory, 111
reciprocal determinism, 189
reciprocity, 13, 212
referral, 61, 63, 189, 218, 267
refraction, 147, 148
refusal, 50
regular decision, 42
relationships, 13, 16, 113, 131, 141, 146, 165, 166, 168, 170, 171, 175, 179, 186, 196, 213, 214, 219, 236, 237, 239, 257, 262, 265, 283, 291, 264, 306, 319, 320, 329, 330, 332
reliability, 65, 106, 109, 112, 118, 119
religion, 74, 86, 168, 216
religious affiliation, 52, 192, 300, 312, 314, 326
remedial courses, 45, 46, 75, 235, 263
resources to facilitate college decision making, 52
respect, 116, 135, 142, 281
responsibility, 3, 65, 66, 91, 133, 153, 155, 156, 170, 178, 187, 196, 205, 224, 239, 250, 265, 279, 286, 311, 321, 323, 325
resume, 3, 24, 94, 197, 198, 217, 304, 307–309, 315, 324, 329

retention rates, 78, 257
retirement, 73, 77, 332
reversibility, 166, 212
rigor, 10, 26, 42–45, 49, 82, 196, 204, 264, 293, 294
rigorous course offerings, 26, 75, 93
role models, 76, 82, 94, 116, 169, 192, 195, 200, 203, 252, 290, 291, 310, 311, 329
role-play, 149, 331
role salience, 280–282
roles, 5, 13, 16, 19, 20, 24, 60, 104, 143, 144, 146, 147, 149, 153, 157, 165, 169, 182, 187–189, 201, 205, 206, 214, 230, 258, 260, 262, 280–283, 286, 295–297, 301, 303, 305, 311, 319
rolling admission, 42

salary, 9, 35, 36, 53, 84, 198, 269, 332
SAT. *See* Scholastic Aptitude Test
scholarship, 21, 24, 39, 88, 125, 130, 182, 250, 251, 285, 292, 296, 334
Scholastic Aptitude Test (SAT), 44, 53, 75, 91, 92, 273, 284, 292, 294, 301, 324
school districts, 70, 92, 104, 241, 257, 263, 327
school environment, 126, 133, 145, 219, 265, 294
school personnel, 14, 34, 67, 70, 88, 89, 130, 202, 203, 235, 238, 239, 286, 289, 292, 305, 307
school population, 28, 229, 290
school to school transition, 15
school to work transition, 15
school website, 248, 313
school-wide initiatives, 296, 317
science, technology, engineering, and math (STEM), 11, 12, 16, 29, 76, 78, 81, 82, 85, 94, 95, 129, 155, 181, 188, 200, 221–224, 289, 325
seasonal and part-time employees, 15
second-language learners, 10, 65, 107
secondary sexual characteristics, 186, 211
selectivity, 38, 42, 45
self- and career awareness, 238, 259, 265
self-assessment, 104, 110, 240, 241, 243, 244
self-awareness, 17, 22, 23, 34, 84, 108, 141, 167, 211, 213, 215, 217, 219, 221, 223, 225, 227, 229, 231, 239, 241, 243, 262, 320
self-concept, 19, 20, 140, 163, 164, 186–188, 194, 195, 212, 213, 215, 216, 218, 238, 260, 262, 267, 272, 280, 282, 303, 304, 321
self-confidence, 140, 145, 170, 197, 199, 219, 239, 285, 294, 304, 323
self-consciousness, 144, 164, 212
self-control, 79, 141, 145, 167, 196, 197, 199, 212, 214, 239, 265
self-directed search, 19, 110, 216, 240

self-efficacy, 76, 77, 79, 81, 82, 91, 105, 108, 110, 147, 191–194, 196, 219, 228, 244, 257, 267, 280, 283–286, 291, 292, 295–297, 301, 302, 306, 317, 321, 328

self-esteem, 126, 140, 166, 226

self-exploration, 84, 108, 214, 219, 238, 240

self-knowledge, 64, 126, 196

self-regulation, 22, 24, 81, 141, 155, 186, 189, 190, 191, 193, 198, 199, 203, 207, 212, 239, 249

self-report instrument, 19, 132

self-worth, 165

senior year, 55, 103, 118, 139, 314, 319, 320, 323, 324, 326

seriation, 166, 171, 187

service learning project, 199

seventh grade, 47, 125, 130, 211, 212, 213, 214, 218, 219, 225, 229, 230, 231

sex, 20, 74, 143, 144, 146, 169, 182, 187, 204, 213, 260

sex type, 20, 143, 144, 169

sexual characteristics, 186, 211

sexual maturation, 215

sexual orientation, 74, 85, 168, 215

sexualization, 187

shame, 141

skill development, 187, 204, 274

social activities, 269, 282

social and enterprising careers, 78

social capital, 12, 16, 17, 21, 91, 168, 193, 194, 212, 213, 216

Social Cognitive Career Theory, 283

social cues, 165, 236

social development, 164, 174, 236

social interaction, 22, 23, 212, 213, 237, 303

social justice, 77, 132

Social Learning Theory, 185, 189, 190, 202, 207

social media, 16, 21, 22, 81, 187, 189, 230, 295

social norms, 165

social skills, 59, 145, 149, 165, 170, 175, 178, 197, 219, 239, 265, 304

social status, 20, 143, 168, 213, 215, 237, 238

social valuation, 20, 193, 194, 215, 216, 238, 260

socialization, 15, 143, 187, 189

socially promoted, 81, 189

socially responsible behavior, 213

socioeconomic status (SES), 5, 10, 16, 26, 36, 41, 49, 74, 93, 106, 172, 180, 216, 221, 284, 289, 307

soft skills, 109, 174

spatial intelligence, 127

spatial relations, 212

special education, 13, 40, 64, 77, 82, 83, 92

speech and language impairment, 82

sports, 15, 69, 127, 154, 164, 176, 177, 182, 185, 202, 217, 285

stakeholders, 12, 14, 24, 25, 26, 29, 33, 65, 118, 121, 130, 153, 175, 196, 198, 204, 211, 218, 225, 227, 239, 244, 258, 316, 333, 334

standardized assessment instruments, 322

standards-based curriculum, 122

state's disinvestment in higher education, 36

statistical summary, 65

status symbols, 193, 216

STEM careers, 11, 16, 76, 78, 81, 82, 85, 94, 95, 129, 155, 181, 200, 221, 223, 224, 289

STEM education, 12

stereotypes, 16, 76, 82, 86, 167, 171, 182, 189, 222, 231

stress management, 248, 250, 251

stressors, 90, 211, 212

Strong Interest Inventory, 111

student activity fund, 307

student loan debt, 37

study habits, 78, 192, 302

study skills, 75, 165, 178, 196, 197, 203, 204, 206, 239, 250, 251, 257, 263, 265, 277, 324

study strategies, 271

subject areas, 46, 129, 244, 245

subjective assessment, 304

subjective data, 116, 244, 303

subject-specific skills, 245, 246

Super's Life-Span, Life-Space Theory, 262, 280, 320

supervision, 92, 93, 201, 231, 244

supplemental lessons, 240, 268

support systems, 27, 80, 307

surveys, 85, 103, 291

taking a year off and avoidance, 50

Talent Search, 47

task attempt, 165

task completion, 24, 321

task performance model, 301

teacher advisory periods, 268

teacher feedback, 284

teacher in-service, 79, 93, 227

teacher involvement, 240

technical careers, 12, 76

technical school, 3, 33, 50, 84, 170, 172, 228, 264, 287, 334

technical skills, 3, 33, 174, 295

testosterone, 212, 278

The College Scorecard, 11, 52

theoretical concepts, 168, 189

thinking skills, 3, 15, 23, 133, 199, 237, 260, 279, 299, 308, 323

third grade, 10, 125, 130, 144, 152, 159, 163–182, 196

time management, 55, 78, 196, 197, 205, 206, 239, 250, 257, 265, 271, 277, 295

Tomás Rivera Policy Institute, 75
training certificates, 228
Training requirements, 182, 197, 240, 242, 244
trait-and-factor approach, 104, 308, 320
transfer, 46, 49, 50
transition
   period, 140, 248, 332
   process, 14, 46, 235, 333, 334
   program, 204, 250, 313
translators, 76, 274
traumatic brain injury, 82
travel, 11, 144, 216
tribal entities, 79
TRIO programs, 47
tuition, 24, 36, 39, 53, 56, 73, 88, 111
tutoring, 16, 43, 47, 199, 203, 237, 263, 290

undermatched when applying for colleges, 41
underserved populations, 279
undocumented students, 67, 87, 88
unemployment, 8, 16, 36
unemployment rates, 6, 7, 84, 157
universality, 206, 296
Upward Bound programs, 46
U.S. Census Bureau, 73
U.S. citizens, 5
U.S. economy, 174
U.S. population, 4, 73, 74

validity, 65, 106, 109, 112, 118, 119
value of a liberal arts degree, 37
value system, 230
Values Card Sort, 113, 219, 220
values inventory, 240, 322, 325, 326
verbal persuasion, 192, 283, 286, 287, 290, 305, 306
vicarious learning, 283, 290, 291, 296, 313, 317, 329

virtual job shadowing, 292
visual impairment, 82
visual learners, 127, 130, 241
vocational and technical schools, 3
vocational choice, 18, 125, 216, 238, 261
vocational identity, 81, 110
vocational interests, 78, 283
vocational personality, 303, 305
vocational training programs, 67
volunteers, 54, 174, 177, 201, 229, 246, 290, 291, 309, 328, 329

weaknesses, 14, 22, 117, 213, 236, 240, 246, 305
weighted grades, 248
Whites, 4, 5, 74
women, 2, 9, 11, 16, 36, 51, 53, 76, 81, 82, 143, 188, 222, 230, 291
work environment, 14, 55, 115, 216
work ethic, 16, 247, 290
work experience, 304, 309
work habits, 155, 171, 196, 257, 263
work roles, 303
Work values, 52, 322
work-bound students, 174
worker, 4, 6, 9, 11, 19, 104, 156, 171, 187, 217, 225, 280, 281, 282, 295
workforce, 1, 2, 3, 4, 6, 9, 12, 22, 27, 36, 48, 51, 73, 131, 166, 174, 307, 315, 316
workplace, 1, 3, 15, 23, 109, 141, 155, 165, 166, 175, 178, 186, 187, 189, 191, 213, 214, 229, 237, 280, 295, 315
workplace etiquette, 174
World of Work map, 112, 241, 242, 245
writing skills, 173, 323

yield, 42
Young's Career Concepts, 12, 155, 144, 194, 217

Zone of Acceptable Alternatives, 20